Visual Basic
for Testers

MARY ROMERO SWEENEY

Visual Basic for Testers

Copyright ©2001 by Mary Romero Sweeney

ISBN (pbk): 1-893115-53-4

Printed and bound in the United States of America 12345678910

Editorial Directors: Dan Appleman, Gary Cornell, Karen Watterson, Jason Gilmore

Technical Reviewer: Harvin Queen

Marketing Manager: Stephanie Rodriguez

Managing Editor: Grace Wong

Editor: Kiersten Burke

Production Editor: Kari Brooks

Page Composition: Diana Van Winkle, Van Winkle Design Group

Artist: Tony Jonick

Cover Designer: Karl Miyajima

Indexer: Valerie Perry

Distributed to the book trade in the United States by Springer-Verlag New York, Inc., 175 Fifth Avenue, New York, NY, 10010

and outside the United States by Springer-Verlag GmbH & Co. KG, Tiergartenstr. 17, 69112 Heidelberg, Germany

In the United States, phone 1-800-SPRINGER; orders@springer-ny.com; http://www.springer-ny.com

Outside the United States, contact orders@springer.de; http://www.springer.de; fax +49 6221 345229

For information on translations, please contact Apress directly at 901 Grayson Street, Suite 204, Berkeley, CA, 94710

Phone: 510-549-5938; Fax: 510-549-5939; info@apress.com; http://www.apress.com

For my Mom, Dolores Romero Leder:
I love you, I admire you; you are my hero.

Contents at a Glance

Contents

Forewords

By Elfriede Dustin

Visual Basic for Testers is a practical book for software test professionals who wish to become proficient in the programming skills necessary to perform software test automation. The book provides solid examples and insightful recommendations specific to software testing. The skills gained by using this book will help you in many ways, whether you continue to use Visual Basic to support test automation or whether you transition your automated scripts to another language or tool.

I have had the opportunity to see a great many projects succeed and others fail during my career in automated software testing. I have noted and documented the reasons for these successes and failures in many presentations, articles ("Lessons in Test Automation," *STQE*, October 1999— or http://www.stickyminds.com) and also in my book, *Automated Software Testing* (Addison Wesley Longman, 1999), in an effort to try to share the knowledge I have gained with others within the software testing community. Mary Sweeney has a similar passion for sharing the lessons and insights she has gained over her professional testing career.

When I first met Mary at a recent Star East testing conference, we were both giving presentations on automated software testing. I quickly learned that Mary is also one who prefers to spend more time "on the floor," where the real work is being done, than in the office. This hands-on enthusiasm for performing automated testing is reflected in the content of her book where she provides real-world technical instruction for improving your automated testing program.

Note that Mary also outlines the fact that no single testing tool is perfect for every situation that may be encountered. Each tool has its own strengths and weaknesses. In the performance of test automation, the test professional needs to exhibit both the skills of a good programmer as well as the characteristics of a successful tester. As noted in my article in *STQE* magazine, one of the top ten reasons for test automation failure is the lack of training or the introduction of training too late in the life cycle.

Visual Basic for Testers offers you the chance to get some of this important training on your own.

Visual Basic for Testers is a book for all those performing software testing who seek to continually improve their test automation and management approach. With this book as a guide, you will perform testing in a quicker and more efficient manner. With the efficiencies gained from applying the instruction provided in *Visual Basic for Testers*, the test team will have more time to devote to high risk areas and will be able to perform more comprehensive testing.

—Elfriede Dustin
Author of *Automated Software Testing* and *Quality Web Systems*
http://www.qualitywebsys.com

By James Bach

You can do a lot of great testing without doing any programming at all. But if you are ambitious, if you want to be a well-rounded virtuoso of testing, you need to learn to code. I started programming professionally when I was in high school. For four years I wrote video games before I said goodbye to that and became a tester. I love testing and I don't miss full-time programming one bit. But, I'm grateful that programming was my stepping-stone into testing. I have more choices and better imagination than I otherwise would.

If you're a good tester and you have good programming skills, then you're something like a superhero. You can see through walls and jump over obstacles. You have super tester strength, speed, and senses. The cape is optional. Everything becomes more testable when you have good tools and you know how to use them. With a programming eye, you see test projects differently. You see more possibilities for interesting tests. You free yourself from testing only in terms of the user interface, you create special test data quickly, and you simulate many users at once. Your testing moves fluidly from manual to automated and back again.

Unfortunately, a lot of tools are too expensive. You may not be provided with the fancy tools necessary to elevate your testing practice. That's where this book comes in. We must invest in education that we can take from job to job. So, learn to use tools that are inexpensive and powerful. Comb through Download.com for useful shareware utilities. Get the resource toolkit for Windows 2000. Get a subscription to *MSDN* if you can. Learn VB. Visual Basic is inexpensive and nearly ubiquitous on Windows platforms. It's something you can carry in your utility belt from job to job.

There's a danger in this. Sometimes testers get so interested in tools that they focus only on those test strategies that are easily automated. Resist that temptation. Testing is not just a mechanical operation of the product, checking for pre-ordained correct results. What's interesting (and important) about testing is that we penetrate illusions. We do this by first imagining what the product might do in various situations, then finding a way to create those situations and track what happens. It takes creative, critical, and practical thinking to see beyond the veneer of splash screens and context menus to understand whether a product will, indeed, faithfully satisfy its users. We testers are like the headlights of the project, illuminating the problems that could otherwise wreck us.

You don't have to learn programming to be a good tester—but it will help and this book is a great start.

—James Bach
Founder and Tester
Satisfice, Inc.
Front Royal, Virginia

Acknowledgments

At first, writing a book appeared to be an impossible task. How could I ever write anything like those thick tomes you see in the computing section of any bookstore? Having done it now, I can tell you how it works. First, imagine taking a germ of an idea for a chapter and then writing it out as best you can. Then you take that product and give to a smart, creative Test Manager and aspiring programmer like **Jason Herres**. Jason provides a lot of incisive comments and suggestions, making red marks all over your work, which you gladly accept because they make you think to yourself, "Whoa, why didn't I think of that?" Then, you send this off to a hard-working, talented, and detail-oriented Tester and Developer like **Harvin Queen** to do a formal tech review. Harv uncovers technical problems with his eagle eye and also makes a few good suggestions. Things are really starting to look better by this time. So, you then take this whole package and give it to a gifted Copy Editor with the patience of an angel, someone like **Kiersten Burke**. By the time Kiersten gets through with your myriad grammatical errors, even a passive voice reads strong. Imagine going through all or part of that same cycle a couple of times for each chapter before it all eventually lands in the hands of Production Editor, **Kari Brooks** and her team, **Diana Van Winkle**, **Tony Jonick**, and **Valerie Perry**. They take the whole thing and make it look so nice with great graphics and icons that you hardly recognize it as the stuff you typed into your beat-up old laptop. After all of this help, imagine how the final product would look compared to your original germ of an idea and then you'll know what I know now: that there isn't any *I* when you're writing—it's a team effort. Thanks to all the members of my team. The cliché is so true: you really can't do it alone.

Believe it or not, along the way, I picked up more help as well. Thanks to **Walt Ritscher** for writing the DCOM section of Chapter 9. Walt also helped review some other chapters. His in-depth Visual Basic knowledge and insight into VB.NET from years of teaching, presenting, and coding in Visual Basic made him a supremely valuable resource. **Dan Hodge**, an old friend and highly experienced and knowledgeable software tester, instructor and developer, took time from his busy schedule to help review some chapters. So did another old friend, **Al Corwin**, (on pretty short notice too). **Lee Wallen** provided some great feedback and also some of the code I used in the examples. **Jason Herres**, **Jonathan Griffin**, and **Kevin Ingalls** also provided code.

Karen Watterson and **Gary Cornell** from Apress publishing gave me this opportunity and provided mentoring along the way—thanks to both for your insight and experience. Many, many thanks also go to **Gary** and to his coauthor, **Jonathan Morrison**, for providing two chapters of their book on VB.NET for the eleventh chapter of this one. Thanks also to **Grace Wong**, Managing Editor, for all of your efforts on my behalf. Thanks to all at Apress for your help and for the professional organization that you run.

It is a great honor to have forewords written by two of the most respected professionals in the Quality Assurance industry, **Elfriede Dustin** and **James Bach**. Both represent the best in the industry; their contributions have had a huge and positive impact on the way QA is performed today. Thank you for your thoughts and for your time. **Bret Pettichord**, **James Bach**, and **Elisabeth Hendrickson**, all three noted industry experts, provided the entire Appendix D with essays on Automated Testing. Don't miss their insightful articles and advice. Speaking of advice, I want to thank the six test engineers who contributed to Chapter 12: **Dan Hodge**, **Jason Herres**, **Harvin Queen**, **Lee Wallen**, **Kevin Ingalls**, **Alan Corwin**, and **Marshall Peabody**. I am grateful for their willingness to share their experiences so readily and so succinctly.

I would also like to acknowledge the Data Dimensions, Inc. training team who helped work on the original courseware that is the basis for this book. Thanks to **David Silas**, **Barbara Winter**, **Eve Gordon**, and **Steve Wolf**.

Now for the "save the best for last" category. Thank you, my dear friend, **Mary Sue Payne**, for being so supportive, and even taking over some tasks I should have done. Thanks to both you and **Jeanine Smith** for continually listening patiently as I went on and on about "the book." You are the best. It amazes me that my kids, **Ryan** and **Keilan**, never once complained about this project, no matter how much time I spent on the computer nor how much whining I did. I love you both, you truly do make everything worthwhile.

I often get asked how I have the time to do all of the stuff I do and write a book too. There's only one answer. Anytime I have ever asked my husband, **Brian Sweeney**, "I'd like to try this, what do you think?", his answer has always been, "Sounds great, go for it!" Then he uncomplainingly picks up the slack, doing more than his share while I do whatever new project I've got going. You are the reason for the wonderful life I lead, Brian. You are my greatest blessing. Thank you.

—Mary Romero Sweeney
June 2001

Introduction

Software testing is a skill. Experience, training, self-study, and a good intuition are what make a good software test engineer. Most test engineers I know are continually striving to learn more about technology. A test engineer is expected to know at least a little about practically everything—from operating systems to networks to databases—in order to be able to find bugs and report them articulately. What I always say to new testers is that this is a great profession for those of us who love to learn continuously. It's like you've never left college—you must study constantly. (Of course, that also makes it a good place to be if you like to feel constantly inadequate! You can never know enough.) So, this book is for that self-motivated test engineer who is intent on continually upgrading his or her knowledge and now wants to learn more about automated software testing.

This book is also for you test leads and managers who want to know what Visual Basic can do for your test project. A not-so-well-kept secret of automated software testing is that the major tools available commercially don't do everything you need them to do, in spite of their advertisements. It's probably unrealistic to expect any tool to be able to fully support the automated testing required for so many diverse applications.

At the Star East QA conference in May 2000, several speakers said that businesses might need two or three of the major tools to accomplish their tasks effectively. This is not good news, of course, since each one of the major automated testing tools is quite expensive. It didn't surprise me to learn during the "Birds-of-a-Feather" sessions that many companies are using one major automated testing tool and filling in the gaps by writing additional automated test scripts in traditional languages such as Java, C++, Perl, and Visual Basic. This is not a new thing. For years, companies, frustrated at not being able to get a tool to do what they want, have found a programmer or two who has said, "Hey, I could just write that myself."

This is not to say that writing your own tools is always the right answer. However, supplementing your automated tools with some scripting done by testers fluent in a traditional language can help a company get more out of its automated testing projects. It is my hope, in these pages, to help you see how you can do just that.

About the Author

After a twelve-year career at Boeing as a software engineer and technical instructor, and a stint as a consultant and contractor, I went to work for ST Labs, an independent testing company, in 1995. I began teaching testers automated testing topics in early 1996. Primarily, we used Microsoft Visual Test 4 for automated testing. It was an exciting time: software testing as a discipline all its own was fairly new and we were on the bleeding edge. Tom Arnold, author of the *Visual Test 6 Bible* (IDG Books, Inc., 1999), hired me—he was just writing the first edition at that time. (I still remember Tom telling me, "If I can write a book, *anyone* can write a book.") It was there that I also met James Bach, the chief engineer at ST Labs, Inc., and was impressed (as I still am) by his thoughtful, common-sense approach to software testing.

At ST Labs, we learned the hard way that automated testing wasn't the solution to every problem; it was not and is not the proverbial silver bullet. We also learned a great number of things that automated testing *is* good for (and we'll explore many of those in this book). One of the key things we learned is that it is a good idea to have at least some programming skills on any testing project, whether automated or not. Not every tester needs to be a hard-core programmer but it helps to have some testers on the team who are fairly proficient programmers for tasks that may come up. It also doesn't hurt to have a few on the team who know a little about software development because even just a little experience helps them look for and ferret out some common programming errors in the software being tested.

So, I started teaching fundamental programming topics to testers and the language of choice was Visual Basic, since it's so widely available and relatively easy to learn and use. The bad news was, none of the textbooks and courseware available on Visual Basic were very relevant to testing. During the course of a class, we found ourselves skipping over some sections of the canned courseware and concentrating our efforts harder in others.

Eventually, the need to write a course specifically for testers became a priority. In 1998, ST Labs merged with Data Dimensions and thus gained a new name. It was as a Data Dimensions employee that I authored a course called "Visual Basic for Testers" and we began to offer this course publicly. As I traveled to each coast teaching the class, I learned much more about how Visual Basic is being used to support automated testing projects.

I wrote a paper for the STAR East conference in the spring of 2000 and presented it there on the topic, "Automated Testing Using Visual Basic." (It is published it on the Data Dimensions Web site at `http://www.data-dimensions.com/Testers'Network/winceright.htm`.) This article generated so much interest that it became apparent a book would be in order—and here it is.

About This Book

This book has a specific, three-fold goal; it will teach the software test engineer:

- How to begin to use Visual Basic as a testing tool, including how to create simple testing utilities and the basic mechanics of writing code to test an application.

- What to look for in a well-written Visual Basic program.

- To understand the software development process and appreciate the efforts of the software developer.

These chapters cover beginning to advanced topics in Visual Basic, focusing on areas that can be used for software testing.

What This Book Is Not

Since the focus of this book is software testing with Visual Basic, we will *not* cover all the development features of Visual Basic. There are many good books for that already. This is not a software testing fundamentals book either. There are many good books available for that as well. This book is intended to bridge the gap between those two types of text so you can learn how to write code in Visual Basic for an automated test project.

For more information on Visual Basic as a software development tool and for more information on software testing, see the reference list in Appendix A (my personal favorites are *Visual Basic 6 from the Ground Up* by Gary Cornell, *Software Test Automation* by Mark Fewster and Dorothy Graham, and anything by Elfriede Dustin).

Who This Book Is For

This book is for software test engineers (usually we just call ourselves testers) who are new to Visual Basic and new to programming in general. It is designed to jump-start the tester into using Visual Basic both for automated software testing and for software development of small programs. This book will not cover any software testing basics—the presumption is that all readers are familiar with fundamental testing concepts. Testing experience is helpful but not required. Software test managers and leads should also be able to derive some good information, especially in Chapters 1 and 12. Although others should be able to gain some good information, I want to emphasize that this book is a primarily for the test engineer on the test bench striving valiantly to ensure software quality.

Where to Start

Although this book is intended for software test engineers with little or no programming experience, you should be able to get some use out of it regardless of your background. Even if you do not have a testing background, you should be able to read and understand the book. However, some of the terms and references to testing concepts may be unclear. There is a References and Resources section in Appendix A that should help you find the information you need.

If you have:

- **No programming experience and no testing experience**: Start at Chapter 1 and proceed through all chapters successively. Read the References and Resources in Appendix A in order to understand the testing terms being used (specifically, Cem Kaner's *Testing Computer Software* is a good place to start). Once you've gained some programming and testing experience, don't forget to read Appendix D with its essays on Automated Software Testing.

- **Testing experience but no programming experience**: Skim Chapter 1, read Appendix D, and then proceed through all remaining chapters successively.

- **Programming experience but no testing experience**: Read Chapter 1 for the testing perspective and then see the following "Chapter Breakdown" section to see where you need to begin depending on experience. If your programming experience is in another language, you should at least skim the earlier chapters starting with Chapter 2. If you have had a programming course in Visual Basic, you should be able to start at Chapter 5.

- **Programming experience and testing experience**: You can skim earlier chapters as needed but can probably jump directly into Chapters 6 through 12 to see what kinds of things you can do with Visual Basic to test databases, access the Windows System Registry, Windows API calls, and the Web. Chapter 11 gives you a heads up on changes coming up in VB.NET with two chapters by Gary Cornell and Jonathan Morrison from their upcoming book, *Programming VB.NET: A Guide for Experienced Programmers* (Apress, 2001, ISBN: 1-893115-992).

Chapter Breakdown

Part One: In the Beginning:
Preparing for Automated Script Writing

Chapter 1: Automated Software Testing Overview

Discussion of automated testing and the role of Visual Basic. Also building an automated testing team and how to create good testing software.

Chapter 2: Getting Started with Visual Basic on an Automated Testing Project

Visual Basic installation notes. What you can do with Visual Basic without a lot of programming background, using Wizards, templates, and internal tools including the Object Browser and the Visual Database tools.

Part Two: The Second Stage: Introduction to Automated Script Writing

Chapter 3: Introduction to the Visual Basic Development Environment

Getting familiar with the toolbar, controls, and all of the windows needed to write VB code. Discusses how to use Help. Contains the first exercises so you can practice. Here, you will write your first simple Visual Basic program.

Chapter 4: Understanding Visual Basic Application Essentials

In order to program in Visual Basic you need to know about programming objects and their properties, methods, and events. You will write an application using some intrinsic VB functions and fundamental programming statements.

Part Three: Beyond the Basics: Now You're Testing!

Chapter 5: Creating Test Utilities

Test utilities are short and simple programs to aid in a testing project. You will use subroutines and functions to write a logging routine and write and read to a file using the Microsoft Scripting Runtime.

Chapter 6: Testing with the Windows Registry

Visual Basic includes some specific commands for accessing a special location in the Windows Registry. You will learn how to use them and how to use a List Box control and an array to do so.

Chapter 7: Introduction to the Windows Application Programmer's Interface (API)

How to use the power of the Windows Dynamic Link Libraries to retrieve system and application information. Specific examples from testing projects are included.

Part Four: Advanced Topics in Automated Test Scripting

Chapter 8: Introduction to Database Testing

Using the Visual Database tools in more depth. Using ADO to connect to and test a database. Accessing SQL Server using SQL-DMO.

Chapter 9: Introduction to Testing COM Components

Understanding COM basics including classes and collections. Creating a COM object for testing. Testing COM components. Overview of DCOM.

Chapter 10: Testing the Web with Visual Basic

How to test Web pages using the Internet Transfer control and the WebBrowser control. Introduction to VBScript.

Chapter 11: VB.NET: Brave New World

A look at the newest version of Visual Basic, including two chapters from a new book by Gary Cornell and Jonathan Morrison.

Chapter 12: From Tester to Tester: Advice to the Visual Basic Automator

This book was written with the help of many testers. In this chapter, I let them speak to you in their own words to give you their advice and lessons learned. This may be the most valuable chapter. Succinct and informative, it also includes a summary of what you have learned in the previous chapters.

Appendixes

Appendix A: Resources and References

Provides the references used in this book and an extensive list for further study.

Appendix B: More Controls

Includes standard file handling within Visual Basic 6.

Appendix C: File Access and Management

Covers a few more essential controls not covered in the chapter projects.

Appendix D: Automated Essay Testing
Includes "Seven Steps to Successful Test Automation" by Bret Pettichord, "Test Automation Snake Oil," a classic article by James Bach, and advice to new Visual Basic testers from Elisabeth Hendrickson.

A Note to Training Organizations and Teachers

Visual Basic for Testers is intended to help in classroom instruction on software testing as part of an overall software-testing curriculum. This book can be used as the basis for an introductory to intermediate-level course in automated software testing in either a corporate or an academic setting. A class based on this text, *Visual Basic for Testers*, is currently taught as part of the software-testing curriculum through the STA Group (`http://www.stagroup.com`) at Bellevue Community College. For more information about using the book as the basis for a course, contact the author at `sweeneyn14@home.com`.

The Practice Files: Answers to Exercises and Demo Code

Each chapter, beginning with Chapter 3, has exercises. Answers for these exercises along with additional code demonstrating chapter topics is available for download from the Apress Web site, `http://www.apress.com`. You will need to answer questions pertaining to this book in order to successfully download the code.

I will post additional topics of interest to testers learning and using Visual Basic on the following Web site at `http://www.VisualMonkey.com/vb4testers` and also at the STA Group Web site at `http://www.stagroup.com`. For comments, questions, or to report errata, contact the author at `sweeneyn14@home.com`.

Part One

In the Beginning: Preparing for Automated Script Writing

CHAPTER 1

Automated Software Testing Overview

Software Testing is no longer a new field—we've come a long way in the past few years. So, why hasn't producing good software gotten any easier? As our testing knowledge has grown, the software we test has continued to grow more complex and the software business more cutthroat. We need to get software out the door quickly, efficiently, and *profitably*. To that end, automated software testing possesses a tempting allure: can we make software testing easier by making it somehow automatic? There are many automated test tool manufacturers who are rushing to meet our needs. Automated software testing tools have grown in capability and, of course, price. Using Visual Basic to test software, therefore, has its own allure. It's a widely used, relatively easy-to-learn programming language. Can it help? Yes—in many ways but certainly not in every way. In this text, we will explore the how, what, when, where, and the all-important why of using Visual Basic for automated software testing.

Software testers wrote this entire book and the code provided. Most examples are derived in whole or in part from actual test projects. This text is very much a tester-to-tester reference. Hopefully, you will find enough to get you started on a successful test project using Visual Basic. To begin, we will need some discussion of automated software testing in general. In this chapter, we will look at some of the important management issues involved when starting automated testing, such as when and when not to automate testing, what kind of personnel requirements you will need to address, and how to build an automated testing team. We will also look at some ground rules for creating good testing software as well as some of the advantages and limitations of using Visual Basic.

What Is Automated Software Testing?

Software testing is the process of "exercising software to verify that it satisfies specified requirements and to detect errors." This definition is the one I like best (it comes from the British Computer Society Specialist Interest Group in Software Testing—BCS SIGIST) because it reflects the value of both finding bugs and ensuring capability. Simply put, that means making sure the software works. Traditionally, most testing has been done manually—that is, a tester sits down and runs the application using defined processes to try to find bugs so that they can be fixed prior to releasing the product. Automated software testing goes a step further. Since basic software testing has gotten more rigorous and more defined, testers have found ways to automate some of the process of testing software by writing software to do it! Of course, many successful testing projects have been completed without ever using automated test scripting. In fact, most applications are primarily tested manually. There is just no substitute for testing the product in the same way that the user would and there is no substitute for the abilities of an able, experienced tester. So, automated testing will never (and shouldn't) replace manual testing of an application. However, used appropriately, automated testing can significantly enhance the testing process.

So, what is automated software testing? Is it the same thing as automation testing? Let's define terms. Automation is an over-used word. *Automation testing* (as automated software testing is often called) could mean testing an Automation object. But what is an Automation object? Depending on what you are reading and your perspective, that can have a few different definitions too. For this reason, I propose calling the process of writing software to test applications, *automated software testing* or simply, *automated testing*. Automated testing is any testing that is done using software. In other words, we write code to test other code. Automated testing includes the use of tools written by others since the tools they have written *are* software that *tests* software. *Automated test scripting* is the process of creating the program code—that is, actually writing the code that will be used to test. Automated test scripts then are the program code used to test the software.

Automated testing is a relatively new area of the testing process—which is, itself, relatively new. Automated testing has been receiving a lot of focus lately due to the ever-increasing complexity and size of software applications that require better and faster ways to test. Rather than replace testers, which might be one of the benefits a manager might expect from automated software testing, automated testing can enhance the testing process with increased capabilities. There are some tedious and time-consuming yet important testing tasks that you may choose not to perform on a test project due to time and budget constraints. For example, verifying the transfer of large amounts of files or data from one system to another could be prohibitive if done manually; writing code to do that makes it achievable. There are many benefits to enhancing a testing process with automated test scripting, here are just a few:

- Performing tedious or repetitive manual testing tasks.

- Running tests in batch.

- Setting a reference to a COM object and testing its interfaces.

- Attaching to a database for data verification testing.

- Accessing and interrogating the Windows Registry.

- Creating testing utilities that support the testing process such as installation, logging, and startup scripts.

Within this text, we will explore all of these uses of automated testing and many more. Not all testing situations can benefit from automated testing. In fact, there are many times when it's not a good idea to automate testing. So, how do you decide when to automate or not? We'll take a look at this in the next section.

When to Automate?

The decision to automate is an important one and necessarily requires analysis and the definition of boundaries between the automated test plan and the manual test plan. Using a programming language like Visual Basic requires additional careful planning since writing test scripts in Visual Basic is essentially software development and can eat up plenty of time in a schedule. (More on the limitations at the end of this chapter.)

How do we determine what to test manually and what to test using automated test scripts? While experience is the best judge, there are also some basic questions you can ask yourselves prior to embarking on an automated test project. The following questions will help determine whether your project is a good candidate for automated testing.

Project and Personnel Issues

- What is the scope of the automated testing piece?

  If your goal is to fully automate all tests, your scope is unrealistic. If you are trying to incorporate automated testing into existing projects or into a new one, it's best to start with small, manageable goals. For example, you can ask your team to write some simple utilities to support your test project using Visual Basic. This has the added advantage of checking their experience level as well. Not all Visual Basic programmers have the same capabilities!

- What is the automated testing skill level of your testing personnel?

  If automated testing is new to your personnel, you need to allow time and budget for them to take classes and learn. You will need to add experienced automated testing personnel to your staff *prior* to your first project. The level of experience will determine the level of automated testing you will be able to undertake. One introductory course in Visual Basic will not be enough to enable your testers to undertake a large project. However, they could use some of Visual Basic's tools and wizards to support a test project and perhaps create and use some simple test utilities.

- What is the availability of your technically skilled testers?

  If you do have technically skilled testers, are they actually available? Many projects start with experienced members who get pulled off for other projects. This may seem like a no-brainer but I have seen this situation occur too many times to think it is just an aberration.

Product Issues

- Is the feature set of the application you are testing relatively stable?

  If not, the scripts you write need to change as often as the application changes. You may find yourself spinning your wheels if you start too soon, using up precious budget. Automated testing works best for products that are relatively stable in file structure, User Interface (UI), and major product components. Testing products that are changing constantly means your test scripts change constantly, too, wasting time and budget.

  Do you plan to test the UI? Is your product GUI (Graphical User Interface)-based?

  Some automated testing tools are geared specifically for the Graphical User Interface. If your project is to test the application's GUI, certain automated testing tools may be a better choice than others. Visual Basic can be used for GUI testing to a certain extent but requires a significant amount of coding to do so (see Chapter 5). For this reason, I would not choose Visual Basic in most cases for extensive GUI-based testing.

- Does your product have areas where tests are run repetitively, greater than ten times per test?

  Any repetitive tasks are candidates for automated testing. Computers perform repetitive tasks well. For example, writing regression tests for high-priority bugs or developing a BVT (Build Verification Test) suite for verification of product robustness after each build are good examples of tests that will be required to be run many times.

- Will your product need to be compatible with multiple platforms?

  Most products need to run on the various versions of Windows: Windows 2000, Windows NT, Windows 95, and Windows 98. There are many other compatibility issues, of course. Automated testing scripts can be written to address some of them.

 NOTE *This point may seem a bit Microsoft-centric. It is true that Visual Basic is a tool for testing mostly Windows-based software systems—there are some exceptions to this, but not many.*

Additional Test Management Issues

- Do you have Visual Basic available to the project?

  If not, can you purchase the proper number of licenses and have them in place in time?

- Can you insert automated testing without affecting existing testing?

  For example, installing Visual Basic and investigating the integration of the Visual Basic scripting with other tests takes time and planning. Can you do this without adversely affecting your total project time and budget?

- Do you have enough time to analyze requirements, code, debug, and maintain test scripts?

  Development of automated test scripts is software development and requires all of the same considerations.

- Who will manage the automated testing for each project and across projects?

  An important consideration is to keep and maintain the work done on a project for future use. For example, scripts for logging test results (covered in Chapter 5) can be used in any project. Identify a group or an individual who will be responsible for ensuring that code that can be reused on other projects is cataloged for future use.

Managing the testing process is a big topic and an important one. There are many excellent texts available, so we won't attempt to compete with them here; check Appendix A: Resources and References for more information on this topic.

 NOTE *Before you go much further, there are two articles in Appendix D that you should read: "Test Automation Snake Oil," a classic by James Bach; and "Seven Steps to Successful Test Automation" by Bret Petticord.*

Automated Software Testing in the Real World

There are many great texts and articles on software testing. Our knowledge store for software testing is increasing, which is a real benefit to us all. However, many of these books and articles specify ideals that may be hard to reach on every project. And many articles seem relevant only to a limited type of test project. This is because software testing is still a relatively new industry, so we are essentially learning as we go. How do we know what's going to turn out to be relevant for the masses? We simply write our experiences and hope we can save someone else some time and energy. After I read some good articles, I am inspired to use their wisdom on my next test project. However, whenever I do get onto a new test project, I am always struck by the difference between what we must do in the real world to get the job done and the ideals we would *like* to meet. Short turn-around and special cases are the norm. For some reason, each particular project is always different from every other even though they all seem to have the same basic constraints: time and budget.

I believe we must make every effort to keep up with the information coming at us from every direction and then necessarily filter it so that we use only what is relevant to our needs on a particular project. Now, that would be a neat trick, wouldn't it? Well, this is actually what we do in the real world, to the best of our abilities anyway. Using Visual Basic and other programming languages on a test project are some of the real-world techniques we end up using when our high-priced automated testing tools just can't get to that important information. This is not meant as a criticism of the automated test tools on the market today—they can't possibly keep up with every need on every test project. I am always surprised at how much they *can* do. It's amazing how well the manufacturers do try to address as many needs as possible. They have come a long way in the last few years, from basic screen capture and recording features to the advanced stress and load capabilities we see today in tools like Segue's Silk Performer and Mercury's WinRunner. However, by default, these tools can't possibly keep up with every need on every test project. Most testing organizations find that at some point they need to resort to using programming-experienced personnel to write code to supplement their testing.

This text introduces you to Visual Basic so that you can use it to address some real-world testing issues in real-time. Hopefully, you will be reading this *before* your next project so that you can put your newfound Visual Basic knowledge to good use without hesitation. If you have this book out just as you are being asked to solve a particularly tricky problem, then good luck, you are engaged in real-world testing!

Building a Team for Automated Testing

What is the makeup of a good test team? Ideally, automated testing personnel and those members of the team using manual processes should not be kept separate. They can enhance each other's capabilities and they do need to keep in close communication. If you are a fairly large company, it is beneficial to have members of the team experienced in different kinds of automated testing, some with applied experience in one or more of the major tools available on the market and at least a couple of testers who have significant programming experience using Visual Basic, C/C++, or other languages.

One large company I consulted for had a sizeable test group dedicated to automated testing. In this group, they hired personnel experienced in several major tools. On each test project, this team determined which tools, if any, were appropriate for that project, as well as the backgrounds and experience required for the test team. They were integrally involved in the setup for all company test projects and monitored each project as it progressed. I have always thought this was the ideal way to proceed. The team was able to keep a repository of test plans and code as well as a detailed history of the projects and their results. They were instrumental in arranging appropriate training in the tools selected for the project as well. This model worked quite well for the company, although, so far, it's the only company I have seen do it quite this way. It takes time and money to set up such a model but has many benefits in the long run.

If you are a midsize company with a team of ten testers, the makeup of your test team could be something like this:

- Four to five testers experienced in traditional manual testing processes.

- Three testers experienced in automated test tools such as Segue, Mercury, and Rational.

- Two to three testers experienced in software development, at least two of whom could be considered advanced programmers.

NOTE *Testers who develop code for use in testing are increasingly gaining titles of their own. This type of testing specialist is sometimes called an* automator *or* Developer-in-Test—*or an* SDE/T (Software Design Engineer in Test) *as Microsoft calls them.*

Of course, there could and should be some overlap. However, don't make the mistake of having nine manual testers but only one person experienced in software development, test tools, and so on. If there is only one person with experience, that person will end up spending all of his or her time coaching everyone else and getting nothing done. It's best to avoid depending too much on a single person or, nearly as bad, only two people in a test project.

What a Tester Needs to Know about Visual Basic Scripting

Although Visual Basic is powerful enough to accomplish some useful testing tasks, you must have knowledgeable testers and programmers to write the code. However, there isn't a lot of information out there yet to help them adapt Visual Basic for testing. Most of the resources are geared for developers, not testers.

Using Visual Basic for testing requires a shift in perspective. A tester can come out of a standard Visual Basic course still wondering how it could ever be used on a test project. These courses and most books concentrate on the controls to use and the ways to create a great, user-friendly application. A tester doesn't care about that so much. What we want to know is how to quickly develop a utility or get to system information and other testing-related data using code. One of the differences between this book and others is that we won't focus on learning a myriad of cool controls or how to develop a slick front end for an application. While these are great things to learn, there are plenty of other books out there that will teach you. Instead, we will focus on the things a tester must know to use Visual Basic as quickly as possible on a test project such as:

- How to access intrinsic Visual Basic functions that return relevant information about files, the registry, the operating system, and so on.

- How to create a front end with basic controls to view test information and results as soon as possible.

- How to access databases quickly and easily.

- How to access the Windows Registry to return relevant application information.

- How to access the Windows API (Application Programmer's Interface) routines to get at important information that can't be accessed through Visual Basic's intrinsic functions.

These are just the beginning, of course, but they represent some of the things the testers who have contributed time and code to this book have used to accomplish their own testing tasks. We will cover all of these and more in the course of this text.

Test Scripts Are Software

When test engineers write automated test scripts, they must take time to define and analyze the requirements. Then the process of writing the scripts actually begins. This process is necessarily interactive as the testers repeatedly run the scripts, then improve and perfect them to meet the ever-changing testing requirements.

After the scripts are working, they must be updated on a regular basis to ensure that they work with new versions of the application being tested. A professional software developer would recognize this process of developing and updating automated test scripts as essentially the same one used to develop software applications:

- Analyze Requirements

- Design

- Code

- Test

- Deliver

- Maintain

Bret Pettichord's article ("Seven Steps to Test Automation Success" in Appendix D) does an excellent job of rewriting the software development process for automated testing projects.

The writing of automated test scripts is software development. Therefore, the skills needed to be a good automator are similar to those required of a good software developer. A good test automator, then, must be both a good tester and a good programmer: quite a challenge.

It is important to recognize that the same rules for developing good software apply to developing good test scripts. Good planning and design are important, as is allowing sufficient time to develop the code and supporting utilities.

Goals of Good Testing Software

Test scripts, like application code, should be:

- Readable

- Reusable

- Maintainable

- Portable

Readability

Using standard naming conventions and constants and creating project standards for code development make code more readable (if these terms are unfamiliar to you, don't worry, we will cover them in Chapters 3 and 4). If code is readable, it can be more readily understood and modified, which makes it easier to work with and to adapt to future projects.

Reusability

Writing routines that can be reused within the same project (and sometimes modified to work within another project as well) can save time and duplication of effort. (However, I don't support creating monolithic libraries.) Some possibilities may include:

- Logging utilities to document test results.

- Front-end or driver routines to make running test suites easy.

- Specialized utilities that make working with your test target easier, such as startup and shutdown routines.

Maintainability

Writing code that is easy to update is important. It allows you to account for a changing application in many ways, including the use of constants, library files, the Windows Registry, and initialization files.

Portability

Writing suites that can be easily changed makes them portable. For example:

- Place path information to resources and data files in the Registry or in an initialization (.ini) file.

- Use Environment variables and Conditional Compilation to allow for changes in platform.

In this text, we will look at several ways to implement these goals.

Creating Successful Testing Software

Of course, one must also allow enough time to debug and test the test scripts. No one writes perfect code. A common pitfall in new automated test projects is that time is allowed to develop automated test scripts but not to test whether or not they work properly!

Keep in mind that once written, automated test scripts also need to be maintained. As the application you are testing changes, the scripts to test that application need to change accordingly.

Since one of our goals is to be able to successfully test a Visual Basic application, we will use the aforementioned "Goals of Good Testing Software" guidelines as we review Visual Basic code. In other words, we will look for elements within the code of a Visual Basic application that make it easier to maintain, read, port, and reuse.

For example, look at the following two code segments:
Segment one:

```
If x = y then z_123
```

Segment two:

```
If dtToday > dtDueDate then
     Call RubjnMonthlyTestReport
End if
```

Can you explain the purpose of the first? How about the second? Is it possible that these two code segments accomplish the same thing? The second segment contains code that you may not understand completely. However, it is clearly more understandable because of the choice of names. Actually, the two code segments could do exactly the same thing. The improved choice of names for variables and proper indentation make the second case easier to understand and thus a better way to write the code.

Code can be written in many different ways. When we review code written by others, we try to determine its readability and therefore the ease with which we can maintain or alter it. When we write code for testing purposes, we will try to levy that same mandate on our own work. We will then reap the same rewards as the developers and in the process learn a bit about why they do the things they do. I will emphasize good programming technique throughout this text. Even when in a hurry on a test project, it is absolutely true that it is just as easy to write code properly as it is to write it poorly.

Why Visual Basic?

Visual Basic is not a testing tool. Visual Basic is a programming language used for software development. Why use Visual Basic for testing—why not use C++? A big advantage to using Visual Basic is that it is a popular language because it is easy to learn and it happens to be the macro language for the widely-used Microsoft Office products. Many other software companies use a form of Basic for their own products. This popularity means there is a wide base of people with a knowledge of Basic, so there should be no shortage of people able to use it or willing to learn. There is also a proliferation of books and resources available for Visual Basic. Although they may not be written specifically for testing, once you get the hang of it, you will find lots of code available in user's groups and books that you can adapt for testing purposes.

Since Visual Basic is not really a testing tool, how is it possible to adapt it for use in testing? Visual Basic has many features that can support the testing process. For example, it has a host of intrinsic functions that can return important information about the test platform and the application under test. Visual Basic's Shell function and SendKeys statement can also be used to run an application and manipulate its GUI (Graphical User Interface). The Visual Database Tools (discussed in Chapters 2 and 8) allow you to connect to a database and examine its structure and data. You can also get very sophisticated with Visual Basic and write essentially anything you want, such as a load testing application. Of course, the tradeoff for a more sophisticated programming endeavor is that you will need both the programmers *and* the time.

Visual Basic can also be used to test many behind-the-scenes operations of the application. For example, scripts can be written to access the initialization (or .ini) files and the Windows Registry. Automated test scripts can verify the correct loading and retrieval of the information from these files. Accessing the Windows API from Visual Basic is a powerful way to both manipulate an application and return important system information. The very fact that Visual Basic is a powerful development tool makes it a promising tool for testing.

Limitations of Visual Basic for Testing

Because it is not intended as a test tool, Visual Basic does not include many of the bells and whistles that most higher-end automated test tools do. For instance, Visual Basic has no inherent support for bug reporting or test design and documentation as many testing tools have. It lacks a recording feature. If you want these kinds of things in Visual Basic code, your test team will have to write them. Once you undertake a significant task like that, you might find you have entered the business of test-tool writing instead of the testing business. Again, Visual Basic should not be considered a substitute for the major test tools but simply a powerful adjunct to them.

Visual Basic is powerful enough to accomplish any testing task as long as you have testers and programmers with the skill and ability to write Visual Basic code. This book is intended to guide you in your efforts.

CHAPTER 2

Getting Started with Visual Basic on an Automated Testing Project

Putting Visual Basic to good use on a test project does not always require extensive programming knowledge. I have often thought that if testers were just familiar with all of the tools and wizards available, there are things they could find out and use that would benefit their testing. In this chapter, we will explore some ways to get started using Visual Basic for testing even if you are new to Visual Basic and have very little programming experience.

Installing Visual Basic

A few words about installing Visual Basic 6. You must first choose the correct edition for your needs. I recommend the Enterprise edition, and that is what this book presumes you have installed. However, most everything we do in this text can be accomplished with the Professional edition. I do not recommend the Learning edition for anything but just that: learning. Even then, it doesn't come with all the features you will want to see.

Visual Basic Editions

Each version of Visual Basic comes in several different editions.

- The **Learning edition** is for beginners. Although it contains the standard control set, it does not contain enough features to effectively develop an application.

- The **Professional edition** has more controls than the Learning edition and has support for creation of basic applications for small businesses.

- The **Enterprise edition** is what businesses need to create full client-server applications. It contains additional controls and add-ins such as Visual Source Safe and so on.

For more information on the editions available, see the Microsoft Web site for Visual Basic at `http://msdn.microsoft.com/vbasic/Prodinfo/`.

Visual Basic Installation Notes

Like most programs, the Visual Basic CDs come with an Installation Wizard. Allow the wizard to guide you through the installation process. If you are a beginner, using all of the defaults is the best way to start. The only exception to this is the Help files. After Visual Basic is installed and just before the wizard ends, it asks if you want to install the Help files. The answer is, of course, that you most definitely *do* want to install Help files. If you have room on your hard drive, install all possible Help and Sample files. What is available will depend on whether you are installing just Visual Basic alone or other Visual Studio applications such as C++ as well. The ability to get Help on *all* topics is of great value for testing applications so take all that you can! You will be able to limit the set of items searched when you select Help, as we will see in the next chapter.

Storage Requirements for Installing Visual Basic 6

If you have a good-sized hard drive, install the "maximum installation" option. This will require 135MB for the Enterprise Edition or 94MB for the Professional Edition. The MSDN install will take 57MB if you select just the Visual Basic Help, but 493MB if you take it all (as I recommend)! If you don't have enough storage space, you will obviously not be able to install all of the MSDN Help. In that case, you can access it from the CD as necessary. This information was taken from the Microsoft Web site. When you install, there are some other options you can select that will increase the size. For more information, see the Microsoft Web site at `http://msdn.microsoft.com/vbasic/Prodinfo/`.

Visual Basic Templates and Wizards

Visual Basic 6 has a toolset that can be used to support testing without doing any coding. Included in this toolset are an abundance of wizards, the Visual Database Tools, the Object Browser, and the T-SQL Debugger. Not only does getting comfortable with this toolset have benefits for testing projects, it also happens to be a good way to get familiar with Visual Basic.

Using the Data Form Wizard

There are many wizards available in Visual Basic. Wizards are added via the Add-in menu item. Not all of them are useful for testing; for instance, the Application Wizard generates a lot of code but needs so much customization that it's easier just to start from scratch. One that can be useful for testers is the Data Form Wizard, which creates a form that will link to an ODBC-compliant database. The form can be set up to view records individually or in a grid format. This can then be compiled into a quickly set up and easy-to-use test tool for inspecting data.

....

ODBC and OLE DB

ODBC stands for Open Database Connectivity. Its official definition from the MSDN Library is:

"A standard programming language interface used to connect to a variety of data sources. This is usually accessed through Control Panel, where DSNs (Data Source Names) can be assigned to use specific ODBC drivers."

Before ODBC, programmers had to use programming languages specific to each database in order to write code to access them. If you were accessing data in just a single database, that was fine but with the need to access many different kinds of data in many different kinds of data stores—such as spreadsheets in Excel or Oracle, SQL Server, Paradox, and Access databases—it became very complex to try to write code to effectively access them all. Why not come up with a standard way to access a database? Thus, ODBC was born and basically revolutionized the ability to access multiple kinds of data. The companies that make databases, like Oracle and Microsoft, provide "drivers" or code modules that access their software in a predefined, standard way. It makes life easier for the programmer. If a database is ODBC-compliant (and most all of them are) you just need to assign a DSN name, which you can basically think of as an alias, for the database. As the definition says, you do this through the control panel of your computer. From then on, you can access that database in a standard way using that DSN.

By the way, there's now another standardized programming language interface, OLE DB. OLE DB is a similar notion to ODBC. It's Microsoft's new component database architecture interface. Why do we need another standardized programming language interface for databases? OLE DB goes further than ODBC to allow access to even non-Windows databases like Unix data stores. We will revisit this when we tackle database testing in Chapter 8.

....

Visual Basic contains a couple of sample databases you can use. It's a good idea to get familiar with Visual Basic capabilities using a sample database rather than messing with real data. If you mess up the sample, it's okay. The Northwind sample database has data that simulates the kind of information you might see in a typical product and sales database. It has several tables of data. One, the Customers table, lists information about customers, such as name, address, state, phone, etc. Table 2-1 shows a sample of some of the data in the Northwind database Customer table.

Table 2-1. The Customers table from Microsoft's sample database, Northwind

CUSTOMERID	COMPANY NAME	CONTACT NAME	CONTACT TITLE	ADDRESS/CITY
ALFKI	Alfreds Futterkiste	Maria Anders	Sales Representative	Obere Str. 57 Berlin
ANATR	Ana Trujillo Emparedados y Helados	Ana Trujillo	Owner	Avda. de la Constitución 2222 México D.F.
ANTON	Antonio Moreno Taquería	Antonio Moreno	Owner	Mataderos 2312 México D.F.

Let's say you are testing this database and want to access the Customer's table, perhaps to add test data. In the next few steps, we will create a form to access the Customer's table using the Data Form Wizard.

1. Select **Microsoft Visual Studio** from the Program group on the Start menu. Then select **Microsoft Visual Basic 6.** The New Project window appears. As you can see in this window, you can create many types of applications using Visual Basic.

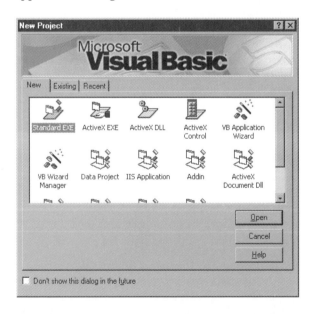

2. Double-click on the **Standard EXE icon**. Visual Basic's IDE (integrated development environment) appears as shown in the following illustration. It already contains a blank form but we will ignore this one to add a data form in the steps below. For now, we won't explore the IDE in great detail; we will go into the components of the IDE more fully in the next chapter.

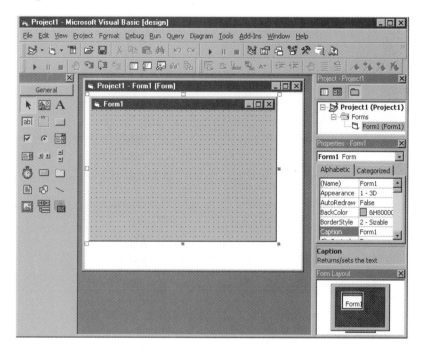

3. From the **Project** menu (located fourth from the left on the main menu), select **Add Form**.

NOTE *This will add a second form to your project since Visual Basic always has a default form. At this point, we will only deal with our new form.*

The Add Form dialog appears as shown in the following illustration.

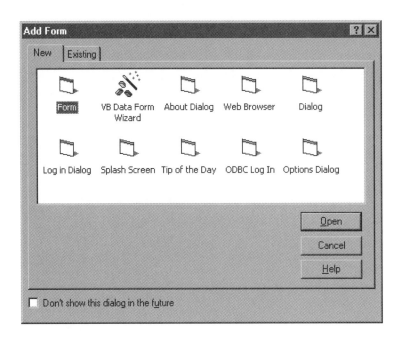

Notice that one of the possible items you can select is the **VB Data Form Wizard**.

4. Double-click on the **VB Data Form Wizard** icon to start the wizard. The first screen asks if you want to use a profile, you don't so just click the **Next** button.

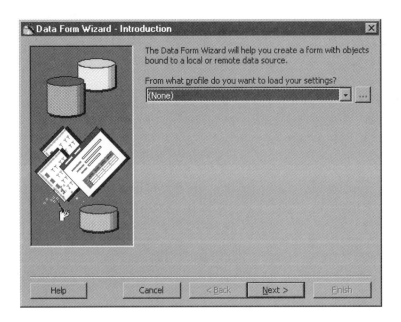

5. Continue to the next screen and select **Access** for the database format (it's the default).

6. Continue to the next screen where you will be asked to select a database. Any file with an .mdb extension will work. If you installed all of the sample files when you installed Visual Basic, you can type in the following full pathname for the Northwind sample database:

    ```
    c:\Program Files\Microsoft Visual Studio\VB98\Nwind.mdb
    ```

7. Continue past the next screen, accepting the defaults. On the Record Source dialog shown in the following illustration, you will need to select a **table** in the database. From the **Record Source** dropdown list, select **Customers** as shown.

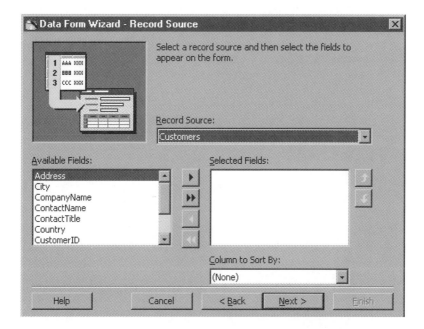

Select as many fields as you want to display from the **Available Fields** list by clicking them and then clicking the **right arrow** next to the list. The fields you select will show up in the **Selected Fields** list box. Just make sure that the Selected Fields list box is not empty and select the **Next** button.

8. Accept all defaults and click **Finish**. Visual Basic creates the form for you and generates a bunch of code, including all links to the data, automatically.

NOTE *You will see a confirmation dialog telling you that your new form has been created. Click **OK** to move past this.*

9. Before you can view the data in the database from your new form, you will have to do just one more thing: select the **Project** menu again and then select the **Project1 Properties** submenu item.

   The Project Properties dialog appears.

   From the **Startup Object** dropdown list in the upper right corner of the dialog, select the new form you just created, **frmCustomers,** as shown in the following dialog.

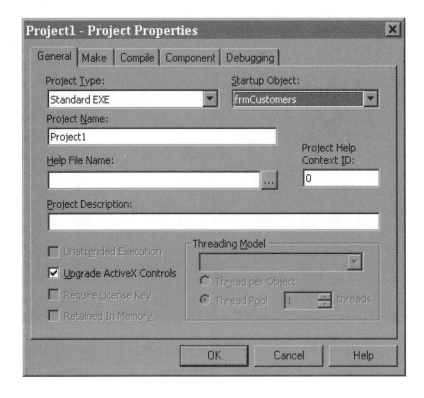

Then click the **OK** button on the dialog to close it. You have just set your new project to start with the customer form you created. Now you are finally ready to run the new program and see the data from the Northwind database.

10. Press the **F5** button on your keyboard to run your new project. You can now click the arrow buttons on the dialog of your new Customers form to view the records in the Northwind database as shown in the following illustration.

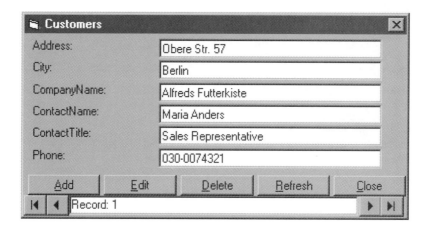

This makes an easy front end for your database. It allows you to view existing data and enter test data quickly and easily without doing any programming. When you are done viewing the data, you can close the window by clicking the 'X' in the upper right corner. When you exit Visual Basic, you will be prompted to save the form and project. You will not need to save this, so you can exit without saving at this point. Saving Visual Basic projects is covered in Chapter 3.

As your Visual Basic experience grows, other wizards, such as the Data Object Wizard and the ActiveX Control Interface Wizard, can help you set up and deploy useful test objects with minimum coding.

Using Form Templates

Form templates are provided to speed the creation of standard types of forms. Not only can you use these to generate common forms such as a splash screen, an ODBC log on (seen in Figure 2-1), an About box, or a Web browser, but the code is generated along with the form. When you created the new form in the last example, did you notice the number of form templates available? These are not produced with a wizard as our data form was but they do have preset characteristics, including plenty of code, which makes them very beneficial in a test project in a project and as learning tools.

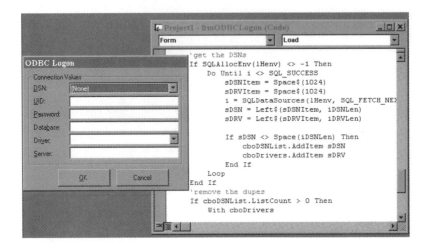

Figure 2-1. An ODBC log on form generated from a template with associated code.

The ODBC log-on form template produces a form like the one shown in Figure 2-1. Some of the code that is generated when the form is created is also shown. The code behind this form handles retrieving and listing the available DSNs (Data Source Names) for database access. The code produced for each of the form templates is a great learning tool. You can copy and paste it when you want to do similar kinds of actions. The code for the ODBC log on form is a bit beyond what we can handle at this point, though. We will use a form template and investigate the code behind it further in Chapter 5. And in Chapter 8, we will again revisit the code behind this form with a better understanding of the techniques that it uses.

Using the Visual Database Tools: White Box Testing Using SQL

The Visual Database Tools allow you to link to an ODBC (Open Database Connectivity) or OLE DB-compliant database. You can view the database structure, for example, its tables, views, and other basic objects. These tools, including the Data View window and Data Environment Designers, support database application testing by allowing you to examine the database back-end with a common interface. This means that if your application has data in SQL Server, Oracle, and Access, you can examine all of these sources using the Visual Database Tools rather than having to log into each DBMS (Database Management System) interface separately. This allows Visual Basic to be a common interface front-end to a database back-end that is accessible via ODBC or OLE DB and that can save you some testing time and perhaps even training time in those database products.

The Visual Database Tools support White Box testing since you can use them to enter and test SQL statements against the database. Figure 2-2 shows the Data View window open with a connection to the Northwind database. Notice that you can see the tables in the database by expanding the Tables folder. Double-clicking on a table will yield a window that returns all data. If you can connect to the Microsoft SQL Server and log on with the proper permissions, you can modify the data and even create new Data objects like tables and views. The Data View window can also be used to inspect Database objects such as Views and Stored Procedures.

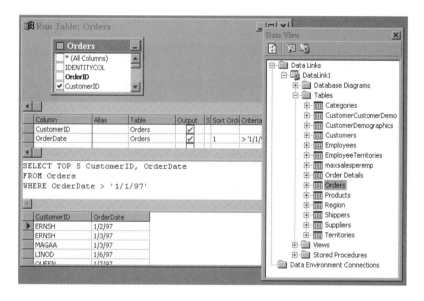

Figure 2-2. The Visual Database Tools windows include the Data View window for linking to a database and the Query Builder window for creating and testing SQL statements.

SQL (Structured Query Language)

SQL is the standard language for retrieving and manipulating data in a relational database. Unlike Visual Basic, SQL is not a full programming language. SQL deals with database access only. If you will be testing databases, you would be well-advised to establish a good grounding in this important language. If you are not sure whether you will be testing databases, keep in mind that all software applications use data and most store this data in some type of database. In Chapter 8, I will present some SQL statements that are practical for testing. There are many good beginning books available for learning SQL—see Appendix A: Resources and References for more information.

Also shown in Figure 2-2 is the Query Builder window where you can create SQL statements for testing data. For example, you can use SQL statements to retrieve duplicate rows and uncover referential integrity leaks, which supports database testing. In the example shown, the last five rows entered into the Orders table are retrieved using a SQL Select statement.

You can get to the Visual Database Tools by selecting the **View ➤ Data View** menu item that displays the Data View window. However, I will defer a step-by-step use of the Visual Database tools until Chapter 8. There, we will explore the use of the Visual Database tools for testing purposes as well as other ways to access and inspect databases.

The T-SQL Debugger: Inspecting and Testing Stored Procedures

The T-SQL Debugger is an add-in to Visual Basic that allows you to open, inspect, run, and debug a stored procedure from a Microsoft SQL Server database.

You can use the T-SQL Debugger if you are quite familiar with SQL Server databases and their objects, such as stored procedures. If you are not familiar with those, you need to do a bit of study on databases and SQL Server before this will be very useful to you. Figure 2-3 shows the T-SQL Debugger window displaying a stored procedure from the Northwind database.

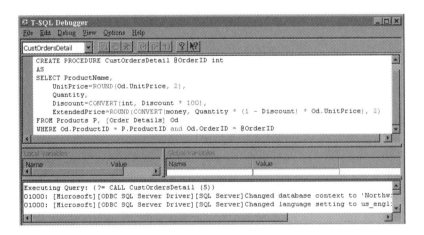

Figure 2-3. The T-SQL Debugger can be used to debug SQL Server stored procedures.

You can use the Visual Database Tools to link to a database and list all of the stored procedures; you can then invoke the T-SQL Debugger to step through the code in one of the stored procedures in the database. This can be useful if you are drilling down into the data to find the source of a bug. It may be that the problem is in the code for a stored procedure called from the database by the application you are testing, rather than in the application's code. The T-SQL Debugger can help you determine the answer. To add the T-SQL Debugger to Visual Basic, follow these steps.

TO TRY THIS

1. Select the **Add-Ins ➤ Add-In Manager** menu item. The **Add-In Manager** dialog with a list of available add-in programs will appear. Notice that you can add quite a few wizards and other applications to Visual Basic.

2. Select the **VB T-SQL Debugger** from the list. With this item highlighted, click the **Loaded/Unloaded** checkbox. This will add the T-SQL Debugger to your Add-ins menu. If you want this to remain in your menu for the next time you start up Visual Basic, also check the **Load on Startup** checkbox.

3. Click **OK** to dismiss the **Add-In Manager** dialog box.

4. Now you can select the **Add-Ins ➤ T-SQL Debugger** menu item. The **Visual Basic Batch T-SQL Debugger** dialog will appear. You will now need to fill in the appropriate connection information to get to your SQL Server database. After that, you can select a stored procedure to access and run.

Figure 2-3 shows the T-SQL Debugger with the contents of a stored procedure. The debugger allows you to insert test data for parameters and then step through the code line-by-line.

We won't cover the T-SQL Debugger in great depth because its use is limited only to Microsoft SQL Server. It's also a bit buggy, so if you use it, do so with caution. For more information on the T-SQL Debugger, see the Visual Basic online Help.

Exploring COM Objects Using the Object Browser

Another useful tool in Visual Basic that doesn't take any programming experience is the Object Browser. Using Visual Basic's References dialog, you can set a reference to a COM (Component Object Model) object. Once the reference has been set, you can use the Object Browser to inspect any properties and methods that the object exports.

....

COM (Component Object Model)

The official definition of COM from the MSDN Library is:

"An object-oriented programming model for building software applications made up of modular components. COM allows different software modules, written without information about each other, to work together as a single application. COM enables software components to access software services provided by other components, regardless of whether they involve local function calls, operating system calls, or network communications."

Many software applications can export information about themselves so they can be used in other software applications. Microsoft Word is a good example of this. The information it exports allows the programmer to access and use Word inside of his or her own programs. For example, you could access an existing Word document and modify it within your VB program once you get experienced enough. For a tester, this is great because you can use VB to access files and other items created by the application you are testing. To be able to export this information, programmers use the COM object model described previously.

Essentially, COM is a hierarchical arrangement of the objects of a software application and their properties, methods, and events. COM handles making these objects available to other software applications. Anyone who knows a bit about COM and programming can create a COM object, so you will find yourself dealing with them as your testing career progresses. In this book, we have a whole chapter that deals with testing COM objects (Chapter 9).

....

Figure 2-4 shows the Object Browser displaying the library of a custom COM object called Housing. The Housing library displays the events, properties, and methods of this object. Notice the definition of the ComputeFee function with its parameter and return value as well as a description of its purpose.

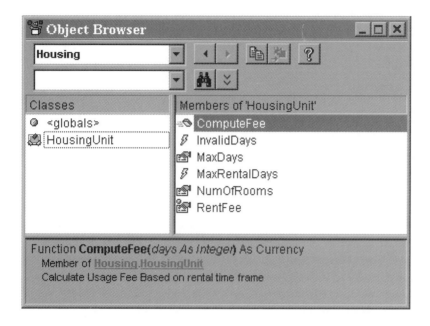

Figure 2-4. The Object Browser displaying the elements of a class.

The Housing object could have been created in any language that supports the COM object model. Setting a reference to an object and viewing the information in the Object Browser can be done in a couple of minutes by a tester with very little Visual Basic training. (Although the tester would have to have a basic understanding of COM.) If you were assigned to test an object like the Housing object, you could use the Object Browser to manually determine the existence of the object and to verify the number and existence of its properties and methods.

The Object Browser also exposes the kind of parameters required and, if the developers have been thorough, can bring up customized help on the objects. Testers can utilize this information to create verification and functionality tests on these objects in Visual Basic code.

Let's start by using the Object Browser to explore a library that is familiar, like Microsoft Word.

TO TRY THIS

1. Select **Microsoft Visual Studio** from the Program group on the Start menu. Then select **Microsoft Visual Basic 6**. The New Project window appears.

2. Double-click on the **Standard EXE icon**.

3. Click the **Object Browser** icon (shown here) from the Standard Toolbar.

 NOTE *To select the Object Browser, you can also press the* **F2** *key or select* **View** ➢ **Object Browser** *from the menu.*

The Object Browser dialog displays. If you click on the **All Libraries** dropdown, you will see a listing of all of the libraries available to Visual Basic by default. These include the VB, VBA, VBRUN, and STDOLE libraries as shown here.

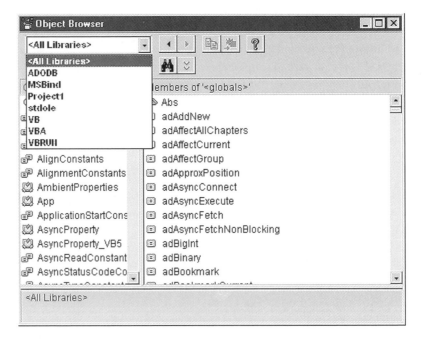

These form the core set of libraries used when you use Visual Basic commands to build applications. The Project1 library is the library attached to your current project. All of the forms, controls, etc. that you create are part of a library. Notice that you do not currently have access to Microsoft Word's Object library. If you did, it would be in this library list.

4. To add a reference to the Microsoft Word Object library, you must have Office products installed. If you do, then using the Visual Basic menu, select the **Project ➤ References** menu item as shown:

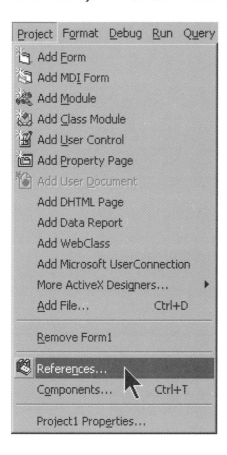

The References dialog box appears.

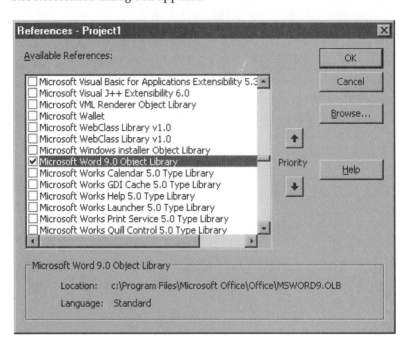

5. Scroll down in the **Available References** list until you find the **Microsoft Word Library** and click its **checkbox** to select it as shown.

   Notice that the Library itself is contained in the file MSWORD9.OLB. It is installed when Microsoft Word is installed. If you are missing this file, you obviously won't be able to reference the library or use it in your applications. If you do have it, you have access to all of Microsoft Word's capabilities from within your Visual Basic applications. This is very powerful for both developers and testers not just because you can access Word but also because you can use this same method to access any object library. Notice the long list of available libraries provided by Microsoft and other companies. There are more available through other manufacturers of software applications.

6. Click the **OK** button on the References dialog to add the library.

7. Return to the Object Browser. If you select the **Available Libraries** drop-down, you will now see Word. If you select **Word** from this list, you will see the Object Browser display the objects contained in the Word library as shown here. Some of them, such as document, dictionary, and Words, should sound familiar—these are all word processing objects as you might expect of a word processor library!

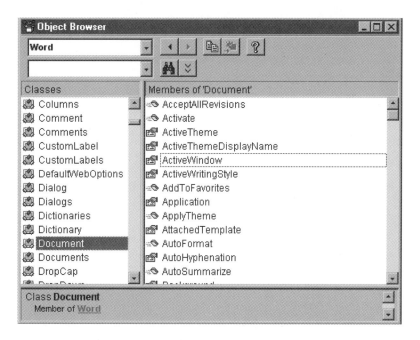

As a tester, you can now verify the existence of COM objects in an application and also determine the existence of the properties, methods, and events of those objects. To do more, you will need to know more about programming in Visual Basic. The remaining chapters in this book will assist you.

The Enterprise Tools

There are a lot of useful tools included in the Enterprise Edition. Some can be very valuable for testing purposes; for example, the APE (Application Performance Explorer) and the OLE/COM Object Viewer. I won't cover these tools here since they belong to the Enterprise package rather than Visual Basic specifically. However, these are worth investigating.

All of the tools we have covered in this section can be used without a line of Visual Basic code. In the next chapter, we'll start looking at simple coding examples to return more key test information.

Part Two

The Second Stage: Introduction to Automated Script Writing

CHAPTER 3

Introduction to the Visual Basic Development Environment

In order to use Visual Basic for testing or any other purpose, you are going to need to learn how to move around in the Visual Basic development environment. In this chapter, you will learn the uses of the major windows within the Visual Basic environment; how to create and run a simple program; and how to use the Help system. Along the way, I will continue to provide explanations and tips that make this information relevant to the tester.

Objectives

By the end of this chapter, you will be able to:

- Start up the Visual Basic development environment.

- Define and use the Design and Run modes in the Visual Basic development environment.

- Create Textbox and Command button controls and set their properties using the Properties window.

- Create an Access key for a control.

- Use basic input and output operations to retrieve information and return it to a user during a test run.

- Use certain editing features and tools of the Visual Basic IDE (integrated development environment) to edit an application.

- Save Visual Basic project files.

- Use the Tools ➤ Options dialog box to customize the Visual Basic development environment.

- Use the Project ➤ Properties dialog box to set Project properties.

- Describe how to get help from the Visual Basic Help system.

Visual Basic History

John Kemeny and Tom Kurtz originally developed the BASIC language in 1964 as a learning tool for students at Dartmouth College. Originally an acronym, BASIC stood for **B**eginner's **A**ll-purpose **S**ymbolic **I**nstruction **C**ode. Compared to Machine-language and Assembly-language, it was much easier to use to teach fundamental programming concepts. Because of this, the use of the BASIC language expanded past the academic. Paul Allen and Bill Gates licensed their own version of BASIC in the mid-1970s for the Altair computer. In 1988, Alan Cooper sold to Microsoft a drag-and-drop shell prototype using BASIC. Alan Cooper's prototype was the beginning of the modern Visual Basic's graphical look and feel. Visual Basic's easy to learn, English-like language and its useful GUI has made it very attractive as a macro language for many applications. Microsoft uses it as the standard macro language, Visual Basic for Applications (VBA), for its widely used Office products. Microsoft dropped the acronym for its product, Visual Basic, intending instead that the name Basic mean a fundamental, straightforward programming language.

Microsoft's Visual Basic, first launched in 1991, is now in version 6. Each version has increased Visual Basic's abilities in application development. Initially released to provide a tool for rapid application development at the cost of rather bulky and inefficient executables, Visual Basic's current executable size and timing in many instances rival that of C++. Visual Basic is powerful and flexible and can still be learned more easily and quickly than can C/C++. As James Fawcette writes in the February 2001 *Visual Basic Programmer's Journal*, "A major part of what has made VB so enormously successful—reaching more developers than all other languages before it combined—is that it has made levels of programming accessible to developers who don't live and breathe development day in and day out." This is exactly what makes Visual Basic a premiere language for the testing community. We test code first and write code second—or third. For automated testing, we need programming languages that are powerful enough to do the job yet straightforward enough to learn quickly. Visual Basic answers that call.

NOTE *VB.NET is the next version of Visual Basic and is scheduled for release in late 2001. It is very different in approach than previous versions of Visual Basic. Chapter 11 covers some of the differences and the implications of these changes for testers. For more information on the current status and features of VB.NET, see the Microsoft Web site at* http://msdn.microsoft.com/vbasic/.

Getting Started with Visual Basic

While this book is targeted to the tester, at some point you will have to learn the fundamentals of working with Visual Basic, as does any new programmer. In this section, we will explore how to work with Visual Basic's IDE (integrated development environment) as well as how to create, edit, debug, save, and run a simple application. In the process, we will also cover some important concepts such as Design mode versus Run mode, focus, events, and event-driven programming.

Starting Up Visual Basic

Visual Basic's IDE can be used to create, debug, and run your testing script code. It includes a number of utilities and tools to support the creating, editing, and debugging processes.

TO TRY THIS

1. Select the **Start** menu and then select **Programs**. Select **Microsoft Visual Studio**, and then select **Microsoft Visual Basic 6**. The New Project window appears. As you see in this window (Figure 3-1), you can create many types of applications using Visual Basic.

NOTE *Depending on the edition installed, you may only need to select Start menu, Programs, and then Microsoft Visual Basic 6.*

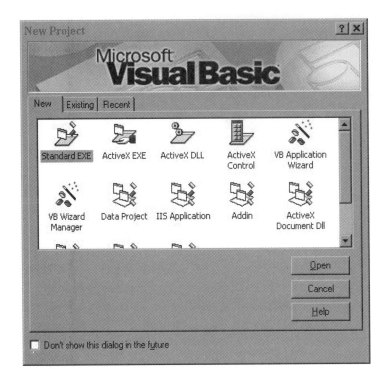

Figure 3-1. The New Project window is the first window to display after launching Visual Basic 6.

Most executables that can be created with Visual Basic can be started with the Standard EXE project. This is the one we will start with to create a simple application.

2.   Double-click on the **Standard EXE** icon to produce the Visual Basic Development Environment window seen in Figure 3-2.

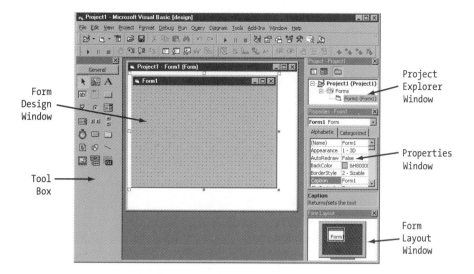

Figure 3-2. The Visual Basic development environment initially displays with five default windows.

Using Visual Basic's Five IDE Windows

The Visual Basic development environment contains five default windows. Each of these has a specific purpose in helping to design a working Visual Basic application:

The **Toolbox** contains controls such as buttons, combo boxes, and text boxes that a user typically sees on an application. These controls are placed on the Form Designer window (usually by double-clicking their icon in the Toolbox).

The **Form Designer** window is the one the user sees when the application runs. Most applications have more than one window. Visual Basic starts with one default window but developers are able to add more.

The **Project Explorer** window shows what modules we currently have in our application. In our case, the default case, we have only one module, the Form module. The Project Explorer window expands with more items as we add more forms and other kinds of modules to our project.

The **Properties** window displays information about the current control, form, or other object that is currently selected. If the form is selected, the Properties window displays the properties that make it look and behave as it does. For example, the BackColor property shows the color that the form currently has. Properties like the BackColor can be changed from the Properties window.

The **Form Layout** window displays the location of all of the application's windows when the user runs the program.

Running a Visual Basic Program

All of the previous steps have been in Design mode. Now we can run the program. When we do this, we are putting it into another mode called Run mode. *Design mode* is where you develop the Visual Basic application. *Run mode* is where you test it out to see what you have done and how it looks to the user. Even though you have made no changes, you currently have an executable Visual Basic program (see Figure 3-3). It is an extremely boring program at this point, but a program nonetheless.

To run the program, press the **F5** key or select **Run ➢ Start** from the Visual Basic menu.

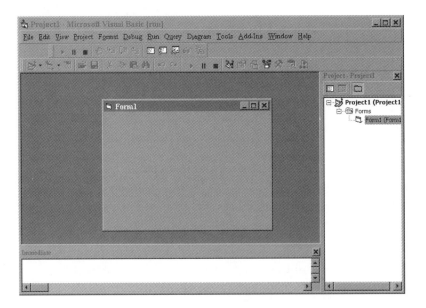

Figure 3-3. Visual Basic in Run Mode with the simplest program you can create.

Notice that the caption of the development environment now contains the word: [Run]. (Did you notice that before running this program, the caption contained the word [Design]?) Layered on top of the Visual Basic development environment you can see the form of our application containing its default caption: Form1.

You get a lot of things for free with Visual Basic right from the start—you can see this by examining the window in Figure 3-3. It has many of Windows' default capabilities. For example, it is sizeable; it also has the Windows control box for maximizing, restoring, and minimizing the window; and it disappears when you click the 'X' in its upper right corner. Run your cursor over the window to verify this. Your cursor will change to a double arrow along the edges of the window, allowing you to size it. Pull down the **System** menu in the upper left-hand corner. You don't have to write any Visual Basic code to get these default capabilities.

In the next section, we will explore what we can do in Design mode to make the program more interesting to the user in Run mode. When you are in Design mode, think of it as being in a big garage, building a car or an airplane. That's where all of your tools are; in our case, these tools are contained in the Toolbox window and in the menu items. You've got all kinds of tools and options for building your system. Think of Run mode as taking the system you have built out for a test drive. During this test drive, you find out how your system looks to a user and how well it works. When you are out for the test drive (Run mode), you've left your tools back in the garage (Design mode), right? That's why you don't see the Toolbox window and why many of the menu items are grayed out in Run mode. You will need to go back to the garage, Design mode, to finish your system. Knowing what mode you are in, Design mode or Run mode, is important. You can always tell what mode you are in by looking up at the caption of the Visual Basic IDE main window.

Visual Basic Application Development

In this section, you will learn the initial steps for Visual Basic application development. In Visual Basic, development of a software application begins with a design of the user-interface—that is, the forms, buttons, and other tools the user sees and uses on the application's forms. As testers, we don't care to learn about a huge range of different tools and all of their possible options and settings, at least at first. To start with, we will want to work with the few basic controls most useful to us to return information quickly. Beauty and bells and whistles can wait, functionality is key. Nevertheless, you will need to change hats here and think like a developer. A developer writes code for a user. In your case, that user may end up being yourself or just a few other testers. A developer always writes code with the user in mind, though. What are the user's capabilities? What actions can you anticipate that the user will take? This will determine what features and code you will add to your application.

Adding Controls to a Form

First things first. Use the **Toolbox** window to select controls such as a Textbox and a Command button to place on the form inside the Form Designer window. You can select controls from the Toolbox simply by double-clicking them.

Double-click a control in the Toolbox to place it on the form. If you click on the Command button control in the Toolbox, a Command button with the default caption "Command1" shows up in the middle of the form.

When a control is first created, it has "handles" on it as shown in Figure 3-4. You can use your mouse to click on these handles and drag to size the control.

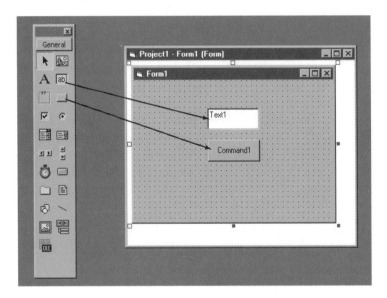

Figure 3-4. Double-click a control in the toolbox to place it on the form. The newest control has "handles" for sizing.

If you click somewhere in the middle of the control, the cursor will change to a drag icon and you can then drag the control to move it to a different location.

Understanding Focus

Figure 3-4 shows a form in Design mode with a textbox and a Command button control. Note that the textbox has handles and the Command button does not. This means that the textbox is currently the control with the *focus*.

Having the focus means that this is the control Windows considers active at the moment. If you were to hit the Delete key now, this control would disappear! It also means that you can now drag one of the handles to size this control. In addition, the properties associated with the control are shown in the Properties window.

 TIP *If you accidentally press the Delete key and delete a control, you can always retrieve it by selecting the **Undo** button from the standard toolbar. You can also undo by selecting **Edit ➤ Undo** or by pressing the **Ctrl** key and the **Z** key simultaneously.*

Figure 3-5 shows what the same form would look like in Run mode. (Remember how to get to Run mode? Press the **F5** key.) Notice which control has the focus now.

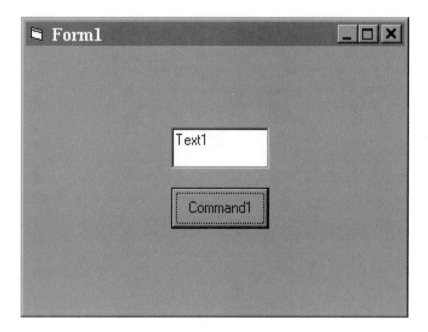

Figure 3-5. The same form as in Figure 3-4 but now shown in Run mode.

You can type text into the textbox and you can click the button but nothing happens. In order to make something happen, you must write Visual Basic code. We have added some controls to make our program *look* like something real but it still isn't very useful. Another problem is the uninformative caption of the button and the boring colors and fonts.

We will make our application more useful by writing code soon. First, let's make it look a little better. How about changing the caption of the button or changing colors and fonts to make it more visually appealing?

Developer or Tester?

Starting to feel like a developer? These issues, such as making an application visually appealing and easy to use, may not always seem so important to some of the test applications we will want to write. After all, in most cases, you probably won't be attempting to sell your test applications to others. These discussions give you valuable insight into the issues that developers deal with every day. These insights can only give you a better understanding of the process, which will make you a better tester. Also, learning quick and easy ways to make test applications simple and appealing to use will be very helpful to both you and your colleagues. It can also make the difference between whether your test application gets used or not. If it's not easy to use as well as functional, it won't get used, and that will be time wasted.

Let's go back to Design mode and discover some ways we can change the look of our program through the use of properties.

Working with the Properties Window

A *property* is an attribute of an object. For example, the color of a form is one of its properties. Other properties are its height and its width. You can think of a property as describing an object. After all, if you were to describe the form in Figure 3-5, you would probably describe how it looks in terms of size and color, for example, "It's gray and it's about four inches wide and three inches tall."

You can change the properties of objects in two ways:

- In Design mode using the Properties window.

- By writing Visual Basic code to change the property while the program is running.

We will explore both methods in this chapter. Perhaps the most straightforward method is to change property values of a control by using the Properties window so we will do that first. Later, we'll change values of the properties using Visual Basic code and then compare the two methods.

Changing Property Values Using the Properties Window

The Properties window shown in Figure 3-6 displays the properties of the form itself. Notice that the form has properties for its appearance and color. You can change these values to alter the appearance of the form.

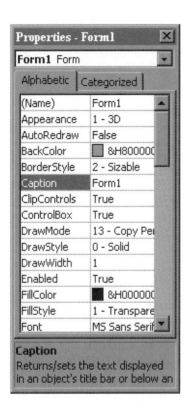

Figure 3-6. The Properties window displaying the properties of a form.

TO TRY THIS

1. Place your cursor in the value next to the **Caption** property. Start typing and you will notice that the caption of the form changes as you type.

2. Next, place your cursor in the **BackColor** property. Notice that there is already a value filled in; this is a number representing the color gray, the default BackColor for a form. Notice that this property value displays an arrow.

3. Click on the arrow in the **BackColor** property. A tabbed **dialog box** displays allowing you to select a color.

NOTE *There are two tabs on the dialog that displays here: System and Palette. If you select colors from the System tab, you will be selecting colors that match the color scheme chosen by the user of the computer. This is the same color scheme that any computer user can change in the Control Panel. If you choose a color from the Palette tab, you can choose any color you want but it won't necessarily match the computer's color scheme.*

4. Select **any color** you would like for your form. You have now changed the BackColor property.

TIP *You can explore more information about these properties by placing your cursor on one of them and pressing **F1**. This will put you into Visual Basic's context-sensitive Help window. You can read about the property and see an example of it used in Visual Basic code. (If this does not place you into Visual Basic's online Help, make sure the Help is actually installed. Installing Help is an installation option— it doesn't happen automatically.)*

If you want to change values for properties of the Command button, simply click on the Command button on the form and notice that the Properties window changes to show the properties of the Command button instead of the form.

You can further change the appearance of the form, Command buttons, or any other object by modifying properties such as the Height, Width, Left, and Top. Take some time to fool around with these and see what happens. Notice that the Properties window helps you figure out what these properties are and do by giving a little explanation at the bottom of the window. You can also search for information about these properties using Visual Basic Help.

Assigning Access Keys

Many controls have Caption properties. The Caption property of a control describes that control to the program's user. The Caption property has a default value—for example, the default caption for a button is Command1. As you can see, the default value of the Caption property is not very descriptive or useful to the user of the application. As the application's developer, you will change it to help the user determine what happens when the button gets pushed (even if the user is just going to be you). A better caption for the button would describe the button's purpose—for example, "OK," "Cancel," or "Exit."

If we create a button on a form and change the Caption property to Exit, you might guess that pressing that button would stop the program. Of course, it won't until we write the code to make it do so. (Patience, that part is coming soon!)

Notice that in the button caption displayed on the form in Figure 3-7, the 'x' is underlined. This allows the user to access the button via the keyboard by simultaneously holding down the Alt key and pressing the 'x' instead of having to click it with the mouse. Now the 'x' is considered the *Access key* for this control.

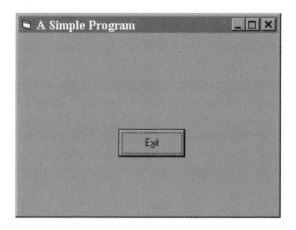

Figure 3-7. A button control with a defined Access key.

The ability to access any control by either using the mouse or pressing a key (or combination of keys) on the keyboard is a standard capability for Windows applications. It allows the user to access controls without using the mouse, an important consideration for those with physical limitations that preclude them from using a mouse. (See the "Accessibility" sidebar later in this chapter) It's also a nice alternative for those without any limitations. People who can type fast often prefer keyboard access since it can speed up data entry. Since it's a Windows standard, many users will expect this capability to exist, therefore, it should be there on all Windows software.

 TESTER'S TIP *Many times testers are called upon to test an application for "user-friendliness," which is a very subjective term but a market expectation nonetheless for today's software applications. Allowing keyboard access is an important metric in testing an application for user-friendliness. Even if the user of an application will only be yourself or another tester, user-friendliness is still important! (See the "Developer or Tester?" sidebar earlier in this chapter.)*

To assign an Access key is easy. Simply place an ampersand in the caption of the control just before the letter you want to be the Access key. For example, in the preceding case, you would place "E&xit" in the button's caption. The ampersand does not show to the user, it is replaced by an underline in the control's caption.

 NOTE *In a Windows 2000 environment, the Access keys do not always show up until the user presses the **Alt** key.*

Accessibility

Ensuring that all applications have keyboard access to all functions (rather than relying on the mouse) is important in accessibility testing. Accessibility testing is gaining more focus these days as companies endeavor to ensure that their products are accessible and usable to those with disabilities. Some people cannot use the mouse so companies must provide alternative methods for accessing applications features. There are other accessibility problems a user might have to deal with, such as limited vision or hearing. Many companies are attempting to address this issue by adding additional features. These features need testing so, at some point, you will likely find yourself testing an application for accessibility. Now you know how the developer provides one form of it: Access keys. For more information about accessibility issues in Windows programming, see Microsoft's Accessiblity Web site at `http://microsoft.com/enable/`.

Understanding Tab Order and the TabIndex Property

The TabIndex property is important enough to require its own heading. When you place a number of controls on a form, then run the program and hit the Tab key several times, you will notice that there is a specific order in which the controls are accessed. This is called the *tab order*. Figure 3-8 shows the TabIndex property highlighted in the Properties window.

Initially, the tab order for controls on the form corresponds to the order in which they are created. You will usually need to change this at some point since you won't always create the controls in the exact order you ultimately want the user to see them. Use the TabIndex property to do this.

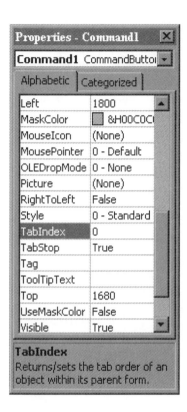

Figure 3-8. The Tab Order property of a control like a Command button indicates the order in which it will be accessed when the user presses the Tab key in Run mode.

The number in the TabIndex property reflects the numeric order in which the control is accessed when the user presses the Tab key. If the TabIndex is 0, then that is the first control to receive the focus when the form initially displays. If it is 1, then it is the second control accessed when the Tab key is pressed, and so on.

Combining Label Controls, Access Keys, and Tab Order

A label control is a control that *cannot* receive the focus, yet, it *does* have a TabIndex property. Why? It turns out that when the system tries to tab to a control that cannot receive the focus, it bypasses that control and goes to the next one in the tab order. This truly is a feature and not a bug! The reason for this is that some controls (like textboxes) do not have captions so setting an Access key for these controls is impossible. Yet, having an Access key is important for those with disabilities like RSI (Repetitive Strain Injury). Users of an application expect to be able to use the keyboard instead of the mouse.

To fix this problem, you can place a label control next to a textbox and put an Access key in the label's caption. You must then make sure that the label control's Tabindex property value is numerically *just before* the textbox's TabIndex property value. Then, when the user selects the Access key and attempts to tab to the label, the cursor ends up in the textbox control next to it. This effectively makes the label control a surrogate Access key for its neighboring textbox control. Why am I making such a big deal out of this? As it turns out, when testing, there have been times when I have had trouble accessing a control in an automated test script by using that control's own property values. Occasionally, I have been able to access the control by using the Access key for the control just preceding it in the tab order.

TESTER'S TIP *One thing to check when testing is whether the developer has set the proper tab order. Improper tab order is easy to do. As you can see, controls get a default tab order based on the order in which they are created. However, since controls can be moved around after being created, a hurried developer can forget to change the tab order. It's possible that a developer might not want to firm up the tab order until late in the development cycle because the UI frequently changes—however, that just makes it all the more important to check for proper tab order prior to product release!*

Now that we know how to change the looks of our controls and form, we are ready to make something happen. To do that, we will work with events in Visual Basic code.

Tab Order, How Important?

The tab order may not seem like a very important item to set. It is, however, one more metric by which user-friendliness can be measured. Once, when helping my mom learn to use the Internet, she complained that she couldn't figure out where she was going on a Web page. As I watched her, I realized that she mostly uses the Tab key to move around rather than the mouse. As a senior-citizen user, she's more accustomed to using typewriter keys rather than that new-fangled mouse, which was jumping her all over the page! So, I tried tabbing around the Web site myself and found that the tab order made no sense at all. It was obvious that the Web-site developer hadn't thought of it. It was a valuable lesson for me that those of us brought up with computers don't always have the same issues as those who don't. Because senior citizens are a growing population of computer users, this is something I test for regularly.

Writing Visual Basic Code

In this section, we will continue our exploration of Visual Basic fundamentals by learning a bit about how to write code. To do this, we need to learn about a new concept: events.

Working with Events: the Code Window

Events are just what they sound like: things that happen, actions. Examples of events in a software application include mouse-clicks, pressing a key, and dragging. Code can be rewritten to respond to these events—that is, the code will run immediately after the event occurs. So, if you want something to happen after a user clicks a button, such as printing a report, you could write code for the *click-event* of that button. The code will then execute when the application's user presses the button.

Earlier programming languages such as COBOL, Fortran, Pascal, and older versions of C were said to be *procedural* as opposed to event-driven. When a software developer wrote code in a procedural language, the developer was driving. In other words, the code ran and forced the user to take a certain step-by-step path through the software application. In these days of multiple icons, users get more choices about what to run and when. *Event-driven programming* allows the user to drive. The user selects an icon by double-clicking it and code runs in response. If the user chooses never to click that icon, its code never runs. If the user clicks a different icon or menu item, the code for that item runs. In procedural-type languages, application development begins by writing instructions to the computer to tell the application where to start and what to do. In Visual Basic, applications are event-driven—that is, the application knows where to start and what to do based on code written in response to events.

To allow an action as a result of a certain event, we add Visual Basic code. Visual Basic is object-oriented enough that you add code to the object that will be acted upon by the event. That is, if you want something to happen when you click a button, then the event is considered the click, and you add your code to the button being clicked.

For example, if you want an action when someone clicks a button, such as bringing up another form, you would add code to the button itself—specifically, you would add code to the button's click-event. You add code to events in the Code window. You must be in Design mode to bring up the Code window. Double-click on any control or the form itself to bring up the Code window, Double-clicking on the button control in our example form brings up the Code window, and places the cursor within the button's click-event handler.

Object-Oriented Programming

Simply stated, *object-oriented programming* means writing programs based on the objects in a software system. For example, a business system may be thought of in terms of its components, such as customers, employees, products, and invoices. Code is written for each object and how it interacts with the other objects. While Visual Basic is not a fully object-oriented programming language, it is considered *object-based*. One of the nicest things about working with Visual Basic is that you can use it to write mostly object-oriented code but it really doesn't *have* to be used for that purpose. Visual Basic itself is written in an object-oriented way but the programmer who uses it doesn't really need to know a lot about object-oriented programming to put Visual Basic to good use. It's good for a tester to know a bit about object-oriented programming because you may be testing such applications. There are some good references for object-oriented programming in Appendix A: Resources and References. You can also try the following link, `http://catalog.com/softinfo/objects.html`, for a good article introducing this concept, "What Is Object-Oriented Software?" by Terry Montlick.

When you double-click on a control in Design mode, your cursor is placed in an empty event handler. This event handler is the default event handler for that control. For example, the button control has a number of events associated with it but its default event is the click-event. In the Code window shown in Figure 3-9, the empty click-event handler for the Command1 button is shown.

Figure 3-9. The Code window for a Visual Basic form and its Object and Procedure boxes.

The code you will write between the two lines starting with sub and end sub is executed when the user clicks the button during Run mode. The Command1 is the name of the control and the Click is the event. Figure 3-10 shows a breakdown of the first line of the event handler.

Event Handle Title   Control Name   Event Name

Private Sub Command1_Click

Figure 3-10. The first line of an event handler indicates the name of the control and the name of the event.

Simple Visual Basic Statements

At times, you will want to make notes to yourself and others about what the program is trying to accomplish. You can do this without affecting what the program does by writing *comments*. Comments are completely ignored by the compiler.

Comments:

```
'This is a comment. Comments are ignored.
'They start with an apostrophe or the word "rem"
'Notice that comments turn green when you type them
'Comments can be used to document your code.
'

Rem This is also a comment
```

One of the most common things you will need to do in any computer program is to report information to the user. You will also need to gather information from the user. *Input statements* retrieve information; *Output statements* report information.

Output statements:

```
Msgbox "Tests are complete, press ok to continue"
Print "Test #1 passed "; time date
Debug.print "This goes to the immediate window"
```

Input statement:

```
Dim strInput As String 'this is a variable declaration; more on this later
strInput = Inputbox ("Please enter the name of the test to run: ")
```

Try typing these Output statements into the click-event of a button. Then press **F5** to run the program and click the button. Figure 3-11 shows the Output statements we discussed in the Code window. (The results in the Immediate window will not display until after the program has been run.)

The form itself is an object that has events associated with it. For example, the Form_Load event will run just before a form or window shows up on the screen. The Debug.Print works the same as the Print statement but will print to another window called the Immediate window. The Immediate window will not pop up automatically while the code is running. To see what has been printed into it, select **View ➤ Immediate Window** in both Run mode and Design mode.

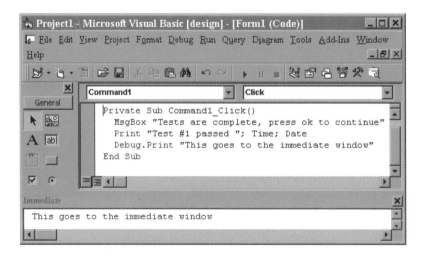

Figure 3-11. Simple Visual Basic statements for outputting information.

The MsgBox command will bring up a window with your message inside of it as shown in Figure 3-12. When the program executes this line, it will bring up the window and the user must click the OK button to continue.

TESTER'S TIP *The Immediate window is one of Visual Basic's debugging tools. It is a good place to print information that you want to see as the program runs but don't want to display to the user of the application. It is especially useful when you are trying to fix problems in your code. We will explore a few more uses of Visual Basic's debugging tools in the next chapter.*

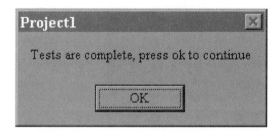

Figure 3-12. A Message box displays as a result of the MsgBox statement.

The Print statement will print text to the upper left corner of the form as shown in Figure 3-13.

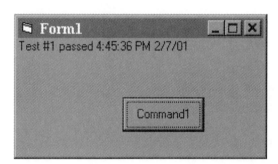

Figure 3-13. The results of the Print statement print to the upper left of the form.

TESTER'S TIP *As you can see, developers write code for the events they presume their users will most likely perform. What about those events the user performs that the developer doesn't antici-pate? In other words, if the user double-clicks the button, should the code run? If the Visual Basic developer does not write code for an event, nothing happens when the user performs that event. Sometimes that is desirable and sometimes it is not! It is important to understand user expectations by checking the test plan and any specifications for the applications you test.*

Saving Your Visual Basic Program

Visual Basic projects have at least two files to save: one file for each form in the project (.frm extension) and another for the project itself (.vbp extension). The following gives you the basic information to save your first Visual Basic program. Select **File** ➤ **Save Project** from the menu. First, you will be prompted to save the form. The default name is Form1 as shown in Figure 3-14.

 NOTE *You will only be prompted to save the project files the* first *time you save. After that, files will be saved automatically to the same location whenever you select **File** ➤ **Save Project** from the menu or click the **Save** icon on the toolbar. After the first time you save, if you want to save to another name or location, select **File** ➤ **Save Project As** from the menu instead.*

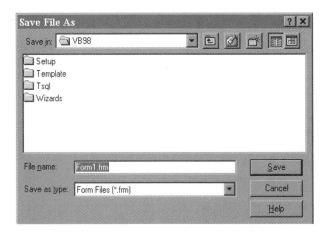

Figure 3-14. Saving a Visual Basic form. When you save a Visual Basic project for the first time, it will initally ask you to save the form (and then the project).

Change the default name from Form1 to something relevant to its use in the project and that will help you remember which project it belongs to. For example, if you are writing a program testing the Notepad, you might call your form NotepadfrmMain.frm

Next, you will be prompted to save the project file as shown in Figure 3-15. The default name is Project1.vbp. Using our previous example, you could name it NotepadProj.vbp. Clicking the **Save** button on the **Save Project As** dialog will save your project.

Notice that the default location is the VB98 folder. You can save your files to any folder. It's a good idea to create one of your own and store them there. Name your folders and files appropriately, keeping them linked by nomenclature to the appropriate spot in your test plan. After saving your files, you can exit Visual Basic knowing that you can retrieve your files and begin editing again wherever you left off.

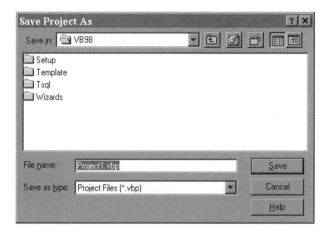

Figure 3-15. Saving the Project file. Choose a relevant name.

When you re-enter Visual Basic, you will be able to reopen the same files from Visual Basic's initial dialog box, New Project, by selecting either the Existing or Recent Files tabs. (See Figure 3-16)

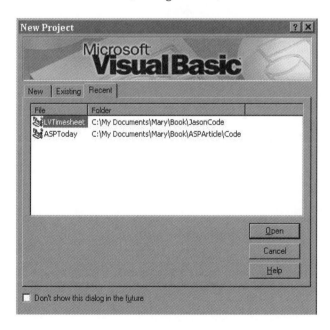

Figure 3-16. The Recent tab on the New Project dialog box lists recently accessed projects. This will speed up the ability to return to the same project whenever you enter and exit Visual Basic.

Setting Up a Good Directory
Structure for Your Visual Basic Files

It can be very helpful to set up a directory structure for your Visual Basic files right away. You will soon find as you learn and use Visual Basic on your testing projects that keeping track of all of the files can be very confusing. Proper versioning is important too—in other words, making sure you know which Visual Basic files test which version or build of your application-under-test. This is especially true if more than one of you is helping to build your Visual Basic test scripts. The following is a suggested directory structure used on many projects by a great tester named Lee Wallen. Basically, he has a top-level directory for the project and within that, two directories: BIN and SRC. In the BIN directory, he keeps EXE extension files and other binary-type files. In the SRC directory, he keeps his Visual Basic files. There are two subdirectories shown here, one for the Project files and one for the form files:

```
XYZProject Directory
- Bin (for holding the compiled .EXE or .DLL etc.)
--XYZSampleApp.exe
- Src
--Projects (all vbp files go in this directory)
--- XYZSampleProj.frm
--Forms (all vb forms go in this directory)
--- XYZfrmSampleForm.frm
```

There are other types of files for Visual Basic projects, such as class files, module files, and resource files. We haven't used these yet but we will. For now, setting up the basic directory structure will be enough. We can add more directories later as needed.

Visual Basic Help

Rumor has it that software developers are so smart they never need to use manuals or the Help system. Nothing could be further from the truth! Most good developers and testers have several well-thumbed reference books on hand and have read through all of the available Help. The Help system and documentation are valuable resources for software developers and especially for testers like you. Visual Basic provides context-sensitive Help as well as the standard Help system.

Using Context-Sensitive Help

Context-sensitive help means help that is specifically tailored to what you are doing right now. If you are trying to set a property or write a line of code, you don't want to have to go through a long hierarchy of Help topics before finding what you need. Context-sensitive help is just a button away—specifically, the F1 button.

TO TRY THIS

1. Open the Code window.

2. Type the command "**MsgBox**" anywhere in the Code window and place your cursor on it.

3. Press **F1**. The Help dialog displays with the MsgBox function description.

Figure 3-17 shows Help information for the MsgBox function. The MsgBox function is explained in text and command syntax is there to help you determine how to correctly write this function.

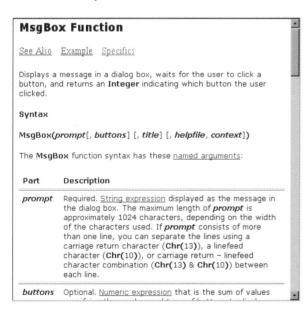

Figure 3-17. Online Help information for the MsgBox function.

Notice that the Help window for the MsgBox function also contains a link to an example. The examples are what I find most useful. The examples use the command in code, most often in a very relevant and useful way. Some of the examples are in the form of a short tutorial, they actually tell you how to copy and paste the example into your own code to see how it works. Additionally, there is a "See Also" link where you will find similar or related commands. These can especially be helpful in fully understanding the original item.

Understanding Command Syntax

To get the most out of Help, it is useful to know about the standard syntax used to describe commands. A common syntax was developed so that all programming manuals could describe how to write commands in the same manner. Command syntax tells you how to correctly formulate your Visual Basic commands. The following line shows the syntax for the MsgBox command used in Visual Basic Help:

MsgBox(*Prompt*[, *Buttons*] [, *Title*] [, *Helpfile*, *Context*])

Let's break this line down into its parts:

MSGBOX Anything in regular text must be provided as shown. Anything not inside square brackets is required. So the word "MsgBox" must appear in this particular command and must be spelled as shown. (Visual Basic is not case-sensitive, however.) This first item is the name of the command being described; each successive item is called an *argument* of this item.

NOTE *The term argument comes from mathematics, meaning the independent variable of a function. In plain English, it means a value that is provided to the command.*

PROMPT This argument is in italics and not inside square brackets, which means that this item is required but the italics signify that you must provide a literal or variable value to satisfy it. How do you know what exactly must be provided for the Prompt? Read down further in Help for the specifics on what is necessary. Notice in Figure 3-17 that the Prompt must be a *string expression* (in other words, some kind of textual value).

[, BUTTONS] Anything in square brackets is optional. This means that the MsgBox command can be used without this particular part. Optional arguments usually perform additional functions. This particular argument would allow the Message box to have additional sets of buttons other than just the OK button.

| The *pipe* symbol looks like a vertical line. If you encounter it in a command definition, it means "or." For example, note the use of the pipe symbol in the following definition:

```
[Public | Private] Const constname [As type] = expression
```

Here, the pipe (vertical line) is used to indicate that the statement can start with either the word "Public" *or* "Private" but not both!

You can access context-sensitive Help from almost anywhere within Design mode. Try accessing it with your cursor on a property in the Properties window—there, you will find more information about an individual property.

Visual Studio Help Issues

Since Visual Studio is an integrated development environment, there may be other software installed, for example, C++ and Java. When you access Contents from the Help menu, you may see topics that relate to these other languages. (See Figure 3-18.)

If only Visual Basic is installed and you search on a particular topic, you may find that certain topics are not accessible or are grayed out. These topics are related to other or noninstalled software. When you install Visual Basic, install all the Help files you have room for. This will save you from being prompted to insert the installation CD. If you do have more Help files installed, you can specify that you want to see only Visual Basic documentation by selecting it from the **Active Subset** dropdown list (see Figure 3-19).

Figure 3-18. If you have Visual Studio, you may have more than just the Visual Basic documentation.

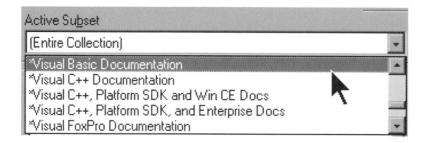

*Figure 3-19. In order to see only Help for Visual Basic (other documentation will be grayed out), specify by selecting only **Visual Basic documentation** in the Active Subset dropdown list in the Help window.*

Customizing the Development Environment

There are a few important ways to customize your environment settings. Some are significant as we begin to write Visual Basic code and others are just nice to know. As is standard in Microsoft products, customization can be accomplished using the Tools ➤ Options dialog box shown in Figure 3-20.

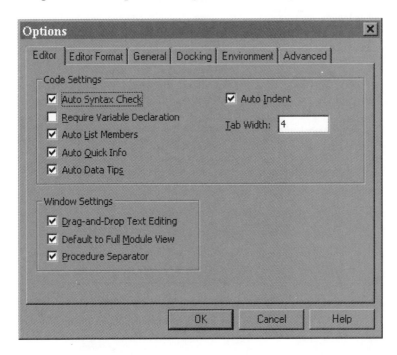

*Figure 3-20. Visual Basic has many options you can set to affect the development environment. Choose the **Tools ➤ Options** menu item to get to them.*

TO TRY THIS

1. Select the **Tools ➤ Options** menu item. Notice that there are six tabs: Editor, Editor Format, General, Docking, Environment, and Advanced.

    The Editor tab contains defaults that you should, for the most part, leave alone. The item on the Editor tab that you *should* change is to check the **Require Variable Declaration** checkbox, which is not checked by default but should be. This is important as we start coding in the next module. It will insert the words "Option Explicit" into all of your Code windows. I'll discuss this in more detail in the next chapter.

2. Select each tab in turn and view the various options. The other tabs have items that you can use to change font size in the Code window, to determine when you are prompted to save files, and so on. Use the **Help** button to get information on the purpose and effect of the various settings you can make on these tabs.

3. To accept the changes you make, click the **OK** button on the Options dialog box. To ignore any changes, select **Cancel**.

Changing Project Properties

Your project is itself just another object. As such, it also has properties that you can set. You cannot set Project properties using the Properties window, however. Set Project properties using the Project Properties dialog box as shown in Figure 3-21.

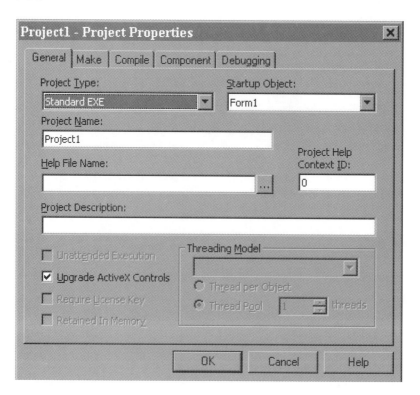

Figure 3-21. The Project Properties dialog box allows you to set properties specific to a single project.

TO TRY THIS

1. To access the Project Properties dialog box, select the **Project ➤ Project1 Properties** menu item. For now, we will only be concerned with a few fields on the General tab:

   Project Name and Description—The default name for every new project is Project1. This is the name that will show up on the Start menu when the project is minimized. You should change this value to reflect what the project does. You cannot use spaces in the project name. Use the Project description field to give a short description of the project's purpose.

   Startup Object—This is the first form the user will see at run time. Remember that every Visual Basic project starts with a single default form, Form1. You can add more forms to your project (which we will do a lot of, beginning in Chapter 5.) As you add forms to your project, they will show up in this Startup Object list. You can assign any of the forms in the project to be the Startup Object.

   Help File fields—These are fields you can use to assign a Help file to this project. Help file development and use is not covered in this text.

2. When you click **OK** on the Project Properties dialog, the settings take effect and the dialog box closes. If you changed an item you want to keep, like the project name, click **OK**; otherwise, click **Cancel**.

EXERCISE 3-1.

A VERY SIMPLE PROGRAM

The purpose of Exercise 3-1 is to practice creating, running, and saving a Visual Basic program. The exercises in this book will usually start by having you run a file that demonstrates what your finished exercise will look like. Depending on your confidence level, you can choose to write the program on your own or follow the steps of the exercise to accomplish it.

You can access the files for the exercises in this book at the Apress Web site at `http://www.apress.com/downloads/downloadPrompt.html`. Once you have done so, you will be able to access all of the files for every exercise. Once you have downloaded the Practice files for this book, notice that there is a folder for each chapter in this book.

1. Open the Chapter3 folder.

2. Run the application file called **SimpleProgram.EXE** by double-clicking it.

3. You are prompted to input your username. Type in your name and click the **OK** button. You will then see a Message box with your name in it.

4. Click **OK**. Now you are looking at a Visual Basic form. Click its **Exit** button. The program closes.

This is how your program will look and behave when it is completed.

Activity One: Creating the Very Simple Program

The following steps will walk you through the creation of a new Visual Basic program like the one you just ran in the previous steps. It will prompt the user for a user name (using the Form_Load event) and then use the Debug.Print statement to print that name into the Immediate window.

NOTE *If you want to create this on your own without following the steps, give it a try! You can check your work against the finished product in the Practice files.*

1. If Visual Basic is not already running, start it from the Windows **Start** menu, select **Programs**, and find the **Visual Basic** icon either from within the Visual Studio programs group or from the Microsoft Visual Basic 6 program group (depending on whether you installed Visual Studio or just Visual Basic 6).

2. Select the **Standard EXE** icon and click **OK**. You are now in Design mode on a new Visual Basic program.

3. **Double-click** the form to display the Code window. Your cursor should already be in the body part of the Form_Load event. If it is not, move it there.

4. Type in the following code (Visual Basic code is not case-sensitive):

```
Dim strUsername as string
StrUserName = Inputbox ("Please enter your username")
Debug.print strUserName
```

5. Run your program by pressing **F5**. Fix any typos or errors in your code. Once those are fixed, run the program again; you should see the InputBox prompting you to type in your user name.

6. Type in your name and press **OK**. Look for your name to show up in the Immediate window. (If you don't see the Immediate window you can display it at anytime by selecting the **View** menu and then the **Immediate** window submenu item. You may have to scroll up in the Immediate window to see your name printed.)

7. Click the '**X**' in the upper right corner of your form to close the program and return to Design mode.

Activity Two: Using a Message Box

Change the previous program to display the user name in a Message box instead of in the Immediate window.

1. In Design mode of the same program, double-click the **form** to return to the Code window. Modify the third line of the code you typed into the Form_Load event so that your code now looks like the following:

```
Dim strUsername as string
StrUserName = Inputbox("Please enter your username")
MsgBox strUserName
```

2. Use the **Help** ➤ **Index** menu item to search for help on **InputBox** (Figure 3-22). Read through the command syntax and text. Look at the example given for this function. Compare the example to the code in step 1.

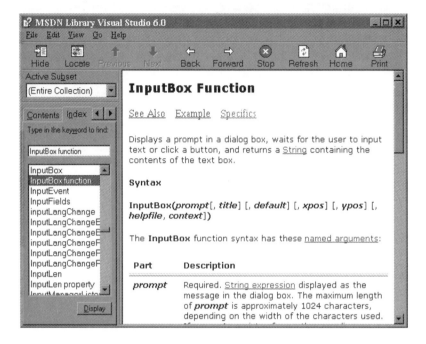

Figure 3-22. Visual Basic online Help for the InputBox function.

Exit the Help system.

3. Run the program again. Now you should see your name displayed in a Message box.

NOTE *The Immediate window was not cleared automatically. If you want to clear it, you will have to do so yourself, and you must be in Design mode. Once in Design mode, open the Immediate window (press **CTRL-G** or select the **View** ➤ **Immediate** menu item), select the text by clicking and dragging (or press **Ctrl-A**), and press either the **Backspace** or **Delete** key.*

4. Click the **OK** button to dismiss the Message box. Click the **'X'** in the upper right-hand corner of the form to return to Design mode.

Activity Three: Adding a Control

In this activity, we will go to Design mode and use the Properties window to change the BackColor property of the form to a different color.

1. Place a button control on the form in the Form Designer window. (Do this by double-clicking the **Command button control** in the Toolbox.)

2. Size your new button control any way you like.

 NOTE *If you try to change the BackColor property of the button it does not seem to have any effect. This is because the button's Style property must first be set to "graphical." (Try this for an extra challenge.)*

3. Change the **Caption** property of your new button control to "E&xit." Notice that an underscore appears under the 'x' in the button's caption. This indicates that the 'x' is the Access key for this control.

4. Double-click your **button control** to go to its click-event in the Code window. Type in the following single-word statement:

   End

5. Place your cursor anywhere on the End statement and press the **F1** key to go to context-sensitive Help. Read about the End statement and the different ways the word "End" is used in Visual Basic. Not all of this will make sense at this point but will as your familiarity grows. Get in the habit of using Help whenever you encounter a new statement.

6. Exit the Help system and return to Design mode. Now run your program again (press **F5** or use the toolbar). You must enter your username again. When you get to the main form, click the **Exit** button. It should end your program and put you back into Design mode.

Activity Four: Saving Files

If you have not done so already, create a folder on your hard drive where you can save all of your files from this text. We will now go through the steps to save your files.

1. Save your project by selecting **File** ➤ **Save Project** from the menu. You will be prompted with two dialog boxes: the first asks to save your form file (.frm extension), give it a relevant name, and click the **Save** button; the second dialog box asks for the name of the project: give your project a relevant name and click the **Save** button.

 NOTE *Do not use the default names for the .frm and .vbp files. Give these more relevant files names. For example, Firstprogram.frm and Firstprogram.vbp.*

2. Exit Visual Basic by selecting **File** ➤ **Exit.**

3. Restart Visual Basic.

4. Reopen your project by selecting the **Recent Files** tab from the starting dialog box.

To View the Suggested Answer to This Exercise

1. From within the Visual Basic, select **File** ➤ **Open Project** from the Visual Basic menu. (If prompted to save your program, do so.) The Open Project dialog box should now be showing.

2. Navigate to the **Practice** files and open the **Chapter3** folder. Inside the Chapter3 folder is an Answer folder.

3. Open the **Answer** folder and double-click on the **SimpleProgram.vbp** file.

4. Go to the **Code** window of the form by double-clicking it. Compare the code you see to what you did in the exercise.

EXERCISE 3-2.

ADDING CONTROLS AND SETTING THE TAB INDEX

The purpose of Exercise 3-2 is to give you practice creating controls and modifying the tab order. (The form you create can be used in an exercise in the next chapter.)

Creating the Form

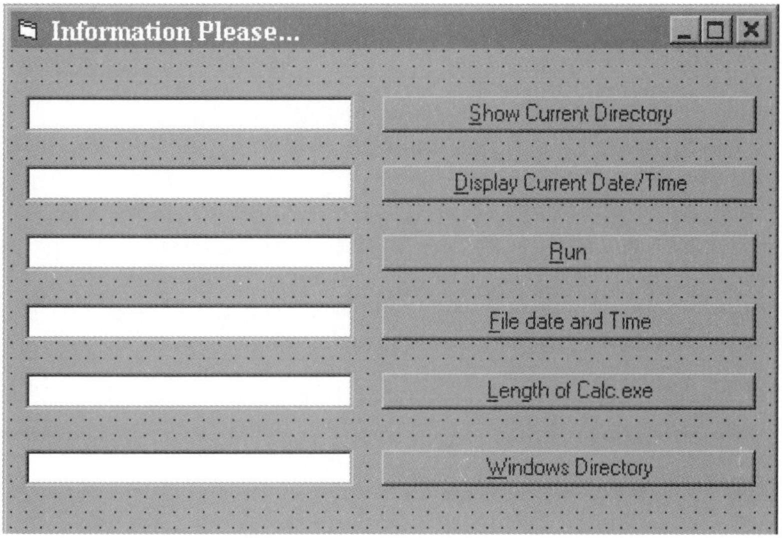

Figure 3-23. Following Exercise 3-2, you will create a form similar to this.

You will create a form that looks similar to the one in Figure 3-23. For now, you won't add any code to the form—that will be done in an exercise in the next chapter.

1. Start up Visual Basic and create a new Visual Basic project by selecting **Standard EXE**.

    If Visual Basic is already running, you can also select **File ➤ New Project** from the menu to start a new project. Careful, do *not* select File ➤ Add Project.

TIP *For best results, read the* entire *following step before attempting it.*

2. Place six textboxes and six Command buttons on the form. Arrange and size these controls to appear approximately like the ones in Figure 3-23.

   To save time in sizing these controls, first size just one of each kind—for example, the Command button—and then:

   - Hold the Shift key and click on each button of that kind to select all of them.

   - Continue to hold the Shift key and select the already-sized button until its control handles are solid.

   - Use the Format ➢ Align menu item and the Format ➢ Make Same Size menu item to make all the others the same.

   Click each of these new controls in turn to select it. Once the control is selected, change its Name property as follows:

NOTE *You can change the name of a control by changing its Name property in the Properties window.*

Give the textboxes the following names in order from top to bottom:

txtCurDir

txtNow

txtRun

txtFileDateTime

txtFileLen

txtWindir

Name the Command buttons from top to bottom:

cmdCurDir

cmdNow

cmdRun

cmdFileDateTime

cmdFileLen

cmdWindir

....

Naming Conventions

Visual Basic doesn't care what you name your controls—the naming convention you use will be important for *you* as the developer of the application. It quickly becomes confusing if you do not have a plan for the consistent naming of controls and other objects in your Visual Basic application. The naming convention used by this book is based on recommendations from Microsoft's *Visual Basic Programmer's Guide.* We use three small letters to indicate what kind of a control it is (so 'cmd' means it's a Command button and 'txt' means it's a textbox). That way, when we refer to these items later on in our code, we won't have to guess at what kind of a control it is, we'll know just by its name. Please be consistent in how you name controls. Your best bet is to follow Microsoft's conventions for Visual Basic. Take the time to read this section. You can find it by going to **Help**, clicking the **Index** tab, and then typing "Object Naming Conventions."

....

3. Select a **textbox** and find its Text property in the Properties window. Select the **value** in the Text property and delete it. Do this for all of the textbox controls on the form.

4. Set the tab order so that the first Command button is the first in the tab order. (Set its Tabindex property to 0.) Set the second Command button's Tabindex property to 1, and so on.

5. For the textboxes, change their Tabindex properties so that they are in the tab order directly after the Command buttons and consecutively follow each other from top to bottom.

NOTE *You will write no code for this form. Creating controls and setting their properties comprises the full exercise.*

6. **Save** the form and project files in your own folder for use in the next exercise. When prompted, name the form file and the project file the following names prefixed with your own initials: **XYZInfoPlease.frm** and **XYZInfoPlease.vbp** (substitute XYZ with your initials).

To compare your form to the suggested answer in the Chapter 3 Practice files, use Windows Explorer to navigate to the following file and then double-click it to open it: Chapter3\InfoPlease.frm.

TESTER'S CHECKLIST

When performing code reviews, look for the following in a well-written Visual Basic application.

Does the Project...

❏ Use Access keys for control captions?

❏ Have a tab order that is easy to follow and use?

❏ Have a sensible color scheme for objects?

❏ Have well-designed forms that are easy to use and understand? Does it contain too many controls or appear too busy?

❏ Use captions that are clear and descriptive?

❏ Follow basic Windows standards, for instance, in assigning Access keys?

Overall, Does the Application...

❏ Have user-friendly features? (Yes, this is very subjective!) Use your own intuition and experience as a user of software. You will get better at this as your experience grows.

Does the Code...

❏ Make appropriate use of comments to document and to clarify? Are there too many comments?

Chapter 3 Review

- What are the five major windows in the Visual Basic IDE?
  See page 43.

- What is the purpose of the Form Layout window? The Form Designer window?
  See pages 43–44.

- Name at least two Visual Basic Output statements.
  See page 58.

- What is an Access key? How do you set an Access key for a control?
  See pages 50–51.

- What is the minimum number of files you will need to save in a typical Visual Basic project? What are their extensions?
  See pages 60–61.

- How can you change the Name property of your project?
  Project Properties dialog.
  See page 68.

- If you wanted to change the font size of the code in your Code window, where could you go to do so?
  Access the Tools ➤ Options menu item to bring up the Options dialog. The font can be set on the Editor tab of this dialog.
  See page 67.

CHAPTER 4

Understanding Visual Basic Application Essentials

In this chapter, we continue our study of Visual Basic fundamentals by covering the essential concepts needed to write test scripts.

Objectives

By the end of this chapter, you will be able to:

- Define the difference between event-driven and procedural programming languages.

- Set properties programmatically at run time.

- Identify how to access and write code for events.

- Explain the difference between a property and a method.

- Create and use event procedures for controls.

- List at least three common coding conventions for a Visual Basic automated test project.

- Explain the importance of coding conventions in an automated testing project.

- Declare and use variables and constants.

- Define the difference between local and module-level variables.

- Create and run a simple, single-form Visual Basic program.

- Use the If statement to make decisions in code.

- Use looping statements to repeat code.

- Create an executable file from a Visual Basic project.

Understanding Objects, Properties, Events, and Methods

Visual Basic is not a strictly object-oriented language like C++, but it *is* based on object-oriented concepts. Visual Basic's environment helps the developer model the real world by allowing you to create and use objects just as you encounter and use objects in your everyday life.

What is an object? There are three things that make an object an object: its properties, methods, and events. For our purposes, an *object* is a thing, a noun. This thing has *properties* that describe it; you can think of properties as adjectives of the object. An object also has actions that it can perform, called *methods*. Because they are actions, methods will be verbs. The object also has *events* that happen to it. The properties, methods, and events of an object define that object.

If you think of yourself as an object (well, you are, aren't you?), then some of your properties would be your height and your hair and eye color. Other objects, say, a chair, would share some of the same properties, such as height and width, but would not share others, like hair color, right? So, not every object has exactly the same properties, methods, and events as every other object. This, of course, models the real world because the real world is filled with all kinds of objects of different shape and description.

Object:	*a thing (noun)*
Property:	*Describes the object (adjective)*
Method:	*An action the object can perform (verb)*
Event:	*An action that happens to the object as a result of some occurrence, like a button-click (verb)*

The actions you perform, such as brushing your teeth or making a telephone call, would be your methods. Events that happen to you might be the "wake up" event that is performed by your alarm clock. You execute a method in response to that event: you shut off the alarm. These are such important concepts that we need to discuss them in depth. In the next section, I'll cover how these ideas of Property, Method, and Event relate to the controls in your Visual Basic program.

Understanding Properties

A real-world object like a chair has properties such as height, width, and color. These properties describe and define the chair. If we were to describe the chair in Visual Basic terms, we might write lines of code like this:

MyChair.Height = 3

MyChair.Color = "Brown"

MyChair.Manufacturer = "Smith Co."

In Visual Basic, an object can be a form or a control such as a Command button or a Text box. An object can also be a database or even a single table within it. The object's properties describe it (Figure 4-1). A Command button has properties such as Height, Width, Caption, and Backcolor. An object then, is a thing that can be described by its properties.

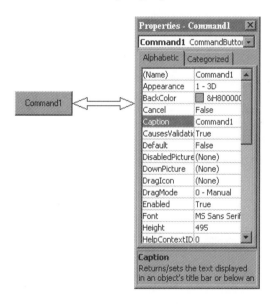

Figure 4-1. An object like a Command button has properties that describe its features, such as height and width.

There are two ways to set the value of a property. The properties of an object can be set using the Properties window. Properties can also be set while the application is running by using a line of Visual Basic code. Say, for example, you wanted to change the color of a form's background to red when the user clicks a button. You could put the following line of code in the button's click-event:

```
Form1.Backcolor = vbRed
```

This line of code is an *assignment statement*—that is, it assigns the value on the right side of the equal sign to the item on the left side of the equal sign. In this case, the Backcolor property of Form1 is assigned the value vbRed. (Notice that we refer to the property of an object using the notation *objectname.propertyname.*) When you read this line of code, you would say, "Form1.Backcolor becomes vbRed."

NOTE *By the way, vbRed is a special value, a constant that is recognized by Visual Basic. It contains a value that represents the color red. There are other constant values available; for example, there is also vbYellow, vbGreen, vbBlue, and so on. There are additional constants that Visual Basic recognizes and they all start with "vb." We will use them as they become necessary.*

You could have selected red from the color palette in the Backcolor property on the form's properties sheet. However, then it would not have changed color in response to the click of the button. It would have been set that way in Design mode, also called *design time.* If you want to have something change while the program is running—that is, during Run mode (also called *run time)*—then you must write code to do it.

Design-Time versus Run-Time Properties

How would you know what properties are available to you to change for a particular control? The list in the Properties box is a start but it does not give you all possible properties for an object. In fact, it lists only properties that can be set during Design mode. There may be more properties for the object; there are some properties that can only be set in code, that is, during Run mode. Since these properties cannot be set during Design mode, they don't show up in the Properties window. However, you can find out what these properties are by looking up the control in the Visual Basic Help system. In the description of the property, it will state if the property can be set during design or run time modes.

For example, if you search in Help for the CommandButton (no spaces), it will give a list of all of the properties available. It will also explain the purpose of each property, its possible values, and what will happen when you change its value.

Assume you have a form with a Command button on it named Command1. If the following line of code was placed in the Load event of the form, what do you suppose its effect will be?

```
Command1.Enabled = False
```

To answer that question, go to Visual Basic's Help system, search for help on the **CommandButton** control, then click on the **Properties** link. The Enabled property of Command buttons is listed there. You will find that setting the Enabled property of a Command button to *False* will cause the button to become disabled, that is, grayed out and inaccessible to the user. Setting the Enabled property to *True* will reverse this and make it available again (see Figure 4-2).

```
Command1.Enabled = True
```

 NOTE *True and False are special values in Visual Basic. They are keywords that will turn blue and will be styled upper- and lowercase when you type them into the Code window. (All keywords are treated this way. For example, if you type "true" in the Code window, Visual Basic will change it to "True.") True and False are actually just keywords that represent numbers. Why? Because computers work a lot better with numbers. True is equal to –1 and False is equal to 0. So, the following code would be equivalent to the line just shown:* `Command1.Enabled = -1`. *Since human beings generally work better with meaningful symbols, True and False (rather than the numbers to which they are equivalent) can and should be used in code.*

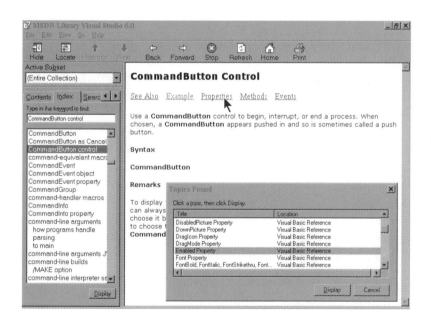

Figure 4-2. The Command button control description and its properties in the Visual Basic Help system.

Understanding Events

Events are actions that happen to an object. For example, when a user clicks a button, that click is an event that happens *to* the button. You can write code to respond to an event when it occurs just as you did in Exercise 3-1 (Chapter 3). When you write code to respond an event, that code is called an *event handler*. Here's an example:

```
Sub Command1_Click()
    Form1.Backcolor = vbRed
    Debug.Print  "the Backcolor of the form is now red"
End Sub
```

The first and last lines of the event handler are the *container* of the handler. If the container is empty, nothing happens when the event occurs. The first line, Sub Command1_Click, indicates the start of the handler for the click-event of the Command1 button. The last line, End Sub, indicates the end of the handler. Inside of the container is the body of the handler and it contains all the code that will run when the event occurs. The word "sub" is actually short for subroutine. There can be many subroutines in your Visual Basic code. They are all sub-parts of the larger program. If you have many buttons, each can have their own set of subs (sort of like many subcontractors working on a big project—they all contribute to the end product).

The first line of code in the event handler, Form1.Backcolor = vbRed, shows the way properties are handled as the result of an event. When the user clicks the Command1 button, the form's Backcolor property will be set to red. The next line calls a method, the Print method of the Debug object, which prints a line to the Immediate window (we saw this line of code in the last chapter).

To understand events, you really need to understand a bit about how Windows operating systems work. In Windows, pretty much everything you see is a *window* (that's why they call it "Windows"). It may seem obvious that a Word document and the Windows Explorer are windows. It may be less obvious that things like command buttons, textboxes, and toolbars are also considered windows by the operating system (OS). The Windows OS monitors all windows constantly for activity, such as when a user types into a textbox or moves the mouse over them. When certain activities occur, Windows knows it and passes a message along to the OS. The OS then broadcasts these messages to other windows. If other windows are programmed to care about that particular event, then they will take action. For example, the Windows OS knows when the mouse moves over a window and broadcasts that event to other windows. In some cases, when the mouse moves over the window, that window (which could be a textbox or a Toolbar button, too) is programmed to change color or do something special such as print a Help message into a label or pop up a tool tip. In most cases, though, an application's windows ignore the mouse moving over them. But that doesn't mean the OS didn't tell them about it! It did. Windows broadcasts messages constantly.

The writers of Visual Basic realized that for most applications a developer would write, there would be no need to deal with *every* Windows message you could possibly get for a control. So, Visual Basic's creators selected certain special messages that they figured the developer would need most. For example, for CommandButton controls they selected common actions to expose as events such as clicking the Command button and moving the mouse over it. To see all of the events exposed by Visual Basic's creators for a Command button, simply drop down the Procedures box in the Code window as shown in Figure 4-3.

For other kinds of objects, the Visual Basic creators selected similar events to expose. If you select other objects in the Code window's Object box, like the form itself, and look at the events for it, you will not see the same list of event procedures as you did for CommandButton controls. This should make sense because not all objects are exactly the same. To understand more about this, select various objects from the Object box in the Code window and explore the different events exposed for the objects. You can then look up those objects and events in Visual Basic's Help system to find out more about how and when they are used.

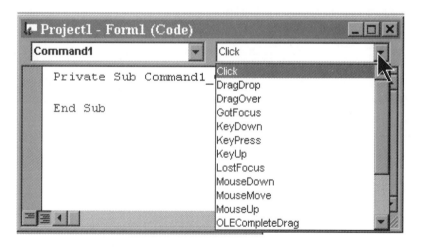

Figure 4-3. The Code window's Procedures box displaying the events exposed for a Command button control.

Understanding Methods

Methods, like events, are also actions. Remember that we defined events as actions that happen *to* an object. With methods, the *object* performs the action.

Because of this, we work with methods in a very different way than we work with events. Think of a method as the verb associated with an object. For example, textboxes have a SetFocus method. When this is called, the textbox sets the focus to itself.

In Visual Basic code, you can write the following lines in the click-event of a button:

```
Debug.Print "Hello there"
Text1.SetFocus
```

At run time, when the user presses that button, the program will print "Hello there" to the Debug (Immediate) window. The next line, `Text1.Setfocus`, causes the cursor to be placed in the textbox named Text1. In this code, Print is a method of the Debug object and SetFocus is a method of the Text1 object. Notice that we use the notation *objectname.methodname*. This notation is similar to how we refer to a property. Think of an object as a container for its properties and methods.

 NOTE *In fact, using the dot or period to refer to an object's properties and methods is not an accident. It represents a drill-hole, that is, a way to "drill" into the object to access its components.*

The literal string "Hello there" is the value provided to the Print method. When we write code to use these methods, we are asking the objects to perform a task. Unlike properties, which must be equal to some value, methods do not have a value because methods are actions, not things. The Print method does need to know what to print so we must provide a value for it:

```
Debug.Print "Hello there"

'notice the lack of an equal sign when we use a method
```

We call this value an *argument* or *parameter* of the method. Since we are not assigning this value *to* anything but simply providing it to the method, we do not use an equal sign.

The SetFocus method tells the textbox to place the cursor inside itself so that it receives the focus. We don't need to provide any value to the SetFocus method. Notice that these methods are both actions, thus they are both verbs.

To write code in response to an event for an object—for example, a button control—double-click that control at design time. The Code window for the form will automatically display. The Code window is shown in Figure 4-4.

Figure 4-4. A Code window contains two dropdown Combo boxes: the Object box and the Procedures box.

As you saw in the last chapter, the Code window contains two dropdown Combo boxes. The one on the left is the Object box. It contains the name of the current object you are working on. The Combo box to the right of the Code window is the Procedure box. It contains a list of all the valid events for that particular object.

Understanding the Difference between Events and Methods

To understand the difference between events and methods, since are both actions related to objects, consider a real-world example: again, think of yourself as an object. Somewhere along the line, someone taught you how to brush your teeth. This is now an action you can perform—no one needs to come and brush your teeth for you, right? In code, you might write this as:

```
JaneDoe.BrushTeeth
```

As mentioned earlier, an event, unlike a method, is not something you can do but something which happens *to* you. Let's say for argument's sake that you wake up every morning to the ring of an alarm clock rather than waking up naturally. So, you have a wake-up event and you perform actions in response to that event. In Visual Basic terminology, this might look the following:

```
Sub JaneDoe_WakeUp()
     JaneDoe.TurnoffAlarmClock
     JaneDoe.GetOutofBed
     JaneDoe.BrushTeeth
End Sub
```

When you work with events, you find them in the Code window and write code to respond to them. When you want to access a method of an object, you write the code for it inside of an event handler using the *Objectname.Methodname* syntax. So, both methods and events are actions related to an object but are handled very differently in Visual Basic code.

Procedural Programming versus Event-Driven Programming

If you hang around programmers long enough, you will hear talk of event-driven programming and its predecessor, procedural programming. I'll briefly try to illuminate what all the talk is about with a little background.

Procedural Programming

Programming languages allow human beings to communicate with computers and tell them what to do. The first-generation programming language is Machine-language, which deals with one's and zero's. Machine-language is pretty tough to write code in, a single instruction can take many lines. Of course, you can make your machine do anything it is capable of in that way. The second-generation programming language is Assembly-language; it allows the programmer to use memory registers to store values and while still tedious to program in, it is very powerful.

The third-generation programming languages such as Fortran, Pascal, Cobol, and C were the first to allow the programmer to write code that used English-like commands and mathematical statements. The commands are translated into instructions (Machine-language) for the computer by a compilation process. There are many books that go into the gritty detail of how this works so we won't delve any further into that process here.

Writing code in third-generation languages lends itself to code that asks the user to do things step-by-step. This step-by-step coding of sequential actions is referred to as *procedural programming*. Since the languages themselves ask the computer to do a series of tasks step-by-step, when the programs need user input, the programmer writes the necessary code to prompt the user for the needed input (such as a username, password, or menu selection). The program waits there until the user responds. If the user doesn't respond, the program continues to wait. Theoretically, it will wait forever. What if the user wants to do something else? Too bad, they either have to respond or quit the program. Thus, applications written using the procedural programming model cannot cope with actions outside the specified order.

Procedural programming is like going to the bakery and taking a number. The bakery (program) handles one customer (task) at a time. What if a customer in the store starts jumping up and down and saying, "Wait, take me first!" or the customer being helped says "I've decided to order lunch at the same time, please hang on and I'll be right back." In either case, the bakery isn't flexible enough to deal with these situations. You must follow their rules or shop somewhere else. This is like procedural programming. In procedural programming, the program will not handle another task other than the one it's got right now. It continues step-by-step and sits and blinks at you until you respond. That is the way programming proceeded for many years, which was okay, too, because the operating systems we had, like DOS, operated from a command line. You only had one command line and only ran one program at a time. That all changed, though, with the advent of graphical-based computer systems.

Event-Driven Programming

Thanks to Xerox-PARC and their development of a graphical-based computer system (along with many others who followed their lead), we now have icons to click and a mouse to click with. Modern operating systems allow us to choose what tasks we want to perform and to move between many different tasks, such as writing a letter on a word processor and stopping midstream to check e-mail. Event-driven programming languages like Visual Basic allow us to take advantage of these capabilities and to write programs allowing users to have choices.

Event-driven programming can be compared to a busy sales office. The phone ringing with a new customer is an event that interrupts whatever other tasks are going on. Imagine that there are plenty of salespeople available to serve customers. An event might be the door opening and a customer walking in. Instead of the customer getting a number, as in the bakery example, a salesperson drops whatever he's doing (wouldn't that be great) and comes to help the customer immediately. When a customer calls (another event), a salesperson drops other tasks or puts those tasks temporarily on hold to address the customer's needs.

Thus, in event-driven programming, the user controls what happens and when. Using Visual Basic, you provide a form with controls on it and attach code to those controls. The user decides at run time when that code actually executes by performing an action that triggers an event. For example, the user clicks a button and the code written for that button's event procedure runs. What if the user *never* clicks that particular button? Well, then your code for that button *never* runs.

As you write code for multiple event procedures associated with controls and forms, you will see a lot of code in the Code window. The order of the event

procedures in the Code window is meaningless. The code for each event procedure is performed in response to an event. Figure 4-5 shows a Code window with
the code for the click-events of two buttons: cmdRun and cmdNow. There are
also some comments and additional variable declarations (I'll cover those later
in this chapter). The cmdRun_Click event and the cmdNow_Click event are completely independent of one another. If you changed the order of these event
procedures in the Code window, for example, you cut the code for the
cmdRun_Click event procedure and pasted it above the cmdNow_Click event
procedure, it would have no effect on how or when the code runs. They will each
run only when their associated event is triggered. This is because Visual Basic
code is event-driven rather than procedural.

Figure 4-5. A Code window containing multiple event procedures.

The Debugger

In order to more fully understand the concepts I have been discussing, I'd like to
introduce a tool that will be helpful in this effort. It can be very useful to see what
is going on in your Visual Basic program by stepping through it line-by-line as it

executes. The Debugging tool in Visual Basic allows you to do that. It is introduced here because the Debugger clearly demonstrates that code actually does
execute in response to an event.

The easiest way to use the Debugging tool is to bring up its toolbar. You can
bring up this or any toolbar by placing your mouse in the toolbar area at the top
of the Visual Basic Development window and right-clicking the **mouse** button.
Then click **Debug** from the pop-up menu.

Once you have brought up its toolbar, you can enter the Debugger by clicking the **Step Into** button on the toolbar as shown here.

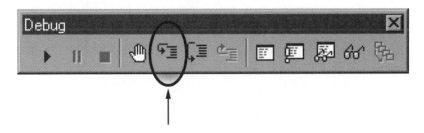

Initially, your program may seem to execute as usual. As soon as an event is
triggered for which you have written a handler, for example, Command1_Click,
your program will execute the first line of the handler and then stop. You are now
in a whole new mode called *Break mode*. Your program is running while in Break
mode but is temporarily halted on the current line of execution.

The Code window shows and a yellow arrow points to the next line of code
that is executed upon clicking the **Step Into** button again. An example is shown
in Figure 4-6. Although the Code window has the focus, your Program window is
still available and you may find it helpful to switch back and forth between them
by using the Windows TaskBar. The Alt-Tab key will also switch you between
available windows.

```
Project1 - Form1 (Code)                          _ □ X
Command2                    ▼    click                  ▼
        Label1 = Environ$("windir")
    End Sub

⇨  │Private Sub command2_click()
    Dim EnvString, Indx
    Indx = 1    ' Initialize index to 1.
    Do
        EnvString = Environ(Indx)    ' Get environment
        Msg = "Environ variable: " & Indx & " is " &
        Picture1.Print Msg
        Indx = Indx + 1   ' increment.
    Loop Until EnvString = ""
```

Figure 4-6. Debugging a Visual Basic program using the Debugger.

If you click the **Step Into** button on the toolbar again, the next line of code is executed and the program again halts. You can use this tool to walk through your program viewing each line as it is executed. This can be of immense help in trying to find and correct code and logic errors.

The Debug toolbar contains other useful buttons and features such as Step Over, Step Out, and the ability to set Breakpoints. I won't cover the entire Debugger in this section because the most important feature (and one you will use the most) is simply being able to step through the program as we have done. We will continue to use the Debugger throughout this text both to find errors and to help understand the flow of code as it executes. For more information on the Debugger, see the Visual Basic Programmer's Guide in the Help system.

EXERCISE 4-1.

USING THE DEBUGGER TO UNDERSTAND EVENTS

The Debugger is a powerful and useful tool for checking your program's execution. In Exercise 4-1, you will use the Debugger to step through the lines of code written in the Simple Program exercise (Exercise 3-1) from Chapter 3. Exercise 4-1 is not intended to demonstrate all debugging features but simply to allow you to use its basic functionality for stepping through programs.

1. Open your Visual Basic project from Exercise 3-1 in Chapter 3 or open the answer by double-clicking the file called **SimpleProgram.vbp** in the Chapter3\Answer folder.

2. Display the Debug toolbar by right-clicking your mouse in the toolbar area. Select **Debug** from the pop-up menu that appears.

3. Click **Step Into** on the Debug toolbar (or press the **F8** key). Since there is code in the Load event of this form, you will see the Code window appear. A yellow line points to the line of code that will be executed next.

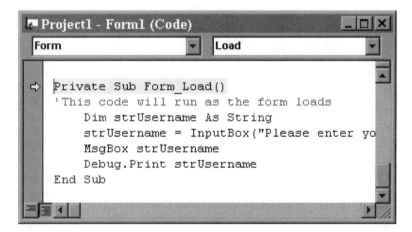

4. Continue to click the **Step Into** button on the Debug toolbar. Note that you may need to click the icons in the Windows TaskBar to change focus back and forth between the executing program and the Visual Basic Code window.

5. Enter your name as usual when prompted and click **OK**. Continue clicking **Step Into** on the toolbar to see each step of the Load event execute.

6. When the program's main window appears, click the **Exit** button. Notice that you are now placed into the Code window again. This time, you will see the yellow line pointing to the first executable line of code in the button's click-event. Keep clicking the **Step Into** until your program quits.

7. *Extra Work*: Look up the Debugger in Visual Basic's Help system and explore the use of other debugging features, such as setting breakpoints, running to cursor, and the use of the Immediate window.

Coding Mechanics

In any software project, whether testing or development, you will have standards to follow. Standards enhance communication among project members and allow new team members to come on board more quickly. Without standard procedures for writing code, naming objects, and so on, a project will soon become chaotic.

We will use industry-wide standard conventions for writing our code in this text. This will also provide you with things to look for if you are called upon to do a code review of an application.

This section covers the use of variables and constants and their scoping issues in Visual Basic. We will then move on to the use of two fundamental coding structures: branching standards and looping statements.

Code Reviews

Code reviews are a regular feature on a software development project. The purpose of this review is to share information among team members, to let team members help each other with difficult coding tasks, and to keep the coding consistent and on target. Having regular code reviews is just as important on an automated-testing project for all the same reasons. Meeting weekly or biweekly with other members of your team to review your automated test scripts for functionality, efficiency, and consistency will help your project immensely. What if you are the only person doing automated script writing in Visual Basic? Show your code and how it works to others, even if they know nothing about coding. The process alone of explaining and demonstrating your code can uncover problems and inconsistencies. If no one on your team is skilled in Visual Basic, ask a person outside of your team who is knowledgeable in Visual Basic to occasionally review your code for errors. (E-mail groups are also a good way to get unofficial code reviews from knowledgeable people.)

Object Naming Conventions

Some basic rules for object names are:

- They can be no more than forty characters long.

- They cannot start with a number.

- They cannot contain spaces or special characters (in other words, no hyphens or slashes, etc.).

It is okay in Visual Basic to name Command buttons things like Fred and Joe. So why do we see a Command button named cmdOK? Well, in looking at this button name, one might guess that this is a standard Command button as opposed to a Radio button or textbox and that its caption is "OK."

So, if you choose the name cmdOK for your Command button, you have chosen a name that is relevant to what that control is and what it does in the program. A common industry convention for naming controls is to use what is commonly called *Hungarian Notation*: we name objects using one to three lowercase characters to indicate what kind of a control it is and then use mixed case for the rest of the characters to describe the use of the control. Table 4-1 lists common prefixes and names for objects on a Visual Basic project.

NOTE *To read the exact specification for Hungarian Notation, type the phrase "Hungarian Notation" into most any search engine and it will take you to the following Web page,* `http://msdn.microsoft.com/library/techart/hunganotat.htm`, *which gives the history of this notation and how to use it.*

You can also read "Object Naming Conventions" in the Programmer's Guide of the Visual Basic Help system for Microsoft's recommendations on how to name Visual Basic objects.

Table 4-1. Common Prefixes and Names for Objects in a Visual Basic Project

OBJECT	PREFIX	EXAMPLE NAME
Command button	cmd	cmdOK
Text box	txt	txtTestName
Label	lbl	lblBookTitle
Form	frm	frmMainEntry
Combo box	cbo	cboListChoices
Option button	opt	optSeverityLevel1
Check box	chk	chkHighSecurity
List box	lst	lstPrintersList

TESTER'S TIP *If you are code-reviewing a Visual Basic application and do not see consistent object naming conventions being used, it could mean inexperienced programmers, which might cause you to more closely look at the code itself for problems.*

Coding Conventions

Coding conventions are ways to write your code so it is easier to understand and maintain. These conventions may vary from company to company and even from group to group. The first thing to do is to check what, if any, existing standards there are for both the development team and the automated test team and then follow them. If there are none, you should try to implement some yourself even if you are the only automated test writer. The following conventions are a good place to start:

- *Indentation.* Good programmers use indentation for clarity—for example, indenting code inside an event procedure makes it easier to see where the procedure starts and ends. The following code demonstrates commonly acceptable indentation for a subroutine. Notice that within the subroutine, indentation is applied to the Do-Loop structure so it is easy to see where it starts and ends:

```
Private Sub command2_click()
    Dim EnvString As String
    Dim msg As String
    Dim Indx As Integer
    Indx = 1   ' Initialize index to 1.
    Do
        EnvString = Environ(Indx)   ' Get environment variable.
        msg = "Environ variable: " & Indx & " is " & EnvString
        Picture1.Print msg
        Indx = Indx + 1   ' increment.
    Loop Until EnvString = ""
End Sub
```

- *Commenting text.* Comments are used to document the author, purpose, modification dates, and other pertinent information about the main code modules. They should also be used to clarify any part of the code that may be difficult to understand. Comments are another tool to help reviewers understand what your intention is—hard as it is to believe, your code might not always be self-explanatory. (Sometimes, after a couple of weeks of hard work, your code isn't even explanatory to yourself!)

  On all software projects there should be some guidelines as to how comments will be used. Otherwise, some project members might not use any and others will use too many. Too many comments can be difficult to maintain and may become outdated. In general, comments should be used for documentation and to clarify any unclear code.

- *Use of templates.* Many projects will require that templates be used to help team members implement the project's coding conventions. These are a good idea to help streamline the process.

All of these are common coding conventions that are good for you to set up and follow on a first-rate automated testing project. They also happen to be things testers can look for when doing White Box testing on a Visual Basic application. As a tester, you should ask for these guidelines and become familiar with them. If the company or project you are working on doesn't have them, you can be the first to suggest and implement these kinds of guidelines! The coding conventions just mentioned are generally accepted industry-wide but are really just a bare minimum. Microsoft has a few more recommendations. To read up on them, see "Coding Conventions, Basic Concepts" in the Visual Basic Help system.

NOTE FOR BEGINNING TESTERS *White Box testing means testing an application with some knowledge of the internals. This may mean that you are given access to the application code, called source code. Learning Visual Basic will give you the ability to do White Box testing of a Visual Basic application. You can use your knowledge of programming in Visual Basic to look for common errors a programmer might perform. Black Box testing has no knowledge of internals. In Black Box testing, you test an application the way any user of the application would. Black Box testing is the most common form of testing; White Box testing requires more technically skilled testers.*

Coding Conventions for Automated Testing

Choosing common coding conventions for your automated testing project is something you can and should do early on in a project. You will be surprised at how many different ways there are to indent and comment code. There can be such wide variation that it makes code review and modification very difficult. Since you will want to use good algorithms over again in other programs, it's important to code them for readability. Coding conventions go a long way towards making code consistent, readable, modifiable, and ultimately, reusable. Creating a coding template for all to use is a good first step in any automated testing project.

You will find that in a tight schedule, coding conventions are disregarded and this, at times, is the cause of certain kinds of bugs. Of course, this will give you an authentic feel for the kinds of errors to look for in software that you test since developers will be operating under the same kinds of time constraints.

Declaring and Using Variables

There are times when coding that you need to store a value. However, you don't always need to store the value in a database or property. Often, you just want a temporary place to store this value and then dismiss it. For example, you may want to store the results of a number of tests, that is, whether they passed or failed and then come back later and create reports or summary information based on those results. A *variable* is an object you can create to store a value in. You must give this storage place a name so that you can use it later. You can create as many variables as you need. In the last chapter, we created a simple variable named strUserName:

```
Dim strUserName as String
```

Think of this line of code as creating an empty space in memory, represented by Figure 4-7. It doesn't make any difference where in memory it is created, you have simply reserved a place and given that place a name.

Figure 4-7. The variable strUserName is created and initially stores an empty string.

Local Variables

The keyword *Dim* is used to declare the creation of a local variable. Think of it as a drawer in which you have determined will (in this case) hold only strings and to which you have given a name. The name strUserName follows the Hungarian Notation convention mentioned in the last section for naming variables.

A *local variable* is one that is created within a procedure—for example, an event procedure. Declaring a variable inside a procedure means that the variable exists only inside the procedure. That is, no other procedures can use or even see this variable. Local variables exist at run time for as long as the routine in which they are declared is running. When the procedure has completed its last statement, the variable is destroyed. When the procedure is called again, a brand new variable is created, used, and destroyed.

In the following bit of code, the variable strUserName is created in the event procedure Command1_Click and is considered local to it:

```
Sub Command1_Click()
    Dim strUserName as String     'variable strUserName is created
    strUserName = "Elvis"         'variable contents are set
    Debug.Print strUserName       'variable contents are read
End Sub                           'variable is destroyed
```

When the Command1 button gets clicked, the Command1_Click event procedure is executed and the variable is created. Its initial value is an empty string by default. Because it is a local variable, it is destroyed at the completion of the procedure, that is, when the End Sub line is executed. If the button gets clicked again, the event triggers and the variable is again created from scratch.

Static Variables

You can also declare variables using the keyword Static. *Static* variables are also local variables so they also only exist within the procedure where they are declared.

The difference between Dim and Static variables is that Static variables are said to be *persistent*. Persistent means that the next time you call the procedure, the local variable—in spite of being destroyed at the end of the procedure—will retain the value it had last time it was used. So, when you click the Command1 button and its event procedure executes the assignment of a value to the variable, the variable is initialized to its previous value, if any. This is easier to see in an example:

```
Sub Command1_Click()
    Static iCount as integer
    Debug.Print iCount
    iCount = iCount + 1   'adds one to the current value of iCount
End Sub
```

In this example, each time you click the button, a number is printed to the Immediate window. Since the variable is Static, its value persists so you should see the numbers printed getting larger by a value of 1.

However, if you replace the keyword Static with the keyword Dim in the prior example, you will get a column of zeroes instead.

TO TRY THIS

1. Create a new Visual Basic application.

2. Place a Command button control on the Form Designer window. Change its Caption property to **Click Me**.

3. Double-click this new button in the Form Designer window to go to its click-event procedure in the Code window.

4. Type the code shown here into the click-event procedure of the new button:

```
Sub Command1_Click()
    Dim iCount as integer
    Debug.Print iCount
    iCount = iCount + 1   'adds one to the current value of iCount
End Sub
```

5. Click the **Run** button on the Visual Basic Tool bar to run your program. Your program's form displays.

6. Click the **Click Me** Command button on your form three times.

7. Display the Immediate window by selecting **View ➤ Immediate Window** from the **Visual Basic** menu.

8. Scroll up and down in the Immediate window to view all of its contents. You should see the following:

   0

   0

   0

9. Go back to Design mode and modify the code in the Command1_Click event, changing the **Dim** keyword to **Static** as follows:

```
Sub Command1_Click()
    Static iCount as integer
    Debug.Print iCount
    iCount = iCount + 1   'adds one to the current value of iCount
End Sub
```

10. Repeat steps 5 through 8. The Immediate window should now display the following:

   0

   1

   2

TESTER'S TIP *Static variables can be useful for White Box testers trying to log how many times a particular event procedure is accessed.*

Data Types

In the Dim statement, the word *String* represents a data type. A *data type* is the *kind* of variable you can create. For example, you might want a variable to store a number so you can do calculations with it. In this case, you might want to create a variable of type Integer. Other times, you might want to store a textual value, like a username. In that case, you would want to choose to create a variable of type String. The data type indicates to the system how much memory space is needed for storage and what kind of item will be stored there.

TESTER'S TIP *One reason to be concerned about choosing the right data type is to ensure getting the right-sized variable. If you consistently choose data types to declare variables that take up more space than you need, your application might become a memory hog, which can cause several possible bugs to occur (such as "Out of Memory"). In the extreme case, this can also cause your program to run slower since it takes longer to process larger variables. This is another example of something that you should watch out for in coding your test software. Also be aware that the developers of the application you are testing may have chosen poor data types and may get these kinds of errors as well.*

Visual Basic is rich in data types. Table 4-2 contains the standard data types you can use to create a variable in Visual Basic.

Table 4-2. Standard Data Types to Create a Variable in Visual Basic

DATA TYPE	SIZE	RANGE	PREFIX
Boolean	2 bytes	True/False	bol
Byte	1 byte	0 to 255	byt
Currency	8 bytes	-922337203685477.58 to 922337203685477.58	c or cur
Date	8 bytes	January 1, 100 to December 31, 9999	dt
Double	8 bytes	-1.79769313486232D308 to 1.79769313486232D308	dbl
Integer	2 bytes	-32,768 to 32,767	i or int
Long	4 bytes	-2,147,483,648 to 2,147,483,647	l or lng
Single	4 bytes	-3.042823E38 to 3.402823E38	sng
String	1 byte per character	0 to 65,535 characters	str
Variant (numeric)	16 bytes	Any numeric value up to range of double	var
Variant (text)	22 bytes + string length	Same range as string	var
Object	4 bytes	Reference to an object	o or obj

The following are examples of local variable declarations using the appropriate prefixes:

```
Dim iCount as Integer
Dim lngNumTests as Long
Dim bytAge as byte
Dim strTestName as String
Dim curSalary as Currency
Dim varMiscellaneous as Variant
Dim bolTestPassed as Boolean
Dim datTestStartDate as Date
Dim sngTestComplTime as Single
```

Visual Basic does not care what you name your variable. The selection of a variable name is up to the programmer—but do select a name that makes it easy to remember the intent and usage of the variable without having to refer back to its declaration. Use the previous examples as a guide.

Variable naming conventions are a critical part of code reviews—they help reviewers to know what a variable does rather than having to look back at the declaration of the variable. A variable name like strTestName is much more readable then a name like x. Remember that in Chapter 1, the section "Creating Successful Testing Software" examined two pieces of code and compared them for readability. Let's look at them again:

Segment one:

```
If x = y then z_123
```

Segment two:

```
If dtToday > dtDueDate then
     Call RunMonthlyReport
End if
```

These two code segments could be written to accomplish exactly the same task. One of the most significant readability elements of code segment two is the choice of variable names. For more information on how to name variables, see "Constant and Variable Naming Conventions" in the Visual Basic Programmer's Guide.

Assigning Values to Variables

All variables are assigned an initial value when created. For numbers, this value is 0. For string variables, the value is "" (empty). Values are assigned to variables in the same way that values are assigned to properties, using an assignment statement as shown here:

```
iCount = 7
strTestname = "Regressions for Build#7"
bolTestPassed = True
strUserName = "Elvis"
```

The object receiving the value is always on the left side of the assignment statement. The value to be received is always on the right. The equal sign in the assignment statement is used to assign a value, which we read as "becomes." So, the first statement should read, "iCount becomes 7;" the next should read, "strTestName becomes Regressions for Build#7;" and so on for the other statements. Figure 4-8 represents how to picture the variables in memory after they have been assigned a value.

Figure 4-8. Two variables, strUserName and iCount, after they have been assigned values.

Converting between Variables of Different Data Types

Because variables have their own data types, working between variables of different data types can sometimes necessitate the conversion of one to another. In the following example, assume txtSalary is the name of a textbox on the form. Let's say the user has entered 12000.00 into the textbox:

```
Dim curSalary as Currency
curSalary = cCur(txtSalary.text)    ' converts "12000.00" to 12000
```

You cannot do numeric operations with text so this code uses the cCur function to convert the text to currency. Now you can use the value in an expression with other numbers such as:

```
Debug.print curSalary * .85
```

There are many other conversion functions to use in Visual Basic. For example, the Str() function converts numeric values to text. Refer to Visual Basic's Help system for more information on conversion functions.

Identifying Shortcuts and Old Code

Many BASIC programmers use shortcuts to declare variables. This has been available since the first BASIC compiler and is generally standard practice. For example:

```
Dim strUsername as String
```

can also be declared this way:

```
Dim strUserName$
```

The '$' is a shortcut for "as string."
Table 4-3 lists shortcuts for the common BASIC data types.

Table 4-3. Shortcuts for the Common BASIC Data Types

DATA TYPE	SHORTCUT
String	$
Integer	%
Long	&
Single	!
Double	#
Currency	@
Variant	blank

The Variant is the default data type. So, if you declare a variable without a data type at all, it is a Variant:

```
Dim X 'X is declared as a variant
```

> **WARNING** *Be careful, the Variant data type takes up the most space in memory. Excessive use of Variants can be very inefficient.*

Shortcutting may be fairly standard practice but I don't recommend it for anyone, especially testers. It is hardly more trouble to spell out the declaration in its entirety and the advantage to doing this is that the code will be more clear and readable. Clarity and readability come in handy as programming progresses to reduce bugs and enhance maintenance.

Code that has been converted from older versions of Visual Basic, such as Visual Basic 3, will frequently contain even more use of the shortcut characters. This code may create and assign variables like this:

```
Myvar$ = "some string"
```

If you see this kind of code, it's a flag that it may have been converted from an older version and should be inspected more carefully.

Local-Level, Module-Level, and Application-Level Variables

If we were limited to only local-level variables, we would not be able to share data between event procedures in our code. There are times when it makes sense to have a value available to all of the event procedures on a form.

For example, a user name might need to be available throughout the entire Visual Basic project in case certain areas of that project are limited to only certain users.

The following code will *not* correctly print the user name to the Immediate window, no matter what the order of execution of events is:

```
Sub cmdUser_Click()
    Dim strUserName as String
    StrUserName = Inputbox("Please enter your username",, "User Name Entry")
End Sub

Sub cmdPrintIt_Click()
    Debug.print "Welcome " & strUserName
End Sub
```

TO TRY THIS

1. Create a new Visual Basic application.

2. Place two Command button controls on the Form Designer window.

3. In the Properties window, change the Name property of one of the buttons to **cmdUser** and its Caption property to **User**. Change the Name property of the other to **cmdPrintIt** and its Caption property to **PrintIt**.

4. Double-click the **cmdUser** button in the Form Designer window to go to its click-event procedure in the Code window.

5. Type the following code for the **cmdUser** button into its click-event procedure:

```
Sub cmdUser_Click()
    Dim strUserName as String
    StrUserName = Inputbox("Please enter your username",, "User Name Entry")
End Sub
```

6. Repeat step 5 for the **cmdPrintIt** button:

```
Sub cmdPrintIt_Click()
    Debug.print "Welcome " & strUserName
End Sub
```

7. Click the **Run** button on the Visual Basic Tool bar to run your program.

8. Click the **User** button and type anything into the InputBox that appears. Click **OK**.

9. Click the **PrintIt** button. What happens? You will *not* see the value you typed into the InputBox displayed in this MsgBox. Why not?

The MsgBox did not display the value you typed in because the variable declared in the cmdUser_Click event was not available outside of that event procedure. It is a local variable and its use is limited to only the code inside the procedure in which it is declared. So, what can we do to correctly access the user name in the cmdPrintIt_Click event procedure? In order to access the value of strUserName in multiple event procedures, we need to make it available and visible to all event procedures on the form. We can do that by making strUserName a module-level variable.

In the Code window associated with the form, there is a section called General Declarations. As its name implies, you can only write declaration statements there.

Variables declared in the General Declarations section are called *module-level* or *application-level variables* and are visible to all of the event procedures inside that form. To declare module-level variables, we do not use Dim, we use the keyword *Private*. To declare application-level modules, we use the keyword *Public*. Figure 4-9 shows a Code window with declarations of a module-level constant and variable.

NOTE *For backwards compatibility, Microsoft allows application-level variables to be declared with the Dim keyword. However, it recommends that Dim be used only for local variables, that is, those declared within subroutines and functions, in order to be consistent. You will see Visual Basic texts using the Dim keyword for application-level variables but that is not recommended. In this book, we will only use the Public and Private keywords for application-level variables.*

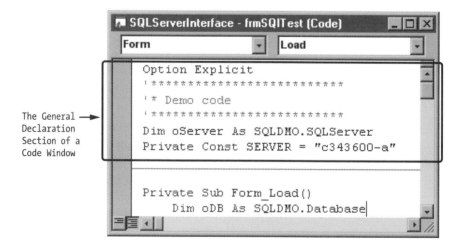

Figure 4-9. The General Declaration section of a form containing module-level declarations.

Examples of module-level and application-level variable declarations include:

```
' Application level (or Global) variables:
Public mstrUserName as String
Public mStrAUTname As String
 ' Module level variables:
Private miSeconds as Single
Private mstrTestResults as Boolean
```

Public and Private variables are also storage locations just like local variables. The only difference is their scope. Both Public and Private variables are available to all procedures inside the module in which they are declared. Public variables are also available to any other code module used in the entire project.

Understanding Scope and Lifetime Variables

Deciding when to declare variables as Dim, Static, Public, or Private can be confusing. This section will help you decide what kind of variable to use and when. Essentially, the determination is made on two important features of the variable, its *scope* and its *lifetime*.

As you have seen, variables are *named storage locations,* that is, a place defined in memory to hold values you want to store.

Scope

The *scope* of a variable determines what parts of the application can see the variable. Scope can be Local, Private, or Public.

- A *Local variable* can be used only within the particular subroutine in which it is declared (created).

- A *Private variable* can be used within the entire module in which it is declared.

- A *Public variable* can be used anywhere within the entire application.

Lifetime

The *lifetime* of a variable is determined at the local level by the keywords:

- **Dim**: temporary—the data is lost after each call of the routine in which it is declared.

- **Static**: persistent—the data remains for subsequent callings of the routine in which it is declared.

The lifetime of a variable is determined at the module and application level by the keywords:

- **Private**: The data persists throughout the life of the module in which it is declared.

- **Public**: The data persists for the life of the project itself.

Table 4-4 summarizes our discussion of scope and lifetime.

Table 4-4. Scope and Lifetime for Visual Basic Variables

VARIABLES	PROCEDURE-LEVEL Local (Dim or Static)		MODULE-LEVEL Private	APPLICATION-LEVEL Public
Location of declaration	Procedure (sub-routine) level.		General Declarations section at top of module.	General Declarations section.
Scope	Available only to that procedure.		Available to only that module's routines.	Available to entire application.
Lifetime	DIM: Value reset every time procedure is called.	STATIC: Values persist.	PRIVATE: Values persist for life of module.	PUBLIC: Values persist for life of project.

I like to compare variable scope to that of a neighborhood. Public variables are those that are available to everyone in the neighborhood. Say a neighborhood shares tools, such as a ladder and a lawn mower, and keeps them in a community shed for all to use. Those items would be considered Public to the neighborhood:

```
Public Ladder as CommonObject 'I am just making up this data type as an example
Public LawnMower as CommonObject
```

Consider each home in the neighborhood a module. Within each home, there are items that everyone who lives in the home can use, for example, the refrigerator and the living room furniture. These would be considered module-level objects and would be regarded as Private:

```
Private LivingRoomChair as HouseholdObject 'I am also making up this data type
Private Refrigerator as HouseholdObject
```

Now, let's say you have children, as I do. You know that within their rooms, they have things that essentially do not exist outside their rooms. No one else in the whole house can use "their" chair, table, bed, clothes, etc. These items would be considered local and would be declared with the Dim keyword:

```
Dim RyansChair as PrivateObject   'this Is a bogus data type as well
Dim KeilansBed as PrivateObject
```

Understanding Option Explicit

You have been working in the Code window quite a bit and by now might be wondering what Option Explicit is doing up in the General Declarations section of the Code window. In a well-written Visual Basic program, these two words are very important to see in every General Declarations section of every module.

Option Explicit will force all variables to be explicitly declared. Every variable we have looked at so far has been explicitly declared. We have done this by writing a declaration statement using Dim, Static, Public, or Private. It is possible without the Option Explicit to write the following line of code *without previously having declared the variable*:

```
X=5
```

Visual Basic, when it encounters this statement, will create a local variable for you. The data type of that variable is Variant. Refer back to the Variant data type description in Table 4-2. Variants take up more space than the other variables: 16 bytes for a numeric variable and 22 bytes minimum for a string. So, leaving off the data type will automatically get you a potentially large and wasteful variable—not a good idea. Leaving off the data type is called *implicit variable declaration*; it is also sometimes called "creating a variable on the fly."

This is poor programming for a few reasons. First, it is possible to accidentally misspell your variable name and create a whole new variable. For example, let's say you created a variable implicitly simply by writing:

```
IntInvoice = 75
```

Then, later on you forget its name and type the following statement:

```
Debug.print intInvoices
```

Notice that we "accidentally" added an 's' to the variable name in this Debug.Print statement. If we actually did this in a program, when Visual Basic encountered this statement at run time (and there is *no* Option Explicit statement), then Visual Basic would create a second variable, intInvoices, in addition to the first variable created, intInvoice. You might believe that you have set your variable to 75 and you expect that "75" will print to the Immediate window—but it doesn't. What *does* print? Nothing. Visual Basic prints the contents of the variable intInvoices, which is a Variant by default with no value at all. So, the contents of intInvoices prints to the Immediate window but you see nothing since intInvoices contains nothing. You get no error message, of course, because Visual Basic did exactly what it was asked to do. Still, you are left scratching your head wondering what you did wrong. Finally, you show it to your team member or spouse or next door neighbor and you feel silly when they say, "Why does it have an 's' when you print it but not when you set it?"

 TESTER'S TIP *Visual Basic programs written using implicit variables can be a sign of neophyte programmers so check code that uses it more carefully during White Box testing and code reviews.*

An easy way to avoid this problem is to use the Option Explicit statement at the top of every Code window in your Visual Basic application. (So far we have only one but we will add more forms soon and each will have its own Code window.) Visual Basic will do this for you (that is, type the "Option Explicit" automatically) if you select the **Require Variable Declaration** checkbox in the **Tools ➤ Options** dialog. Unfortunately, it isn't the default so you will have to make sure you check it yourself. Figure 4-10 shows the Require Variable Declaration checkbox in the Options dialog box.

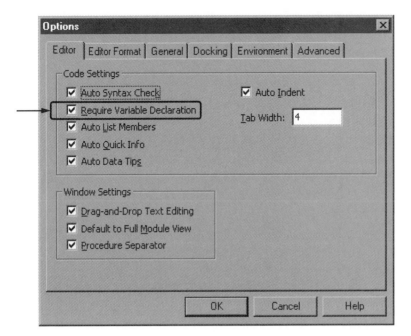

Figure 4-10. The Options dialog box from the Tools menu. It's good programming practice to always have the Require Variable Declaration checkbox checked.

Constants

Constants, like variables, are storage locations to which we give a name. Constants are aptly named because their values can never change. Constants are a part of any well-written program. Like variables, they can be local-level, module-level, or application-level. The same scoping rules apply.

Here are some examples of constant declarations:

```
Private Const mTAXRATE = 0.085
Const mAppUnderTest = "XYZ Application"
Const msngDELAYTIME As Single = 1.5
```

If you leave off the Private keyword when creating a constant in the General Declarations section, the default is a Private constant anyway. That is, if you want a constant to be Public, you must use the Public keyword. Notice that in the declaration of the msngDELAYTIME constant in our example declarations, you can force Visual Basic to use a particular data type. If you do not specify one, a default data type is assigned—but what is assigned may not be what is most efficient for that variable. It is best to assign the data type of the constant as was done in the declaration of the msngDELAYTIME constant.

Because you cannot assign a new value to a constant, you will never see it on the left side of an assignment statement. But of course, you will see it on the right side of an assignment statement because its value can be read:

```
Option Explicit
Const mAppUnderTest = "XYZ Application"
Const msngDELAYTIME As Single = 1.5

Sub Form_Load()
    Me.Caption = mAppUnderTest
'Me refers to the current object
'in this case, the form
End Sub
```

TO TRY THIS

1. Create a new Visual Basic application.

2. Double-click the form in the Form Designer window to go to its Code window.

3. Type the following code into the Code window:

    ```
    Const mAppUnderTest = "XYZ Application"
    Sub Form_Load()
        Me.Caption = mAppUnderTest
    End Sub
    ```

> **NOTE** *When you double-click on the form, the Form_Load event's first and last lines are already created for you. You will not need to type the* Sub Form_Load *and* End Sub *lines again.*

4. Click the **Run** button on the Visual Basic Tool bar to run your program. The caption of the form should say "XYZ Application."

5. Go back to Design mode and place a Command button control on the form in the Form Designer window.

6. Double-click the **Command** button control to go to the Code window for its click-event. Type the following code inside the click-event procedure:

```
Msgbox "The Application Under Test is: " & mAppUnderTest
```

7. Run the program again by pressing **F5**. Your application's form appears.

8. Click the **Command** button on your form. Notice that the name appears in a Message box as well as in the form's caption.

Using Branching Statements

There are times when you need to make a decision in the code. For example, if the first test you run fails, you may want to exit your testing application. If it doesn't fail, you may want to run others. In fact, you may make the decision to run all kinds of different tests based on whether or not certain tests pass or fail. To make a decision while code is running, you need a branching statement.

There are two kinds of branching statements, the If-Then-Else construct and the Select-Case construct. Why two? You can do anything with If-Then-Else. However, sometimes the Select-Case statement provides a bit more readability and is preferred in certain kinds of situations, as we will see as our programming skills progress.

If-Then-Else

There are two forms of the If-Then-Else statement: single line or block. The following gives the formal command syntax for If-Then-Else:

```
If condition Then [statements] [Else elsestatements]
```

Or, you can use the block form syntax:

```
If condition Then
   [statements]
[ElseIf condition-n Then
[elseifstatements] ... ]
[Else
   [elsestatements]]
End If
```

For instance, in our user name example, what happens if the user inputs the wrong user name? We would want to display an error message. If the user inputs the correct user name, we might want to send a welcome message.

The following If-Then-Else code would accomplish that:

```
Option Explicit
Public strUserName as String
Sub Form_Load()
    StrUserName = InputBox("Please enter your user name")
    If strUserName = "Elvis" then
        MsgBox "Welcome! " & strUserName
    Else
        Msgbox "Invalid User Name"
        End 'ends program immediately
    End if
End Sub
```

TO TRY THIS

1. Create a new Visual Basic application.

2. Double-click the form in the Form Designer window to go to its Code window.

3. Type all of the If-Then-Else code just shown into the Code window.

4. Click the **Run** button on the Visual Basic Tool bar to run your program.

5. Type in "**Elvis**" at the prompt. What happens?

6. Stop the program by clicking the **End** button on the Visual Basic toolbar.

7. Run the program again. This time, type in anything *except* "Elvis" at the prompt. What happens?

Select-Case

Another branching statement is the Select-Case statement, which will also make decisions based on a condition. Its structure is shown here:

```
Select Case testexpression
[Case expressionlist-n
   [statements-n]] ...
 [elsestatements]]
End Select
```

The following would perform the same selection as in the previous example:

```
Select Case strUserName
    Case "Elvis"
        MsgBox "Welcome! " & strUserName
    Case Else
        Msgbox "Invalid User Name"
        End  'statement ends the program immediately
End Select
```

> **NOTE** *The Select-Case and If-Then-Else branching statements are complex statements because they are able to contain other statements. Due to this fact, they must have an end, that is, a way to signal to the processor that this complex statement is finished. This is why both statements have an "end" part. The If-Then-Else must have an End If and the Select-Case structure ends with an End Select.*

If-Then-Else is the statement you will see and use the most. Select-Case is common to most programming languages and is frequently used in error-handling routines as we will see later in this text.

Programming with Loops

Another commonly used programming structure is the loop. There are many times when you will want to perform the same code multiple times and consecutively. For example, we might want to write a simple stress test to log into an application over and over. We could use a looping construct to perform that same code ten times, one hundred times, one thousand times, or more rather than having to do it manually with a whole lot of testers.

Looping is sometimes called *iteration* or *repetition*. These terms are synonymous. Each means to repeat a set of steps in your code.

Looping a Specified Number of Times (Counted Iteration)

You can specify the number of times a loop will repeat using a For-Next loop.
The formal syntax for the For-Next loop is:

```
For counter = start To end [Step step]
    [statements]
[Exit For]
    [statements]
Next [counter]
```

For example, the following will print the words: "Stop Testing" five times to the Immediate window:

```
Dim icount as Integer
'iCount will be used to count how many times we have executed the loop
For icount = 1 to 5
    Debug.Print "Stop Tests", iCount
Next iCount          'increments iCount automatically
```

- In the second line, for iCount = 1 to 5, 1 is considered the *lower bound* of the loop and the 5 is the *upper bound*. These values can be integers or floating-point numbers. More commonly they are byte or integer values since those data types provide for whole numbered variables that take up a small amount of space.

- The next iCount is the last line of the loop. It handles automatically adding one to the loop counter, iCount. Adding to the counter is called *incrementing* the counter. If the counter is an integer, the increment must always be an integer and is by default incremented by 1. If a non-integer, numeric data type is used, such as Single or Double, then the default increment is still 1 unless otherwise specified. However, the Single and Double data types will allow you to increment by decimal numbers like .25. To see all of your options for incrementing, check the Visual Basic Help system for the For-loop.

- The third line is in the body of the loop. Any lines of code between the For and Next lines are executed every time the loop executes. Notice in this example that we will print out the value of iCount. What would you expect to see?

TO TRY THIS

1. Create a new Visual Basic application.

2. Place a **Command** button control on the Form Designer window.

3. Double-click the new button in the Form Designer window to go to its click-event procedure in the Code window.

4. Type all of the code shown here into the click-event procedure of the new button:

```
Dim icount as Integer
For icount = 1 to 5
    Debug.Print "Stop Tests", iCount
Next iCount
```

5. Click the **Run** button on the Visual Basic Tool bar to run your program. Your application's form displays.

6. Click the Command button on the form.

7. Display the Immediate window by selecting **View** ➢ **Immediate Window** from the **Visual Basic** menu.

8. Scroll up and down in the Immediate window to view all of its contents. You should see the following:

```
Stop Tests    1
Stop Tests    2
Stop Tests    3
Stop Tests    4
Stop Tests    5
```

These steps execute the code in the button in a loop. The numbers printed represent the value of the iCount variable for each consecutive time the loop executed.

TIP *For extra practice, try running the Debugger (refer back to the "Debugger" section and Exercise 4-1 earlier in this chapter) and watch the loop execute line-by-line.*

Writing Conditional Loops

Frequently, you will not know how many times you need to execute a loop. Whether or not to iterate will depend on some condition.

Conditional looping can have the condition at the bottom as in the following example or at the top. The formal command syntax is:

```
Do
    [statements]
    [Exit Do]
    [statements]
Loop [{While | Until} condition]
```

Or, you can use this syntax for testing at the top:

```
Do [{While | Until} condition]
    [statements]
    [Exit Do]
    [statements]
Loop
```

Code Review Practice

The following example uses the intrinsic function Environ and loops through all of the environment variables on a platform, listing them into a Picture box control:

```
Dim EnvString, Indx, Msg          'using shortcuts for variable declaration
Indx = 1  ' Initialize index to 1.
Do
   EnvString = Environ(Indx)      ' Get environment variable.
   Msg = "Environ variable: " & Indx & " is " & EnvString
   Picture1.Print Msg
   Indx = Indx + 1                ' increment
Loop Until EnvString = ""
```

NOTE *To try this example, create a new Visual Basic application and place a PictureBox control on the form. Create a Command button and place the previous code into its click-event. You can also run the program from the Practice Files. To do so, open the Chapter4\Demos folder and open and run the EnvironEx.vbp program.*

The following are notes about the previous loop:

- The Dim statement uses shortcutting. Two variables are declared on the same line. The declaration shown has the same effect as if the following had been typed instead:

```
Dim EnvString as variant
Dim Msg as variant
Dim Indx as variant
```

  Referring back to our data types in Table 4-2, we know that Variants take up the most memory. This kind of shortcutting saves typing but makes the code less readable and less efficient, not to mention harder to edit. Since EnvString and Msg are obviously strings, the String data type would have been a more efficient choice for them. The Indx variable should have been defined using either the Integer or Byte data types.

- The loop used is a conditional Do-loop with the conditional test at the bottom of the loop. The indentation makes it easy to see which statements are repeated. Everything between the keyword Do and the keyword Loop is repeated each time the loop executes.

- The loop will repeat until the variable EnvString is equal to blank, fulfilling the condition. So, the number of times the loop executed might be different for different systems depending on the number of environment variables on a particular platform.

- The loop counter is not automatically incremented in a conditional loop. In fact, a loop counter is not required at all in conditional loops. In this case, it is necessary because environment variables in Windows are numbered. Environ(1) would return the text of the first environment variable. Environ(2) would return the text of the second environment variable, and so on.

- If the Environ function returns an empty string, there are no more environment variables to list and the program exits the loop.

- Is this "good" code? Compare this code with the recommendations for coding conventions and object naming conventions discussed in previous sections. The code uses indentation properly—but what about clear, consistent, and appropriate names for variables? Hungarian Notation is not used in this code sample. The choice of data types is also not efficient since Variant has been chosen as the default. There are comments but are they helpful? I would rate this code as below average. Where did it come from? It is derived from an example from the Visual Basic Help system! It is important to note that not all code examples in the Help system or other books and references you find on Visual Basic will always use good programming techniques. Be wary!

Using the Shell Function to Run One Program from Another

So far, we have covered fundamental Visual Basic concepts and statements. Now we know just about enough to start using Visual Basic and the commands we have learned in a testing environment. We need one more very important function first, the Shell function. This is important to testers because it is the command that will run an application from within Visual Basic. There are many times when testers will need to do this, either to start the application you are testing or to launch another program for test support such as the Windows Registry.

To use the Shell command, you must provide the pathname of the executable (.exe) file you want to run.

The Shell function has the following syntax:

```
Shell(pathname, [,windowstyle])
```

The `windowstyle` argument is used to specify whether or not to give the new program's window the focus and to determine how it is displayed. Table 4-5 lists possible ways to display the window.

Table 4-5. Visual Basic Constants for the Shell Command

CONSTANT	DESCRIPTION
VbHide	Window is hidden from view but has the focus.
VbNormalFocus	Window has the focus and has its default size and position.
VbMinimizedFocus	Window is minimized with the focus.
VbMaximizedFocus	Window is maximized with the focus.
VbNormalNoFocus	Window is its default size and position but does not have the focus.
VbMinimizedNoFocus	Window is minimized and does not have the focus.

The following code will run the Notepad accessory:

```
Dim lRetVal as Long
lRetVal = Shell ("c:\windows\notepad.exe",vbNormalFocus)
```

Shell is a *function*. The difference between functions and other types of Visual Basic commands is that a function always has to return something to you. In this case, the Shell command will return the Task ID of the program it ran. The *Task ID* is a unique number that identifies the running program. Because the Shell function returns the Task ID, we must have a place to put it. The Dim statement used in the previous code creates a variable to hold the Task ID.

Let's say we want to perform some tests on the Notepad accessory. Follow these steps to start the Notepad from within your Visual Basic code:

1. Start up Visual Basic and create a new project.

2. Place a button on the default form.

3. Add the following code to the button's click-event:

    ```
    Dim lRetVal as Long
    lRetVal = Shell ("c:\windows\notepad.exe",vbNormalFocus)
    ```

4. Press **F5** to run the program.

5. Click the button on the form. You will be able to watch the Notepad accessory start.

NOTE *Once you start the Notepad accessory, you will have to close it manually. In the next chapter, I will introduce the SendKeys statement, which will allow you to close the Notepad from within your code.*

Creating an Executable File from a Visual Basic Project

Once you have finished your Visual Basic project, you can compile it into an .exe file. To do so, perform the following steps:

1. Select the **File** menu and then select the **Make <Project Name>** submenu item. The **Make Project** dialog box is displayed.

    The default name, Project1, is displayed in the Filename textbox. Change this to a name that is descriptive of your project.

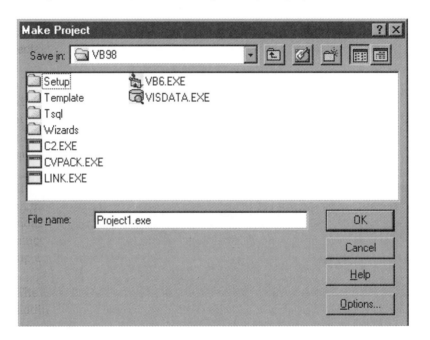

2. Click **Options** to select compilation options. This will bring up another dialog box that will allow you to set a version number, comments, and other options to document your application. When you are finished, click **OK** to close this dialog box.

    Click **OK** on the **Make Project** dialog to compile your application into an .exe file.

NOTE *The default name of your .exe will be the same as the name of your project and the same as your .vbp file. You can change the name of your .exe to something relevant that you will remember. Make sure that you leave its extension as .exe, however, and remember what you have named it so that you can find it later!*

4. Once your .exe is complete, close Visual Basic. It may prompt you to save your .vbp and .frm files, go ahead and do so.

5. Find your new .exe file using Windows Explorer and double-click it. Since it is an executable file in its own right, it will run independently of Visual Studio.

NOTE *This method of creating the .exe is useful for running the application on your own system or you can also copy this .exe and use it on another computer that has a full installation of Visual Basic 6. For porting this to machines without Visual Basic 6 installed, use the Package and Deployment Wizard (see the Microsoft Visual Studio 6 Tools program group) because files in addition to the .exe are needed.*

EXERCISE 4-2.

INFORMATION PLEASE

Exercise 4-2 will apply your knowledge of the preceding section using variables, constants, branching, and assignment statements. In addition, we will use several intrinsic functions of Visual Basic that can be useful on a testing project. These functions demonstrate some of the power built into Visual Basic.

Before beginning the exercise, look up all of the following topics in the Visual Basic Help system:

CurDir

Now

FileDateTime

FileLen

Environ$

Shell

TIP *Use context-sensitive Help by typing the preceding topics into a Code window, then place your cursor on each one in turn and press* F1.

1. Run the file **InfoPlease.exe** from the Chapter 4 folder in the Practice Files.

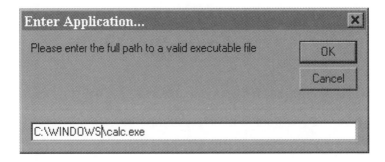

2. Type in the full pathname of the Calc.exe accessory on your system (on Windows 95/98 it is usually in **C:\Windows\Calc.Exe**) and click **OK**.

TIP *To find the correct location of the Calc.exe accessory, use the* Windows Start *menu and click the* Find *menu item. Type in "Calc" to find the correct full pathname for this accessory.*

Note the functionality of the buttons on the window.

This is how your completed project will look.

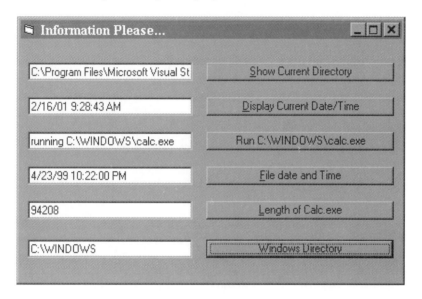

Steps to Create the InfoPlease Program

1. Open the project InfoPleasetempl.vbp in the Chapter 4 folder in the Practice Files.

WARNING *This program is only partially complete and will not run without errors. Your task is to complete the program so that it will run successfully. The next steps will guide you.*

2. Create a module-level string variable called mstrAppName. Now run the program. Click the buttons to see how they work. Return to Design mode.

3. Click once on each button and note its name (not the caption) in the Properties box.

4. In Design mode, double-click on the **cmdNow** button. Note the code there. It accesses the Now function and returns its value into the txtNow textbox. The code for the cmdFileDateTime, cmdFileLen, and cmdWindir Command buttons are also created for you.

5. Double-click the new **cmdCurDir** button in Design mode to go to the Code window. Enter the code to assign the return value of the CurDir function to the Text property of the txtCurDir textbox.

6. In the Code window, look at the form's Load event (Form_Load). It already has code to prompt the user for their user name. Use an If-Then statement to write the code in order to verify that the user has entered an application name. In this If-Then statement, check to see whether the application name is blank (mstrAppname = ""); if it is, write the code to send a warning message and exit the program. Test your work by running the program. *Do not move onto the next step until this part works.*

   Also, do *not* change the existing code. Add your If-Then code after the green comments.

7. In Design mode, double-click the new **cmdRun** button to go to its click-event procedure in the Code window.

   • Dimension a local variable called lngReturn of data type Long:

   ```
   Dim lngReturn as long
   ```

   • Write the code to assign the text "running…" to the Text property of the txtRun textbox:

   ```
   TxtRun.Text = "Running…"
   ```

   • Add the following additional code to this event procedure:

   ```
   lngReturn = Shell(mStrAppname, vbNormalFocus)
   Debug.Print mStrAppname & " Started"
   Debug.Print "Task ID: " & lngReturn & " started at: " & Now
   ```

   • What is happening in this code? What is the purpose of the '&'?

8. Run and Test your program until it works like the .exe (**Chapter4\Info-Please.exe**) you ran at the start of this exercise.

> **NOTE** *If you encounter the "File Not Found" error message, you haven't typed a correct file name into the InputBox that starts the program. You can eliminate this by typing a correct file name; don't forget to include its full path. Or, for an extra challenge, look up the InputBox function in the Visual Basic Help system and modify the function call to include a default value.*

9. Create an .exe file from this new project.

10. Pick appropriate names for your new files. Use the **File ➤ Save As** menu item to save your work.

> **TIP** *Create a new folder for yourself. Save all your work into this new folder to keep your work separate from the lab's templates and answers—this way, you can restart if necessary*

Extra Work: Return to Design mode. Use the Debugger to execute your program line-by-line. Attempt to execute all lines of code written.

> **NOTE** *Compare your answer to the suggested answer for this exercise found in the Answer folder inside of the Chapter 4 folder in the Practice Files.*

TESTER'S CHECKLIST

When performing code reviews, look for the following in a well-written Visual Basic application.

Does the Project . . .

❑ Have a Coding Conventions document or attachment?

❑ Provide templates to team members to facilitate use of common coding conventions?

Does the Code . . .

❑ Follow the coding standards required by the Coding Conventions document? Or use consistent indentation?

❑ Use standard object and variable naming conventions?

❑ Use Option Explicit in every module?

❑ Limit the use of Variants?

❑ Use a style that makes it readable by a programmer with approximately one year of programming experience?

❑ Make proper use of the defaulting of data types for variables? Is it consistent?

❑ Allow for portability between operating systems? That is, does it break when ported from one Windows OS to another?

Code Review Practice

Open up the Visual Basic project named EnvironEx in the Chapter 4 folder. Use the aforementioned criteria to do a code review. What is your assessment?

Chapter 4 Review

- How are Properties set at run time?
  See page 84.

- Explain the process for writing the code to respond to the click-event of a Command button.
  See page 89.

- What is the difference between a property and an event?
  See page 89.

- What is the difference between event-driven and procedural programming?
  See page 90

- List three common coding conventions for a Visual Basic software project.
  See pages 98–99.

- List two to three keywords that may be used in variable declaration.
  See pages 100–102.

- What is the difference between local and module-level variables?
  See pages 108–112.

- How would you repeat a series of code statements fifty times?
  Using loop structures.
  See pages 119–122.

- What are the steps to create an executable file from a Visual Basic project?
  See pages 126–127.

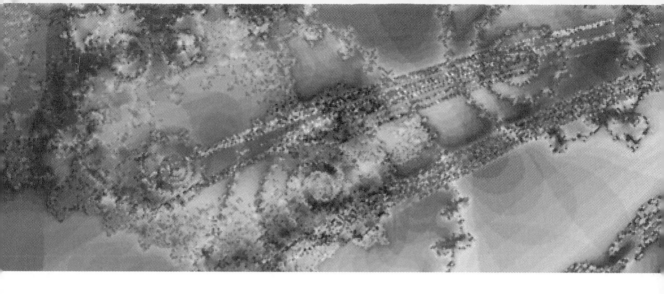

Part Three

Beyond the Basics: Now You're Testing!

CHAPTER 5

Creating Test Utilities

On any automated testing project, if you have to write every line of code from scratch every time, you'll never finish. If you start early in the project to identify tasks that can be written and stored as utilities and used repeatedly, it will save you time and headaches. An additional benefit is that some of these utilities are usable on other projects. Remember from Chapter 1 that one of the goals of good software is *reuse*. Actually, the whole reason we are automating testing in the first place is to increase our testing capabilities with code and to avoid doing certain tests over and over manually, right? So, it makes sense to create pieces of code generic enough to be used more than once.

To create and use these utilities, you will need to learn to use a common programming structure called the procedure. You will also need to use a Visual Basic object called a Standard module in order to store your utilities. In this chapter, you will use these procedures and modules to begin a utility library. I will also introduce some ideas for practical utilities, for example, logging routines and an application-startup routine. Along the way, you will learn some additional techniques to round out your test, such as adding timing and using the SendKeys statement to send keystrokes to an application. After that, the sky is the limit; you can create many different kinds of utilities with the techniques you will learn in this chapter.

Objectives

By the end of this chapter, you will be able to:

- Explain why the creation of utilities is important on a testing project.

- Define the difference between a subroutine and function.

- Build simple test utilities using subroutines and functions.

- Describe the purpose and scope of a Visual Basic Standard module.

- Create and use a Visual Basic Standard module.

- Describe the difference between a Standard module and a Form module.

- Add a new Form module to a Visual Basic application.

- Explain the use of the Show and Hide methods for forms.

- Explain the use of the Load and Unload statements.

- Read from and write to a text file using the Microsoft Scripting Library.

- Explain the importance of logging on an automated testing project.

- Add code for simple timing to your test script.

- Use the SendKeys command to simulate user input.

Creating and Using Procedures

Many lines of code are useful enough to be used more than once, not just in one project but in others as well. Rather than cutting and pasting, it makes sense to write the steps down and put them in a library where they can be accessed or called repeatedly. After all, the idea behind automated testing is to avoid duplication of labor. This same philosophy can be applied to reusing code, why reinvent the wheel?

We call each discrete set of steps a *procedure*. There are two kinds of procedures: *subroutine procedures* and *function procedures*. We have already worked with a special-purpose subroutine procedure, the *event procedure*. The event procedures we have worked with have the keyword Sub in their first line. Sub is short for *subroutine*. The procedures we have worked with have been attached to a control or form in our Visual Basic project, for example, Public Sub Form_Load. This procedure runs just before the form displays so whether or not it runs depends on the form. Now, you will learn how to create your own generic procedures that are not attached to any specific object. These generic procedures will prove to be a very powerful way to expand the usefulness of your code. Before you do, though, you need to engage in some planning to make sure you are headed in the right direction.

Planning Your Procedures

Before actually sitting down and writing a bunch of routines, you need to do some planning. What exactly is the task you are trying to accomplish? How can you organize this task into manageable parts and write the code to implement it? Your initial task definition will come from the Test Plan and your Test Lead in the form of a test case. Then, assuming the test case you have been given includes automating all or part of the test case, you will have to sit down and plan how you write the code to accomplish it. Software planning is not a trivial task and there are many books available on how to do it effectively (see Appendix A: Resources and References). However, to get started, you will have to do what is done on essentially all software projects (I first listed these steps in Chapter 1):

- Analyze requirements (from the Test Plan and Test Lead).

- Design your automated tests.

- Write the test code.

- Test the test code—yes you must test your tests!

- Deliver (implement the test).

- Maintain the test code.

You may iterate on these steps many times for some automated test code, depending on the task.

In Chapter 4, I described subroutines as sub-parts of the larger program, such as many subcontractors working on a big project. That's how you can think of all procedures. Before creating a procedure, you need to sit down and design the kinds of tasks you want procedure to perform. This is not a trivial process. Good planning is a part of any good program.

For now, let's get started simply. In most tests you automate, there will be some essential starting tasks to perform such as checking system statistics and, of course, properly starting the application under test. At the end, there will be some clean up tasks—for example, shutting down the application and printing out test results. In the next few sections, I will show you how to create some simple routines to start your application and to log test results. So, your current design might be:

- StartProgram

- RunTest

- LogTests

Next, you will learn how to create the subroutine and function procedures to implement these tasks.

Creating and Using Subroutine Procedures

In the last exercise (Chapter 4, Exercise 4-2), you wrote code that ran an application using the Shell command and printed status information into the Immediate window. It is very likely that the same code might be useful again for a different test. You can make this code more general by converting it into a general subroutine. We have been using subroutines all along in the form of event procedure subroutines; however, we can also write them independent of particular events. These are not attached to any control on the form. You can create a subroutine by simply typing it into the Code window. (Where within the Code window? Anywhere except inside another procedure):

```
Private Sub StartProgram()
End Sub
```

That's all there is to creating a subroutine! Like the event procedures we have already worked with, the subroutine has a *container* (the Sub and End Sub lines) and a *body* (all the lines between the Sub and End Sub lines). Simply typing in the preceding code created a procedure—which is pretty useless at this point until you write more code inside those two lines to tell it what to do. What do you want it to do? At this stage, you should write what the routine will do in comments. This will help you focus your efforts and keep your routines simple and direct:

```
Private Sub StartProgram()
'this routine will start the Calculator accessory with normal focus.
'It will log the starting time to the debug window similar to this:
'Shell Calculator
'debug print "Calc Is started" Now
End Sub
```

The preceding comments are a form of *pseudocode*. Pseudocode is not real code but statements in English (or your native language) descriptive enough to allow you to write real code—it's a part of the planning and design process that developers also use to help write organized code.

```
Now you can write the code using real Visual Basic statements:
Private Sub StartProgram()
'this routine will start the Calculator accessory with normal focus.
'It will log the starting time to the debug window similar to this:
    Dim lngReturn As Long
    'The following line works for Win9x systems, for
    'WinNT or Win2K system be sure to Include the correct path to calc
    lngReturn = Shell("Calc.exe", vbNormalFocus)
    Debug.Print "Calc Started"
    Debug.Print "Task ID: " & lngReturn & " started at: " & Now
End Sub
```

NOTE *This snippet of code is written for a Windows 95 and Windows 98 platform. On Windows NT, the path for the calculator is different. The full path to Calc.exe on Windows NT is c:\winnt\calc.exe. The full path on Windows 2000 is c:\winnt\system32\calc.exe. Code in the Chapter 6 Practice files shows how to customize this so that it will be portable to any system.*

Now, the question is when does this new subroutine run? Event procedures run in response to an event. Since the StartProgram subroutine we just wrote is not an event procedure and is therefore not associated with any control, there is no event that will automatically cause it to run.

When you want the StartProgram subroutine to run, the first thing you must ask yourself is when? This is event-driven programming remember? Once you have determined when you want it to run, choose the correct event procedure from which to run it, then you can simply type the name of your StartProgram subroutine into that event procedure. Using programming terms, we say we are *calling* the procedure when we do this. Generic routines you create yourself won't run unless called. Let's say you want your new StartProgram subroutine to run when the user clicks a button. To call the new subroutine, you can create a button and type the call into the click-event of this new button:

```
Private Sub cmdRun_Click()
    StartProgram        'executes a call to the procedure
End Sub
```

You can call the StartProgram subroutine as many times as you want from within any event procedure. This technique is useful if you want to run the same code more than once within your project. Instead of cutting and pasting, you can now call the StartProgram subroutine and it will execute and run the Calculator accessory. It will print status information to the Immediate window every time it is called.

TO TRY THIS

1. Create a new Visual Basic project.

2. Place a Command button on the form and change its Name property to **cmdRun**.

3. In the form's Code window, type in the following code for the cmdRun_Click event and the StartProgram subroutine:

```
Private Sub cmdRun_Click()
        StartProgram          'executes a call to the procedure
End Sub


Private Sub StartProgram()
    Dim lngReturn As Long
    'The following line works for Win9x systems, for
    'WinNT or Win2K system be sure to Include the correct path to calc
    lngReturn = Shell("Calc", vbNormalFocus)
    Debug.Print "Calc Started"
    Debug.Print "Task ID: " & lngReturn & " started at: " & Now
End Sub
```

NOTE *Be sure to include the correct path to the calc.exe program for the operating system you are using.*

4. Press **F5** to run your program. Click the button. What happens? (You should see the Calculator program run.)

You have written a general subroutine called StartProgram. You could call it again from any other spot in your program by simply typing its name. Since it's not attached to any particular control, it is located in the General section of the Form module as shown in Figure 5-1.

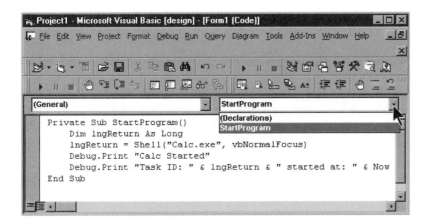

Figure 5-1. General subroutines are located in the General Declarations section of the Code window.

 TESTER'S TIP *When reviewing Visual Basic code, one of the first things to do is to review the subroutines created by the developer. You will find a list of those routines in each form by going to the Code window and selecting* General Declarations *in the Object box. The Procedure box will then have a list of all of the general procedures.*

Using Arguments

Of course, the code for our new StartProgram subroutine only runs whatever program you have typed into it next to the Shell command. What if we'd like to have the StartProgram subroutine run other applications, not just the Calculator? If we want to make this routine more general, we can add an *argument* that allows us to fill in the name of the application we want to run. An argument is a way to give some information to the subroutine in order for it to do its job. In programming terms, when we give a value to subroutine, we are *passing* the argument to the routine. Think of passing the butter to your brother at the dinner table. That's exactly what it means (only not with butter). To pass an argument means to provide a value to the subroutine. We would like to be able to call the StartProgram subroutine and just give it the name of the application to run—that is, pass it the name like this:

```
Private Sub cmdRun_Click()
    StartProgram "calc.exe"                    'correct calls for Win9x systems
    StartProgram "notepad.exe"
    StartProgram "c:\winnt\calc.exe"           'correct for WinNT4
    StartProgram "c:\winnt\system32\calc.exe"  'correct for Win2K
End Sub
```

Once we have an argument for our StartProgram subroutine, we can use it to run any valid executable program in the same way simply by passing the correct pathname to the executable program. Before we can see this happen, we will have to make a couple of important modifications to the body of the subroutine. The StartProgram subroutine needs to be able to accommodate this new argument. Here is how it is modified to accept an argument (the changes are in bold):

```
Private Sub StartProgram(App As String)
    Dim lngReturn As Long
    lngReturn = Shell(App, vbNormalFocus)
    Debug.Print App & " Started"
    Debug.Print "Task ID: " & lngReturn &  "started at: " & Now
End Sub
```

Notice that we replaced "Calc.exe" with the word "App". App is an argument declared in the *Formal Argument list* of the subroutine. The first line of the subroutine lists all of the arguments between parentheses; if there is more than one argument, commas separate them. Each one is given a name and a data type. The declaration of an argument (App as String) looks a lot like a variable declaration, doesn't it? However, arguments are not the same as variables. Variables create storage. Arguments are only placeholders. This is why you don't see the keywords Dim, Private, or Public in the declaration of an argument. Those keywords imply the creation of space in memory. The argument is there to represent a value that will be given to the routine when the program runs.

What is really important when we declare an argument for a procedure is to declare what *kind* of value is needed, in other words, the data type of the argument. Of course, we need to refer to it in the code we write for the subroutine so we must also give it a name. At run time, however, the argument name will be replaced with the actual value passed into it. Got it? It will be easier to understand after working with a few examples.

Now that you can write a subroutine, you will find many useful things to do with them. For example, there is no command in Visual Basic to pause for a few seconds. That is something we occasionally want to do when testing, pause while we wait for the dialog box to display or to give enough time for a network connection. We can create our own Pause subroutine that will perform this task for us. In fact, using arguments, we can make a subroutine that will pause for any amount of time we give it. To do this, we will make use of two intrinsic Visual Basic functions, Timer and DoEvents:

```
Private Sub Pause(PauseTime As Double)
    Dim StartTime As Double
    StartTime = Timer
    'timer is intrinsic VB function
    Do While Timer < StartTime + PauseTime
        DoEvents   'allow system to perform other tasks
    Loop
End Sub
```

In this code:

- *Timer* is a function that returns the number of seconds since midnight so its value is continually changing. Capturing its value before our task and then again afterwards allows us to time how long a task takes to run.

- *DoEvents* is a Visual Basic statement that releases the system at run time to perform other tasks, such as update the system clock and repaint windows. Without DoEvents, the system cannot do other tasks as the loop runs. The program will hang (lock up), usually requiring you to end the task with a Ctrl-Alt-Delete key sequence.

You can insert a delay anytime you want simply by calling this subroutine and passing to it the number of seconds you want to delay:

```
Private Sub cmdRun_Click()
    Pause 5 'a call to our new Pause sub
    StartProgram "calc.exe"
    Pause 5
    StartProgram "notepad.exe"
End Sub
```

TO TRY THIS

1. Using the program you created in the last "To Try This," modify your cmdRun event procedure to look like the following (be sure to use the correct path to the Calc.exe and Notepad.exe accessories on your system):

```
Private Sub cmdRun_Click()
    Pause 5 'a call to our new Pause sub
    StartProgram "calc.exe"
    Pause 5
    StartProgram "notepad.exe"
End Sub
```

2. Create a Pause subroutine that looks like this:

```
Private Sub Pause(PauseTime As Double)
    Dim StartTime As Double
    StartTime = Timer
    'timer is intrinsic VB function
    Do While Timer < StartTime + PauseTime
        DoEvents
    Loop
End Sub
```

3. Modify your StartProgram subroutine to look like the following:

```
Private Sub StartProgram(App As String)
    Dim lngReturn As Long
    lngReturn = Shell(App, vbNormalFocus)
    Debug.Print App & " Started"
    Debug.Print "Task ID: " & lngReturn & "started at: " & Now
End Sub
```

4. Press **F5** to run the program again. Wait five seconds. You should see the Calculator accessory appear; then, after another five-second delay, the Notepad accessory will appear.

TIP *Use the Debugging tool we discussed in Chapter 4 to step through your code line-by-line. The Debugging tool has a feature that allows you to see the current value of a variable while debugging simply by dragging your cursor over it. As you step through your code, you will see the values being passed into the arguments of your subroutine. This is an excellent way to understand what's going on.*

Understanding Function Procedures

Functions are similar to subroutines in many ways. Functions, like subroutines, are also procedures and must also be "called" to be executed. The main difference between functions and procedures is that a function *always* returns a value. Another difference is that functions can be used in an arithmetic expression. For example, the following is a function for calculating the average of three numbers. It takes three arguments and returns a value representing the average of those three numbers:

```
Private Function AvgSize(F1 As Long, F2 As Long, F3 As Long) As Long
    AvgSize = (F1 + F2 + F3) / 3
End Function
```

 TESTER'S TIP *Taking an average value is a common testing task. For example, you may test the performance of a certain task of an application (such as logging into an application) by measuring how long it takes to complete. How can you be certain that the performance you saw is typical? Often we will perform the test multiple times and then take an average. This is just one example; you will likely find many others.*

Note that a function, unlike a subroutine, has a single value that it returns (the extra "As Long" after the Formal Argument list indicates the data type of that return value). In short, the arguments listed inside the parentheses must be *passed to* the function "(F1 As Long, F2 As Long, F3 As Long)" and the "As Long" following the Argument list is what the function *gives back*. Notice also that our function AvgSize has declared three arguments, each specified with its name and data type and separated from the other by commas.

Another difference between subroutines and functions is that somewhere within the body of the function, you will see the name of the function on the left-hand side of an equal sign. On the right side will be a value that ends up being what the function returns. Since the function must return a value, we must assign the function a value in the body of the code. The following is the line that does this for our AvgSize function:

```
AvgSize = (F1 + F2 + F3) / 3
```

One use of our new AvgSize function might be to calculate the average size of a created file. The code in Listing 5-1 uses the intrinsic Visual Basic function FileLen to find the sizes of three executable files. We then call the AvgSize function to find the average of these three values.

Listing 5-1. An event procedure that calls the AvgSize function.

```
Private Sub Command1_Click()
'declare three variables to hold the sizes of 3 files In bytes
    Dim lFileSize1 As Long
    Dim lFileSize2 As Long
    Dim lFileSize3 As Long
'The FileLen function Is an Intrinsic VB function which will return the length
'of a file In bytes
    lFileSize1 = FileLen(Environ("windir") + "\calc.exe")
    lFileSize2 = FileLen(Environ("windir") +  "\notepad.exe")
    lFileSize3 = FileLen(Environ("windir") + "\regedit.exe")
'The following line calls the function AvgSize and returns Its value Into a label
'control for display.
    Label1.Caption = AvgSize(lFileSize1,lFileSize2,lFileSize3) 'the call
End Sub
```

Argument Names

In the function example demonstrated here, why are the names of the actual arguments different than the names used inside the function? That is, inside the function, the three arguments are called F1, F2, and F3 but when we call the function, we declared three variables named lFileSize1, lFileSize2, and lFileSize3. Why do we use different names—don't we *have* to call them the same name? The answer is no, we don't, as you will see when you try it yourself. The names of the arguments in a function are simply placeholders. When you call the function (or a subroutine with arguments) you can pass in a literal value like 2 or you can pass in a variable.

The important thing is that the actual argument be the correct data type specified by the function in the Formal Argument list. The Formal Argument list is the first line of the function or subroutine. That first line is considered the declaration of those arguments. You *can* give the formal arguments and the variables that you pass into the procedure the same name, but you don't have to.

Notice that the call to the function is on the right side of an assignment statement. This means that it will be providing a value to what is on the left side of the assignment statement. There must be some place to put the return value of the function. So, Label1's Caption property receives that value. Notice also that, unlike subroutines, when a function is called, there *must* be parentheses around the Argument list:

```
Label1.Caption = AvgSize(lFileSize1,lFileSize2,lFileSize3) 'the call
```

TO TRY THIS

1. Create a new Visual Basic project.

2. Place a label control on the Form Designer window. Size it appropriately but do not change its name from its default, Label1.

3. Place a button control on the Form Designer window. Do not change its Name property either—its name will be Command1. Change the Caption property if desired.

4. Double-click on the **Command** button in Design mode to go to its click-event procedure. Type in the code from Listing 5-1. (You can use any three files of your choice rather than the ones used. Be sure to specify the full path for each.)

5. Create a new function procedure by typing the following anywhere in the Code window (do not type it within another event procedure, of course):

    ```
    Private Function AvgSize(F1 As Long, F2 As Long, F3 As Long) As Long
        AvgSize = (F1 + F2 + F3) / 3
    End Function
    ```

6. Run your program (press **F5**).

7. Click the **Command** button. The value you see represents the average size (in bytes) of the three .exe files: Calc, Notepad, and Regedit. You can verify this by checking their sizes using the Windows Explorer.

Since a function returns a value, we can take that value and immediately do a calculation with it; for example, multiply it by some factor. In contrast, we cannot use a subroutine call in an expression. For this reason, always use a function to perform a task that must return a value.

The following would be a legal line of code:

```
Print AvgSize(3,2,1) * 20
```

This line uses the AvgSize function in an expression—something you cannot do with a subroutine. The numbers 3, 2, and 1 are passed into the AvgSize function. The result of the function will be 2. Since it's the average of 3, 2, and 1, that value is then multiplied by 20. So, 40 will be printed to the Immediate window by the Print statement.

Procedure Scoping

You may have noticed that when an event procedure is created, it has the Private keyword preceding the word "Sub" like this:

```
Private Sub Form_Load()
End Sub
```

When we created our own general functions and subroutines, we also used the Private keyword. The Private keyword is used to specify the *scope* of the routine, that is, from where in the application it can be called. Actually, every subroutine or function can be designated either Private or Public in scope. If you leave off the designation, its scope will be Public by default. If a procedure is declared Private (as all of the event procedures are), then that procedure can only be called from within the form in which it is declared. So far, we have been working with an application that only has one form so it really hasn't been an issue. However, we will soon be adding new forms and other kinds of modules to our application. If we want to call our new general routines from code in some other form in the application, we need to make sure that the routine is declared as Public.

Understanding Code Modules

All code in Visual Basic is stored in Code modules. So far, we have used only one kind of Code module, the Form module. Most applications are more complex and require more than one form. Each form has its own Code module associated with it. Also, as an application grows, you will find there is general code that you want to run from multiple forms. This code can be stored in a Standard module. There are actually three kinds of modules where code can be written in Visual Basic: Form modules, Standard modules, and Class modules. Using Class modules, you can create your own objects and store code associated with them. In this chapter, we focus on Form and Standard modules; Class modules will be covered in Chapter 9.

Creating and Using Standard Modules

Once you start to amass useful functions and subroutines, you will want to use them in more than one form or perhaps in more than one project. So far, you have written all of your subroutines and functions inside of one form and have declared them with the Private keyword. If you create the routines with a Public scope, you can access them from anywhere in your Visual Basic application. Rather than have Public procedures in a Form module though, it makes sense to move your general functions and subroutines to a general location, a sort of library file. There, they will be easier to locate and maintain. In Visual Basic the place to store general routines is in a Standard module.

Standard modules are like one big General Declarations section. Like a Form module, a Standard module has a Code window where functions and subroutines can be written; the difference is that the Standard module does not have a visible interface, that is, a Standard module does not have a form part, just a code part. It's a place for code only. You can store general subroutines, functions, constants, and variables in a Standard module. If you make these objects Public, they can be accessed from any place in your application.

Standard modules add another file to your project with a *.bas* extension. To add a Standard module:

1. Select the **Project** ➤ **Add Module** menu item. The Add Module dialog is displayed as shown in Figure 5-2.

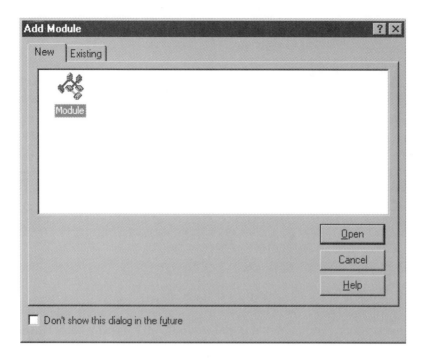

Figure 5-2. The Add Module dialog.

 NOTE *You can select the* Existing *tab of the Add Module dialog to add already existing .bas files into your project. This will allow you to use Standard modules previously created by yourself or others, which supports the concept of code reuse—a good programming technique for both developers* and *automated test-script writers.*

2. Click the **Open** button.

Your Project window (Figure 5-3) has changed; a new file called Module1 has been added. In addition, a new Code window has been added. The new Code window is for the new Standard module and is just like the other Code windows we have used except that they were attached to forms. The module has properties just like a form has properties, but not as many. One of the properties is the name of the module so you can change the name to something more descriptive. For example, if you place a lot of math routines into a Standard module, you might want to name the module something like modMathRoutines.

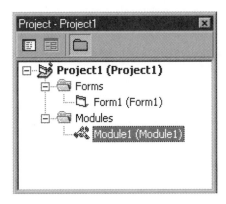

Figure 5-3. The Project window after a new Standard module has been added.

At this point, you can move your general subroutines to the Standard module. The calls to the routines do not have to change; Visual Basic is able to locate them in the Standard module. Once this module is saved, it can be imported into other projects, thus allowing for code sharing of useful routines on your testing project.

Adding Existing Modules to Projects

Another great benefit of all modules is the ability to add them to other projects. Once you have created a set of useful utilities in a Standard module, you can import that module into other projects. This saves you not only creation time but also maintenance time because the same module file can support multiple applications.

> **WARNING** *Look out—if you import the same module into multiple applications or change it within one application to suit that application's needs, you must realize it is changed for all other applications as well. If you don't want this, then once you have imported it into an application, be sure to save it with a different name. To do so, right-click the* **Standard** *module in the Project Explorer window and select* **Save As** *from the pop-up menu.*

Here's how you can add an existing module to a Visual Basic project:

1. Select the **Project ➤ Add Module** menu item. The Add Module Dialog displays. Notice that it has an Existing tab (see Figure 5-4).

2.   Click on the **Existing** tab.

Navigate to the module you want to add, select it, and click **Open**. The module is now added to your Project window.

 WARNING *If the module you are adding has the same name as another module, you will get an error message. The solution is to rename the module in your application first (change its Name property in the Properties window) and then import the new module.*

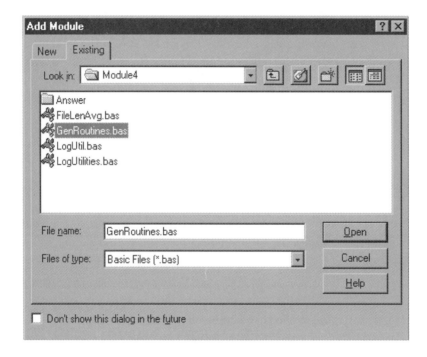

Figure 5-4. You can select Standard modules to add to your project using the Existing tab of the Add Module dialog.

Your whole project now has the power of the functions, subroutines, and constants already created in this module, all you have to do to use them is to add the appropriate calls to these routines. This is why it is critical to make sure your functions, subroutines, constants, and variables are properly scoped in all modules, that is, declared as Public or Private correctly. You want to make sure that you can access the things you need to. This is also why comments will become your best friend—it may seem hard to imagine but in the future, you could have tens or hundreds of modules you've written and keeping them straight (project management) is difficult! That's why good commenting is a great habit to have. It is not always for other automated test writers, sometimes it is for yourself.

 TESTER'S TIP *Speaking of project management, you should also enforce version-control for your files. It can quickly become chaotic trying to remember which Visual Basic script goes with which product build. Especially when you have a lot of people writing them. Microsoft's Visual Source Safe is software that can provide this kind of version management. There are other software packages that will do the same. Or, you can enforce version control yourself but it can become quite complicated in a large project.*

Understanding Form Modules

Forms are also modules. Form modules and Standard modules work identically in the way that variables, constants, subroutines, and functions are declared and used within them.

The major difference between a Form module and a Standard module is that the Form module contains a visual interface. That is, it contains a screen that the user can see at run time. Standard modules are simply code storage areas and are never be seen by the user. As mentioned earlier, you can think of them as a library where general code is stored.

The ability to import and export modules in your project applies to Form modules as well as Standard modules. You can create new forms in your project in the same way that you created a new Standard module. It's easy.

To add a new form:

1. Select the **Project ➤ Add Form** menu item. The Add Form dialog displays.

   Notice that you can create a number of forms based on templates as shown in Figure 5-5. For example, you could create a Splash screen and an About box by selecting these items. You will find that they come complete with controls and code.

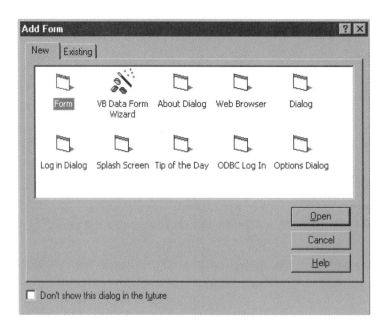

Figure 5-5. The Add Form dialog allows you to create a new form from scratch or from a template. You can also choose an existing form by selecting the Existing tab of this dialog.

TIP *There is even a wizard available, the Visual Basic Data Form Wizard, to help you set up a form that directly accesses a database table, (see Chapter 2 for the steps to set up that form).*

2.   Select the default form and click the **Open** button. The Code window for the new form appears. Notice that your Project window also changes to reflect the addition of the new form. It has a default name of Form1.

Now that you have a new Form module, you might think you could run your program and this new form would appear, perhaps after the first form is dismissed. However, it doesn't appear on its own. You must write code to handle when the new form displays in the program. To display a new form, we will use the Show method. The following line of code will display our new form:

```
Form1.Show
```

Next, we will explore Visual Basic's four statements that handle displaying and hiding forms.

Displaying Forms

Table 5-1 summarizes the four Visual Basic commands used to manipulate forms in an application.

Table 5-1. Commands to Display or Hide a Form

COMMAND	DESCRIPTION
Show Method	Displays a form. If the form has never been loaded, it loads the form and then displays it.
Hide Method	Sets the form's Visible property to False. Does not unload the form, therefore the form still resides in memory.
Load Statement	Places the form in main memory but does *not* display it. Activates the Load event.
Unload Statement	Unloads the form from main memory and activates the Unload event.

The Show method of a form displays that form. The Hide method of a form hides that form. Placing the following code in the click-event of a button displays a new form:

```
Form1.Show    'will display Form1 provided it already exists.
```

Then you can place the following code in the click-event of a button on Form1:

```
Form1.Hide    'will hide Form1 but leaves It In main memory
```

Unloading a Form versus Hiding a Form

If you want to dismiss a form, you could use the following statement instead of the Hide method:

```
Unload Form1
```

Although the Unload statement and the Hide method appear to do the same thing, there is an important distinction between them. The Unload statement unloads the form from main memory while the Hide method does not.

Using the Unload statement to dismiss a form frees more memory for your application; however, the price you pay is that the next time the form is displayed, the system will have to reload it into memory. This might mean that the form will take longer to display. Whether or not it takes longer to display depends on whether the form itself has a lot of graphics or perhaps a lot of code that does database access. These kinds of actions will cause a significantly longer loading process.

If you use the Hide method, you will *not* unload the form from main memory. The form still resides in memory; it just isn't visible (this is equivalent to setting the form's Visible property to False). The next time the form's Show method is used, the form doesn't need to be reloaded and so it may appear more quickly. Developers occasionally use this technique to give the application the appearance of better performance. The price you pay in this case is that memory won't be freed while the form is not visible; it continues to take up main memory. So, you may see an overall performance impact due to that technique, especially if you do it with multiple forms in the application.

There is no right or wrong way to use Hide versus Unload, it's just a tradeoff. Is the form you are planning to display used frequently enough in the application to warrant leaving it in main memory? If so, then hide it using the Hide method. Otherwise, unload it using the Unload statement to free up memory. Other considerations might include your users' expected operating environment: are they using machines with enough memory to function efficiently with one or more hidden forms residing in memory?

Loading a Form versus Showing a Form

The Show method is the only way to display a form. A Load statement *loads* the form into memory but does not display it. If the form has already been loaded (having been shown before or by the use of the Load statement), then Show only needs to display the form. If the form has never been loaded before, the Show method handles both loading and displaying the form.

If Show loads and displays a form, when would you use the Load statement? You can use the Load statement to preload a form into main memory so that when its Show method is performed it will display quickly. For example, when an application launches and a Splash screen is showing, you can call the Load statement to load any frequently used forms into memory. Most users expect the Splash screen to take a few seconds and this is plenty of time for your code to load forms into memory for quick display later. This little trick gives the appearance of faster performance.

 TESTER'S TIP *As you can see, it easy for a Visual Basic developer to load a form and never unload it. This will leave the form in main memory even after the main application completes. So, one test case you should be sure to perform on every Visual Basic application you test is whether there are any forms still loaded in main memory after the application completes. You can perform this simple test by checking the Windows Task Manager on Windows NT and Windows 2000 systems. On Windows 9x systems, you can do a Ctrl-Alt-Del (press the* Ctrl, Alt, *and* Delete *keys simultaneously) to bring up a dialog that will show what programs are currently active.*

EXERCISE 5-1.

In Exercise 5-1, you will add a Form module to an existing Visual Basic application. You can use the application you worked on from the last exercise or you can use any existing or new Visual Basic application to do this. There is no template or exercise files for this exercise.

Steps to Complete the Exercise

1. In an existing Visual Basic application, place your cursor in the Project window.

2. Right-click the **Project** window.

3. Select **Add** ➤ **Form** from the pop-up menu. The Add Form dialog displays (see Figure 5-5).

4. Double-click on the **About Dialog** template icon. Note that a new form called frmAbout now appears in your Project window. The new Form object appears in the Form Designer window.

5. In the Form Designer window, double-click anywhere on your new form to go to its Code window. Review the code behind the form. How much of it can you understand?

6. Go to the General Declarations section of the new form. Note all of the declarations including the Function declarations from the ADVAPI32 dynamic-link library like the following:

   ```
   Private Declare Function RegCloseKey Lib "advapi32" (ByVal hKey As Long) As Long
   ```

   The frmAbout form uses these declarations to link to the Windows System Registry. You will learn more about the Registry in Chapter 6 and about dynamic-link libraries in Chapter 7.

7. Select the main form in your application. Place a button somewhere on this form.
   This new button will be used to show the frmAbout form. In the next steps, we will add code to do that.

WARNING *Now that you have two forms, be careful to place the button on the correct form. Place it on the main form in your application; do* not *place the button on the new frmAbout form! You can always tell what form you are working with in Design mode by looking up at the caption of the Form Designer window, it tells you the name of the form.*

8. Set the Caption property of this button to &About. Set the Name and other properties of this new button as you desire.

9. In the click-event of your new button, write the code to access the frmAbout form. Use the Show method:

```
FrmAbout.Show
```

10. Run the application; click your new button. If the form does not appear, check that the name and spelling of the form match your code and try again.

11. Once your new About dialog is showing, click its **System Info** button. Note all the system information it displays.

12. Go back to Design mode. Double-click the **System Info** button in Design mode to go to its event procedure. Review the code to see how it uses the API calls to access system information.

13. Save your work. You now need to save the new form. Give it an appropriate name of your choice.

Creating a Logging Utility

One of the most important tasks we have as test engineers is to report results. So far, the only information we have reported has gone to the Immediate window. That's great—however, we are going to need more to do full reporting on test results for our clients and/or for our own management. We will take logging in stages. First, we will standardize test results logging by creating a basic Logging utility that continues to use the Immediate window. Later, we will upgrade the utility to write out to a file instead.

Since results logging is so important to testing, you will find that your Logging utilities will increase in number, size, complexity, and sophistication just as your test scripting does. It is important, then, to be proactive and consider how to write these utilities so they can grow with the project. The following code is a very simple subroutine for logging information to the Immediate window:

```
Sub Logit(strLogText As String)
'the following logs a string of information to the Immediate window
'along with the date and time and a log number
Static lLogNum As Long
    lLogNum = lLogNum + 1
    Debug.Print lLogNum, strLogText, Now
End Sub
```

The first thing to do with a Logging utility is to create it as a subroutine or function even if it is at first very simple. Place your new utility in a Standard module that you will use only for logging and reporting. (In Chapter 9, we will make this a Class module and explore the benefits of doing so.) A project can contain multiple modules and it makes sense to use these modules to organize logically related routines.

Once you have placed your logging routines into a module, you can log information to the Immediate window in a standard way quite easily by simply calling your logging subroutine:

```
Logit "This string went to the Immediate Window"
```

Your Immediate window contains the following output:

1 This string went to the Immediate Window 4/23/99 3:14:03 PM

File Handling

In order to upgrade your logging routine, you need to understand how to open and output information into files. File handling can be useful to a tester in many ways, test results logging is just one of them. For example, many applications you test will use files for logging of their own or for error reporting or will create temporary files that may be useful in testing the application. Knowing about file handling techniques will allow you to access and read these files.

Results logging for your own tests is a good way to get familiar with working with files in Visual Basic, so that's where we will start. In order to do quick and efficient file handling, you will need to learn to work with the Microsoft Scripting Library.

Using The Microsoft Scripting Library to Access Files

Starting with Visual Basic 6, we can access files and folders using the familiar *Object.Method* syntax. (For previous versions, there are standard file management commands. See Appendix C.) We add a reference in our application to the Microsoft Scripting Library and get access to a very useful object called the File System object (FSO). The FSO allows us to set the properties, methods, and events of files and folders in the same way as other kinds of objects in Visual Basic. You can create, move, alter, and delete file folders. You can also open text files for reading and writing and return basic information like creation date and time. In our case, we will use the FSO to create a file and to write test results into it.

Setting a Reference to the Scripting Library

The Scripting Library is not a part of the Visual Basic language per se but you can access it by setting a reference to it. To set this reference, select the **Project ≻ References** menu item from Visual Basic's standard menu to bring up the References dialog shown in Figure 5-6.

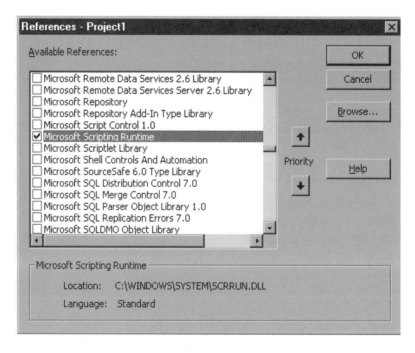

Figure 5-6. The Project References dialog allows you to set a reference to many different available object libraries. Here, the reference is set to the Microsoft Scripting Library.

Notice that the Scripting Runtime is located in the SCRRUN.DLL file installed in the Windows System directory.

Inspecting an Object Library with the Object Browser

Having set this reference, you can now view the structure of the library and the available properties and methods by using the Object Browser. Clicking the Object Browser button on the standard toolbar will display the Object Browser window (see Figure 5-7).

Figure 5-7. The Object Browser button on the Standard toolbar.

The Object Browser displays the libraries available to your Visual Basic program. The Scripting Runtime library allows access to the Windows file system by exposing files and directories as objects with properties and methods. (*Exposing* means to make available.) As you can see in the Object Browser window displayed in Figure 5-8, the Scripting library has a File System object with methods like OpenTextFile, GetFolder, GetFileName, and so on.

Figure 5-8. The Object Browser displaying the Microsoft Scripting Library objects.

The Object Browser displays the hierarchy of the objects and for each method, property, and event, displays the syntax and information to access each at the bottom of the window. You can get more information on these properties, methods, and events by highlighting them and then pressing the ⟨?⟩ button. Help will display that explains how to use and access the component.

The File System Objects (FSO)

The File System object is composed of multiple objects, each of which has useful properties and methods we can use to manipulate files. Table 5-2 from the Microsoft Visual Basic Help system describes the five objects contained in the File System.

Table 5-2. File System Objects

OBJECT	DESCRIPTION
Drive	Allows you to gather information about drives attached to the system such as how much room is available, what its share name is, and so forth. Note that a *drive* isn't necessarily a hard disk. It can be a CD-ROM drive, a RAM disk, and so forth. Also, drives aren't required to be physically attached to the system; they can also be logically connected through a LAN.
Folder	Allows you to create, delete, or move folders, plus query the system as to their names, paths, and so on.
Files	Allows you to create, delete, or move files, plus query the system as to their names, paths, and so on.
FileSystemObject	The main object of the group and is full of methods that allow you to create, delete, gain information about, and generally manipulate drives, folders, and files. Many of the methods associated with this object duplicate those in the other objects.
TextStream	Enables you to read and write text files.

Creating the File System Objects in Code

In order to access the powerful functions provided by the File System object, you must first create what is called an *object variable*. An object variable is similar to the variables we have created earlier in this text but it is able to hold a much more complex kind of object. The variables created so far hold a single value that can be stored and referenced later as needed. Object variables are created with a similar syntax but the object created is more than just a single value, it is a container that can hold an entire object with its own properties and methods, like a Command button or a even a Form. The object variable we will create next will hold a powerful File System object with all of its own associated properties, methods, and events for file handling.

The following code creates an object variable that will be used to hold a File System object and gives it the name fs:

```
Dim fs As FileSystemObject
```

Now we have an overall object for creating and working with files. In order to represent a specific individual file, though, we need to create a *Text Stream object*. In the following line of code, a Text Stream object variable is created and is given the name tLog. The Text Stream object will represent the actual file:

```
Dim tLog As TextStream
```

To write to a text file, the objects must be set appropriately. The two object variables just created will hold more than a single value, they will each hold a reference to a complex object. This is different than the kinds of variables we have created prior to this point so we will use a different syntax to set this kind of variable:

```
Set fs = CreateObject("Scripting.FileSystemObject")
```

The *Set* statement is used to assign an object to an object variable. We have to use the Set statement because we are doing more than just assigning a simple value to the variable, we are creating an entire and complex object and assigning the variable to reference this object. We set the fs variable equal to the return value of the function CreateObject. The CreateObject function will return a reference to a new File System object. Using the new File System object, we have the power to create, open, and work with many different files. We will just open one for now. In order to do that, we use a method of the File System object, the CreateTextFile method, to set the tLog variable to a specific file:

```
Set tLog = fs.CreateTextFile("c:\fResults.txt", True)
```

In the previous statement, we set the tLog variable, which is an object variable of type TextStream, to the results of the CreateTextFile function of the File System object, fs. This method will actually create a text file and return a Text Stream object that can be used to access this file. In plain English, we have essentially assigned the tLog object variable to the file c:\fResults.txt. (The *True* argument indicates that we can overwrite the file if it exists.) Now when we want to access the fResults.txt file, we can use our object variable tLog. To write to our new file, we can use the WriteLine method of our text stream object:

```
tLog.WriteLine ("This will go to the file")
```

The WriteLine method of the Text Stream object, tLog, will send a text line to the file with an end-of-line character. Other methods that we get with our Text Stream object can write characters and blank lines to the file.

To close the file, we can call the Close method of the Text Stream object:

```
tLog.Close
```

The code just discussed shows how to create, write to, and close a file.

TO TRY THIS

1. Create a new Visual Basic project and add a button to the default form.

2. Set a reference to the Microsoft Scripting Library (see the preceding "Setting a Reference to the Scripting Library" section).

3. Add the following code to the button on the form:

```
Dim fs As FileSystemObject
Dim tLog As TextStream
Set fs = CreateObject("Scripting.FileSystemObject")
Set tLog = fs.CreateTextFile("c:\fResults.txt", True)
tLog.WriteLine ("Testing is Fun!")
tLog.Close
```

4. Open the file c:\fResults.txt using the Notepad accessory. You should see the words "Testing is Fun!"

What about writing to a file that already exists? You follow much the same process in code. However, instead of using the CreateTextFile method of the FSO, you can use the OpenTextFile method. OpenTextFile will open an existing file for reading, writing, or appending more data into whatever data already exists in the file:

```
Set tLog = fs.OpenTextFile("c:\Log.txt",ForAppending)
```

The OpenTextFile method has two significant arguments:

- **C:\log.txt** is the full file name for the file to be opened.

- **ForAppending** specifies that the file will be written to, but will not change any existing data in the file.

Listing 5-2 combines what we have learned about opening and accessing a file. The If-statement ensures that the file is created the first time the routine is called. After that, the file is opened using the OpenTextFile method.

Listing 5-2. A subroutine, LogToFile, which handles logging test results to a text file.

```
'declare necessary variables and object variables for logging
Private Const LOGFILE = "c:\testresults.txt"
Private fs As FileSystemObject
Private tLog As TextStream

Private Sub LogToFile(strLogText As String)
'Logging to an output file
    Static lLogNum As Long
    Set fs =  CreateObject("Scripting.FileSystemObject")
    lLogNum = lLogNum + 1
    If lLogNum = 1 Then
        Set tLog = fs.CreateTextFile(LOGFILE, True)
        tLog.WriteLine ("Starting Tests on " & Appname & " " & Now)
    Else
        Set tLog = fs.OpenTextFile(LOGFILE, ForAppending)
    End If
    tLog.WriteLine (lLogNum & " " & strLogText)
    tLog.Close
End Sub
```

This subroutine can be called in your test code to write a line to a text file on your system. If you write test results using this subroutine, at the end of your tests, you will have a text file full of results that you can print or upload into a database or spreadsheet for further processing. Now you have the code for writing to a file for logging purposes. What about reading from an existing file? It's likely on an automated testing project that you will want to investigate a text file by reading it since applications may use text files for logging status or error information. In the next section, we will open an existing text file and read from it.

Reading from a Text File

To read from a file, you follow pretty much the same steps as accessing a file to write. Instead of using the OpenTextFile function with the *for appending* parameter, you use OpenTextFile with the *for reading* parameter:

```
Set tLog = fs.OpenTextFile(LOGFILE, ForReading)
```

The Text Stream object has methods to read the entire file, to read the file one line at a time, or to read a specific number of characters. The method for reading the entire file can be quite expensive in terms of memory resources, especially if the file is large. So, the code in Listing 5-3 bypasses the ReadAll method and shows how to read a text file into your Visual Basic program line-by-line. The code outputs the information retrieved from the file into the Immediate window.

Listing 5-3. The Readlog subroutine will read a text file into your Visual Basic program.

```
Sub ReadLog()
'*  The following routine writes both to the debug
'*  window and also opens the notepad to display the output
    Dim strHold$
    Set fs = CreateObject("Scripting.FileSystemObject")
    Set tLog = fs.OpenTextFile(LOGFILE, ForReading)
    Debug.Print "Output from File: "
    Do While Not tLog.AtEndOfStream
        strHold = tLog.ReadLine
        Debug.Print strHold
    Loop
    tLog.Close
    'open notepad and display the current output
    Shell "notepad.exe " & LOGFILE, vbNormalFocus
End Sub
```

NOTE *The code in Listing 5-3 is a subroutine that presumes the existence of the LOGFILE constant. LOGFILE needs to be created and set to a valid pathname. The code in Listing 5-2 creates this constant and will be used in the exercise files so you will get a chance to see how this works.*

Now you have the ability to create some useful logging operations for your tests. If you place these routines into a module, you can use that module in any automated test applications you write. This supports reuse of code and allows you to log information in a standard way. As you determine you need more sophisticated logging, you can expand these routines if necessary. For example, you might eventually change the routines to log to a database. (Database access is covered in Chapter 8.) The structure is already in place so you can upgrade these routines later, as necessary.

NOTE *The Scripting Library does not allow access to binary files. In order to access a binary file, you must use the standard form of file access used in previous releases of Visual Basic. Appendix C contains code using standard file access and management and has an example for binary, random, and sequential files.*

Now that you have learned how to create routines for logging test information, you are just about ready to write code to test an application. In the next section, you will learn a little bit about how to do some simple manipulation of an application and then use your new routines to log your results.

Simple GUI Testing Using SendKeys

One task you may want Visual Basic to support is simulated user action on the application's Graphical User Interface (GUI). Extensive GUI testing can be tricky and time-consuming so you may want to consider more sophisticated tools if you want to automate testing of the GUI. However, if you choose to do some simple and short GUI tests, Visual Basic does provide functions for doing so. You have already used the Shell statement to open the application but how about performing some simple user tasks such as clicking buttons and typing text?

GUI Testing Tools

There are many tools on the market for performing automated testing, some are expensive and some are free (shareware). Most of these tools provide a way to manipulate an application's GUI by pointing, clicking, dragging, typing into textboxes, and so on, in an application's windows just as a user might. In fact, some of these tools provide sophisticated recording of your own actions and then produce a script that will repeat those actions, reporting results and providing many options. You could write similar tools in Visual Basic but it is not a simple task and would take a significant investment of time and resources. To find out more about the tools already available for GUI testing, try ApTest's Web site at http://www.aptest.com/resources.html.

The SendKeys statement does just what it implies, it sends keyboard commands to a window. The following line of code sends the characters H-e-l-l-o-sp-T-h-e-r-e-! from the keyboard to the screen. If a window on the screen (such as Notepad) has the focus, it types the words "Hello There!" into it:

```
SendKeys "Hello there!"
```

Figure 5-9 displays the results of this statement in the Notepad accessory.

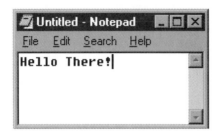

Figure 5-9. The results of the SendKeys statement.

Listing 5-4 displays the code from the Chapter5\Demos\Sendkeys.vbp demo file.

Listing 5-4. Using the SendKeys command to manipulate the Notepad accessory.

```
Option Explicit
Private Sub cmdSendKeys_Click()
    Dim lReturnValue&, I%
    lReturnValue = Shell("notepad.exe", 1)
'Change the path to notepad, if necessary
    Pause 1
    AppActivate lReturnValue  ' Activate Notepad.
    SendKeys "Hello there!"
    SendKeys "%{F4}" ' Send ALT+F4 to close Notepad.
    Pause 1
    SendKeys "{tab}"
    SendKeys "{enter}"
End Sub
```

In Exercise 5-2, you will use the SendKeys statement along with all you have learned about creating utilities to set up some simple GUI manipulation of the Calculator accessory.

NOTE *It is possible to get more sophisticated GUI tests using calls to the Windows API libraries if necessary. However, this will take a significant amount of coding effort, and I don't recommend doing much GUI testing this way (see the "GUI Testing Tools" sidebar in this chapter). Chapter 7 presents an introduction to using the Windows API libraries.*

Adding Timing to Your Tests

Remember the Timer function? It is an intrinsic Visual Basic function that returns the number of seconds that have elapsed since midnight. We used it in a loop to calculate a pause. (See the "Understanding Subroutine Procedures" section earlier in this chapter.) You can add that code to any test you do to calculate an approximate amount of time that will be sufficient for comparison purposes. In order to do this, add the following code prior to the action you want to time:

```
'declare 3 variables for holding start, end and elapsed time values:
Dim lngStartTime as Long
Dim lngEndTime as Long
Dim lngTimeElapsed as Long
'Capture the starting time:
LngStartTime = Timer
```

At the end of the task you are timing, you can place the following code:

```
LngEndTime = Timer
LngTimeElapsed = lngEndTime - lngStartTime
```

TESTER'S TIP *You can use timing in a lot of ways. One of its biggest uses is in Performance Testing. You can time how long a task in your application takes, record that value, and then compare it to values taken for the same task after subsequent builds of the application.*

The code in Listing 5-5 uses the Timer function to time how long it takes to start the Notepad accessory.

Listing 5-5. Adding code to time a task is an important testing duty.

```
Private Sub cmdRun_Click()
    Dim lngStartTime As Long
    Dim lngEndTime As Long
    Dim lngTimeElapsed As Long

    lngStartTime = Timer
'don't forget to add full path name to Notepad, necessary on WinNT and Win2000
    Shell "Notepad.exe", vbNormalFocus
    lngEndTime = Timer
    lngTimeElapsed = lngEndTime - lngStartTime

    MsgBox "Time to launch Notepad " & lngTimeElapsed

End Sub
```

Relatively speaking, it takes no time at all to start Notepad so you will probably get a 0 for the elapsed time when you launch Notepad. However, that won't be true for most tasks you want to time. This a technique you can use for timing tasks in general.

TESTER'S TIP *When you use the Timer function for tests, you will want to eliminate other variables. Timing from one platform to the next using various device configurations can vary significantly. When running timing tests, you'll want to standardize on a particular configuration.*

Using the Timer Control

Although the Timer function is useful, there are situations when it makes sense to perform a task at a specified interval. Visual Basic contains a control called the Timer that you can place on your form to trigger an event at a timed interval. You can add this control to the form by double-clicking it (see Figure 5-10).

The Timer control will not display to the user at run time. It's a hidden object during Run mode so you will only see it in Design mode. The purpose of the Timer control is to add a link to the system timer. It will fire off an event at an interval you specify. Once you place a timer on the form, you can set the interval for it by using its properties. The Timer object has one event: the Timer event that fires whenever the specified interval elapses. There are some good uses for this in testing. For example, you can ping a server or a Web site to determine its state. (More on this in Chapter 10.)

Figure 5-10. The Timer control.

A demonstration of the use of the Timer control is contained in Practice Files this book. The Chapter5\ Demos\TaskBarTimer folder in the Practice Files contains code for a stopwatch-type program called TaskBarTimer.vbp. Open this file to examine and run the code. Figure 5-11 shows the TaskBarTimer demo project in Design mode. The Timer control is in the upper right-hand corner.

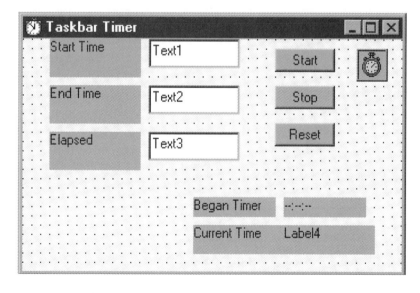

Figure 5-11. The TaskBarTimer demo project in Design mode (courtesy of Kevin Ingalls).

The TaskBarTimer program can come in handy for the simple timing of manual tasks whenever you can't find your stopwatch. The code in this program uses the standard Visual Basic Timer object. Additionally, timing can be accomplished even better with shareware tools available from the CCRP (Common Controls Replacement Project) Web site at `http://www.mvps.org/ccrp`. There are many great tools and controls available from this Web site—with some restrictions. Some of them require advanced Visual Basic knowledge to use so keep checking there as your Visual Basic experience grows.

Documenting Your Tests

You have enough information in Visual Basic to get started automating a few simple tests. However, there is still one more very important topic to cover that should be a part of every automated testing project: documenting your tests. This is different than reporting results. *Test documentation* means ensuring that your test script clearly describes its purpose and expected and possible outcomes. Comments in your Visual Basic code can be used to document this information. These comments should also clearly indicate what test case is being implemented and be able to map this information to a specific place in the overall test plan. Comments should clearly explain who wrote the script, when, why, and explain any modification history. The following is a sample of the kinds of comments you might use to document your tests:

```
'************************************************************************
'*   XYZProject Tests
'*   Test Case:  XYZ_ADOVerify XYZ01A
'*   Date:  2/1/2000
'*   Modification History:
'*   Date:           Automator:          Build#:         Remarks/Changes:
'*   3/1/2000        MRSweeney           1               Initial Test
'*
'*   Inputs/Setup:   Set reference to ADO object library
'*                   Set reference to TestUtilities object
'*                   Ensure creation of File DSN to attach to XYZDB
'*   Outputs:  L.LOGFILE = "c:\windows\desktop\XYZLog.txt"
'*   Component Under Test:  XYZDB.
'*   Method Under Test:  XYZ Database Verification Test
'*   Description:  The purpose of this test is to verify the number of Invoices
'*       in the XYZ database
'*   Remarks:  See test case for Procedural Steps
'************************************************************************
```

Additionally, each subroutine, function, and event procedure in your test project should contain a few lines of comments to explain its purpose. It is important to standardize the kind of comments each test project will use for documentation. A good way to do this is to set up a sample or template module with comments. This should be done prior to any coding and can be started while waiting for the first test build release from the developers to the test team.

Creating a coding template for your tests and setting up other guidelines we have seen, such as object and variable naming conventions, and writing test support routines such as logging routines, are all part of a testing *framework*. A testing framework is the structure and support you create surrounding your tests. Putting some thought into planning and devising this framework appropriately can help you develop a structure that will speed up development of the actual test scripts. Testers always ask, "What can be done *before* the application is ready to test?" Setting up this framework is part of the answer. As the chapters in this book progress, we will discuss other items that can be added to your testing framework.

EXERCISE 5-2.

TESTING THE CALCULATOR

In Exercise 5-2, you will write a program that manipulates the buttons on the Calculator accessory. In this exercise, you will start with a template. You then add two existing Standard modules. You add subroutines to these modules to read from and write to a test results file. You will also add code to manipulate the Calculator GUI using the SendKeys statement.

Run the file **Chapter5\Exercise5_2\CalcTest.exe** from the Practice Files. The program's main window has two buttons; notice that one is disabled.

- Click the button **Test Calc**.

> **WARNING** *Do not move your mouse while the tests run! Moving the mouse during this time might conflict with the code since it is also moving the mouse.*

- When complete, the Calculator closes.

- Now the button **View Log** is enabled. Click it and review the output displayed.

- Notice that the time elapsed is displayed on the form.

Figure 5-12 shows how your program should look when complete.

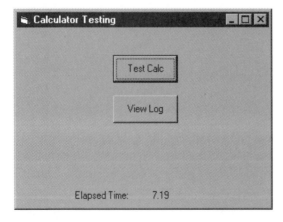

Figure 5-12. The answer to Exercise 5-2 should look similar to this when you are finished.

(The complete answer to the following exercise is in Chapter5\Exercise5_2\Answer\CalcTest.vbp in the Practice Files. Check it if you need a hint!)

Follow These Steps to Write the Code

1. Open the project CalcTestTempl.vbp in the Chapter5\Exercise5_2 folder. Review the form's controls. There are two buttons, cmdCalc and cmdLog, and two labels. Review the existing code.

> **WARNING** *This template program will not run until you complete it by following the remaining steps.*

2. Look up the SendKeys statement in Help. Scroll down in the Help window and study the table that lists all of the key codes for keyboard items. Exit the Visual Basic Help system.

Adding Logging Utilities

3. Import two Standard modules into this project: GenRoutines.bas and LogUtilities.Bas. These two modules are located in the Chapter5\Exercise5_2 folder in the Practice Files. (To import, use the **Project ➢ Add Module** menu item from the Standard menu and select the **Existing** tab.) Once the modules have been imported you can see them in the Project window.

> **NOTE** *At this time, you may want to save the whole project, form, and both module files to a new location. It's a good idea to save your work as you complete each significant step. In the following instructions, substitute your own names when saving the files.*

4. Your new LogUtilities module has an existing subroutine called Logit, which writes output to the Immediate window. Review the code in Logit. LogUtilities also contains a subroutine called ReadLog. This routine opens a text file, reads it line-by-line, and writes this information to the Immediate window. You will not change either of these two subroutines.

5. Create a new subroutine called LogToFile. LogToFile will have a single argument of type String:

    ```
    Sub LogToFile(strLogText As String)

    End Sub
    ```

    In subsequent steps, you will add code to LogToFile so that it will access a text file.

6. Open the **Project ➤ References** menu item. Locate and check the **Microsoft Scripting Runtime** checkbox in the Project References dialog box. (You will need to scroll down quite a ways.) Click the **OK** button to save the reference and close the dialog.

7. Open the Object Browser and display the Scripting Library. Review the objects, methods, and properties in the Scripting Library. Find the CreateTextFile and OpenTextFile methods of the Text Stream object. Note the syntax of these methods. Find the full definitions of these methods in Help. Exit or minimize the Object Browser.

8. Add the following declarations to the General Declarations section of your LogUtilities module:

    ```
    Private Const LOGFILE = "c:\testresults.txt"
    Private fs As FileSystemObject
    Private tLog As TextStream
    ```

    The declarations create both the File System and Text Stream objects you will need to access a text file.

9. Add the following code to the body of your new subroutine, LogToFile. The code opens a text file and writes into the file using the Text Stream object:

    ```
    Static lLogNum As Long

    Set fs = CreateObject("Scripting.FileSystemObject")
    lLogNum = lLogNum + 1
    If lLogNum = 1 Then
        Set tLog = fs.CreateTextFile(LOGFILE, True)
        tLog.WriteLine("Starting Tests on " & Appname & " " & Now)
    Else
        Set tLog = fs.OpenTextFile(LOGFILE,ForAppending)
    End If
    tLog.WriteLine (lLogNum & " " & strLogText)
    tLog.Close
    ```

Adding a Start Program Routine

10. Open the Code window for your GenRoutines module. Modify the Start-Program subroutine so that it is a function that returns the Task ID of the program it starts. The function should look similar to the following:

```
Function StartProgram(App As String) As Long
    Dim lngReturn As Long
    lngReturn = Shell(App, vbNormalFocus)
    LogIt App & " Started " & "Task ID: " &  lngReturn
    LogToFile App & " Started " & "Task ID: " &  lngReturn
    StartProgram = lngReturn
End Function
```

This function works much better than a subroutine for our purposes. The Shell command returns the Task ID of the application that is started. In the previous code, this value is assigned to the variable lngReturn. This value is, in turn, assigned to the return value of the function in the statement:

```
StartProgram = lngReturn.
```

(This Task ID value is important. Later in the code, it is used with the AppActivate statement to set the system's focus to the Calculator program.)

NOTE *Look up AppActivate in the Visual Basic Help system for more information. It is used in the code later in this exercise.*

11. Add a global module-level constant to your GenRoutines module called Appname. Set this constant equal to Calc.exe:

```
Public Const Appname = "calc.exe"
```

(For Windows NT platforms, include the full path to the Calculator application).

12. Open the Code window for the Form module. Add the code to the cmdLog_Click event to run the ReadLog subroutine. Since ReadLog has no arguments, the code in the cmdLog_Click event procedure is just one word:

```
ReadLog
```

13. The Form_Load event contains the following line of code:

```
cmdLog.Enabled = False
```

This code disables the cmdLog button so the user cannot attempt to view the log before the test has been run. Now we need to modify the code so that the cmdLog button is enabled (in other words, set to True) when the test has completed running. Insert the following line of code to enable the cmdLog button. Where is the best place to insert this line?

```
cmdLog.Enabled = True
```

14. Run the program and debug until it works. Set breakpoints at the top of the LogToFile and ReadLog routines in the LogUtilities module. To understand how it works, use the Debugger to step through this code as it runs.

15. To check your work (or get a hint), check the code in CalcTest.vbp in the Answer folder in Chapter5\Exercise5_2.

    Extra Work. In the cmdTest_Click event, use the Timer function and the StartTime variable defined for you to add the code to calculate the length of time it took to run this event. Load the results into the lblTime.caption property.

TESTER'S CHECKLIST

When performing code reviews, look for the following in a well-written Visual Basic application.

Does the Project...

❑ Use Standard modules to contain logically related reusable routines?

❑ Maintain, use, and manage Standard modules to eliminate redundancy and promote code reuse?

❑ Remove all forms from memory after the application completes?

Does the Code...

❑ Use understandable names for functions and subroutines?

❑ Create functions and subroutines that are single-purpose? (Large, cumbersome procedures are less reusable and intelligible. Routines should have a single, clear purpose.)

❑ Consistently document Form and Standard modules with header comments?

❑ Use the Microsoft Scripting Library or an appropriate database file for logging information?

Code Review Practice

How does your own code stack up so far? Do a self-test on your own code or ask a fellow tester to do it. Review the code for the exercises you have completed using the checklist(s) provided in this chapter and all previous chapters.

Chapter 5 Review

- Explain why the creation of utilities is important on a testing project.
  See page 137.

- What is the difference between a subroutine and a function?
  See page 147.

- Describe the purpose and scope of a Visual Basic Standard module.
  See page 151.

- How do you create a Visual Basic Standard module?
  See pages 151–153.

- What is the difference between a Standard module and Form module?
  See page 155.

- Explain the use of the Show and Hide methods for forms.
  See pages 157–158.

- Explain the use of the Load and Unload statements.
  See pages 157–158.

- How do you set a reference to the Microsoft Scripting Runtime?
  See page 162.

- Write the line of code to create a File System object using the Microsoft Scripting Runtime and the line that sets this value.
  See page 165.

- What steps must you follow to write a line to a text file using the File System and Text Stream objects?
  Create and set a text stream object.
  See page 165.

- Write the SendKeys command to press the Enter key on the keyboard.
  Sendkeys "{enter}".
  See page 170.

CHAPTER 6

Testing with the Windows Registry

At one point or another, all testers find themselves investigating the Window's System Registry; it's a valuable place for viewing application installation settings, options, and statistics. It tracks settings for every application on your machine. On network computers, it tracks the settings for every user. Now that you are a programmer in Visual Basic, your applications are now subject to it also. In this chapter, I introduce the Registry and explore how to access it and put it to use in testing. In this chapter we'll look at some new functions for retrieving information from a special Registry key reserved for use only by Visual Basic applications. These new functions are very useful when testing Visual Basic applications yet they only allow us into a small part of the Registry dedicated to Visual Basic. So we'll return to the Registry again in Chapter 7 to see how to access any part of the Registry using the Windows API routines. Also in this chapter, we will continue our exploration of the Visual Basic language by introducing a new data structure, the array, and discuss how to introduce error handling into your code.

Objectives

By the end of this chapter, you will be able to:

- Explain why a tester might need to use the Windows System Registry.

- Use the following four Visual Basic Registry functions to retrieve, set, and delete Registry settings for Visual Basic applications:

    GetSetting

    SaveSetting

    GetAllSettings

    DeleteSettings

- Create an array to hold lists of information.

- Use a list box control to display multiple rows of data.

- Describe the purpose of the Err object in error handling.

- Implement a simple error handler using the On-Error statement.

Introduction to the Windows System Registry

The Windows System Registry is a hierarchical database that stores a considerable amount of information about the computer on which it resides, including:

- What applications are installed and customized information about them.

- User profiles for machines used by multiple people.

- What hardware is installed on the machine.

- System information such as usage of the system ports (like modem and printer ports).

Most applications you test will load important information into the Registry starting at installation. While an application runs, it often also accesses the Registry to store user-specific customization options like preferred font and window sizes. Verifying this information can be an important part of a testing project. We may also need to use the Registry for our own purposes as our tests run, storing our own path information and customization options. Tester Lee Wallen explained how a testing project he was on used three servers: a development server, a test server, and a staging server. He stored critical information for each server in three separate locations in the Registry and accessed them throughout the testing process to keep information straight between all three servers.

Registry Utilities

There are existing Registry utilities that testers should be aware of. For example, RegMon will show the user what reads and writes are occurring within the Registry and which applications are doing the reads and writes. The information is in real time. This information is handy for testers because you may need to validate whether or not an application is logging information to the Registry appropriately. You can find our more about RegMon at the Sysinternals™ Web site (be sure to check out the licensing restrictions for commercial use) at http://www.sysinternals.com/ntw2k/source/regmon.shtml.

There are other utilities at Sysinternals that might prove useful to testers as well. How is this handy for someone programming in Visual Basic for testing? It helps to be aware of what is available so you know what you *don't* have to write and can better decide what you actually need.

There's a Windows utility called RegEdit that allows you to access the Registry. The RegEdit utility can be launched from the Start ➤ Run menu item on the Windows TaskBar.

To start the RegEdit utility:

1. Select **Start** ➤ **Run** from the Windows TaskBar.

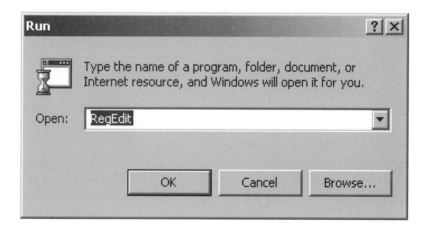

2. Type "**RegEdit**" and click **OK**. The Registry Editor dialog displays.

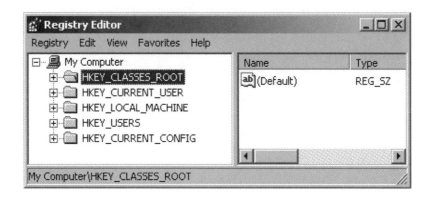

WARNING *Do not attempt to manually modify the Registry until you know exactly what you are doing. If you corrupt system information in the Registry, you will have to restore it before your system will even boot. Take the time to read how to backup and restore the Registry in the Registry Help files prior to working with it. Always backup the Registry prior to making any changes.*

The Registry consists of top-level keys called *hives*. (Named so because of their structural resemblance to beehives.) Hives are composed of keys, subkeys, and value entries. The keys and subkeys are denoted by folder icons, and work essentially the same as the folders we see in the Windows Explorer in that they contain other subkeys and values. The first four hives are:

HKEY_CLASSES_ROOT

HKEY_CURRENT_USER

HKEY_LOCAL_MACHINE

HKEY_USERS

These four keys are always considered open. An *open* key means that applications may add their own keys and data to these main hives. If you click on these hives in the RegEdit utility, you will see that they expand to include keys for all kinds of useful information and probably a bunch of things that won't (at first) make a lot of sense.

Starting with Version 4, Visual Basic applications have been able to store information into a special location reserved for them:

HKEY_CURRENT_USER\Software\VB and VBA Program Settings

Each Visual Basic application can create a subkey under this key. If you are testing a Visual Basic application, this is an important place to check for entries specific to that application. It's not mandatory for an application to use it, however, so you won't necessarily find anything there. It's also entirely possible for an application to bypass this and create subkeys for itself in any of the open hives. The RegEdit utility has a Find dialog that you can use to search for keywords in keys, values, and data. (There are also some third-party utilities available for Registry manipulation.) A common technique is to use the import/export capability of the Registry itself to print a text file containing the state of the Registry prior to installing or running the application and then doing the same afterwards. Comparing these two text files will tell you which keys are changed by the application. Otherwise, you may have to rely on your application's documentation or ask the developers if and where Registry information for the application you are testing is stored.

NOTE *Visual Basic developers can access other parts of the Registry using a set of library routines called the Windows Application Programmer's Interface (API). You will learn how to do this yourself in Chapter 7.*

Visual Basic provides four commands for retrieving and manipulating the settings as shown in Table 6-1.

Table 6-1. The Four Commands for Retrieving and Manipulating Visual Basic Registry Settings

COMMAND	DESCRIPTION
GetSetting	Retrieves a Registry entry.
SaveSetting	Creates a new or saves an existing Registry entry.
GetAllSettings	Returns an array of Registry entries.
DeleteSetting	Deletes a Registry entry.

Creating and Saving Application Settings

As a tester, you will more often *read* existing settings for the application you are testing rather than create, save, or delete them. However, it is instructive to perform these tasks anyway. First, to gain a better understanding of development issues and also because it can be quite useful to your own test scripts to use the Registry to store information that might change from build-to-build or version-to-version of the product being tested. The kinds of information you might want to store in a testing project include items such as the full pathname to the software under test, recent test dates, test priority settings, and the list goes on. Using the Registry to store this data allows you to take it out of your code and therefore makes your code more portable. Writing portable software means you will end up modifying it less, a goal of good programming.

The SaveSetting statement saves information to the Registry. SaveSetting has the following syntax:

```
SaveSetting appname, section, key, setting
```

SaveSetting has the arguments shown in Table 6-2.

Table 6-2. Arguments for the SaveSetting Statement

ARGUMENT	DESCRIPTION
appname	String expression containing the name of the application or project to which the setting applies.
section	String expression containing the name of the section where the key setting is being saved.
key	String expression containing the name of the key setting being saved.
setting	Expression containing the value that key is being set to.

If the setting already exists, it is updated; if it does not exist, SaveSetting creates it.

The following code in the Unload event of a form stores the date of the latest test run:

```
Private Sub Form_Unload(Cancel As Integer)
      SaveSetting "Calc", "TestInfo", "LastTestDate", Now
End Sub
```

TO TRY THIS

1. Create a new Visual Basic program and type the following line into the Form_Unload event of the default form:

   ```
   SaveSetting "Calc", "TestInfo", "LastTestDate", Now
   ```

2. Run the program using the Debugger. (Press **F8**). You won't see anything happen until you close the window because the unload event of the form runs as the form closes.

NOTE *For an introduction to Visual Basic's Debugger, see Chapter 5.*

3. Close the form by clicking the 'X' in the upper right corner of the form.

4. Step through the Form_Unload event by continuing to press **F8**. You will see the code you entered executing. When complete, you will be returned to Design mode. You can now close Visual Basic.

5. Check the Registry using the **RegEdit** utility. Navigate to the following key:

   HKEY_CURRENT_USER\Software\VB and VBA Program Settings

   Open this key and underneath you should find a new subkey named Calc with a subkey under it called TestInfo. Note the value under this subkey; it should be today's date and current time.

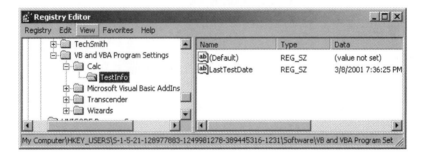

6. Exit the Registry.

7. Run your program again, this time without the Debugger—just press **F5** to start.

8. Check the Registry again by repeating step 5. You will find the entry updated with a new time.

Retrieving Visual Basic Application Entries

In the last section, you learned how to set a value in the Registry. As I mentioned earlier, perhaps the most frequent and important task you will perform with the Registry is *reading* Registry entries. This is because you will likely need to verify information in the Registry against expectations required for the software under test. Using the Registry, you can verify that the installation was successful and that customization options are set correctly. (Keep in mind that the commands in this chapter only access a limited portion of the Registry specific to Visual Basic applications. For other non-Visual Basic applications, we'll examine Registry entries using calls to system functions, in Chapter 7).

Settings can be retrieved in two ways: individually or in a list, depending on whether you are looking for the value of a single setting or all of the settings under one key. We will see how to do both.

Retrieving Single Registry Settings

To retrieve an individual setting, use the GetSetting function. The following line of code calls GetSetting to retrieve the LastTestDate setting value for the Calc application under the subkey TestInfo:

```
strTestDate = GetSetting("Calc", "TestInfo",  "LastTestDate", Now)
```

The GetSetting function has the following syntax:

```
GetSetting(appname, section, key, [default])
```

The default is optional, you can provide a value in that argument to use as the default in case there is no value in the Registry. If you use the Now function in this argument, then the first time your test runs, the current date and time will be returned rather than no value at all. If there is a value in the Registry, the default argument is ignored.

What if the Registry key you are looking for does not exist? What if you have misspelled one of the arguments? It's important to note that the GetSetting function does not return an error in these cases. It will return nothing at all unless, as I mentioned, a default value is provided.

> **NOTE** *Before starting the following "To Try This" section, first, make sure you have performed the steps in the last "To Try This" because the following presumes you already have a Calc key and a TestInfo subkey in the Registry.*

1. Create a new Visual Basic application. Type the following code into the Code module of the default form:

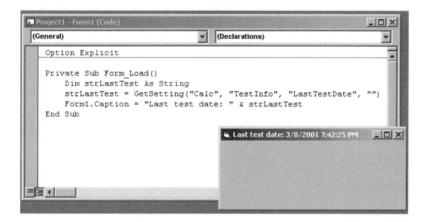

```
Private Sub Form_Load()
    Dim strLastTest As String
    strLasttest = GetSetting("Calc", "TestInfo", "LastTestDate", "")
    me.caption = "Last test date: " & strLastTest
End Sub
```

2. Run the program (**F5**). You should see the value of the LastTestDate setting in the caption of the displayed form.

Retrieving Multiple Settings

If you want to retrieve the whole list of settings from under a Registry subkey, using the GetSetting function to retrieve each one, one-at-a-time will work but is cumbersome. Instead, you can use another function, GetAllSettings, to retrieve the list of values under a subkey. However, before you learn that trick, you will need to understand how to work with lists of information in Visual Basic. Up to this point, you have learned only about storing one value at a time in a single variable. Certainly, you can create multiple variables to hold lists of values but, again, that is difficult to manage. It would be nice to use a structure that allows us to store and manipulate a list of values. Fortunately, there is such a structure common to programming that's been around for a long time: the array.

Creating Lists with Arrays

In programming, whenever you need a list of items, think, "array." An *array* is a variable but a more sophisticated variable than those we have used so far. Think of any list you use regularly, such as your own To Do list, and then try to imagine a way to represent that in code. Your To Do list is a single thing, one list, which contains multiple items. You can represent this list in code using an array. The following code declares an array of strings that could hold five items of your To Do list:

```
Dim astrToDoList (1 to 5) as String
```

The declaration for an array looks just like a declaration for a variable except for the parentheses and what's between them. The name of the array is still something you choose yourself just as you choose the name of variables yourself. And just like naming standard variables, try to choose a name relevant to what the use of the array will be and which also makes it obvious that it is, indeed, an array. In this case, I preceded the name with a lowercase "a" to indicate that this is an array and different from simple variables. The (1 to 5) part of the declaration is called the *index* of the array and tells how many items, or elements, the array has. An *element* is an individual item within an array. It can be dealt with as though it were a simple variable by using the name of the array and its element number—for example, astrToDoList(1). The specification of the index (1 to 5) says that the array has five elements. Think of this new variable as looking like this:

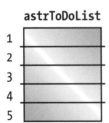

astrToDoList

Just as you might keep track of each item on your To Do list by giving it a number, each element of an array has a number. The number assigned to an element is called the *index* or *subscript* of that array element.

To set an individual element's value in the array, you must use its index or subscript. For example:

```
astrToDoList(3) = "Pick up milk"
```

astrToDoList

1	
2	
3	*"pick up milk"*
4	
5	

You work with each individual element of an array as though it is a single variable. Except, of course, you must always provide the subscript of the array element in order to specify which element of the array you are working with:

```
Debug.Print astrToDoList(3)
```

The following are other legal array definitions. Note that array declarations follow the same scope and lifetime rules as other variables:

```
Public aTestResults (1 to 20) as String     '20 string elements
Private aSales(1990 to 2000) as Currency     '11 currency elements
Dim aTemperatures (-50 to 50) as Single      '101 single-precision float elements
Dim aCounters (14) as Integer                '15 Integer elements
```

Notice also that the index of the array does not have to start at 1. In fact, if you leave off the lower bound of the array index as in the last example, the lower bound defaults to 0. Assuming the previous declarations, the following code would set some of the values in the aTestResults array:

```
ATestResults(1) = "Test No. 1 Passed"
ATestResults(2) = "Test No. 2 Failed"
ATestResults(20) = "Test No. 20 Passed"
```

Fixed-Size versus Dynamic Arrays

The array examples we have seen so far declare a *fixed-size* array. This means that the array will always stay exactly the same size. It is possible to declare an array that can change size, called a *dynamic* array. To declare a dynamic array, you don't put any index values between the parentheses. The following declaration creates a dynamic array:

```
Dim astrTestResults () as String    'declares a dynamic array
```

When a declaration like this is made, it tells Visual Basic that, at some point, you will be using an array by that name in your code. Since you have not specified any size for the array, how will Visual Basic know what size to give it? Before using the array, you must size it with a ReDim statement such as:

```
ReDim astrTestResults (1 to 100) as String     'resizes a dynamic array
```

This might seem somewhat redundant but the advantage is that you can resize the array later, making it either bigger or smaller by issuing another ReDim statement. All of the arrays we looked at previous to this one were given a size on their first declaration. This makes these arrays fixed-size arrays. Fixed arrays, of course, cannot be resized so you can never ReDim them.

Multidimensional Arrays

The previous arrays are all single-column lists. What if you want to store information in a table format? You can create a table of information by adding another index to the array. The following declaration creates an array with five rows and two columns:

```
Dim aintGrid (1 to 5, 1 to 2) as Integer
```

Notice in the declaration of the multidimensional array that the row's index is declared first and then the column's index.

There is certainly more to learn about arrays and they have many applications for both the software developer and the tester. For now, we have covered enough to use them for our immediate purpose which is to retrieve a list of Registry settings.

See the Visual Basic Programmer's Guide in the Help system for more information on arrays and see Appendix A: Resources and References for some good supplementary texts on application development in Visual Basic.

Arrays and the GetAllSettings Function

Now that you know a little bit about how to create and use an array, we can use one to hold the return information from the GetAllSettings command. Listing 6-1 retrieves all of the Registry titles and values under a key called TestInfo.

Listing 6-1. Using a dynamic array to hold the return value from the GetAllSettings function.

```
Private Sub Form_Load()
    Dim astrSettings() As String    'creates a dynamic array of strings
    Dim iCount As Integer
    astrSettings = GetAllSettings("Calc", "TestInfo")
    For iCount = 0 To UBound(astrSettings)
        Debug.Print astrSettings(iCount, 0), astrSettings(iCount, 1)
    Next iCount
End Sub
```

To understand this code, you need to understand the structure of the data returned by the GetAllSettings function. The function returns a two-column list of information:

AppName	Calc
AppPath	C:\windows\
LastTestDate	\<actual date and time value>

Notice that this is a two-dimensional array. The first column contains the name of the Registry item and the second column contains the actual value. The rows are numbered with the first row being row zero. (Most things computers work with start at 0 rather than 1.)

In Listing 6-1, an array of strings was declared to hold the list that GetAllSettings returns:

```
Dim astrSettings() As String   'creates a dynamic array of strings
```

This is a dynamic array: it is created without any indicated size. We do not want to specify how big the list is since it could change depending on how many values are listed under the Registry subkey.

By leaving the parentheses empty, we have allowed the dynamic array on the left side of the assignment statement to be automatically sized by the GetAllSettings function so that it will handle the array returned. We do not need to resize the array with a ReDim statement because the return value from GetAllSettings does that for us:

```
astrSettings = GetAllSettings("Calc", "TestInfo")
```

The For-Loop runs through each row in the list in turn using a variable called iCount as the loop index. The iCount variable is used to tell how many times the loop has been executed. The UBound() function used in the For-Loop takes an array as its argument and always returns the upper bound of the array—in this case, 2, the number of the last row:

```
For iCount = 0 To UBound(astrSettings)
    Debug.Print astrSettings(iCount, 0),  astrSettings(iCount, 1)
Next iCount
```

The body of the loop prints first the value name and then the value itself. The first time through the loop, iCount's value is 0 so we are printing the value in row zero and column zero: astrSettings(0,0), which prints "Appname." Then, a comma is printed, which inserts a tab between the two items in the Debug window. Next, astrSettings(0,1) accesses the data in row zero, first column and "Calc.exe" is printed.

The second time through, the loop does the same thing only now iCount's value is 1 so the values in the next row of the array are printed. The output to the Immediate window looks like this:

AppName   Calc.exe
AppPath   c:\windows\
LastTestDate   <Actual date and time value>

Displaying Multiple Values Using List Boxes

In the previous examples, we printed results to the Immediate window. This is useful if you need to get quick results. However, if you want to create a more easily viewable set of results and display them on your form, you can use another control that Visual Basic provides, the list box.

You can use a list box control to display the return values from an array. *List boxes* and their cousins, Combo boxes, are controls used to display lists of values. The list box is perfect for us in this case since the GetAllSettings function returns a list. To change the example in the last section (which printed to the Immediate window) so that it prints into a list box instead, simply place a list box control on the form. To do so, double-click on the **ListBox** icon in the toolbox as shown in Figure 6-1.

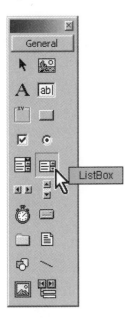

Figure 6-1. The ListBox control can be added from the Toolbox.

The default name for a list box is List1. The recommended way to name a list box is with the prefix "lst" (that's a lower case "L," by the way, not the number 1), as in lstSettings. Both list boxes and Combo boxes have a method called *AddItem* that we can use to load individual items into the control.

For example, the following two lines load a list box named lstFruits with two rows:

```
lstFruits.Additem "apples"
lstFruits.Additem "pears"
```

Getting back to our Registry example, assume we place a list box on our form and rename it something more appropriate like lstSettings. The following code would display the Registry settings in the list box:

```
For iCount = 0 To UBound(astrSettings)
    lstSettings.AddItem astrSettings(iCount, 0) & " " & astrSettings(iCount, 1)
Next iCount
```

Notice that we had to combine the values (using the & operator) instead of using the comma to separate them. The use of a comma to insert a tab is unique to the Print method.

The results displayed in a list box are shown in Figure 6-2.

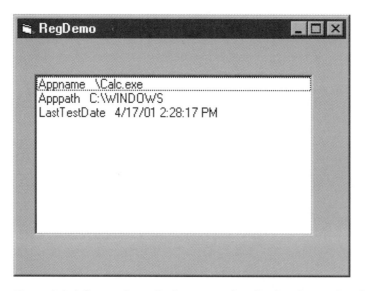

Figure 6-2. A form using a list box control to display the results of the GetAllSettings function.

Deleting a Registry Setting

At times it is necessary to delete Registry settings. For example, if you have created Registry settings to contain application testing information on a platform, when you are done testing, you will probably want to clean up and delete them. You may at times also need to reset the Registry back to an initial state.

To delete a Registry setting, use the DeleteSetting statement, which has the following syntax:

DeleteSetting appname, section, key

The following code deletes the LastTestDate subkey from our previous example:

```
Private Sub cmdDeleteKey_Click()
    DeleteSetting "Calc", "TestInfo", "LastTestDate"
End Sub
```

What if you try to delete a setting that does not exist? In that case, an error is generated by the system at run time. (This is different than the GetSettings function. Recall that the GetSettings function does *not* return an error if you ask it to return a nonexistent setting.) If you use DeleteSettings to try to delete a setting that does not exist, it generates an error that brings up a system dialog box (see Figure 6-3) and essentially stops your program. The generated error, "Run Time Error 5 Invalid Procedure Call or Argument," is not very descriptive. You can make this situation easier to deal with at runtime by *trapping* the error. It's about time to introduce error trapping and handling into your code. This will be beneficial in working with the Registry functions and throughout the rest of your code.

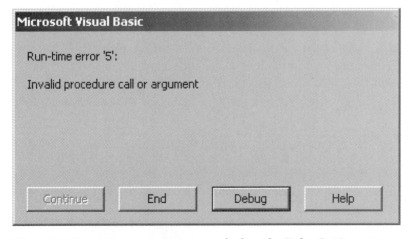

Figure 6-3. A run time error is generated when the DeleteSettings statement attempts to delete a setting that does not exist.

Error Trapping

> **NOTE** *Error trapping and handling changes significantly in VB.NET. See Chapter 11 for more information.*

All implementations of the Basic language allow you to perform error handling in much the same way. The basic process for trapping and handling errors includes three parts:

- Setting the error trap.

- Writing the error trap handler.

- Exiting the trap.

So, to implement standard error handling in Visual Basic, follow these steps:

1. Set up the error trap using the On Error statement:

    ```
    On Error Goto ErrHandler
    ```

    This line goes at the top of the subroutine or function, right after the first line. It specifies what to do when a run time error occurs. It tells the system to go directly to a label in your code. You specify the name of the label. Here, I chose ErrHandler but you could use any name as long you later provide a code label that matches it (see step 2).

2. Set up a *handler* for the possible errors you may receive. The handler section of the error trap will be where code is written to deal with the possible errors received. To set up this handler section, we use a code label:

    ```
    ErrHandler:
    ```

The code label can be called anything you want but it must have a colon after it and it must be the same as what was specified in the On Error statement—that is how Visual Basic differentiates it from a variable. Code labels are located at the bottom of the subroutine. The program jumps to this error handler only if there is an error generated somewhere in the code above it.

3. Inside the handler, handle the possible errors received using a branching statement:

```
If Err.Number = 5 then
    Msgbox "Not a valid Setting, Try again..."
Else
    MsgBox "Err # " & Err.Number & " " & Err.Description
End If
```

4. To exit the error handler, use the Resume statement:

```
Resume
```

Or,

```
Resume Next
```

Step 3 uses an If-statement for the error handler. More commonly, a Select-Case statement is used in error handlers. The following code would accomplish the same thing:

```
Select Case Err.number
    Case 5
        Msgbox "Not a valid setting, try again..."
    Case else
        Msgbox "Err # " & Err.Number & " " & Err.Description
End Select
```

Listing 6-2 attempts to delete a Visual Basic Registry setting. If the setting does not exist, a System Error 5 is generated and trapped by the program. The trap displays an Error Message dialog box using the MsgBox statement. If we hadn't done this, we would have gotten a "System Error" message and the program would have stopped. The added code that creates and handles the error is in bold.

Listing 6-2. Code to delete a Registry setting and handle a run time error if the setting does not exist.

```
Private Sub cmdDeleteKey_Click()
On Error GoTo ErrHand
    DeleteSetting "Calc", "TestInfo", "LastTestDate"
    MsgBox "Deleted LastTestDateSetting Successfully"
Exit Sub
ErrHand:
    If Err.Number = 5 Then
        MsgBox "Not a valid setting, unloading the form will re-enter it"
    Else
        MsgBox "Err # " & Err.Number & "" & Err.Description
    End If
End Sub
```

Using the ERR Object

Listing 6-2 uses the Err object. The Err object always exists in Visual Basic; you do not have to create it yourself and it is automatically loaded with the last error generated. Simply check its Number property to see which error number was generated. Listing 6-2 checks the value of the Err.Number property of the Err object inside the handler using an If-statement.

Notice that the only error we specifically deal with is Error 5. The code handles all other errors that may be received by bringing up a Message box with the error number. It also prints out the text of the message using the Description property of the Err object.

Important properties of the Err object include the following:

Err.Number	The error number of the last error.
Err.Description	The text of the last error.
Err.Source	The project name.

How would you know what all the possible error numbers are? The Visual Basic Help system has a "Trappable Errors" section.

There are some additional actions you can take in response to an error. The following statements can be used only in error handlers:

Resume	Resumes execution to the line of code causing the error.
Resume Next	Resumes execution to the line of code immediately after the error.

Listing 6-3 demonstrates the SaveSetting, DeleteSetting, and GetAllSettings commands used in this chapter. It is available in the Practice Files for this chapter. It can be typed into a Form module that contains a Command button control named cmdDeleteKey and a list box control named lstSettings. Full code sample for examples used in this chapter can also be accessed in the Practice Files Demo folder for this chapter.

Listing 6-3. Using the SaveSetting, DeleteSetting, and GetAllSettings commands to read and manipulate Visual Basic Registry settings.

```
Option Explicit
Private Sub Form_Unload(Cancel As Integer)
'demonstrate the use of the SaveSetting statement
'save 3 settings for the "Calc" application into the Registry.
    SaveSetting "Calc", "TestInfo", "Appname", "\Calc.exe"  'all the rest go to
                                                            'TestInfo subkey
    SaveSetting "Calc", "TestInfo", "Apppath", Environ$("windir")
    SaveSetting "Calc", "TestInfo", "LastTestDate", Now
End Sub


Private Sub Form_Load()
'demonstrate the use of the GetAllSettings function
    Dim astrSettings() As String  'creates a dynamic array of strings
    Dim iCount As Integer          'declare the index
    astrSettings = GetAllSettings("Calc", "TestInfo")
    For iCount = 0 To UBound(astrSettings)   'loop to print the settings
        Debug.Print astrSettings(iCount, 0), astrSettings(iCount, 1)
        lstSettings.AddItem astrSettings(iCount, 0) & " " & astrSettings(iCount, 1)
    Next iCount
End Sub


Private Sub cmdDeleteKey_Click()
'the following code demonstrates the use of the
'DeleteSetting statement and error handling
On Error GoTo ErrHand
    DeleteSetting "Calc", "TestInfo", "LastTestDate"
    MsgBox "Deleted LastTestDateSetting Successfully"
Exit Sub
```

```
ErrHand:
    If Err.Number = 5 Then
        MsgBox "Not a valid setting, unloading the form will re-enter it"
    Else
        MsgBox "Err # " & Err.Number & "" & Err.Description
    End If
End Sub
```

Accessing Other Registry Keys

The preceding information applies only to Visual Basic applications. Even then, a Visual Basic application might not use these settings. As I mentioned earlier, the developer can also use the Windows API library routines to set other parts of the Registry. As a tester, you might want to check other parts of the Registry for that and for other reasons, such as checking installation options for the applications you are testing or checking internationalization settings. Using the Windows API libraries is discussed in the next chapter.

EXERCISE 6-1.

CREATING A REGISTRY MANAGEMENT UTILITY

In Exercise 6-1, you will complete a utility program for accessing Visual Basic settings in the Registry.

Run the file **Chapter6\Exercise\VBRegistry.exe** from the Chapter 6 Practice files. This runs a Registry Manager utility created for this book.

First, use the Registry Manager utility to set a new Registry value. Use the default values in the Appname, Section, and Setting textboxes to create the new value by clicking the **Save New or Existing Setting** button. Type your name into the Input box that displays.

Open up the System Registry using the **RegEdit** utility from the TaskBar's **Start ➤ Run** menu. Verify that the new setting has been added. Remember that Visual Basic stores its settings under the following key:

HKEY_CURRENT_USER\Software\VB and VBA Program Settings

(Look for a key called "New Appname.") Switch back to the **Registry Manager** utility (the Visual Basic program). Use this utility to add and delete settings until you are satisfied that you understand its functionality. Verify your steps with the RegEdit utility.

This is how your program will look when complete:

Follow These Steps to Write the Code (Or Try It on Your Own)

1. Open the file **Chapter6\Exercise\VBRegTempl.vbp** of the Practice Files.

> **NOTE** *This program is a template and although it will run, it won't work properly until you finish it by following the remaining steps.*

2. Open the Code window and read the comments at the top. Review all of the existing code. *The code is incomplete*; the following steps guide you through to completion.

3. Review the SaveSetting statement and its arguments and example in the Visual Basic Help system.

4. Scroll to the code for the cmdAdd_Click event. Review the existing code. What does it do? It basically verifies that correct data is entered into the textboxes. It is here to add a new Registry setting. Once the code determines that the textboxes have been filled in appropriately, the user is prompted to add a value for the new Registry setting.

5. Add the single line of code that uses the SaveSetting statement to save the values in the txtAppname, txtSection, and txtSetting textboxes as well as the strSetting variable (returned from the InputBox command) to save a new setting into the Registry. This line of code should be the last line in the cmdAdd_Click event procedure.

6. Test your work by running the program and clicking the **cmdAdd** button (captioned "Save New or Existing Setting"). If it does not work, modify or debug until it does.

7. Scroll to the **cmdShowValue_Click** event procedure. Review the existing code, which checks that values are entered into the textboxes.

8. After this code, add code using the GetSetting function (review the syntax and example in the Visual Basic Help system first) to retrieve the setting and return it into the **lblValue.caption** property. (lblValue is a label on the form that is used to receive a Registry value in its caption. Notice its location.)

9. Add code after your GetSetting function to verify that something was returned. Use an If-statement. Remember that GetSetting does not generate an error but simply returns an empty string if the arguments are invalid. Test your work by running the program and clicking the **cmdShowValue** button (captioned "Show Setting Value").

10. Scroll to the cmdDelete_Click event in the Code window. At this point, you can assume the user has typed a setting to delete in the txtAppname, txtSection, and txtSetting textboxes. Use the Visual Basic Help system to review the DeleteSetting syntax. Then use the DeleteSetting statement to delete the setting. (You can skip the next step and go directly to step 12 or you can try step 11 for a challenge.)

11. *Optional Challenge*: DeleteSetting can delete a single item and its value or an entire subkey under the Visual Basic key. How can you write the code to handle either case? In other words, if the user enters a specific setting into the Individual Setting Title (txtSetting) textbox, then you would write code to delete just that setting. However, if the user does *not* enter a value into the txtSetting textbox then write the code to delete the whole subkey. Review the way this is handled by the Registry Manager program example you ran at the start of this exercise: **Chapter6\Exercise\VBRegistry.exe**. (The answer is in the Answer folder.)

12. Notice the error-handling code contained in the **cmdDelete** routine. Comment out this code, then run your code and attempt to delete a nonexistent setting. What happens? Uncomment the code. Run it again. Now what happens?

    Challenge: Change the error handler's If-statement to a Select-Case statement that accomplishes the same task.

13. Exit the Code window and view the form designer. Place a list box control on your form. Place it just above the cmdList Command button (captioned "List Multiple Settings"). Size it appropriately. Change its **Name** property to lstSettings.

14. Return to the Code window. Scroll to the cmdList_Click event procedure in the Code window. It verifies that the txtAppname and txtSection textboxes are correctly filled in and contains the declaration of a local dynamic array named astrSettings. The cmdList_Click event procedure also has a line that uses the list box's clear method to clear its values: `lstSettings.Clear`.

15. After the `lstSettings.Clear` line, write the code using the GetAllSettings statement to retrieve all the settings indicated by the user in the txtAppname and txtSection textboxes into a dynamic array.

16. Test your work by running your program. Click the **cmdList** Command button (captioned "List Multiple Settings"). Debug until it all works. Compare your work to the answer in the **Chapter6\Exercise\Answer** folder.

TESTER'S CHECKLIST

When performing code reviews, look for the following in a well-written Visual Basic application.

Does the Project...

❏ Use the Registry to store path and application information (as opposed to hard coding this information)?

Does the Code...

❏ Document Registry calls with clear comments and appropriate constants?

❏ Have a consistent and understandable Registry subkey hierarchy?

❏ Use error handling in key areas to handle run time errors?

Chapter 6 Review

- Explain at least one reason why a tester might need to access the Registry.
  See page 184.

- What are the four Visual Basic Registry functions? Describe the purpose of each.
  See page 187.

- Write the declaration statement to create a dynamic array of strings.

  ```
  Dim aMyArray () as String
  ```

- What is the purpose of a list box control?
  See page 197.

- Describe the purpose of the Err object in error handling.
  See page 202.

- What are the two statements needed to set up an error trap?
  See page 200.

CHAPTER 7

Introduction to the Windows Application Programmer's Interface (API)

Application software developers need to be able to interface with the operating system in order to provide their applications with capabilities such as sophisticated graphics and communications. Microsoft Windows operating systems provide the software developer access to many powerful routines. The Windows API routines are a set of libraries filled with routines that provide the interface to the operating system, hence the name Application Programmer's Interface. The Windows API really is the programming interface between an application and the operating system. As testers, we can use these routines to check on operating system statistics such as memory allocation and status. We can also use them to manipulate an application in ways that Visual Basic alone cannot; when you access the many routines in the Windows API, you are actually extending Visual Basic's capabilities.

The Windows API were, for the most part, written in C++ and provided for C/C++ application developers. Visual Basic developers can use them also but that wasn't the original intent. You see, the authors of Visual Basic tried to provide most everything the developer would need to write applications in an attempt to create a language that is much simpler and easier to learn and use than C++. They accomplished this goal with resounding success—Visual Basic is an excellent and powerful product. However, if you spend much time writing code in Visual Basic, you will find that in spite of the best efforts of the Microsoft Visual Basic development team, you will eventually need to go beyond what is provided. Since most of the Windows API routines were not written with the Visual Basic developer in mind, using them can be tricky due to differences in the way Visual Basic and C++ handle things such as arguments and string data. We will explore many of these differences in this chapter.

Objectives

By the end of this chapter, you will be able to:

- Describe the Windows API usefulness for testers.

- List some Windows API routines useful to a testing project.

- Prototype and use some basic Windows API routines.

- Create and use a user-defined type.

Windows API Overview

This chapter is a simple introduction to get you started using the Windows API libraries with Visual Basic. Further study and lots of practice are required to successfully work with these routines. There are some good resources for that purpose listed in Appendix A: Resources and References of this book. This chapter should be enough to get you started effectively using these routines in your test scripts. Before you can really understand what the API routines are and how to use them, you will need to know some basics about libraries in general.

Understanding Static and Dynamic Libraries

Library routines are those routines you can use from within your program but are already prewritten and thus outside of your own program code. In programming, there are two kinds of files you can use to include library routines: static and dynamic library files. We have already used one kind of static library file; Chapter 4 introduced Visual Basic's Standard module as a place to store subroutine and function procedures that can be used throughout your application. Visual Basic's Standard module is a *static* file. We are able to place any general routines for testing, such as logging routines, into the Standard module. Using Visual Basic's ability to import and export Standard modules, multiple applications can use this general code. When the application is compiled, the code called from the Standard module file is compiled into the application's executable (.exe) file. Every application that uses the Standard module gets the routines that it uses from the module compiled into its executable file—in other words, it gets its own copy of the routines.

One advantage to using a static file like the Standard module is that the code in the Standard module is checked for syntax errors and any problems with the call to the routines are resolved at compile time. Of course, one disadvantage is that the executable file includes this code and is larger because of it. Using a routine from a static library is kind of like buying a book from a bookstore: with each book you purchase, your own library grows larger. Your neighbor may have also purchased the same book. Each of you must now provide a space for the book to reside in so your respective libraries grow larger. What's the alternative to using a static library? Using a *dynamic* library. Using our previous example, what if, instead of buying your own copy of a book, you and your neighbors decide to check out the book from the public library to share? In this case, there only needs to be one copy of the book and you can lend it back and forth as needed. In fact, you can return the book to the library and check it back out again and again. Many others can use the same book by doing the same thing. Using a dynamic library follows this public library model in which files are shared. The dynamic library is available in memory to multiple applications. The applications can link to this file at run time instead of at compile time. The advantage to this arrangement is that there only needs to be one copy of a routine in the dynamic library and each of the applications share the copy as needed. So, the size of each application using this dynamic file can be smaller than if it had its own static copy. Of course, one disadvantage might be a higher likelihood of run time errors. At compile time, the only checking that can be done by the system is to ensure that the call to the routine inside the dynamic file is correct. If there are problems inside the routine, there will be an error at run time. Figure 7-1 displays a simplified graphic of the relationship of the source, executable, static, and dynamic library files.

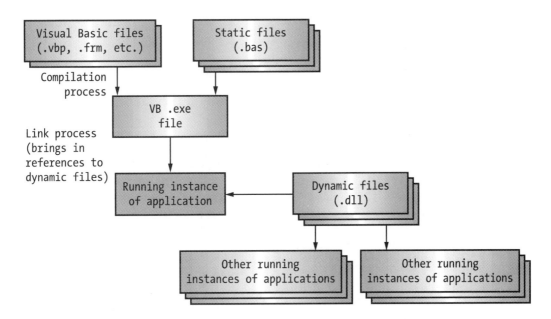

Figure 7-1. Static files compile into the executable while dynamic files are linked at run time.

The Windows API Dynamic-Link Library Files

The Windows API routines are located principally in three libraries: USER32.DLL, GDI32.DLL and KERNEL32.DLL. These libraries come with the operating system and are located in the Windows System directory.

The DLL extension stands for dynamic-link library. A DLL is a library of routines external to your application that can be called from your application. A DLL is a dynamic library because it can be linked at run time, unlike a static library such as the Standard module (.bas) files (which we have used in our applications up to this point). Another great thing about DLL procedures is that they can be modified and improved by their developer without your having to recompile your code.

The following is a description of the kinds of functions each of the three major Windows API libraries contains:

USER32   Contains routines relating to windows management such as menus, cursors, messages, timers, communications.

GDI32   The Graphics Device Interface Library contains functions for drawing, display, font functions, etc.

KERNEL32   Contains routines for memory management, task management, etc.

There are other supplemental DLLs in addition to the three main libraries (see the "Additional Windows API Libraries" sidebar). All DLL files for the Windows API are located in the Windows System directory. They are installed with the Windows operating system.

Additional Windows API Libraries

Although the core functionality of the Windows 32-bit API is divided into the three major libraries mentioned (USER32.DLL, GDI32.DLL, and KERNEL32.DLL), there are a number of smaller libraries and a whole slew of extension libraries. Microsoft wanted to add features and capabilities to the Windows operating systems rather than update the existing libraries so they simply added additional DLLs. The following are considered part of the basic operating system:

COMDLG32.DLL   Provides support for common dialogs such as the open and close dialogs you see in many applications.

LZ32.DLL   Supports file compression.

VERSION.DLL   Supports file version control.

The following are some major extensions to the basic libraries but again, this is not a complete list, especially since more can be added at anytime.

COMCTL32.DLL	Holds newer Windows controls such as the Tabbed Dialog control and the Treeview control.
MAPI32.DLL	This is the DLL that provides support for adding electronic mail capability.
NETAPI32.DLL	Holds functions for accessing and managing networks.
ADVAPI32.DLL	Holds advanced API extensions such as calls to manipulate the Windows System Registry.
ODBC32.DLL	The library containing the functions to access ODBC (Open Database Connectivity)-compliant databases.

For more information on current Windows 32-bit API libraries, see the Microsoft Developer's Network Web site on the Win32 API at
`http://msdn.microsoft.com/library/psdk/portals/win32start_1n6t.htm`.

Exploring the Windows API Routines

Because they are not part of the Visual Basic language, the Windows API routines are not documented in the Visual Basic Help system. If you have a full installation of Visual Studio including C++ and you installed the C++ Help files, then you will find documentation on the Windows API routines. This is practical for finding out which routines exist and their purpose. However, the syntax used in the C++ Help is, of course, for C++ programmers only. Another downside is that not all of the routines in the API libraries are usable or useful for Visual Basic programmers. How can we find out what is available for and usable in Visual Basic?

The most definitive reference on Windows API programming can be found in Daniel Appleman's book *Visual Basic Programmer's Guide to the Win32 API* (see Appendix A: Resources and References). It's well written and informative with many examples and a lot of code on the accompanying CD. I consider this book to be a required reference for testers writing Visual Basic. The only downside for us is that it is not written from a testing perspective, it targets software developers. So, the rest of this chapter will be kind of like a specialized subset of that book to get you started learning and using Windows API routines that are valuable for testing.

Useful APIs for Testing

There are over seven hundred available Windows API routines but you don't need to know about all of them. Some routines that have proved useful for testing include:

GlobalMemoryStatus	Returns information about the current memory state.
GetWindowsDirectory	Returns the current Windows directory.
GetActiveWindow	Returns a handle to the active window.
GetSystemMetrics	Returns system information such as resolution.
RegOpenKeyEx	Opens a Registry key.
RegQueryValueEx	Returns a specific Registry setting.
RegCloseKeyEx	Closes a Registry key.
SendMessage	Allows you to send direction to a window.
GetVersionEx	Returns the current operating system version.

The Windows APIs listed here are only a few you may find helpful. Examples of all of these are included in the following text as well as in the Chapter7/Demos folder in the Practice Files.

Using API Routines

First, you need to find out about the API routine from either a book like this one, the Windows SDK Help, a Visual Basic Web site (see Appendix A: Resources and References), or by word of mouth. Once you have identified the routine you want to work with and what it does, you can then follow these steps to insert it into your application.

Steps to Call a Windows API Routine

1. Although API calls are linked at run time, the system must know the name of the routine to use and where to find it. So, the first step in using an API routine is to prototype it with a Declare statement. The following statement declares that the GetSystemMetrics API is used:

```
Private Declare function GetSystemMetrics lib "user32.dll" alias"GetSystemMetrics" _
        (byval nIndex&) as long
```

This statement goes into the General section of a Form or Standard
module. Notice that the GetSystemMetrics function resides in the
USER32 DLL.

2. Now that the API has been declared, it can be called like any other
    function:

```
Msgbox "Resolution is: " & GetSystemMetrics(0) & ", " & GetSystemMetrics(1)
```

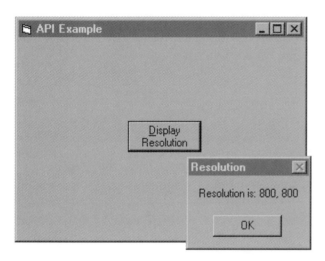

How would you have known what arguments are required for this API call
and what it returns? Its description must be found in a text like Appleman's or in
the Windows Software Development Kit (SDK) Help.

Although Visual Basic does not provide help on the Windows API routines, it
does offer a utility that makes it easier to supply the correct syntax when you
work with them. The API Text Viewer shown in Figure 7-2 can save a lot of typing
and typos.

NOTE *If you installed Microsoft Visual Studio, you can locate the API
Text Viewer tool in the Microsoft Visual Studio program group under
Microsoft Visual Studio 6 Tools. If you installed from the Visual Basic
6 CD, it is located in the Visual Basic 6 program group under Visual
Basic 6 tools.*

The API Text Viewer allows you to search for and then copy and paste the
correct Declare statements needed for Windows API calls.

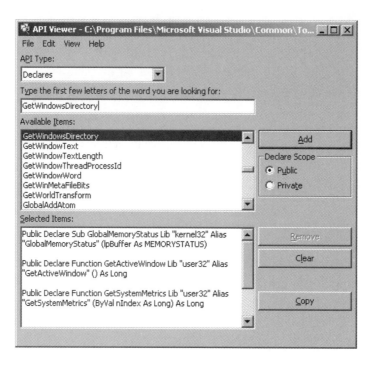

Figure 7-2. The API text viewer is a Visual Basic tool for getting the correct declaration syntax for Windows API routines.

Using the API Text Viewer

There is no help to speak of in the API Text Viewer utility. There are some instructions for using the API Text Viewer that come with Visual Basic. These instructions are located in C:\Program Files\Microsoft Visual Studio\ Common\Tools\Winapi\APILOAD.txt. The first step in using the viewer is to load a file containing the declaration statements. Select **File ➣ Load Text File** from the menu and load the Win32API.txt file. If you end up using the API Text Viewer a lot, you can convert the file into a database, which will run faster but is unnecessary—searching the text file is pretty fast, too.

The following text from the APILOAD.TXT file should get you started using this utility:

"The Dropdown at the top of the form allows you to view Constants, Declares, or Types. By selecting an entry and choosing the **Add** button, you can add an item to the Selected list at the bottom of the form.

To copy items from the Selected list to the clipboard, simply click the **Copy** button. All of the items in the list will be copied. Subsequently, you can include them in your modules by selecting **Paste** from the module Edit menu. To remove an entry from the Selected list, choose the **Remove** button."

Calling API Routines with User-Defined Type (UDT) Arguments

The GetSystemMetrics API call only asks you to provide a simple, single numeric argument. Many Windows API routines require more than one argument and these arguments sometimes require more complex structures than just a single variable. If you work with the Windows API routines a lot, you will encounter arguments that require the use of a *structure variable*. Because of this certainty, it's time to learn about the structure variable: how to create it, assign values, and utilize it within a procedure call, particularly within a Windows API procedure call.

A structure variable is a variable composed of multiple parts. In order to create a structure variable, we must first declare a new type to specify these multiple parts or *components*. For example, the following code defines a structure type, also called a user-defined type (UDT):

```
Type PersonType
    Name as String
    Age as Integer
End type
```

At this point, there is no storage created. A UDT is simply a template. It defines what your structure variable will look like when created. It's a nice structure for allowing logically related information to be kept together in one variable. Because the UDT definition is a template, it cannot be created within a procedure; it must be declared in the General Declarations section of a Code module. The following line of code creates the structure variable as defined by the UDT we just set up:

```
Dim Person1 as PersonType
```

Figure 7-3 displays a graphical way to think of the structure variable defined by creating Person1.

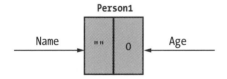

Figure 7-3. The structure variable Person1 as defined by a UDT has two components, Name and Age.

Person1 is a variable composed of two components: Name and Age. We can declare as many variables of this new type as we need. In other words, we could create a structure variable called Person2, another called Person3, and another called something else using the Dim statement in the same manner as we did for

Person1. Each of these structure variables would have its own Name and Age components. UDTs have been compared to cookie cutters. The UDT cookie cutter defines the shape and size of the cookie but it is not a cookie. When you actually create the cookie by declaring the variable, you get something that looks just as the cookie cutter defined it and you can customize it. Customizing a real cookie means adding icing or sprinkles so that each cookie starts the same but can be made different from the others. Setting the individual values of each component customizes the structure variable defined by a UDT.

To set or read the values in a structure variable's component, we use the period (.), or dot, to indicate that we are finding a value within the variable:

```
Person1.Name = "Elvis Presley"
Person1.Age = 66
```

Notice that we assign values according to the data type of the component. For example, when the UDT for PersonType was created, we assigned the String data type to the Name component. So, when assigning the component, we assign a string value to the Name component, `Person1.Name = "Elvis Presley"`.

What does this have to do with calling Windows API routines? A structure variable can be passed as an argument to a subroutine or function. In fact, structure variables are used quite frequently in Windows API routines as a way to pass multiple values in a single argument. This is a convenient way to reduce the number of arguments a routine can have.

For example, the GlobalMemoryStatus API uses a structure type to define all the memory statistics it uses. Listing 7-1 declares the MEMORYSTATUS UDT with eight components and then declares the GlobalMemoryStatus API that resides in the Kernel32 DLL.

Listing 7-1. The Windows API routine, GlobalMemoryStatus, uses the MemoryStatus UDT.

```
Type MEMORYSTATUS
    dwLength As Long
    dwMemoryLoad As Long
    dwTotalPhys As Long
    dwAvailPhys As Long
    dwTotalPageFile As Long
    dwAvailPageFile As Long
    dwTotalVirtual As Long
    dwAvailVirtual As Long
End Type
Declare Sub GlobalMemoryStatus Lib "kernel32" (lpBuffer As MEMORYSTATUS)
```

Even though this declaration of the GlobalMemoryStatus API has only one argument, we know that the argument has eight components because it is of the MEMORYSTATUS type and the definition of the MEMORYSTATUS type, with eight components, just precedes the declaration.

Listing 7-2 assumes the declaration of the MEMORYSTATUS type from Listing 7-1, creates a variable of the MEMORYSTATUS data type, and accesses its components to set the values of three textboxes on a Visual Basic form.

Listing 7-2. Using the MemoryStatus UDT.

```
Private Sub Command1_Click()
  Dim Memstuff As MEMORYSTATUS
  Memstuff = GetMemData
  Text1.Text = Str(Memstuff.dwMemoryLoad)
  Text2.Text = Str(Memstuff.dwTotalPhys)
  Text3.Text = Str(Memstuff.dwAvailPhys)
End Sub
```

TO TRY THIS

1. Create a new Visual Basic project.

2. Place three textboxes and one command on the form (do not change their Name properties).

3. *Optionally*, place three label controls next to the textboxes and change their Caption properties to **Memory Load**, **Total Phys. Memory**, and **Available Phys. Memory**.

> **NOTE** *Do not change the Name properties. For simplicity, just leave the default names, Text1, Text2, and Text3.*

4. Right-click on the form in Design mode and select **View Code** from the pop-up menu.

5. Type in all of the code shown in Listings 7-1 and 7-2.

WARNING *Remember that UDTs cannot be created inside of a sub-routine or function, they must be created at the top of the module in the General Declarations section. If you create a UDT within a sub-routine or function, you will get the error message "Can't define types inside of procedure." Move the code outside of the procedure to fix this problem.*

6. Run the program and click the button. You should see a display of the current memory status in the textboxes.

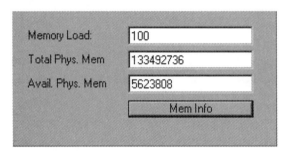

Using Windows API Functions for the Registry

The Visual Basic Registry functions we used in Chapter 6 were limited to a single, specific key. If we need to access other parts of the Registry, we need to call routines from one of the associated libraries of the Windows API the ADVAPI.DLL, which has routines that can access and manipulate the Windows System Registry.

Working with the Registry functions may seem daunting when you first look at the code because there are many things you need to do to set up the arguments, such a creating constants and UDTs. Later in this chapter, we will explore how to go about setting things up yourself. But here, since the work has already been done, we will just copy the code and see it work.

One of the more common tasks a tester will need to perform is to list all of the items underneath a key in the Windows Registry. We performed a similar task in Chapter 6 using the special Visual Basic Registry commands that are limited to working with only one specific registry key. Now we will explore code that examines the subkeys under any key in the Windows Registry.

For example, Listing 7-3 opens the HKEY_CURRENT_USER\Software key and enumerates all of the subkeys underneath.

Listing 7-3. Accessing the Software key under the Windows Registry's HKEY_CURRENT_USER hive.

```
Private Const KEY_ENUMERATE_SUB_KEYS = &H8
Private Const KEY_NOTIFY = &H10
Private Const READ_CONTROL = &H20000
Private Const SYNCHRONIZE = &H100000
Private Const STANDARD_RIGHTS_READ =(READ_CONTROL)
Private Const KEY_QUERY_VALUE = &H1

Private Const KEY_READ = ((STANDARD_RIGHTS_READ _
  Or KEY_QUERY_VALUE Or KEY_ENUMERATE_SUB_KEYS _
  Or KEY_NOTIFY) And (Not SYNCHRONIZE))

Private Const HKEY_CURRENT_USER = &H80000001

Private Type FILETIME
    dwLowDateTime As Long
    dwHighDateTime As Long
End Type

Private Declare Function RegOpenKeyEx Lib "advapi32.dll" Alias "RegOpenKeyExA" _
        (ByVal hKey As Long, ByVal lpSubKey As String, _
        ByVal ulOptions As Long, ByVal samDesired As Long, phkResult As Long) As Long

Private Declare Function RegEnumKeyEx Lib "advapi32.dll" Alias "RegEnumKeyExA" _
        (ByVal hKey As Long, ByVal dwIndex As Long, ByVal lpName As String, _
        lpcbName As Long, ByVal lpReserved As Long, ByVal lpClass As String, _
        lpcbClass As Long, lpftLastWriteTime As FILETIME) As Long
Private Declare Function RegCloseKey Lib "advapi32.dll" (ByVal hKey As Long) As Long

Sub cmdEnum_Click()
    Dim ft As FILETIME
    Dim keyhandle As Long
    Dim res As Long
    Dim iCount As Long
    Dim keyname As String
    Dim classname As String
    Dim keylen As Long
    Dim classlen As Long
```

```
res = RegOpenKeyEx(HKEY_CURRENT_USER, "Software", 0, KEY_READ, keyhandle)
    If res <> 0 Then
        MsgBox "Can't open key"
        End
    End If

    Do
        keylen = 2000
        classlen = 2000
        keyname = String$(keylen, 0)
        classname = String$(classlen, 0)
        res = RegEnumKeyEx(keyhandle, iCount, keyname, keylen, 0,classname, _
                classlen, ft)
        iCount = iCount + 1
        If res = 0 Then
            lstEnum.AddItem Trim$(keyname)
        End If
    Loop While res = 0

    Call RegCloseKey(keyhandle)
End Sub
```

TO TRY THIS

1. Create a new Visual Basic project.

2. Create a list box control named lstEnum and a Command button named cmdEnum.

3. Type the code in Listing 7-3 into the form's Code window. (Look out for typos!)

If typing all of the code in Listing 7-3 seems a daunting task, the project EnumKeyAPI.vbp in the Practice Files Chapter7\Demos folder demonstrates the code in Listing 7-3. Figure 7-4 shows the EnumKeyAPI project in Run mode. It displays a list of the keys under the HKEY_CURRENT_USER\Software key—in other words, a list of the currently installed software. Of course, this list will likely be different for every machine.

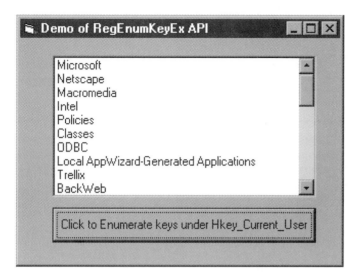

Figure 7-4. The EnumKeyAPI project in Run mode.

To understand what's going on in the code, you must understand a little more about the Windows Registry. Listing 7-3 declares three routines from the Windows API: RegOpenKeyEX, RegEnumKeyEX, and RegCloseKeyEX. Before you can work with any key in the Registry, you must first open it, hence the reason for calling RegOpenKeyEX. This function returns a *handle* to the key. Think of the handle as just that, a way to hold and work with that key. A handle to a Windows Registry key is simply a number that uniquely identifies that key. The following code repeats the call to RegOpenKeyEX from Listing 7-3:

```
res = RegOpenKeyEx(HKEY_CURRENT_USER, "Software", 0, KEY_READ, keyhandle)
```

The arguments of this call to RegOpenKeyEX specify which hive we are opening and which key underneath the hive. We specify that we are opening the key for reading with the KEY_READ argument. The keyhandle argument will hold the handle to the key returned to us by Windows. Notice that same argument value is passed into the RegEnumKeyEX function in the following call also from Listing 7-3:

```
res = RegEnumKeyEx(KeyHandle, iCount, KeyName, KeyLen, 0,ClassName, _
    ClassLen, ft)
```

The KeyHandle argument is the first argument in the call to RegEnumKeyEX and it tells Windows which key we are trying to access. The RegEnumKeyEX function, when called within a loop (as it is in Listing 7-3), will return successive values of the subkeys into the KeyName argument. The remaining code within the loop handles placing these values into a list box for display.

NOTE *In Listing 7-3, one of the arguments required for the RegEnumKeyEX required a UDT definition. Even though we didn't need the information returned from this argument, it had to be provided. So, the FileTime UDT was declared and its argument was provided but its return value was not used.*

EXERCISE 7-1.

In Exercise 7-1, you will write the code to make a simple call to a Windows API routine. This call returns the version of the Windows operating system you are currently running. You will use the GetVersionEX API routine.

- Run the file **Chapter7\Exercises\APILab.exe** from the Practice Files. The program's main window has a single button.

- Click the button **OS Version**.

- The current version of your operating system prints into a label on the form.

- Close the window.

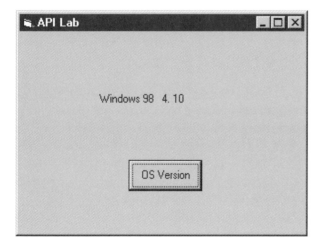

This is how your program will look when complete.

Follow These Steps to Write the Code

1. There is no template for this exercise; create a new Visual Basic project.

2. Add a single button to the form. Change its Name property to **cmdOS**. Change its Caption property to **OS Version**.

3. Add a single label to the form. Change its Name property to **lblOS** and its Caption property to blank (remove all text from the Caption property of the label).

4. Type the following code into the General Declarations section of your form's Code window:

```
Private Type OSVERSIONINFO
    DWOSVersionInfoSize As Long
    dwMajorVersion As Long
    dwMinorVersion As Long
    dwBuildNumber As Long
    dwPlatformID As Long
    szCSDVersion As String * 128
End Type

Const VER_PLATFORM_WIN32_NT = 2
Const VER_PLATFORM_WIN32_WINDOWS = 1
Const VER_PLATFORM_WIN32S = 0

Private Declare Function GetVersionEx Lib _
        "kernel32" Alias "GetVersionExA" _
        (lpVersionInformation As OSVERSIONINFO) As Long
```

 NOTE *Instead of typing the code, you can use the API Text Viewer from the Microsoft Visual Studio program group, Microsoft Visual Studio 6 Tools. If you installed from the Visual Basic 6 CD, then it is located in the Visual Basic 6 program group under Visual Basic 6 tools. You will need to add the keyword* **Private** *to the function and UDT declarations.*

5. Create a local string variable in the click-event of the button. Create a local variable of the UDT type:

```
Dim strAns As String
Dim OSData As OSVERSIONINFO
```

6. Set a component of the UDT as follows:

```
OSData.DWOSVersionInfoSize = 148
```

7. Now add the call:

```
GetVersionEx OSData
```

8. Use a branching statement to determine on which platform you are running. The GetVersionEX API call loads your UDT structure variable with data. The component that contains the current operating system version is the dwPlatformID component. It is loaded with one of the values in the constants you created at the top of the form. You can choose an If-Then statement or a Select-Case statement. To get you started, the following would be the beginning of the If-statement (the answer has a Select-Case):

```
If OSDATA.dwPlatformID = VER_PLATFORM_WIN32_NT then
    strAns = "Windows NT " …
```

9. The constants available are listed in Table 7-1 along with the text you should place into a string. You can then catenate this string (in the next step) to the version components.

Table 7-1. Constants for Microsoft Versions

CONSTANT	OPERATING SYSTEM	VALUE
VER_PLATFORM_WIN32_NT	Windows NT	2
VER_PLATFORM_WIN32_WINDOWS	Windows 95	1
VER_PLATFORM_WIN32S	Windows	0

NOTE *Windows 95 and Windows 98 both return 1 into the dwPlatformID argument (so you can use the VER_PLATFORM_WIN32_WINDOWS constant to check for either operating system). However, then you cannot differentiate between Windows 95 and 98. If you want to check for Windows 95, the value of the dwMinorVersion component will be 0; for Windows 98, the value of dwMinorVersion will be greater than 0.*

10. Now load the label caption with the answer. We can also add in the values of the MajorVersion and MinorVersion components. They contain the version number of the operating system. Your code should look something like this:

```
lblOS.Caption = strAns & " " & Str(OSData.dwMajorVersion) & "." & _
    Str(OSData.dwMinorVersion)
```

11. Run your program and click the button. You should see your current operating system version displayed.

12. Compare your answer to the answer in the Chapter7\ Exercises7_1\Answer\Apilab.vbp project in the Practice Files.

13. Name and save your files.

Working with the Windows API: Beyond the Basics

While it is possible to simply copy examples of calls to the Windows API routines without understanding how the calls are working (as we did in the last section), that won't suffice for long. An understanding of a few basics will increase your ability to use calls to the Windows API in your test applications. An added benefit is that many of these basics also apply to calling and using routines from any DLL. For example, consider the following declaration of a the GetFileVersionInfo function from the VERSION.DLL API library:

```
Private Declare Function GetFileVersionInfo _
    Lib "Version.dll" Alias "GetFileVersionInfoA" _
    (ByVal lptstrFilename As String, ByVal dwHandle As Long, _
        ByVal dwLen As Long, lpData As Any) As Long
```

This routine will return the version of a file. The GetFileVersionInfo routine can be very useful for testers trying to ensure that the application being tested is the correct version. However, examining the declaration is a little confusing. First, what is the Alias and why does the declaration repeat the function name with an 'A' after it (GetFileVersionInfoA)? The arguments required don't look too bad at first. The lptstrFilename argument is a string, which you might guess is the string containing the file name to be checked—and you would be right. But what about the other arguments? It is difficult to determine what to provide when calling this routine. For example, what kind of data type is Any? Also, what is the meaning of ByVal and why is it used so much? To answer these questions we need to cover a few fundamentals of API handling.

Understanding Windows API Arguments

The following are a few basic tips for working with the Windows API procedures to help you become more proficient in using them. We will examine some of the critical differences between Visual Basic and C declarations, such as differences in the argument lists, data types, Unicode versus ANSI routines, and even the True and False keywords.

Working with Strings

One of the things that can trip you up right away when working with calls to DLL routines from the Windows API is working with String arguments. There are two important issues to deal with:

- Understanding strings and the use of the ByVal keyword

- Sizing strings

Understanding Strings and the Use of ByVal

Most of the Windows API routines that have string arguments expect a string to be passed in the format of a C++ string. C++ strings are terminated with a null value, that is, the ASCII value of 0. Visual Basic strings are *not* null terminated but if the ByVal keyword is specified in the argument, Visual Basic will add a null to the end of the string being passed. That's why you see so many ByVals in the declarations for API calls for Visual Basic. You do not have to do anything special to the string being passed, just declare and set its value as usual (as long as ByVal is used).

ByVal does not mean the same thing when used with numeric arguments; Visual Basic does not attach a null to a number. With numeric arguments, ByVal means that when the numeric variable is passed to the routine, it is only a *copy* of the variable and not the actual variable. In this case, ByVal means literally "by value." The value of the variable is passed but not the actual variable location. This protects the variable from being changed or modified by the routine.

The GetSystemMetrics declaration we saw in the last section uses ByVal for its integer argument:

```
Private Declare Function GetSystemMetrics lib "User32.DLL" alias _
    "GetSystemMetrics" (byval nIndex&) as long
```

The code to call GetSystemMetrics is:

```
Dim iTest as Long
ITest = 1
Debug.print GetSystemMetrics(iTest)
```

In this code, iTest is declared as a Long integer. Its value is set to 1. Then it is used as the actual argument to the GetSystemMetrics function call as shown. Because of the ByVal keyword in the declaration of the argument, what is actually passed is a copy of iTest containing the value 1. That way, if GetSystemMetrics were written to modify the variable passed to it, it would only be modifying the copy and the contents of iTest would remain the same even after the call to GetSystemMetrics.

When passing arguments to routines, the default is ByRef, meaning that the actual variable is passed in (actually, a pointer to the variable is passed but it amounts to effectively the same thing). We don't have to type "ByRef" since it is the default. If specifying ByVal protects your variables from being written to, then why isn't ByVal the default? Think of an office where you have an important document. If you want to protect it, you can make copies of the document and keep the actual document under lock and key. However, to make all of those copies, you need to buy a copy machine and perhaps even hire a secretary. This creates extra overhead for your office, right? It's the same with passing arguments. When an argument is passed ByRef, there is less overhead. When you have to make copies of values before passing them, you pay the price with extra overhead in terms of memory and storage.

Sizing Strings

Another important fact about working with strings from DLL routines concerns when the routine has an argument that will hold return data. The string you provide for the argument in this case must be made large enough to hold the return value. This is nonintuitive for Visual Basic programmers since we don't usually have to worry about that. But when working with DLL routines built for C, you will usually need to size the string first. You can do this by created a fixed-length string and making it a size larger than you think you will need. For example, the GetWindowText API returns the text of a window in its second argument. To make sure there is enough room for all of the text that may be returned, the writer of the following code declares a fixed-length string of 100 characters, and then passes it to the GetWindowText routine:

```
Dim r as long
Dim sWindowText As String * 100
r = GetWindowText(hWndOver, sWindowText, 100) ' Window text
```

This is the most common error in working with strings and DLL routines. If the length of the string were not specified, there would be no error message; the routine would just return nothing into the sWindowText argument. Very frustrating! Be sure to create a fixed-length string larger than the return value you expect and also to add enough extra spaces to consider the null character at the end of the string. I usually create the string very large initially, like 256 characters. Once I get the return value, I chop the string back to the correct length needed for successful retrieval simply by counting the characters in the actual return value and adding on an extra space for the null.

Understanding the Any Keyword

The Any keyword is provided by Visual Basic to allow for routines that can accept multiple data types in a single argument. The lpData argument in the GetFileVersionInfo declaration shown earlier is an example. When the GetFileVersionInfo routine is called, the data type of the lpData argument will be equivalent to the data type of the variable passed to it. It is up to the user of the routine to make sure that what is passed into it makes sense.

The only way to know what kinds of data types a Windows API routine will accept without error is to look up its description. The best resources for this are the aforementioned Appleman book or *Visual Basic Programming with the Windows API* by Pappas and Murray (see Appendix A: Resources and References) or the Windows SDK. I prefer either the Appleman or Pappas and Murray texts since they are written specifically to call Windows API from Visual Basic.

By the way, if you are incorrect in the data types you pass to a routine, you may encounter a run time error such as a GPF (General Protection Fault). If this occurs, you will lose everything you have coded into your project up to the last time you saved. So, save your work frequently, especially when coding API calls!

Understanding Aliasing

The Alias keyword is just what it sounds like: you can rename a DLL routine anything you want by using an alias. This can be useful in situations where the routine name conflicts with a Visual Basic keyword. For example, there is a Windows API routine called SetFocus that conflicts with the Visual Basic method of the same name. The following partial declaration would handle it:

```
Public Declare Function Joe Lib "user32" Alias "SetFocus" (ByVal hwnd As Long) As Long
```

In this case, I named my function Joe just to be silly but it could be done. When this function is called during run time, Visual Basic would know to actually use the SetFocus routine from the USER32 DLL:

```
Joe(hMyHandle)      'a call to the SetFocus API
```

ANSI versus Unicode

Conflicts with Visual Basic keywords and Windows API routine names are pretty rare and yet, in the API Text Viewer, practically every routine uses aliases. Why? There are actually two or three versions of the same routine in the DLLs in Windows NT. There is usually one version that works for ANSI strings and another that works for Unicode strings. ANSI is the typical way Visual Basic passes strings (although Visual Basic uses Unicode internally). ANSI strings handle the standard English character set, up to 256 characters. Unicode is for use with double-byte character sets (DBCS) and can handle up to 32,767 characters—plenty to handle languages with lots of characters like Japanese. Unicode can handle smaller languages like English as well, which is why it is called Unicode—it's able to handle universal languages.

In the GetFileVersionInfo routine, we see that the actual routine used from the DLL is GetFileVersionInfoA, the version of the routine that will work with the ANSI character set. There is a corresponding routine called GetFileVersionInfoW. The 'W' stands for wide, meaning the Unicode character set since it is bigger. The 'A,' of course, stands for ANSI. Windows 95 can only work with the ANSI version. However, Windows NT can use either version. To make your code more portable, simply call this routine as GetFileVersionInfo and use the alias to specify which actual routine, GetFileVersionInfoA or GetFileVersionInfoW, you really want. When porting between systems, you need only change the declaration in the .bas file if you want to switch to Unicode (or vice versa) rather than change it in every call to the routine.

API Return Values and the Meaning of True and False

Many Windows API functions use their return value to return the information requested (as you might expect). For example, GetSystemMetrics is a function that returns a value equal to the resolution, provided you give it the correct input argument. However, many more Windows API routines use the return value of the function to indicate whether or not the function ran correctly. Then, when you call it, you provide a Boolean variable to handle the function's return value and to check whether the routine ran with or without errors. So, if you check a call to a Windows API routine the way you might typically do for a Visual Basic routine, you could run into problems.

NOTE *An important difference between Visual Basic and Windows routines is that Visual Basic considers True to be –1 and False to be 0, whereas Windows considers 0 to be False and any nonzero value to be True.*

The function GetFileVersionInfo uses its return argument for this purpose. A call to GetFileVersionInfo might look like the following:

```
rc = GetFileVersionInfo (strFile$, 0&, lBufferLen&,sBuffer(0))
If rc = 0 then
    Debug.print "API call failed"
End if
```

The If-statement in the preceding code will correctly determine whether or not the call completed successfully. Consider what would happen if the preceding code had been written with an If-statement like this:

```
'incorrect check of API return value
If rc <> -1 then
    Debug.print "API call failed"
Endif
```

This code is incorrect because it is possible for the routine to run properly with a return value that is nonzero and *not* –1. However, the prior code would still mark it as failing. So, now you know the difference between True and False—in Visual Basic and C++, that is.

Visual Basic and C++ Declaration Conversions

Since we know that most Windows API routines are written for C++ and, indeed, all of the Windows SDK Help is written with C syntax, it is beneficial to know which Visual Basic data types to use when C data types are specified. For example, consider the definition of our old friend the GetFileVersionInfo routine in the Windows SDK Help:

```
BOOL GetFileVersionInfo(
LPTSTR lptstrFilename, // pointer to filename string
DWORD dwHandle, // ignored
DWORD dwLen, // size of buffer
LPVOID lpData // pointer to buffer to receive version info. );
```

If you looked up GetFileVersionInfo in the Windows SDK Help, you would get the preceding syntax. To find out how to declare this in Visual Basic, you can use the API Text Viewer. If that's not available, then what Visual Basic data types do you provide when declaring the API routine in your code? Table 7-2 lists numeric and character conversions from C++ declarations to Visual Basic declarations.

Table 7-2. Numeric and Character Conversions from C++ Declarations to Visual Basic Declarations

C++ DECLARATION	VISUAL BASIC DECLARATION (32 BIT)
Char chMyChar	ByVal chMyChar as Byte
BYTE chMyByte	ByVal bytMyByte as Byte
Short nMyShort	ByVal iMyShort as Integer
WORD wMyWord	ByVal iMyWord as Integer
Int iMyInt	ByVal lMyInt as Long
UINT wMyUInt	ByVal lMyUInt as Long
BOOL bMyBool	ByVal lMyBool as Long
DWORD dwMyDWord	ByVal lMyDWord as Long
LONG lMyLong	ByVal lMyLong as Long
Float MyFloat	ByVal sMyFloat as Single
Double MyDouble	ByVal MyDouble as Double
VARIANT myVar	ByVal vMyVar as VARIANT
VARIANTARG MyVar	ByVal vMyVar as VARIANT
HWND hWnd	ByVal hWnd as Long

String handling follows the rules we discussed earlier in this chapter. Basically, all strings in C are pointers to characters with a null termination character and are represented by the LPSTR data type or some variation of it such as LPCSTR, LPCTSTR, and LPTSTR. As you have seen, in general, most DLL routines expect null terminated strings, that is, C strings. Visual Basic can work with arguments using these data types by providing Visual Basic strings designated with the ByVal keyword.

Writing API Wrappers

Once you have gone through all the work of determining correct arguments and setting up the API, it makes sense to save yourself and your coworkers from having to do the same thing next time you need the same kind of information. You can write a wrapper routine for calling this function that simplifies the call later on.

For instance, it turns out that to actually get the full file-version information we want for a particular file, we need to use some other Windows API routines from the same DLL. Listing 7-4 calls the GetFileVersionInfo routine using related APIs to put the result into an understandable format.

Listing 7-4. Writing a Wrapper function for the GetFileVersionInfo Windows API routine.

```
Public Function GetFileVersion(strFile$) As String
'Author: Jonathan Griffin, Data Dimensions, Inc.
   Dim sBuffer() As Byte
   Dim lVerPointer As Long
   Dim udtVerBuffer As VS_FIXEDFILEINFO
   Dim lVerbufferLen As Long

   'Find out if there is any version info available
   lBufferLen& = GetFileVersionInfoSize (strFile$, lDummy&)
   If lBufferLen& < 1 Then
      GetFileVersion$ = "Not Available"
      Exit Function
   End If

   '**** Store info to udtVerBuffer struct ****
   ReDim sBuffer(lBufferLen&)
   rc& = GetFileVersionInfo (strFile$, 0&, lBufferLen&, sBuffer(0))
   rc& = VerQueryValue (sBuffer(0), "\", lVerPointer, lVerbufferLen)
   MoveMemory udtVerBuffer, lVerPointer, Len(udtVerBuffer)
   '**** Determine File Version number ****
   FileVer = _
      Format$(udtVerBuffer.dwFileVersionMSh) & "." & _
      Format$(udtVerBuffer.dwFileVersionMSl, "00") & "." & _
      Format$(udtVerBuffer.dwFileVersionLSh, "00") & "." & _
      Format$(udtVerBuffer.dwFileVersionLSl, "0000")
   GetFileVersion$ = FileVer
End Function
```

Listing 7-4 prepares all the necessary information and even formats it. Now we have our own GetFileVersion function, which handles the calls to the Windows API procedures. We call this kind of function a *wrapper* since it wraps up the calls to the API routines in a nice, neat package, effectively hiding the details from the user of this routine. All the caller has to do is provide a valid filename to this function. Creating wrappers for all the DLL calls you commonly make and then storing them in a module will greatly enhance your ability to quickly set up automated tests. To examine and run the code in Listing 7-4, open the **UseApi.vbp** file from the Chapter7\Demos folder in the Practice Files. For more examples of how to write and use Wrapper functions, open the **Chapter7\Demos** folder in the Practice Files. There is a program called apiexamples.vbp, which contains Wrapper functions for some of the examples we have used in this chapter. It is intended to help you understand Wrapper functions and also to give you a little more experience working with calls to the Windows API routines.

Windows API Examples for Testing

It is all very well to talk about how useful the Windows API can be for testing purposes. However, it's usually a lot easier to get ideas when you have had a chance to see a few good examples. In this section, we will explore code written in Visual Basic that has been used on test projects, some simple and some more challenging.

Example 1: Sending a Message to a Control

In Chapter 5, we learned a little about how to manipulate the Calculator program, clicking its buttons using the SendKeys command. Actually, the SendKeys command is a wrapper itself written by the Visual Basic developers to simplify the call to a Windows API routine called SendMessage. The SendMessage function is a bit more complicated to call and use than the Visual Basic SendKeys command. It is also more powerful because we can tell a control to do just about anything we need it to do. If you are determined to use Visual Basic as a GUI testing tool, you will need to spend a lot more time working with the SendMessage routine from the USER32 DLL. Listing 7-5 displays some code to use the SendMessage routine to tell a Combo box control to drop down. The usual action of a Combo box is to only drop down when clicked by the mouse or when the user uses the down arrow. In this case, the code tells the Combo box to drop down when the Combo box receives the focus. (For this example, assume there is a Combo box on the form with the name cboDemo.)

Listing 7-5. Manipulating controls using the SendMessage Windows API routine.

```
Private Declare Function SendMessage Lib "user32" Alias "SendMessageA" _
    (ByVal hwnd As Long, ByVal wMsg As Long, ByVal wParam As Long, lParam As Long) _
        As Long
```

```
Private Sub cboDemo_GotFocus()
'This code demonstrates how to send a message to a combobox, making it
'"drop itself" down. It calls the SendMessage Windows API routine
'from the USER32 DLL
    Const cb_SHOWDROPDOWN = &H14F
    Dim ret As Long
    ret = SendMessage(cboDemo.hwnd, cb_SHOWDROPDOWN, 1, ByVal 0&)
End Sub
```

TO TRY THIS

1. Create a new Visual Basic standard project.

2. Add a Combo box control to the form and change its Name property to **cboDemo.**

3. Add the following code to the Form_Load event:

```
Private Sub Form_Load()
    cboDemo.Text = "Select a treat:"
    cboDemo.AddItem "Apples"
    cboDemo.AddItem "Peaches"
    cboDemo.AddItem "Pumpkin Pie"
End Sub
```

4. Add all of the code from Listing 7-5 to the Code window (comments are optional, of course).

5. Add other controls as desired such as other Command buttons, textboxes, etc., and change the Tabindex property so that the cboDemo Combo box is not the first in the tab order—in other words, make sure its TabIndex property is *not* 0.

6. Run the program and press the **Tab** key until the focus is on the Combo box. You will see it drop down automatically once it has received the focus.

You can also run a prewritten demo, SendMessageDemo.vbp, of this example from the Chapter7\Demos folder. Figure 7-5 shows the SendMessageDemo.vbp application in Run mode.

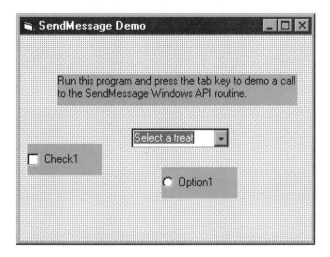

Figure 7-5. The SendMessageDemo.vbp file demonstrates the use of the SendMessage Windows API routine.

Example 2: Visual Basic Spy Utility

When you run your cursor over the top of a window, the operating system does a lot of work to send messages about what is there and what is going on. You can retrieve some of this information and find out more about the objects on the application window using Windows API routines. A number of programmers have developed *Spy routines* to find out the number and kinds of controls on a dialog, the class name of the control (for example, the Button class), and other pertinent information. Why is this important for testing? Sometimes controls are standard Microsoft Windows controls, other controls are specialized versions of controls, and still others are not really controls at all but simply painted bitmaps. Knowing a little more about which is which can help a tester determine how to test the control for proper functionality.

Listing 7-6 is a piece of a Visual Basic Spy program written by WorldMaker.com, which uses a number of calls to Windows API routines. (This code is shareware and is available in the Chapter7\Demos folder of Practice Files.) It assesses the current location of the cursor at run time and returns information about the window it happens to be over, including the Windows class, handle, parent window information, window style, and so on.

Listing 7-6. Determining Microsoft Windows information with API routines in a Spy program.

```
Private Sub Timer1_Timer()
'This code Is excerpted from FreeSpy32, contributed by WorldMaker.com
    Dim r As Long
    Dim pt32 As POINTAPI
    Dim ptx As Long
    Dim pty As Long
    Dim sWindowText As String * 100
    Dim sClassName As String * 100
    Dim hWndOver As Long
    Dim hWndParent As Long
    Dim sParentClassName As String * 100
    Dim wID As Long
    Dim lWindowStyle As Long
    Dim hInstance As Long
    Dim sParentWindowText As String * 100
    Dim sModuleFileName As String * 100
    Static hWndLast As Long
    Const GWL_STYLE = 0
    Call GetCursorPos(pt32)
    ptx = pt32.x
    pty = pt32.y
    hWndOver = WindowFromPointXY(ptx, pty) 'Get window
    If hWndOver <> hWndLast Then            'If changed
                                           'update display
        hWndLast = hWndOver                ' Save change
        Cls                                'Clear the form
        Print "Window Handle: "; hWndOver  'Display window handle
        r = GetWindowText(hWndOver, sWindowText, 100)
        Print "Window Text: " & Left(sWindowText, r)
        r = GetClassName(hWndOver, sClassName, 100)
        Print "Window Class Name: "; Left(sClassName, r)
        lWindowStyle = GetWindowLong(hWndOver, GWL_STYLE)
        Print "Window Style: "; lWindowStyle
        ' Get handle of parent window:
        hWndParent = GetParent(hWndOver)
        ' If there is a parent get more info:
            If hWndParent <> 0 Then
                ' Get ID of window:
                wID = GetWindowWord(hWndOver, GWW_ID)
                Print "Window ID Number: "; wID
                Print "Parent Window Handle: "; hWndParent
```

```
          ' Get the text of the Parent window:
          r = GetWindowText (hWndParent, sParentWindowText, 100)
          Print "Parent Window Text: " & _
             Left(sParentWindowText, r)
          ' Get the class name of the parent window:
          r = GetClassName (hWndParent, sParentClassName, 100)
          Print "Parent Window Class Name: "; _
                Left(sParentClassName, r)
       Else
          ' Update fields when no parent:
          Print "Window ID Number: N/A"
          Print "Parent Window Handle: N/A"
          Print "Parent Window Text : N/A""
          Print "Parent Window Class Name: N/A"
       End If
    ' Get window instance:
    hInstance = GetWindowWord(hWndOver, GWW_HINSTANCE)
    ' Get module file name:
    r = GetModuleFileName(hInstance, sModuleFileName, 100)
    Print "Module: "; Left(sModuleFileName, r)
  End If
End Sub
```

Listing 7-6 is a routine that will return information about an application's windows. This information consists of items such as classname, Window handle, and Window text. The routine uses a number of calls to the Windows API. The Windows API routines used are declared in a separate module, which is contained in the Chapter 7 Practice Files for this book.

··

Understanding Windows Handles

A number of the calls to the Win32 API routines require retrieving or providing a handle to the window. So just what is a *windows handle*? The Visual Studio Product Documentation defines a handle as "a number assigned to a window that is used by the operating system to keep track of the attributes of the window." In layman's terms, a handle is a number assigned to a window—the kind of number assigned in a long integer—so, any number between approximately plus or minus two billion. Since computers work better with numbers than with anything else, a number is used to represent a window rather than a string value (like the window's caption). Windows handles are assigned to a window when it is created and are used to identify that window as long as that window is in memory. When the window is destroyed, the handle number is released. This is like taking a number to get help at a store: the salespeople identify you by your number for that sale. The salespeople don't care about your name (in fact, that could be confusing because there might be many people with the same name). So, they refer to you as Customer 7 (or whatever number is on your ticket). When you leave the store, your number is released. If you come back (even later that same day), you will be assigned a new number. This is the way that windows handles work: a new handle number is assigned to a window each time it is created.

The term "handle" is used in other places in programming. Remember the section "Using Windows API Functions for the Registry" earlier in this chapter? The number that uniquely identifies a Registry key was also called a handle. This is not the same thing as a Window handle but it is a similar idea—a number that identifies a particular item to Windows.

Listing 7-6 demonstrates calls to these Windows API routines:

GetWindowWord	Returns information from the Windows structure for a window.
GetModuleFileName	Returns the full pathname of a loaded module.
GetClassName	Retrieves the classname of a window.
GetWindowText	Retrieves the caption of a window or a control.
GetCursorPosition	Retrieves the current position of the cursor.
WindowFromPoint	Returns the handle of the window that contains the specified point.
GetParent	Determines the parent of a window.

Figure 7-6 shows the FreeSpy32 program returning information about the Static control that contains the results of a calculation on the Calculator accessory.

The FreeSpy32 program makes good use of several Windows API routines. To run this program, open the **Chapter7\Demos** folder from the Practice Files and double-click on the **FreeSpy32.vbp** file. The full source code for this program is contained in the Chapter7\Demos folder and makes a good learning tool for using the Windows API routines. This code is shareware and may be used for learning and noncommercial purposes only through the courtesy of Worldmaker.com.

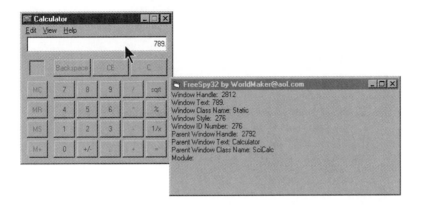

Figure 7-6. Using the FreeSpy32 program to access a control on the Calculator accessory.

Example 3: Inspecting the Entire Registry Using Windows API

Interrogating the Registry for installed hardware is another common testing task since it is important to know which devices an application can and cannot work with. Listing 7-7 accesses the HKEY_LOCAL_MACHINE Registry key to retrieve information about the available printers on the system. The cmdShowPrinters_Click routine calls the RegEnumKeyEx Windows API routine to list all of the printers and then displays them in a Message box.

Listing 7-7. Using Windows API routines to determine available printers.

```
Option Explicit
Private Const HKEY_LOCAL_MACHINE = &H80000002

Private Type FILETIME
      dwLowDateTime As Long
      dwHighDateTime As Long
End Type
Private Const READ_CONTROL = &H20000
Private Const KEY_QUERY_VALUE = &H1
Private Const STANDARD_RIGHTS_ALL = &H1F0000
Private Const KEY_ENUMERATE_SUB_KEYS = &H8
Private Const KEY_NOTIFY = &H10
Private Const SYNCHRONIZE = &H100000
Private Const STANDARD_RIGHTS_READ = (READ_CONTROL)
Private Const KEY_READ = ((STANDARD_RIGHTS_READ Or _
      KEY_QUERY_VALUE Or KEY_ENUMERATE_SUB_KEYS Or KEY_NOTIFY) And (Not SYNCHRONIZE))
Private Const ERROR_SUCCESS = 0&
```

```
Private Declare Function RegOpenKeyEx Lib "advapi32.dll" Alias "RegOpenKeyExA" _
        (ByVal hKey As Long, ByVal lpSubKey As String, ByVal ulOptions As Long, _
         ByVal samDesired As Long, phkResult As Long) As Long
Private Declare Function RegEnumKeyEx Lib "advapi32.dll" Alias "RegEnumKeyExA" _
       (ByVal hKey As Long, ByVal dwIndex As Long, ByVal lpName As String, _
        lpcbName As Long, ByVal lpReserved As Long, ByVal lpClass As String, _
        lpcbClass As Long, lpftLastWriteTime As FILETIME) As Long
Private Declare Function RegCloseKey Lib "advapi32.dll" (ByVal hKey As Long) As Long

Private Sub cmdShowPrinters_Click()
'The following code Is excerpted from the book
'Visual Basic Programmer's Guide to the Win32 API by Dan Appleman
    Dim ft As FILETIME
    Dim keyhandle&
    Dim res&
    Dim curidx&
    Dim keyname$, classname$
    Dim keylen&, classlen&
    Dim msg$
    Dim reserved&
    res = RegOpenKeyEx(HKEY_LOCAL_MACHINE, _
            "SYSTEM\CurrentControlSet\Control\Print\Printers", _
            0, KEY_READ, keyhandle)
    If res <> ERROR_SUCCESS Then
        MsgBox "Can't open key"
        Exit Sub
    End If
    Do
        keylen& = 2000
        classlen& = 2000
        keyname$ = String(keylen, 0)
        classname = String(classlen, 0)
        res = RegEnumKeyEx(keyhandle, curidx, keyname$, keylen, reserved, _
            classname$, classlen, ft)
        curidx = curidx + 1
        If res = ERROR_SUCCESS Then
            msg = msg & Left(keyname, keylen) + vbCrLf
        End If
    Loop While res = ERROR_SUCCESS
    Call RegCloseKey(keyhandle)
    MsgBox msg, 0, "Printers"
End Sub
```

The ShowPrinters routine searches the Windows Registry for available printers. The cmdShowPrinters_Click event procedure issues a call to the ShowPrinters routine. Figure 7-7 shows the results of the call to the ShowPrinters routine.

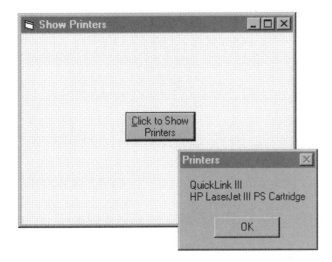

Figure 7-7. Running the code from the ListPrinters.vbp program to list available printers.

You can review and run the code from Figure 7-7 by opening the ListPrinters.vbp program in the Chapter7\Demos folder in the Practice Files.

It is certainly valuable to see other installed hardware on a system, such as modems, sound cards, and CD-ROMs. In the Chapter 7 Demos folder, there are further routines for performing these kinds of tasks in the Windows Registry. Please note the documentation to ensure with which operating systems they will run correctly.

Example 4: A Registry Search Utility

Searching the Registry for a specific value can help determine whether software has been installed or uninstalled properly, another familiar testing task. One of the limitations of the RegEdit utility is that although you can search for a specific value using the **Search** ➤ **Find** and **Search** ➤ **Find Next** menu items, you must continually select **Find Next** to find *all* instances and this can be tedious as well as time-consuming. To answer that problem, expert tester Lee Wallen created the RegFind utility. Written in Visual Basic, of course, it uses calls to Windows API routines to access the Registry but its sophistication goes beyond what we have covered in this chapter. It is presented on the Chapter7\Demos folder in the Practice Files with the full source code as a learning aid and as a useful utility to share (with some restrictions). Lee has graciously allowed it to be reproduced here. Figure 7-8 displays the RegFind utility.

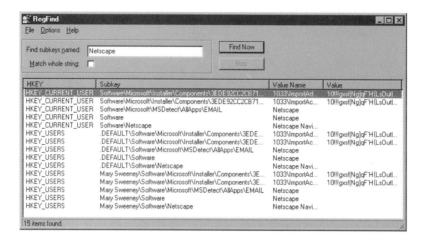

Figure 7-8. The RegFind utility will search the Registry for a specific value. The file to run it is RegFind.exe, located in the Practice Files of the Chapter7\Demos folder.

Calling Other DLL Procedures

You can call routines from other DLLs in a fashion similar to how you have called the Windows API routines in this chapter. DLLs can be created by application developers—usually in C++ but also in Visual Basic—and can contain many useful routines specific to the application you are testing. Check with the developers of the application software you are testing to see what, if any, DLLs are available. The developers will need to provide you with the basic information necessary to call the routines successfully and you can supplement that information with the knowledge gained in previous sections of this chapter to help you determine the correct way to call them using Visual Basic.

EXERCISE 7-2.

USING ADVANCED API CALLS

In Exercise 7-2, you will write a Wrapper function for a Windows API routine. You will open a template that contains the code to list the available printers on a system. You will then rewrite the code so that it is called from a function contained in a Standard module. Finally, you will write the code to place the results into a list box and display it.

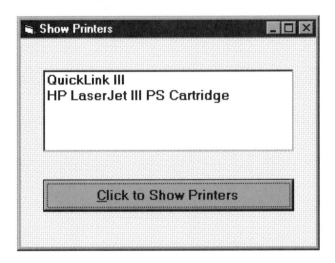

This is how your program will look when complete.

Follow These Steps to Write the Code

1. Open the file **Chapter7\Exercises7_2\ListPrintersTempl.vbp**. This is a working program that will list the available printers into a Message box. It already contains a Command button named cmdShowPrinters and the code to access the Windows Registry in order to retrieve a list of the available printers on the system. In the following steps, you will wrap the existing code inside a general function and place this function inside a Standard module. This will make the code more reusable.

2. Add a list box control just above the cmdShowPrinters Command button for the form and change its name to **LstPrinters**. Change the Height property of the LstPrinters list box to about **1500** and the Width property to about **4000**.

3. Create a new Standard module and name it **RegistryRoutines**.

4. Add a new, empty function into the new Standard module you have created with the name ShowPrinters as in the following:

```
Public Function ShowPrinters() As Variant

End Sub
```

5. Select all of the code within the cmdShowPrinters_Click event handler (do not cut the Sub cmdShowPrinters_Click() and End Sub lines) and leave the empty container of the event handler. Paste this code into the Show-Printers function (created in the step 4) in the Registry Routines Standard module.

6. Cut all of the declarations at the top of the Form module and paste them into the top of the Standard module. You have basically gutted your Form module's code so the only code remaining should be the empty CmdShowPrinters_Click() event procedure (and perhaps a few comments). The remaining code in the Form module should look like this:

```
Option Explicit
Private Sub cmdShowPrinters_Click()

End Sub
```

7. Place the following code into the cmdShowPrinters_Click() event procedure:

```
Dim iCount As Integer
Dim astrPrinterArray() As String   'create an array to hold results from the
                                    'ShowPrinters function
astrPrinterArray = ShowPrinters
For iCount = 1 To UBound(astrPrinterArray)       'load the list box
    lstPrinters.AddItem astrPrinterArray(iCount)
Next iCount
```

8. You will have to modify a few lines in the ShowPrinters function now located in your Standard module in order to print the list of available printers into an array instead of calling the MsgBox function. To accomplish this, add the following array declaration after the other Dim statements within the ShowPrinters function:

```
Dim aretArray() As String   'creates a dynamic array
```

9. Find the following line of code within the ShowPrinters function:

```
msg = msg & Left(keyname, keylen) + vbCrLf
```

Delete this line and replace it with the following:

```
ReDim Preserve aretArray(1 To curidx) As String
aretArray(curidx) = Left(keyname, keylen)
```

10. Find the following line of code within the ShowPrinters function:

```
MsgBox msg, 0, "Printers"
```

Delete this line and replace it with the following:

```
ShowPrinters = aretArray   'return the Array
```

11. Locate the `Exit Sub` line of code and change it to `Exit Function`.

12. Run the program and debug as necessary. You should see a list of currently available printers on your system.

> **NOTE** *For this to work, you will need to have some printers available. If you see an empty list box, check to be sure you have printers installed by looking at the system Control Panel.*

13. Compare your answer to the answer in the Chapter7\Exercises7_2\Answer folder in the Practice Files.

14. Name and save your files. You will have three files: the Form file (.frm), the Standard module file (.bas), and the Project file (.vbp).

Additional Work

You can import the two Standard modules, mGetFileVersion.bas and mGetRegistryValues.bas, from the Demos folder into your new project as well. Explore these files; they contain the code to use many other Windows API routines. Try to write calls to these routines.

> **TIP** *There is a lot of good code in the Demos folder for this chapter that you can use to get started writing calls to different Windows API routines.*

❏ Are any calls to DLL routines declared in a Standard module (supporting ease of maintenance, clarity, readability, and reuse)?

❏ Are calls to complex API routines wrapped inside other functions or subroutines for easy reusability?

Chapter 7 Review

- Describe the Windows API libraries and explain how these libraries can be useful to a tester.
  See pages 211–215.

- List some Windows APIs that may be valuable to a testing project.
  See page 216.

- What are the important differences between Visual Basic and C strings and why does it matter?
  See pages 231–234.

- Where can you go to find out how to precisely specify a Windows API routine to use in your automation tests?
  See pages 217–218.

- What is a wrapper routine? Why is it important on an automated testing project?
  See page 237.

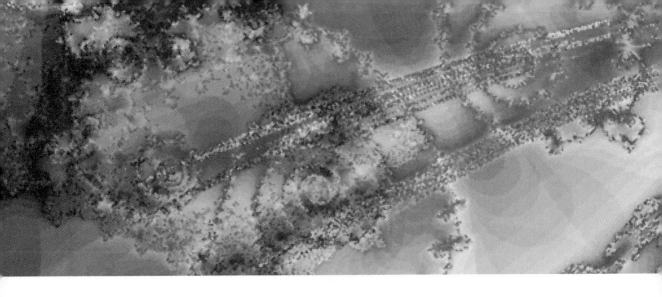

Part Four

Advanced Topics in Automated Test Scripting

CHAPTER 8

Introduction to Database Testing

The testing of software applications usually includes accessing and verifying data of some kind. This is true of any kind of software application you can think of these days, including, of course, Web applications. In fact, out of necessity, more focus is being placed these days on end-to-end testing of large software applications. *End-to-end testing* traces the flow of information and any bugs encountered from the user of the system, the client, all the way through to any data accessed and then back again to the original client. Going through the entire system may include passing through multiple servers and accessing heterogeneous data stores. For example, a client system such as a browser on a home computer accesses an application stored on a Web server. This Web server, in turn, passes the client's request for information—say, a price on a product—to a database server. The database server returns the request back to the Web server, which, in turn, passes the information back to the client. Testing this kind of arrangement can be complex as the tester tries to determine the source of bugs in the system's multiple layers. It is important to be able to understand and work with of all types of data to be effective at end-to-end testing. This data can be stored in many ways—for example, spreadsheets, text files, and databases. Relational database management systems (DBMS) such as Oracle, SQL Server, Informix, Sybase, etc. are used to store data for large, client-server type systems. However, many applications include data from older, nonrelational database systems. Because of this exceedingly wide field of possible data sources, we will have to limit the focus in this chapter to data stored in ODBC-compliant databases.

Understanding data involves more than can be presented in one book. To be effective at database application testing, you will also need some database background—in other words, a thorough knowledge of database design and Structured Query Language (SQL) as well as practical training and experience with a database management system (DBMS).

Visual Basic can be a very functional means to access and verify data in an ODBC-compliant relational database in several ways. First, Visual Basic contains a number of useful tools to reference and view a database and even modify its structure and data. It can also be used to programmatically access data using a variety of data access methods. In this chapter, we will start by exploring the use of the Visual Database tools for data access and then use ADO (ActiveX Data Objects) programming to manipulate data in a SQL Server database.

NOTE *See the "ODBC and OLEDB" and "SQL" sidebars in Chapter 2.*

Objectives

By the end of this chapter, you will be able to:

- Use the Visual Database tools to access database components.

- Use the Visual Database tools' Query Builder window to execute some queries useful for testing.

- Use ADO code to open and access a database.

- Access the SQL Server SQL-DMO (Distributed Management Objects) library.

Database Application Testing Using the Visual Database Tools

Visual Basic 6 can be used to support database testing both with and without doing a lot coding. The tools that don't involve a lot of coding include the Data Form Wizard and the Visual Database tools. In Chapter 2, you learned how to use the Data Form Wizard to create a quick front end for a database. In this section, you will learn how to use the Visual Database Tools to access many types of databases and even to modify SQL Server databases. This will afford you a common way to access heterogeneous data so you can examine the state of the data and execute and test queries against it.

NOTE *The Visual Database tools available in the Visual Basic 6 Enterprise edition are also available in Visual InterDev, Microsoft Visual J++, and Microsoft Visual C++ 6 Enterprise editions.*

The Visual Database tools in Visual Basic are comprised of three major components: the Data View window, the Query builder, and the Data Environment designer.

Using the Data View Window

Creating a data link in the Data View window is an easy way to quickly set up a connection to a database. Once the database is open, you will be able to retrieve database objects like tables and views. This will give you a look at the structure of the database so that you can verify the presence of those same database objects. You will also be able to inspect the data and perform queries as mentioned earlier.

TO TRY THIS

1. Select the **View ➤ Data View Window** menu item or you can click the **Data View window** icon from the Standard toolbar.

2. Click on the **Add a New Data Link** icon within the Data View window.

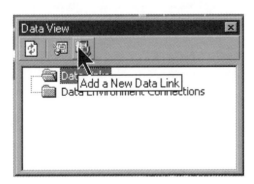

The **Data Link Properties** window appears with the **Data** tab displayed. From this window, you can select the OLE DB data provider for many different kinds of databases including Oracle and SQL Server. The most general one is the OLE DB data provider for ODBC databases, which will allow you to connect any ODBC database. (See Chapter 2 for a discussion of ODBC and OLE DB.)

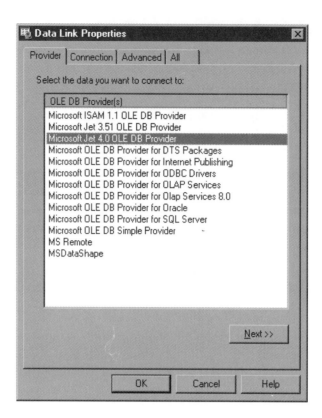

3. The Jet database providers allow us to connect to a Microsoft Access database. That is what we will select for this example since Visual Basic installs sample databases of this type (as long as you have selected that option when you installed Visual Basic). Select **Microsoft Jet 4.0 OLE DB provider**, then click **Next>>**. This takes you to the **Connection** tab of the same window (so you could have just clicked on the Connection tab also).

4. From the Connection tab, browse to the database you want to investigate. This part of the dialog will look different depending on what you selected in the previous Data tab. Since you selected a Jet provider, you are prompted only for an Admin account and password. By default, Access databases have an Admin account with no password so you can usually just specify the default here. For this example, you will link to the sample Northwind database located in the following file when Visual Basic installs: **C:\Program Files\Microsoft Visual Studio\VB98\NWIND.MDB**. You can browse to this file or type it directly.

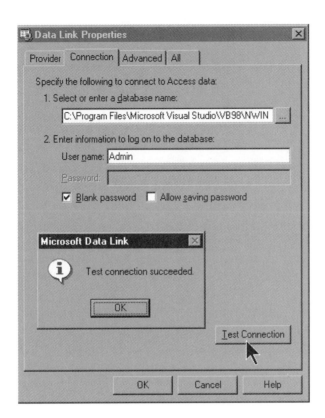

TIP *You can test the connection to the databases by clicking the* Test Connection *button on this same dialog. If the connection is successful, it will display a Message box indicating success. If not, you will have to check with your system administrator to determine the correct database and logon specifications required.*

5. From here, you can simply click **OK** and continue; however, there is one more important point to discuss on the **Advanced** tab of this dialog. By default, the Microsoft Access permissions are set to **Share Deny None** on this tab. This means that neither read nor write access can be denied to others and you also have read and write access to the database (as long as the username you specified in step 3 also has that capability). When testing, you don't usually want to modify data unless you are specifically adding test data to do so. My recommendation, in most cases, is to set your access to **Read** access on a production database. This will not allow you to change database values. If you change this value now, however, you won't be able to change data—which we are going to do in a later task. So, for now, you can leave the default access, **Share Deny None**. Click **OK** to close the dialog.

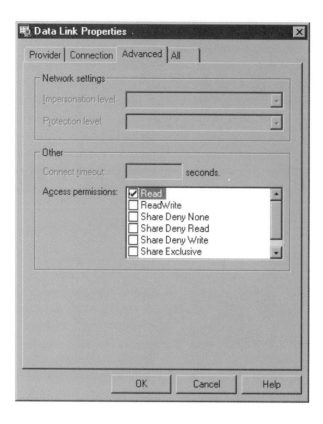

6. In the Data View window, expand the **Data Links** folder, expand the data link you just created, and then expand the **Tables** folder. You can now expand any table to see its list of fields (columns). Double-clicking the table will open a new window, the **Run table** window (which is referred to as the Query Builder window in Help but does not contain that name in its caption), and display the current contents of the table.

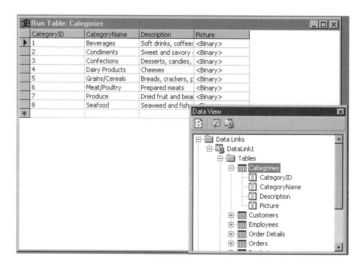

NOTE *Double-clicking a table opens the whole table. For a sample database, this action is okay; however, when accessing a very large table, this operation may take quite awhile. There are other kinds of queries that will return useful information but don't return all of the rows in the table. We will explore other queries practical to testing next.*

Using the Query Builder Window to Execute Database Queries

Creating a data link and investigating the database structure and contents as we have just done is a valuable first step in database access. You can follow pretty much all of the same steps as in the last section to access any ODBC database. This gives you a common way to access these databases so it isn't always necessary to learn each one of their individual DBMS software.

It is even more valuable to be able to execute queries against the database. The Run Table window that displays when double-clicking on a table in the Data Link window is really the Query Builder window cleverly disguised! Adding more panes to this same window will allow you to create and execute queries within it. There are quite a few valuable SQL queries for testing that will return information about the database. The next steps demonstrate how to use the Query Builder window to do just that using the data link created in the previous section.

TO TRY THIS

1. Make sure you have created the data link from the last section, "Using the Data View Window." Then click on the caption of the **Run Table** window (Query Builder) to make sure it has the focus.

NOTE *The Run Table window pops up by double-clicking on a table in the Data View window. If you closed the Run Table window earlier, simply click on any table from the Data View window.*

2. Select the **View ➢ Show Panes** menu item and select the **Diagram** and **SQL** panes. Now the Query Builder window is set to build and run SQL

statements. The Diagram pane of the Query Builder window displays the tables in the query and, if there is more than one table, any relationships between them. The SQL pane shows the current SQL statement. It can be modified to any valid SQL statement.

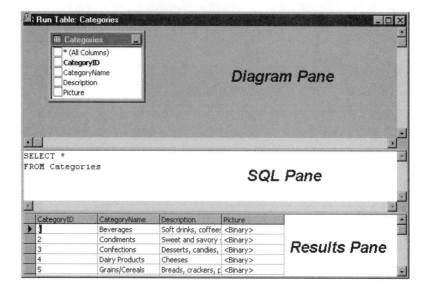

3. Modify the SQL statement in the SQL pane so that it reads:

```
Select Count(*) from Categories.
```

This statement will return the number of rows in the Categories table.

4. Right-click in the **Diagram** pane (or the **Results** pane) and select **Run** from the pop-up menu. The Results pane will show the answer to the query.

There are a number of SQL statements that are valuable for testing. The following are just a sample using the data in the Northwind database (to try them, repeat steps 3 and 4 from the preceding task).

- To return the most recently ordered items from the Orders table:

```
SELECT *
FROM Orders
WHERE orderdate =
        (SELECT MAX(orderdate)
                FROM orders)
```

- To find records with duplicate primary keys in a table (there are no such duplicate records in Northwind tables. However, this is a good check for other databases where referential integrity of the data is suspect):

```
SELECT employeeid
FROM employees
GROUP BY employeeid
HAVING COUNT(employeeid) > 1
```

- To find orphan records, that is, Orders that have no Employee assigned (again, this result should yield zero rows [no data] in the Northwind database):

```
SELECT e.EmployeeID, o.Orderid
FROM employees e RIGHT OUTER JOIN
    orders o ON e.employeeid = o.employeeid
WHERE e.employeeid IS NULL
```

- You can also drag tables and views from the Data View window and drop them onto the Diagram pane of the Query Builder window. This is a quick way to run predefined queries without knowing a lot of SQL. To give this a try, place your cursor on any table in the Data View window, click it once, drag it just over the Diagram pane of the Query Builder window, and let go. From there, you can modify the SQL statement if desired.

To get the most out of these tools, you should learn more about SQL. There are many excellent books on SQL, for further information on learning this language, see Appendix A: Resources and References.

Relational Database Objects Primer

If you are unfamiliar with relational databases, you will need to get up to speed on the basics before doing any significant amount of testing. There are courses available at community colleges and many good books that can help you get up to speed; Appendix A of this book has some good resources.

To get you started, here is a description of some of the major objects in a relational database:

Tables: All data in relational databases is stored in table format. The rows of the table represent one record's worth of data. For example, each row in a Customers table would contain information about a single customer. The columns of the table represent individual pieces of data about the customer, such as the customer's name, address, and so on.

Views: A view is an alternate way to look at data from one or more tables in the database. A view's contents are generated by a query and usually contain a subset of columns from one or more tables. A view is considered a virtual table because it can be treated as though it were a table even though it isn't. For example, a view can store the SQL code to find all customers in the customer's table who live in Washington. That information actually resides in the customer's table but since it is defined in a view, we can look at it in the view as though it is a table of its own. So, a view is really just a query that is stored and has a name.

Stored Procedures: A stored procedure allows the database programmer to write a set of SQL statements and give them a name so that they can be used over and over without having to rewrite them each time they are needed. Stored procedures can contain most any SQL statement and can be used to perform simple or complex database tasks.

The Data Environment Designer

You can do a lot of data interrogation using just the Query Builder window—it's quick and easy. The Visual Database tools also provide an alternate way to access databases visually through the use of the Data Environment designer. It is set up in much the same way but with some extra steps. The value of these extra steps is that unlike the data link, you get a Connection object that you can refer to in your Visual Basic code. You can programmatically manipulate the Connection object to perform database tasks. You can also create Command objects to attach to a connection and drag and drop those Command objects to create forms based on the data. Although these activities might be valuable in testing, they are, of course, largely useful for application software development. There are a number of ways to access databases programmatically in Visual Basic. To cover all of them may be confusing so I will focus on methods that are either simple or very powerful. The data link is a very simple method that does not require a lot of code. To perform programmatic access, I will use the ADO object library commands since this library provides great flexibility and power.

Testing Databases Using ActiveX Data Objects (ADO)

There is a real alphabet soup of methods to access databases in code. Microsoft started out with DAO (Data Access Objects), which is built primarily to access Microsoft's proprietary Jet database engine used by Microsoft Access. RDO

(Remote Data Objects) had, for a long time, been the method to access data in a client-server system. RDO provides commands to access multiple types of databases since it is really just a wrapper around the ODBC API. (I warned you this was an alphabet soup!)

ODBC was built to accommodate databases of varying types. There has been so much proprietary database access that businesses found it difficult to access all the data they needed in a single program. ODBC answered this by creating drivers for databases that allow the access of data in a common way. (See Chapter 2 for a discussion of ODBC.)

Since Microsoft had DAO and RDO working just great, why did they come up with something new like ADO? Actually, ADO itself is a wrapper around OLE DB (see Chapter 2). ODBC (and its wrapper RDO) only allows for data access across Windows databases. This does not address the need to access heterogeneous data across multiple platforms such as UNIX-based systems and other non-Windows operating systems. The intent of OLE DB is to allow data access across even these varying operating systems. So, this is effectively a step beyond ODBC towards multiple-platform, heterogeneous database systems.

For testers, ADO is a good choice for data access since it allows us to learn a single method to access a variety of databases.

With all of these acronyms, it's easy to get confused. The chart in Figure 8-1 summarizes the common Windows data access methods and how ADO compares to them.

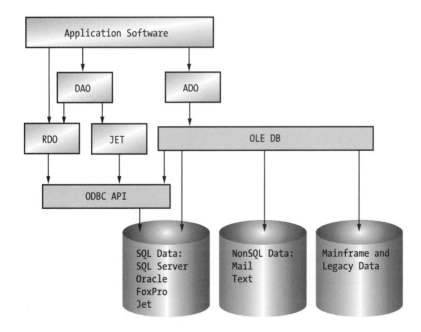

Figure 8-1. Comparison of Data Access methods for Windows programming.

Understanding ADO Architecture Basics

The ADO programming model has two important objects necessary to open a connection to a database and obtain a set of records: the Connection object and the Recordset object. ADO does have other objects, such as an optional Command object and an Error object. However, the only two that are really necessary to make a connection are the Connection and Recordset objects. The interesting thing about them is that they are not related hierarchically. You can have a Connection object that sets up a connection to a database, then creates sets of data—that is, Recordset objects—and attaches them to this connection. However, you can also just create a Recordset object and set it up with a connection when you create it. You can set it again at a later time to attach to a different connection. This allows for great flexibility in programming. If you find this confusing, don't worry, you can set up a connection to a database and then obtain a recordset from it very easily. You don't have to worry about disconnecting them unless you get to a point in programming in which you want to do so.

It's usually best to start with an example, but first, we will need to do some set up. To use the ADO library, you must set a reference to the Microsoft ActiveX Data Objects Library by selecting the **Project ➤ References** menu item and place a check in its box in the Project References dialog (Figure 8-2).

NOTE *Figure 8-2 shows a check in the box of the Microsoft ActiveX Data Objects 2.6 Library. Versions of the library available to you may vary depending on what is installed on your machine. Check the box with the highest-level version you have available. Earlier versions are there for backwards compatibility with applications that may use them.*

Once you have set the reference, you can view the ADO objects and their corresponding properties and methods (similar to what we did with the Microsoft Scripting Runtime library in Chapter 5) in the Object Browser (Figure 8-3).

NOTE *Press F2 in Design mode to get to the Object Browser, or* View ➤ Object Browser, *or click its icon on the Standard toolbar.*

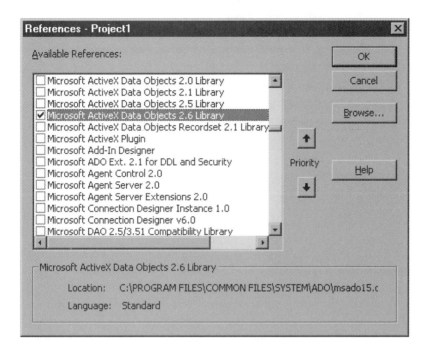

Figure 8-2. Setting a reference to the ADO library using the Project References dialog.

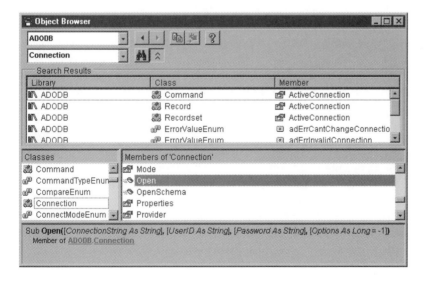

Figure 8-3. The ADO library.

Using the Connection Object

The Connection object is used to set up the information necessary to attach to a database. It has a number of properties used to specify this information, such as username and password, as well as, of course, the location of the database. The Open method of the Connection object is used to actually create the connection. There are two ways to connect to the database. One is to use a Data Source Name (DSN) and the other is to directly specify the database using a DSN-less connection.

NOTE *The Connection object has other uses as well. In addition to opening a connection, it can be used to execute SQL statements by using its Execute method. Once the connection is created, set, and open, you can specify a SQL statement to execute such as:*

```
cnn.execute _
    "Insert into categories (CategoryName) values ('Tester Products')"
```

Creating a Data Source Name (DSN)

Think of a Data Source Name as a kind of alias to a database. You create a DSN to preset the logon information for the database you want to access. You can include password and other access information in the DSN and give it a name of your choice. Then, in your Visual Basic code, you can reference this name and use it to logon to the database. Data Source Names can be created from the Control Panel. For Windows 95/98 systems, set up a DSN in the ODBC data sources area. When you double-click there, the dialogs do a good job of explaining how to set up the DSN. You will need to have an appropriate logon for the database as provided by your system administrator.

To create a DSN for a database:

1. Open your computer's Control Panel starting from the Windows TaskBar by selecting **Start** ➢ **Settings** ➢ **Control Panel**. In Windows 95/98, double-click on the **ODBC Data Sources** icon. In Windows 2000, select **Administrative Tools** and then **Data Sources** (ODBC).

2. There are three different kinds of DSNs to choose from: System, File, or User DSNs, depending on the visibility you need for this database. The System DSN is the most global; the User DSN is the least global. The dialog explains the options; choose whichever is most appropriate. If you can't decide, select **System**, then click **Add**. A list of database drivers will display in the next dialog.

3. Select a driver for the kind of database you want to use such as Oracle, SQL Server, or Access and click **Finish**. You will then be prompted to create a name for the DSN. You can make that up but it should be something you will remember such as NWindDSN.

4. If you have selected the Microsoft Access driver, you will need to browse to find the Access .mdb file. Other databases drivers will walk you through a series of forms you will need to examine to enter logon information for the database.

If you have set up the DSN correctly, you will see it appear in the list. You can then use the DSN in your code to simplify calls to the database. It is possible to create a DSN-less connection, however. We will explore both ways.

Accessing a Database Using a DSN

To open an ODBC-compliant database that has an available DSN, the connection can be set with the following two lines:

```
Dim MyConn As New ADODB.Connection
MyConn.Open "YourDSN", "Admin", ""
```

In this code, MyConn is created as an object variable of the Connection class. Then, the Open method of this new object is used to connect to the database. The first argument of the Open method, YourDSN, refers to a DSN that can be created through the Control Panel's ODBC settings (see the previous sidebar, "Creating a Data Source Name"). Usually, the developer will have already created this DSN so you will simply need to find out what it is. The second argument of the Connection object's Open method is where you specify the username to connect to the database—in this case, Admin. The third argument is the password to log onto this database; in this case, there is no password for the Admin account. (That probably won't always be the case!)

Accessing a Database without a DSN

It is possible in ADO to create a DSN-less connection by specifying all of the connection criteria when you set the Connection object. For example, the following code demonstrates opening a connection to the SQL Server sample database,

Northwind, using a DSN-less connection, and logging onto the SQL Server sa (system administrator) account, assuming there is no password:

```
Dim MyConn As New ADODB.Connection
MyConn.Open "Driver={SQL Server};Server=;Database=Northwind;UID=sa;PWD="
```

In order for this to work, you must have Microsoft SQL Server installed because when the Server argument is left blank as shown, the default is to look for a local server—in other words, a server on your machine. Otherwise, you must specify the name of a server you can access. In that case, you don't need SQL Server installed on your machine but you must have access to a SQL Server database installed on the server you are connecting to. If you want to use a trusted connection to SQL Server, which means logging on using your NT or Windows 2000 username and password, then you leave both the UID (user identification) and the PWD (password) arguments unset.

NOTE *Your SQL Server database administrator determines whether you can log onto SQL Server with a trusted connection or with a SQL Server connection (called* **SQL Server authentication***).*

Once the connection is established, our next step is to retrieve a set of records for testing.

Using the Recordset Object

The Recordset object can be used to issue a SQL statement to retrieve exactly what it sounds like: a set of records. Once you have a set of records, you can think of them like a card file of index cards: you can process them one-by-one and look up information in them. To get this set of records, we must first create the Recordset object variable and set it equal to a new, empty recordset:

```
Dim MyRs As ADODB.Recordset
Set MyRs = New ADODB.Recordset
```

Before retrieving the actual records for the recordset, you need to specify where the records will be processed—either on the client or the server. If you specify that you want to process on the client, you can save server resources so, in general, you will usually choose client-side processing. To set this, use the CursorLocation property:

```
MyRs.CursorLocation = adUseClient
```

You can also specify a cursor type. A *cursor* is essentially a pointer that points to the current record in a recordset. There are different kinds of cursors and depending on which you choose, you can specify how the data is retrieved. For example, you can choose a cursor that will allow you to see changes made by others, or not. Choices for cursors are:

Static—A fast cursor because you get a snapshot of the data as it exists at the moment you capture it. You will not get to see any additions or deletions to the data that other users may be making while you work.

Forward Only—This is the fastest cursor because it is a static cursor that can only go forward through the recordset. This cursor is appropriate for writing code to generate a report.

Dynamic—The slowest but most powerful cursor. You can move in any direction in the recordset and see all changes, additions, and deletions.

Keyset—Just like a dynamic cursor, you can move any direction in the recordset and see modifications made by other users to a particular record. However, you won't be able to see the addition of new rows to the data.

The cursor type will determine our ability to modify or view the data. For testing, you will be viewing data largely for verification rather than modification purposes; this allows you to choose a fast cursor. The static cursor is fast, even though it doesn't allow for viewing modifications performed by others. The ADO library provides four constants to access the four types of cursors: adOpenStatic, adOpenDynamic, adOpenForwardOnly, and adOpenKeyset. The following code sets the CursorType property of the MyRs recordset to a static cursor:

```
MyRs.CursorType = adOpenStatic
```

Now we can open the recordset. We use a SQL statement to determine the records to view. This SQL statement will retrieve all of the records from the Customers table in the database:

```
MyRs.Open "Select * from Customers", MyConn
```

Notice that the Connection object is an argument for the recordset's Open method. This is how you connect the Recordset object to the connection. Now we have a set of records to work with and from here on, we will use the MyRs Recordset object properties and methods to access this set of records. The next code sample shows a few of the properties and methods we can use to work with our recordset:

```
MyRs.MoveFirst 'moves to the first record
MyRS.MoveNext  'moves to the next record
Debug.print MyRs.RecordCount   'returns the # of records In the recordset:
Debug.print MyRs!Fieldname     'Will return the value of a field in the recordset
If MyRs.EOF then               'determine whether the cursor is at the end of the file
    MyRs.Close                 'close the recordset
Endif
```

The syntax for all of these properties and methods can be found by exploring the ADO type library in the Object Browser.

Now you can write code to test the database. Suppose that one test requirement is to determine that a certain number of rows exist in a table within the database. The code in Listing 8-1 will open the database, count the number of rows in a table, and determine whether or not the actual number of rows found is equivalent to what is expected.

 NOTE *The code in Listing 8-1 presumes the existence of the LogUtil.bas module. The code will not compile correctly without it. The full text of this project can be viewed and run from following file in the Practice files:* Chapter8\Demos\ADORecordVerif.vbp.

Listing 8-1. Testing the Northwind sample database by verifying row count in the Customers table.

```
Option Explicit
'****************************************************************
'* Northwind Test.
'* Verify that the expected number of records
'* in the Customers table, matches the actual number of records.
'* Dependencies: LogUtil.bas must be available
'* References: This project sets a reference to the Microsoft SQL-DMO object
'* library. It also sets a reference to the Microsoft scripting
'* run time library in order to perform the logging routines from
'* the logutil module.
'****************************************************************
Private Sub cmdShowResults_Click()
    ReadLog
End Sub

Private Sub Form_Load()
    Dim MyConn As New ADODB.Connection
    'MyConn.Open "NWindDSN", "sa", ""    'This line uses a DSN. This DSN must
                                        'be preset up to access the
                                        'Northwind sample Database on any SQL Server
    MyConn.Open "Driver={SQL Server};Server=;Database=Northwind;UID=sa;PWD="
            'The line above uses a DSN-less connection and
            'presumes you have a local server with SQL Server installed
            'If you can connect to a remote SQL Server, place its name after
            'the 'Server=' argument
    Dim MyRs As ADODB.Recordset
    Set MyRs = New ADODB.Recordset
    MyRs.CursorType = adOpenStatic
    MyRs.CursorLocation = adUseClient
    Const iEXPECTED As Integer = 91 'set number of expected items

    LogUtil.Appname = "Northwind DB Test"  'set Public application variable
    MyRs.Open "Select * from customers", MyConn
    If (Not (MyRs Is Nothing)) Then
        ' empty recordset?
        If (Not MyRs.EOF) Then
            MyRs.MoveFirst
        End If
```

```
      ' verify results
      If MyRs.recordcount <> iEXPECTED Then
          LogToFile "***Test Failed. Actual records: " & MyRs.recordcount & _
                    "; Expected records: " & iEXPECTED
      Else
          LogToFile _
              "Test Passed. Actual records: " & MyRs.recordcount & _
                    "; Expected records: " & iEXPECTED
      End If
   End If
End Sub
```

Notice that the logging of test results in Listing 8-1 is accomplished through the use of the Logging utilities module created back in Chapter 5. You can try this example by running the **ADORecordVerif.vbp** project file from the **Chapter8\Demos** folder.

Revisiting the ODBC Logon Form Template

In Chapter 2, I discussed how the many form templates and wizards provided by Visual Basic can be great learning tools. Now that you know a bit about accessing the ADO library and calling the Windows API routines (from Chapter 7), the code generated when you create a new form in a project from the ODBC Logon form template should be more intelligible. Listing 8-2 displays the code behind an ODBC Logon form.

Listing 8-2. The code generated when you add an ODBC Logon form from the template to your Visual Basic project.

```
Option Explicit
Private Declare Function SQLDataSources Lib "ODBC32.DLL" _
        (ByVal henv&, ByVal fDirection%, ByVal szDSN$, _
         ByVal cbDSNMax%, pcbDSN%, ByVal szDescription$, _
         ByVal cbDescriptionMax%, pcbDescription%) As Integer
Private Declare Function SQLAllocEnv% Lib "ODBC32.DLL" (env&)
Const SQL_SUCCESS As Long = 0
Const SQL_FETCH_NEXT As Long = 1


Private Sub Form_Load()
    GetDSNsAndDrivers
End Sub


Private Sub cmdCancel_Click()
```

```
    Unload Me
End Sub


Private Sub cmdOK_Click()
    Dim sConnect    As String
    Dim sADOConnect As String
    Dim sDAOConnect As String
    Dim sDSN        As String

    If cboDSNList.ListIndex > 0 Then
        sDSN = "DSN=" & cboDSNList.Text & ";"
    Else
        sConnect = sConnect & "Driver=" & cboDrivers.Text & ";"
        sConnect = sConnect & "Server=" & txtServer.Text & ";"
    End If


    sConnect = sConnect & "UID=" & txtUID.Text & ";"
    sConnect = sConnect & "PWD=" & txtPWD.Text & ";"

    If Len(txtDatabase.Text) > 0 Then
        sConnect = sConnect & "Database=" & txtDatabase.Text & ";"
    End If


    sADOConnect = "PROVIDER=MSDASQL;" & sDSN & sConnect
    sDAOConnect = "ODBC;" & sDSN & sConnect

    MsgBox _
    "To open an ADO Connection, use:" & vbCrLf _
        & "Set gConnection = New Connection" & vbCrLf & _
    "gConnection.Open """ & sADOConnect & """" & vbCrLf & vbCrLf & _
    "To open a DAO database object, use:" & vbCrLf & _
    "Set gDatabase = OpenDatabase(vbNullString, 0, 0, sDAOConnect)" & vbCrLf & _
    "Or to open an RDO Connection, use:" & vbCrLf & _
    "Set gRDOConnection = " & _
        "rdoEnvironments(0).OpenConnection(sDSN, rdDriverNoPrompt, 0, sConnect)"

    'ADO:
    'Set gConnection = New Connection
    'gConnection.Open sADOConnect
    'DAO:
    'Set gDatabase = OpenDatabase(vbNullString, 0, 0, sDAOConnect)
    'RDO:
    'Set gRDOConnection = _
        rdoEnvironments(0).OpenConnection(sDSN, rdDriverNoPrompt, 0, sConnect)
End Sub
```

```vb
Private Sub cboDSNList_Click()
    On Error Resume Next
    If cboDSNList.Text = "(None)" Then
        txtServer.Enabled = True
        cboDrivers.Enabled = True
    Else
        txtServer.Enabled = False
        cboDrivers.Enabled = False
    End If
End Sub

Sub GetDSNsAndDrivers()
    Dim i As Integer
    Dim sDSNItem As String * 1024
    Dim sDRVItem As String * 1024
    Dim sDSN As String
    Dim sDRV As String
    Dim iDSNLen As Integer
    Dim iDRVLen As Integer
    Dim lHenv As Long            'handle to the environment

    On Error Resume Next
    cboDSNList.AddItem "(None)"

    'get the DSNs
    If SQLAllocEnv(lHenv) <> -1 Then
        Do Until i <> SQL_SUCCESS
            sDSNItem = Space$(1024)
            sDRVItem = Space$(1024)
            i = SQLDataSources(lHenv, SQL_FETCH_NEXT, _
                              sDSNItem, 1024, iDSNLen, sDRVItem, 1024, iDRVLen)
            sDSN = Left$(sDSNItem, iDSNLen)
            sDRV = Left$(sDRVItem, iDRVLen)

If sDSN <> Space(iDSNLen) Then
                cboDSNList.AddItem sDSN
                cboDrivers.AddItem sDRV
            End If
        Loop
    End If
    'some additional code has been removed for this listing
    'see the ODBC logon form for the rest.
End Sub
```

When the ODBC Logon form is displayed, the Form_Load event runs and executes a call to the subroutine GetDSNsAndDrivers. If you examine this sub-routine, you will see it uses calls to Windows ODBC32.DLL API routines, SQLAllocEnv, and SQLDataSources to list all of the available DSNs and drivers. This is information you might want to include as setup information when running your tests since it may vary from system-to-system. The code in the cmdOK_Click event creates a connection string and has code that will allow you, the programmer, to choose between an ADO connection, a DAO connection, or an RDO connection by uncommenting the correct lines. The ADO code option can be used to open a DSN or DSN-less connection depending on the field values filled in on the form by the user. Figure 8-4 displays the ODBC Logon form.

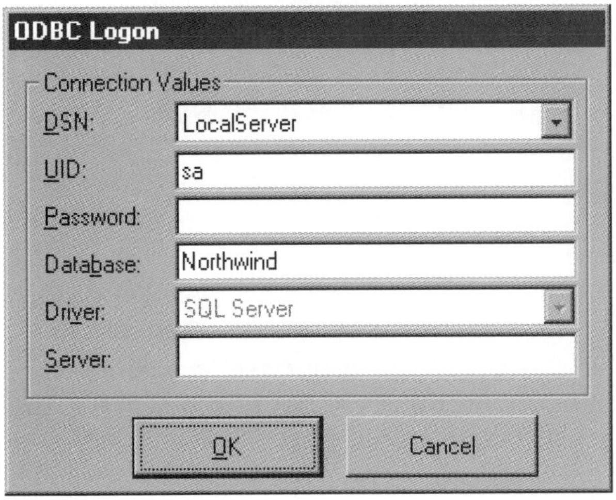

Figure 8-4. The ODBC Logon form generated by a form template.

I hope you have noticed that there is a lot of work being done here by the form template code, which you can copy and paste rather than writing it from scratch. The ODBC Logon form and its associated code can be modified to suit your needs for logging into a database.

Another way to let Visual Basic generate code for you is to use the Data Form Wizard. In Chapter 2, we used it to quickly connect to a database and to view data in a prebuilt form. The Data Form Wizard has an option to connect to remote ODBC databases and then produces an option to generate ADO code for the connection. If you select this ADO code option when using the wizard, then create the form and view the code behind it, you will find code to create the connection and Recordset objects. You will also find the code to move between records on a form and bind the data to those fields. If you need to do anything like this, this code is a good starting point. Listing 8-3 displays a portion of the code generated by this wizard for the Form_Load event.

Listing 8-3. A portion of the code generated from by the Data Form Wizard.

```
Dim db As Connection
Set db = New Connection
db.CursorLocation = adUseClient
db.Open
"PROVIDER=MSDASQL;driver={SQL Server};" & _
    "server=C343600-A;uid=sa;pwd=;database=Northwind;"

Set adoPrimaryRS = New Recordset
adoPrimaryRS.Open _
"select ProductID,ProductName,SupplierID,CategoryID, Unitprice from Products", _
                    db, adOpenStatic, adLockOptimistic
```

Testing SQL Server Databases Using COM

There's another way to get at the structure and data of a database and that is if the database exports a COM library. If it does, the database can also be accessed by setting a reference to it as we have done with other applications that export libraries, like Word and Excel. SQL Server since version 6 exports its COM architecture through a library called the SQL-DMO. (DMO stands for Distributed Management Objects.) SQL-DMO is a powerful and fast way to access SQL Server once you have become familiar with the basic library objects. In fact, SQL Server's own Enterprise Manager software, a front end to the DBMS itself, is written using SQL-DMO. Figure 8-5 shows setting a reference to the SQL-DMO library in the Project References dialog. Doing this will give you access to all of the SQL database objects and allow you to write code to connect to a SQL Server database.

There is another object library for SQL Server, SQL-NS. This is the Namespace library and includes objects that can be used to access wizards and dialogs from the SQL Server Enterprise Manager. Both the SQL-DMO and SQL-NS libraries install with SQL Server. The SQL-DMO COM object library is displayed in the Object Browser as shown in Figure 8-6.

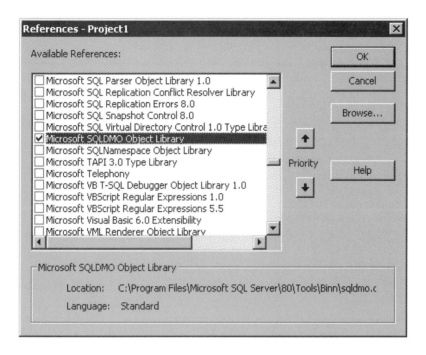

Figure 8-5. Setting a reference to SQL Server's SQL-DMO library.

Figure 8-6. The SQL Server DMO object library.

Listing 8-4 accesses a SQL Server using the COM objects exposed by the SQL-DMO library.

Listing 8-4. Code to access a SQL Server and list all of its available databases in a list box.

```
Option Explicit
'The following code was written by Walt Rischer, President of the NW VBDA
' (Visual Basic Developer's association)
Private oServer As SQLDMO.SQLServer   'Create the Server object:
Private Const TestServer = null   'set this value to your actual server
                                  'or It will default to the local server
Private Sub Form_Load()
    Dim oDB As SQLDMO.Database
    Set oServer = New SQLDMO.SQLServer
    oServer.Connect TestServer, "sa"   'connect to the server as system admin
    lstDatabases.Clear
    For Each oDB In oServer.Databases
      lstDatabases.AddItem oDB.Name     'list all databases on the server
    Next
End Sub
```

In Listing 8-4, an object is created to connect to a specific server in the Form_Load subroutine. The code can then access any of the exposed properties and methods of the object. The code above uses the databases collection in the connected SQL Server and loops through it, loading each database name (using the Name property) into a list control.

Listing 8-5 calls the PingSQLServerVersion method of the Server object to determine the version of the SQL Server installation.

Listing 8-5. Code to interrogate a SQL Server and return its version using the SQL-DMO object library.

```
Private Sub cmdPingIt_Click()
'this routine uses the PingSQLServerVersion function to determine
'The correct version of the server.
'Author: Walt Rischer
Dim strMessage As String
Dim lVersion As Long
```

```
On Error GoTo errhand  'error handling
    lVersion = oServer.PingSQLServerVersion(SERVER, "sa")
    Select Case lVersion
        Case SQLDMOSQLVer_80  'this constant only exists in SQL 2000;
                              'if using SQL 7 or earlier version you must comment out
            strMessage = "SQL Server 2000"
        Case SQLDMOSQLVer_70
            strMessage = "SQL Server 7.0"
        Case SQLDMOSQLVer_65
            strMessage = "SQL Server 6.5"
        Case Else
            strMessage = "unable to determine version " & lVersion
    End Select
    MsgBox strMessage
Exit Sub
errhand:
    MsgBox "Unable to connect to server " & vbCrLf & _
              " Error: " & Err.Number & " " & Err.Description
End Sub
```

In the procedure cmdPingIt_Click (Listing 8-5), the PingSQLServerVersion method of the Server object is used to return the current version of the Server. This application is a simple utility for returning general information about a SQL Server, its available databases, and its version—useful information on a test project. It's a good start on a utility you may want to customize for your own SQL Server test project. You can access this utility in the Chapter 8 Practice file by opening the project Chapter8\Demos\SQLServerInterface.vbp.

Figure 8-7 shows the main form of the utility using the code in Listings 8-2 and 8-3.

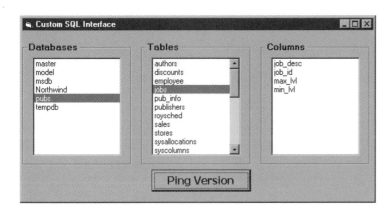

Figure 8-7. Walt Rischer's simple SQL-DMO utility.

Does all of this seem like a lot of coding work? What are the advantages to accessing a database using ADO or COM libraries like the SQL-DMO, especially when using the Visual Database tools is fast and easy? Using the Visual Database tools is easy but must be performed manually. Once you have written the code to test a database using ADO or the COM libraries, you can use the code again and again. With code, the value is that you may only have to occasionally change a few values, such as table names or expected row counts, and then run it without taking the time to do manual investigation.

Using the SQL-DMO and other COM object libraries effectively requires a little more knowledge of the structure of COM including classes and collections. I will cover this in greater detail in Chapter 9.

The Many Ways to Test Databases Using Visual Basic

So far, we have seen that we can use the Visual Database tools, the ADO library, and in some cases, COM libraries to access databases for testing purposes. I chose to present the ADO library because of its advantages in accessing data of all types but you could also choose to use DAO or RDO to access databases from within Visual Basic. It is also possible to use the ODBC32.DLL library to write code to test a database as we saw in the ODBC Logon form template code. Writing code to access the ODBC32.DLL would definitely require advanced programming skills.

Yet another way to test a database programmatically is to access the API provided specifically for that database by the developers. Not *every* application has its own set of API, but many times, they do. You will have to check with your application's developers to determine if such API exist. This would also likely require more advanced programming skills.

EXERCISE 8-1.

QUERYING A DATABASE USING VISUAL DATABASE TOOLS AND ADO

The purpose of Exercise 8-1 is to increase your familiarity with the Visual Database tools and ADO programming by comparing their use. First, you will create a connection to a database using a data link and execute a query using the Query Builder window. Then, you will write ADO code to accomplish a similar task. You will also modify the data in the database (this will work since the database you will connect to is a Microsoft Jet database) and then run your ADO code to verify the change.

Follow These Steps to Complete the Exercise

1. Start a new Visual Basic project.

2. Follow steps 1 through 4 from the previous section, "Using the Data View Window," in this chapter. You will be creating a data link to the **Microsoft Jet 4.0 OLE DB Provider** and specifying the **C:\Program Files\Microsoft Visual Studio\VB98\NWIND.MDB** database. When setting the Data Link properties from the Data Link Properties dialog, select the **Advanced** tab and click the **Read/Write** checkbox.

WARNING *You* **must** *select read/write capability because you will be adding data to the database later.*

3. In the Data View window, expand the **Data Links** folder, expand the data link you just created, and then expand the **Tables** folder.

4. Double-click the **Orders** table. The Query Builder window will be displayed. Click the **title bar** of this window to make sure it is selected.

5. Select the **View ➤ Show Panes** menu item and select the **Diagram** and **SQL** panes.

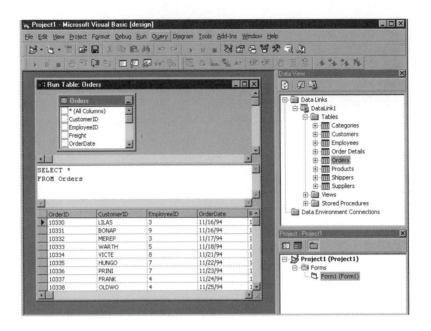

6. Next, you will add SQL code into the SQL pane to return the mostly
    recently ordered items in the database. To accomplish this in the SQL
    pane, erase the **Select * from Orders** command by highlighting and
    backspacing. In its place, type the following command exactly as shown
    here:

```
SELECT *
FROM Orders
WHERE orderdate =
        (SELECT MAX(orderdate)
     FROM orders)
```

> **NOTE** *When typing into the SQL pane, you need not use the "_"
> underscore character to continue lines. You are not typing Visual
> Basic code into the SQL pane, you are typing SQL code. SQL state-
> ments have different syntax—the line-continuation character is not
> required in SQL syntax.*

7. Right-click in the **SQL** pane and select **Run** from the pop-up menu as
    shown:

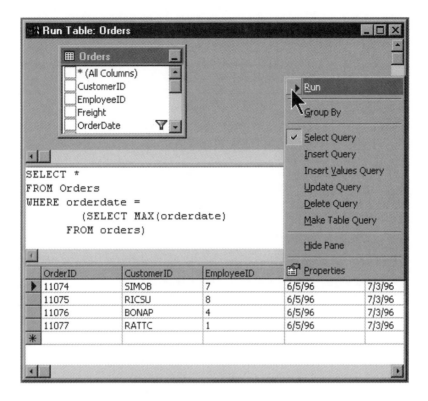

Take note of how many records and their values have been returned. Now we will write ADO code to execute the same statements programmatically.

NOTE *Do not close this window, you will return to it later in order to add data to the database.*

---

8. Select the **View ➤ Object** menu item from the Standard menu. This will display the default form for the project.

9. Add two buttons to the form. In the Properties window, change the following properties of these two new buttons as follows:

   • Name property: **cmdADO**; Caption property: **Click to Start ADO Test**

   • Name property: **cmdResults**; Caption property: **Click to View Test Results**

10. Open the Code window for the form and create the following two object variables:

```
Private cnnNW As adodb.Connection
Private rsMaxOrders As adodb.Recordset
```

11. Press **F5** or select the **Run ➤ Start** menu item. You will get the following compile error dialog:

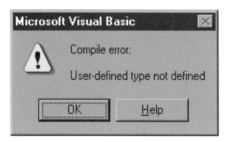

I wanted you to see this error at least once. You will receive this error anytime you try to use objects from a library for which you have not yet set a reference. Click **OK** to dismiss the error dialog.

12. Set the reference to the **Microsoft ActiveX Data Objects** library by selecting the **Project ➤ References** menu item and checking the appropriate box. This test will require some logging so add a reference to the **Microsoft Scripting Runtime library** also. Then click **OK** to close the dialog. (You can now try running the program again. Nothing much will happen since you have not done anything but you will not get the error message this time.) Return to the Code window for the remaining steps.

> **NOTE** *You will find several libraries that say "Microsoft ActiveX Data Objects" with different version numbers. Which to choose? Select the highest-level version; at this writing, this is the* Microsoft ActiveX Data Objects 2.6 library. *The others are there for compatibility with code that may have been written to use them. Since you are writing new code, select the highest library version available.*

13. Add the LogUtil Standard module you created in Chapter 5 Exercise 5-2 or you can add one that is already waiting for you in the Chapter8\Exercises folder by selecting the **Project ➤ Add Module** menu item. The **Add Module** dialog displays. Select the **Existing** tab, find the **LogUtil.bas** file, and double-click it to add it into your project.

14. Next, you will add code to the click-event of the cmdADO button to open a connection to the Microsoft NWIND sample database that installs with Visual Basic 6 in the Program Files\Microsoft Visual Studio\VB98 library. This sample database is a Jet database (.mdb) so the provider is Microsoft.Jet.OLEDB.4.0. You will also add code to open a recordset with the same SQL command we used to return the most recently ordered items in the database, as well as add code to log the number of records found to a log file.

If you want to try to accomplish this on your own, ignore the following code and use the previous chapter as a guide.

Or, you can type the following to the cmdADO_Click event:

```
Dim strRow As String
Dim fldHold As Variant
Appname = "Northwind DB (.mdb) "
cnnNW.Provider = "Microsoft.Jet.OLEDB.4.0"
cnnNW.ConnectionString = "C:\Program Files\Microsoft Visual Studio\VB98\NWIND.MDB"
cnnNW.Open

rsMaxOrders.Open "Select * from orders where orderdate = " & _
                 "(select max(orderdate) from orders)", cnnNW, adOpenStatic


rsMaxOrders.MoveFirst
LogToFile "Found the following number of records: " & rsMaxOrders.RecordCount
Do While Not rsMaxOrders.EOF
    For Each fldHold In rsMaxOrders.Fields
        strRow = strRow & fldHold & " " 'load a string with all fields in this row
    Next fldHold
    strRow = strRow & vbCrLf  'carriage return after each row
    rsMaxOrders.MoveNext      'move to the next row in the record set
Loop
LogToFile strRow              'log to the test results file
'clean up
rsMaxOrders.Close
cnnNW.Close

Print "Test complete!!"
LogToFile "Test Completed " & Now
cmdResults.Enabled = True
cmdADO.Enabled = False
```

15. Add the following line into the cmdResults_Click event so that the log file can be viewed when this button is clicked:

```
ReadLog
```

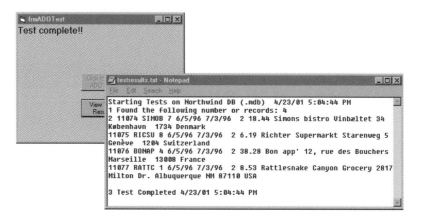

The answer for this code is located in Chapter8\Exercises\Answers\ ADOExercise8_1.vbp. Do not close out of Visual Basic, the next exercise continues on with the same files.

EXERCISE 8-2.

ADDING TEST DATA

In Exercise 8-2, you will continue your work with the Orders table in the North-wind database. You will add a new row to the Orders table using the Visual Database tools and then verify its existence by running the ADO code you created in Exercise 8-1. This exercise presumes you have accomplished Exercise 8-1.

Follow These Steps to Complete the Exercise

1. Switch back to the Query Builder window. (If you closed it, open the Data Link window by selecting the **View ➤ Data Link** menu item and expanding the data link and tables folders. You can then double-click on the **Orders** table to produce the Query Builder window once again. Use the **View ➤ Show Panes** menu item to show the SQL and Diagram panes.)

2. You will enter a new row into the Orders table using a SQL statement. This row will have an OrderDate column equal to the most recent order so it should show up in our query to return most recent orders. You may have to adjust the date depending on how current the data in your database is. In the following statement, the orderdate is 6/5/96; modify this date, if necessary, to make sure it's the same as the most recent order-date. Erase whatever value is in the SQL pane and type the following SQL Insert statement into the SQL pane:

```
INSERT INTO Orders
    (orderid, customerid, employeeid, orderdate, requireddate,
    shipvia)
VALUES (77777, 'BONAP', 7, '6/5/96', '7/3/96', 2)
```

3. Right-click in the **SQL** pane and select **Run** from the pop-up menu to execute this query. If you have any problems, check the syntax and try again. Once the query has successfully run, you will receive a message box saying, "1 row affected by last query." This means the new row was inserted correctly. Click **OK** to dismiss this message box.

4. Now run your own project (from Exercise 8-1 or you can run the answer from Chapter8\Exercises\Answers\ADOExercise8_1.vbp). When the Query Builder window has the focus, the Run menu item and toolbar button are disabled. To run the project first, click the **View** ➤ **Object** menu item to again view your Visual Basic form. You can now run the project by selecting **F5** or the **Run** ➤ **Start** menu item

5. Your test results should now show that another row qualifies.

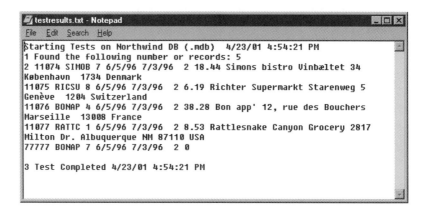

```
testresults.txt - Notepad                                    _ □ ×

File  Edit  Search  Help

Starting Tests on Northwind DB (.mdb)  4/23/01 4:54:21 PM
1 Found the following number or records: 5
2 11074 SIMOB 7 6/5/96 7/3/96  2 18.44 Simons bistro Vinbæltet 34
København  1734 Denmark
11075 RICSU 8 6/5/96 7/3/96  2 6.19 Richter Supermarkt Starenweg 5
Genève  1204 Switzerland
11076 BONAP 4 6/5/96 7/3/96  2 38.28 Bon app' 12, rue des Bouchers
Marseille  13008 France
11077 RATTC 1 6/5/96 7/3/96  2 8.53 Rattlesnake Canyon Grocery 2817
Milton Dr. Albuquerque NM 87110 USA
77777 BONAP 7 6/5/96 7/3/96  2 0

3 Test Completed 4/23/01 4:54:21 PM
```

EXERCISE 8-3.

TESTING USING SQL-DMO

In Exercise 8-3, you will access a SQL Server database using the SQL-DMO library.

 WARNING *Microsoft SQL Server 7 or 2000 or the client components must be installed (so that you may access another SQL Server across a network) before you can begin the exercise. If you do not have access to any SQL Server, you will not be able to perform this exercise.*

Follow These Steps to Complete the Exercise

1. Open the **Chapter8\Exercises\SQLServerInterface.vbp** file in the online Practice files.

2. Start the Visual Basic debugger by pressing **F8**. Review the code by stepping through it line-by-line with the debugger. As you step through the code, use your cursor to view the contents of the object variables and properties.

3. Open the **Object Browser** and select the **SQL-DMO** library. Look up the Server object and view its properties. Look up the databases and tables collections and read the available Help for these objects.

4. Add a new button anywhere on the form and name it cmdGetData.

5. Add the following code to display the number of rows in the Sales table in the Pubs database:

```
Private Sub cmdGetData_Click()
    MsgBox "Number of Sales in Pubs: " _
        & oServer.Databases("Pubs").Tables("Sales").Rows
End Sub
```

6. Compile, debug, and run your code. Save your files.

7. An answer to this exercise is in the project Chapter8\Exercises\Answer\SQL_DMO8_3.vbp.

To verify your answer, try connecting to the Pubs database via the Visual Database tools.

TESTER'S CHECKLIST

When testing a relational database:

❑ Use the Visual Database tools to quickly and easily connect to an ODBC-compliant database and visually verify data. Use ADO or SQL-DMO to connect to a database programmatically if you need to save and run automated scripts to test the database.

❑ Save queries you have found that find data problems. Start with those SQL queries the in section, "Using the Query Builder Window to Execute Database Queries" earlier in this chapter. These queries can be used programmatically by using ADO or SQL-DMO or they can be used within the Visual Database tools.

❑ Use the ODBC Logon form template to quickly perform database connection tasks. Remember, you can copy and paste the code from this form for your own use. The Data Form Wizard also generates code for quick database access.

❑ Become proficient at database design and SQL.

Chapter 8 Review

- Describe how the Visual Database tools can be used to support testing of a database application.
  See page 256.

- List two ways to access a database using Visual Basic code.
  See pages 264 and 278.

- Explain the difference between accessing a database via SQL-DMO and ADO.
  See pages 264–282.

- List the steps to connect to a database using the SQL-DMO.
  See pages 278–282.

- List the steps to connect to a database using ADO.
  See pages 269–272.

CHAPTER 9

Introduction to Testing COM Components

The best way to learn ActiveX technology is not to initially deal separately with each type of ActiveX component, but instead to first understand thoroughly the core COM technology.

—Dan Appleman
Developing COM/ActiveX Components with Visual Basic 6

> **NOTE** *The "COM Components and DCOM" section of this chapter was written by Walt Ritscher. Walt is a lecturer, trainer, and developer who is well versed in a wide variety of software tools, including Visual Basic, ASP, and, most recently, .NET. As a senior instructor at Bellevue Community College, he teaches an assortment of COM and programming courses. Walt has collaborated on software projects both large and small and currently works on developing .NET training courses and materials. He is also the founder and president of the Visual Basic Developers Association (VBDA), the largest VB group in the United States.*

The Common Object Model (COM) is the system that Microsoft has created for defining software objects that can interact with one another. This model now proliferates throughout Windows software. As testers of Windows applications, we will be operating under this architecture for a long time; even when the new DotNet (see Chapter 11) architecture becomes fully adopted, the testing community will need to understand and test COM objects for existing applications and for interoperability of the new with the old. That's just part of the testing game. In this chapter, we will explore COM more formally, discussing its key components such as classes and collections. You will learn not only how to access them for testing but also how to create and use them for your own purposes. To really be successful using and testing COM, you will want to study further. Some excellent resources for doing so are listed in Appendix A: Resources and References.

Objectives

By the end of this chapter, you will be able to:

- Understand the basics of the Microsoft Component Object Model.

- Create a Class module containing testing utilities.

- Create a simple COM Object library for use in testing projects.

- Understand the basics of working with and testing collections.

- Set a reference to a COM object and test some of its properties and methods using Visual Basic code.

COM Basics

COM builds software in terms of objects and interfaces to them so that other languages or systems can use these objects. Microsoft calls this process automation. We have already used COM libraries many times; the Microsoft Scripting runtime, the ADO Object library, and the SQL-DMO Object library are all examples. Now we will explore the core concepts in order to test COM objects and also to create our own.

When I introduced the idea of an object back in Chapters 2 and 3, I said that an object could be defined by its properties, methods and events. The COM concept embraces that idea on a larger scale. Essentially, COM allows the developer to model an application after the real world using objects that have properties, methods, and events. The objects we have been using—for example, the File System object we used in Chapter 5 and the Database object we used in Chapter 8 —exist in libraries that are hierarchical and contain many classes of objects within objects. In COM, objects can contain other objects in much the same way as things in the real world. For example, a house is an object and within that house are rooms that can be considered objects. Within those rooms are furnishings that also can be considered objects. Similarly, within a Database object there are Table objects and within these Table objects there are Field objects. So, COM allows us to work with multiple objects in a structured way. Figure 9-1 shows the simple hierarchy of a real-world House object alongside the hierarchy of a Database object and some of the objects it might contain.

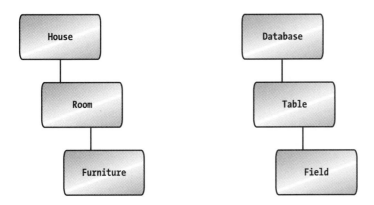

Figure 9-1. A comparison of a Database object and a House object demonstrating that software objects are hierarchical in nature, just as many real-world objects are.

Understanding COM Classes

Using our last real-world example, we know that a house contains rooms. In COM language, we would say that a House object contains Room objects. We also know that there is usually going to be more than just one room in any house. But what does it mean to *be* a room? In the real world, we know what it means for an object to be called a room because we have been in many of them. However, if we want to create a software representation of something like a room, then we must describe to the computer precisely what that means. We can start with the fact that a room must have at least three walls, a floor, and a ceiling. If we set up these requirements, we are setting up the properties of a room, that is, what makes a room a room. If we do something like this with software objects, in software terms, we're setting up the properties for the Room class. The American Heritage Dictionary defines *class* as "a set, collection, group, or configuration containing members regarded as having certain attributes or traits in common." When we set up a software class, we describe the common attributes and traits of the objects that class represents using properties, methods, and events. Just like there are classes of objects in the real world (such as the class of animals called mammals and the class of water-dwelling life forms called fish), there are classes of objects in COM.

Figure 9-2 shows our house and database, each with a few representative properties that define its attributes and traits.

Think of a class as a template for how an object belonging to that class will look and behave. It's like the blueprint for the house we have been discussing. The blueprint is not the house; it simply defines its characteristics. When you create the house, you are creating an object, or *instance,* of the House class. With one set of blueprints, you can build many actual houses—just look at all of the McDonald's franchises around and you are seeing instances of the McDonald's Franchise class!

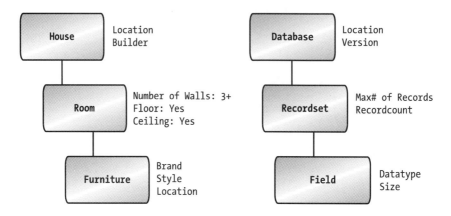

Figure 9-2. The House and Database objects with corresponding properties.

Understanding COM Collections

COM also includes the notion of *collections* of objects, which allows us to create, manipulate, access, and manage objects in a group. We have already worked with some collections; for example, when we investigated the SQL-DMO library in Chapter 8, we saw a database collection within the Server object. We were able to access this collection of databases and find out the names of each database that existed on the SQL Server and then we printed those names into a list box. Programmers can also create useful collections specific to an application. For example, a business application may deal with an Invoice object for customer sales. In such a system, each invoice could be created as an individual object and accessed in that way. Additionally, COM also allows us to create a group of these objects, for example, an Invoices collection. We can easily perform functions on the entire group such as totaling all of the invoices and printing that value. Working with collections of objects can be a much easier way to perform operations that must be done to each and every item in the group or to the group as a whole. It is a handy way to work with sets of objects just as we do in the real world.

For example, using our house analogy, a real-estate development company might consider all of its houses part of a Houses collection. Treating these objects as members of a collection can make it easier to access and retrieve information about the houses as a group, such as how many houses there are and the total number of employees assigned to each. There can also be collections within collections. Within a house, which is, itself, part of a collection, there can be a Rooms collection and within each room, a Furniture collection. So, our earlier diagrams (Figures 9-1 and 9-2) can represent either a single instance of a house, a room, and a piece of furniture, or the hierarchy of the collections of those objects. Figure 9-3 shows our House objects represented as part of a larger collection.

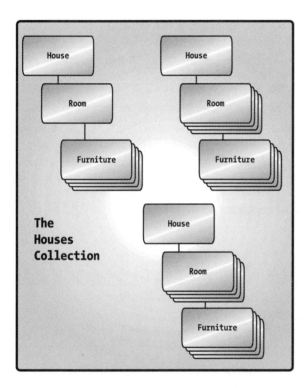

Figure 9-3. A representation of a collection of House objects.

Working with an Established COM Library

Now that you have a basic idea of objects, classes, and collections, it's time to get some actual experience. Perhaps the fastest way to get familiar with COM is to start accessing an established COM library such as that provided by Microsoft Excel. Excel exports a hierarchy of objects that are familiar to any user of spreadsheet software: worksheets, cells, ranges of cells, and so on. In Chapter 5, you learned how to set a reference to the Microsoft Scripting Library to perform file access. Once the reference to it was set, you were able to view the objects and methods of the Microsoft Scripting Library using the Object Browser. You can do the same for Microsoft Excel.

TO TRY THIS

To access the Microsoft Excel Object library, you must have Microsoft Excel installed on your computer. Then:

1. From the Project References dialog, set a reference to the Microsoft Excel Object library. Notice its location is in the Microsoft Office Folder under Program Files. Object Libraries usually have an .OLB extension, although, they aren't limited to this extension—for example, an .OCX file also represents a library.

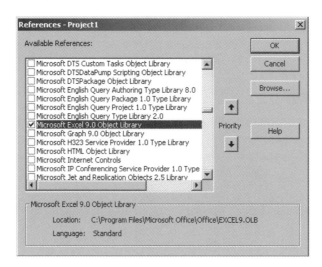

2. Display the Object Browser as shown below with the Excel library.

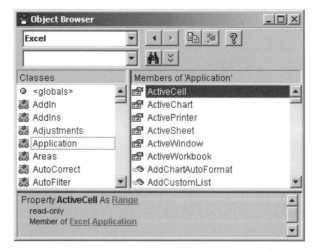

The next step is getting familiar with the objects and their corresponding properties and methods. If we were actually testing Excel, this would be easy enough using the Object Browser and the many books available on Excel automation. However, you may not always be fortunate enough to test a product that is so well established and documented. If the application you are testing exports COM objects, you must rely on the documentation provided by the developers and discover as much as you can about the Object library by using the Object Browser. This will be difficult since the Object Browser doesn't tell you things such as which properties must be set before others, unless there's Help provided. If the developers have been thorough, you will have access to Help on the objects, since Help can be coded into the application during development.

Microsoft Excel does have Help available for its library objects (but then, Excel is a major application and it should). Help won't necessarily always be available for a custom-created COM object. To find out if there is Help on an item in a library, select the item in the **Object Browser** and press **Shift-F1** (or you can click the **question-mark** (**?**) button in the Object Browser). If Help has been supplied the Help dialog will appear with information specific to the item you have selected. If Help is not available, then if you are lucky, the developers of the object have been thorough enough to send a message indicating that fact—if not, nothing happens when requesting Help on the item, no error message, nothing! If you are testing a custom-created COM object, checking to see if Help has been provided is one of the first things to look for. Not only because it can be very useful in helping you to understand the object and its functionality but also because it's a sign of thorough and conscientious coding.

TESTER'S TIP Documentation Expectations for Testers: *It is important to find all possible sources of documentation for the application you are testing. In a perfect world, there would be a very complete software specification that tells in great detail everything the application must be able to do. In reality, this is a rare occurrence. Even if there is a specification, it may not always be up-to-date or complete. Software developers are frequently under pressure and in a hurry so it's difficult to get complete information from them or from the other* stakeholders *(those people with a significant role in the application's development and success). So, it is up to the tester to find the information to create proper test cases in any way possible. A software specification is the first place to look but it is also necessary to look in other places if the answer isn't found there. For example, if the developer has provided Help on a COM object, then that is one important place to look for additional information on the intended functionality of that object. You might be wondering, why don't I just ask the developer? A good dialogue with the developer will answer questions but it is also important to be well informed so that the right questions can be asked and the valuable time of the developer is not wasted.*

Coding for COM

Once you have set the reference to an object's library and familiarized yourself with its available methods and properties, you can start to write code. To use the object's library, also called a COM component, you must declare an object variable, which creates an instance of the object. You will generally also create object variables for some lower-level objects within the library as well.

Listing 9-1 shows an example of how to access the Excel Application object and set some properties in order to interrogate an Excel document.

Listing 9-1. Code to create and set Excel objects.

```
On Error Resume Next    'ignore errors for now
Dim oTimeApp As Excel.Application
Dim oTimeWorkBook As Excel.Workbook
Set oTimeApp = GetObject(, "Excel.Application")
If Err.Number <> 0 Then 'If Excel is not running then
Set oTimeApp = CreateObject("Excel.Application") 'run it
End If
Err.Clear   ' Clear Err object in case error occurred.
On Error GoTo 0 'Turns off error handling
Set oTimeWorkBook = _
oTimeApp.Workbooks.Open(App.Path & "\timesheetexample.xls")
```

As the code in Listing 9-1 shows, Excel exports an Application object that you can reference to create a running instance of Excel or to connect to an existing one. The Application object is at the top of the Excel library hierarchy and is used to get a programmatic handle to Excel. This Application object is created by the following variable declaration:

```
Dim oTimeApp As Excel.Application
```

You can then set the oTimeApp Application object with the Set statement using either the GetObject method or the CreateObject method. The GetObject method can be used to access an instance of Excel that is already running:

```
Set oTimeApp = GetObject(, "Excel.Application") 'look for a running copy of Excel
```

If you use the CreateObject method to set your Excel Application object, you will launch a new instance of Excel:

```
Set oTimeApp = CreateObject("Excel.Application") 'run it
```

NOTE *The ability to create an object variable of type Excel.Application is only available because you previously set the reference to Excel's Object library. If you haven't set this reference, the above code will generate the Error message "Unrecognized data type." To set the reference, use the **Project ➢ References** dialog.*

Be sure to clean things up when you are done. Memory has been allocated to these objects. The following lines of code will free up assigned memory:

```
Set oTimeWorkBook = Nothing
Set oTimeApp = Nothing
```

Declaring Object Variables: Early versus Late Binding

There are two ways you may see object variables declared in Visual Basic. In this book, I have declared object variables and set their values in two statements:

```
Dim myobject as ObjectType
Set myobject = New ObjectType
```

There is another way to do it in just one line:

```
Dim myobject as New ObjectType
```

At first, the second way might seem easier since it is just one line and easier to type. But every time Visual Basic encounters a variable declared in this way, it must test whether or not an object reference has already been assigned to the variable. This is because the object is set with *late binding*. When two lines are used to declare the variable, the object is set immediately in a process called *early binding*. All you really need to know is that late binding can make the application run significantly slower. There are very few times when late binding is advisable. In general, write your own code with the early-binding syntax and, when testing, look to see if the developer's have done this as well. For more information on early and late binding, see the Visual Basic Help system.

TO TRY THIS

1. Create a new Visual Basic project. Save it immediately into your own practice directory with a name of your choosing.

2. Create a new Excel spreadsheet in the same directory where you saved the Visual Basic project (or you can move an existing spreadsheet into this directory).

3. Set a reference to the Microsoft Excel 9 Object library using the **Project ➤ References** dialog.

4. Add a new button to the default form. Change the Name and Caption properties of the button to the following:

    -   Name property: **cmdExcelDemo**

    -   Caption property: **Excel Automation demo**

5. Add the code in Listing 9-1 to the click-event of the button.

6. Change the last line of the code you just entered to include the full pathname of any Excel spreadsheet. (Or you can simply leave the line as is and use the TimeSheetDemo.xls file from the Chapter9\Practice Files folder. This file must be in the same directory as your Visual Basic project.) If you choose to change it, your new line will look something like this:

    ```
    Set oTimeWorkBook = _
    oTimeApp.Workbooks.Open("c:\MyPracticeFiles\MyExcelSpreadsheet.xls")
    ```

7. Add the following code to the click-event of the button just before the End Sub:

    ```
    MsgBox "Opened Excel successfully!"
    oTimeApp.Visible = True
    'clean up memory:
    Set oTimeWorkBook = Nothing
    Set oTimeApp = Nothing
    ```

8.   Run the program. You should see your spreadsheet displayed. Your Visual Basic program just created the necessary objects to launch Excel and display an existing spreadsheet. (Compare your work to the ExcelDemo.vbp project in the Chapter9/Demos/SimpleExcelDemo folder.)

To summarize, if you want to access a COM object exported by the application you're testing, set a reference to the Object library that contains the desired object, then create an object variable and set it. Once you have set the reference, you can then access the important properties and methods of the object. When you are done accessing the object, clean up all resources used in your code. Behind the scenes, a lot of memory has been allocated to the objects you used. You can release any memory resources that have been allocated for an object by using the Set statement to set it equal to the keyword Nothing.

You will test custom COM objects later in this chapter, but first, you will learn more about COM objects by creating one of your own.

 TESTER'S TIP *Developers may forget to clean up resources in their code. If this occurs, you will see errors such as "Out of Memory" occur. You may also see "File locked" errors because the object is holding onto a document like an Excel spreadsheet and has not released it before other code tries to access the same file! All of this just because the developer forgot to set objects equal to Nothing when done! It's easy to make these kinds of errors so it's something to look for when testing COM components. If you have access to source code, look to see that objects are properly released.*

Creating a Class

When you want to create a new object, you need to define what it means to be that object. Setting up a class is the way to define the characteristics of an object.

TO TRY THIS

1. Create a new standard Visual Basic application.

2. From the **Project** menu, select **Add Class Module**.

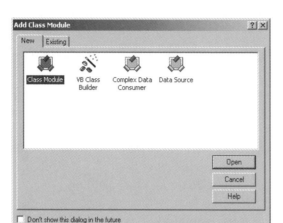

3. Double-click on the **Class Module** icon. Note that a new Class module icon now appears in your Project window. Also notice that a Code window for the new class opens.

4. In the Properties sheet for your new Class module, change the name of the Class module to **cTestClass**. You now have an empty class. In later steps, you will add properties to define the characteristics of this class.

TIP *Keep this new project for use in the following sections.*

Creating Simple Class Properties

Let's say you want to create a COM object for use in testing. What kinds of things would make up the properties of that object? The things that may change from test project to test project are candidates, such as the name of the application being tested and, perhaps, the name of the log file in which to record your test results. If you set these up as properties of your Test object, you can then create the Test object and set them when you need them.

The simplest way to create the properties of a class is to create a variable for each property you want to include in the class.

TO TRY THIS

1. Add a String variable called APPNAME to the Class module you just created by typing the following line of code into the Code window for the cTestClass module you created in the previous section:

```
Public APPNAME as String
```

2. Add a button to the default form in your project. Type the following into the click-event of the button:

```
Dim MyTestObject As cTestClass
Set MyTextObject = new cTestClass
MyTestObject.APPNAME = "My Application"
MsgBox "Application Name Is: " & MyTestObject.APPNAME
```

Did you notice as you typed MyTestObject in the third and fourth lines of the preceding code that Visual Basic recognized the MyTestObject object and dropped down a list of its properties? In this case, there is only one property, APPNAME. The point here is that even with just a single line inside of a Class module, you have created a simple class. And with only a few lines, you created an object of this class and accessed a property.

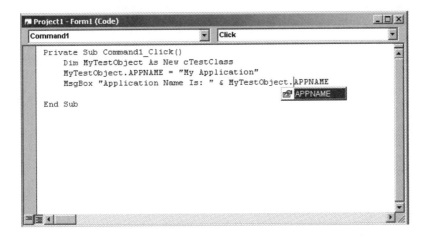

3. Run the program. A Message box will display with the value of the APPNAME property: "My Application".

4. Save this application. You will be prompted to provide a filename for the class as well as the form and project.

While this is a simple way to create a property, the problem with creating it in this way is that there is no protection for the property. In our case especially, the variable created in the preceding steps is a string variable and so can be set to anything, not necessarily the legitimate pathname to an application. The variable we have created can also be set multiple times for a single Test object. What if you wanted to set limits on the variable? In our case, we might want to restrict the property to be set only once at the start of a test in order to get the name of the application being tested and then make it a read-only variable that can't be changed. That way, the variable could not be mistakenly set to an incorrect value. There may be many other reasons for the creator of a class to restrict values of properties. For example, if there is an Age property in a Person class, the creator may want to limit the range of that value to something reasonable for human ages, such as a value between 0 and 125. If you want to protect a property value, you can use a special-purpose procedure called a property procedure.

Creating Class Properties Using Property Let and Property Get

Chapter 5 introduced a programming construct called a procedure. You learned that in general programming, there are two kinds of procedures: function procedures and subroutine procedures. In Visual Basic, there is another kind of procedure called a *property procedure*. The procedures Property Let and Property Get are used to create the properties of a class. They are special-purpose procedures allowing us to write code to manage setting the values for Private variables located inside a class. The advantage of using property procedures over Public variables for properties, is that property procedures allow us to set restrictions on the values that can be placed in properties and on how these properties can be used.

In the following code, the original variable APPNAME is changed to a Private scope instead of Public. (Its name is also changed slightly to mstrAPPNAME because we will continue to use APPNAME as the property name but in a different way.) When this variable is declared as a Public variable (as done in the last section), then its value could be easily changed outside the module in which it is created—which is both good and bad. It's good because then the value can be set properly when needed; however, its Public scope allows it to be accessed from anywhere in the application at anytime so it can be set to an invalid value (for a discussion on scope, see the "Procedure Scoping" section in Chapter 5). To solve this problem we could change the scope of the variable to Private. However, this makes its value inaccessible from outside the module it is created in and that might make it impossible to set its value when needed. The Property Let and Property Get procedures solve this problem by setting and retrieving the value of the variable, allowing you to add customized code to manage the contents of the variable. If you use APPNAME as the name of the Property Let procedure, you can continue to reference the property in your code by the name APPNAME. So, to set the value of the mstrAPPNAME variable, the user of the Class module will have to call the procedure `Property Let APPNAME` instead of directly setting the variable as shown in the following code:

```
Private mstrAPPNAME As String
Public Property Let APPNAME(ByVal strApp As String)
    mstrAPPNAME = strApp
End Property
```

The `Property Let APPNAME` procedure takes in a single string argument value and, in turn, sets mstrAPPNAME, a Private variable, equal to that value. In this code, there is no protection for the variable so it isn't easy to see the value added by creating this property procedure yet. If you want to add code to restrict the use of the variable, you can write conditional code that will not allow the variable to be set to a value you don't want. For example, the following change to the `Property Let APPNAME` procedure will allow it to be set only one time (added code is in bold):

```
Private mstrAPPNAME As String
Private bolFlag As Boolean

'Note: Boolean variables are Initialized to the value FALSE by default

Public Property Let APPNAME(ByVal strApp As String)
    If bolFlag = False Then
        mstrAPPNAME = strApp
        bolFlag = True
    End If
End Property
```

This code adds another Private variable, bolFlag, to the class but this variable will *not* be exported as a property unless we provide Property Let and Property Get procedures for it. The Private variable bolFlag is used only to determine whether or not the APPNAME property has previously been set and if so, does not allow it to be set again. Now our property APPNAME is protected in a way that it could not have been had we left this property a Public variable in this class.

In order to allow the user of this class to read the value of the APPNAME property, we will have to provide a Property Get procedure. The Property Get procedure is similar to a function procedure in both syntax and functionality. Its sole purpose is to retrieve the value of a Private variable of a class. Since it only retrieves a value, it is usually unnecessary to add any additional code other than the single line within the procedure body as shown here:

```
Public Property Get APPNAME() As String
    Set APPNAME = mstrAPPNAME
End Property
```

It is not necessary to do anything special to access these new procedures and that is intentional. The whole point of the special procedures for class properties is to allow you to access the properties in a way common to all other properties of objects used in Visual Basic while managing protection for them. So, the code you wrote in the previous "To Try This" to access the APPNAME property when it was a Public variable will still work.

TO TRY THIS

1. Use the project you created in the previous "To Try This." Comment out the declaration of the variable APPNAME in the Code window for the cTestClass and type in the following declarations:

    ```
    Private mstrAPPNAME As String
    Private bolCount As Boolean
    ```

2. After these declarations, add the following code into the class cTestClass Code window:

    ```
    Public Property Let APPNAME(ByVal strApp As String)
        If bolCount = False Then
            mstrAPPNAME = strApp
            bolCount = True
        End If
    End Property

    Public Property Get APPNAME() As String
        APPNAME = mstrAPPNAME
    End Property
    ```

3. Run the project. The code should run the same and display the value of the APPNAME property (which is really just exporting the value of the Private variable mstrAPPNAME).

4. To make sure the protective code you wrote allows the value of the APPNAME property to be set only once, add the following to the click-event of the button before the `End Sub`:

```
MyTestObject.APPNAME = "Another Application"
MsgBox "The new Application Name Is: " & MyTestObject.APPNAME
```

5. Run the project again. This time, after dismissing the first Message box with the name, you should see a second Message box that displays the contents of the APPNAME property. However, it will still read "My Application," since its contents were set the first time. The code you wrote to set the variable to a different name was not effective because the variable was protected by the code in the Property Set procedure.

 TIP *Use the Debugger to walk through this code to observe how and when the Property procedures are called and the value of mStrApp-name is set. Using the Debugger in this way can be really helpful to understanding how this all works. For more information on how to use the Debugger, see "The Debugger" section in Chapter 4.*

The class you have created in these examples is not very sophisticated or complete—it only has one property and no methods or events! Methods appropriate for this Test object might include the kinds of routines we have created for test utilities in Chapter 5. Candidates for routines might include logging routines and those for checking Windows API routines for system status, like memory state. Once you have determined what kinds of routines you would like to include in your own Test object, they can be implemented in your class as subroutines and functions. In Exercise 9-1, you will convert some of the routines created in earlier chapters into methods of your test class. Before you do this, however, we will explore how to make a class more generally available by converting it into an ActiveX component.

Converting a Class into an ActiveX Component

When a class is contained within a project (as it has been in all of our examples so far), it is directly accessible and usable to that project only. If you want to make this class available to other projects, you could, of course, import the Class module into those projects, as we have done with Form and Standard modules in previous chapters (see the "Adding Existing Modules to Projects" section in Chapter 5). However, with Class modules, there is a better way to accomplish this. You can convert the class into its own project, only this time, not a Standard EXE project but an ActiveX DLL or ActiveX EXE project. Both of these kinds of projects, when compiled, will create entries in the Windows System Registry. Placing an entry for a class in the Windows Registry allows it to be accessed by multiple applications simultaneously. In fact, this makes your class (now called an ActiveX component) a dynamic library file (as opposed to a static library file) and there are many benefits to this. When a class is created as an ActiveX component and registered, not only can this component be accessed by other applications but also these applications can access the component at run time rather than compile time. Accessing a component at run time helps to make the calling application executable smaller since it doesn't have to carry all of the code around with it in its own executable. (For a more detailed discussion on the differences and benefits of static versus dynamic library files, see the "Understanding Static and Dynamic Libraries" section in Chapter 7.) This arrangement also promotes reusability, one of our criteria for good code (see Chapter 1, the "Goals of Good Testing Software" section).

I mentioned that you could convert the class to either an ActiveX DLL or an ActiveX EXE project—what's the difference? Briefly, the ActiveX DLL component can run in the same process space as the application that calls it. The ActiveX EXE component, being a separate executable, runs in its own process space. (See the sidebar "What Is a Process" later in this chapter.) Running in the same process space is the fastest way to access ActiveX components. However, one limitation is that the component cannot run stand-alone (see the "COM Components and DCOM" section later in this chapter). We will focus on the ActiveX DLL for this discussion but there are advantages and disadvantages to each that bear further study if you plan to create your own. By the way ActiveX, in this case, is just another moniker for a COM object.

You can directly create an ActiveX DLL project by selecting the **ActiveX DLL** icon from the New Project dialog. This creates a new project with a single class and no Form or Standard modules. It is ready to add code for properties and methods to the class. Also, additional Class modules can be added to the project just as Microsoft Excel has multiple classes available as we saw when we looked at its library. You do not have to start with an ActiveX DLL or EXE project, though, to convert an existing class into an ActiveX component. You can create an

ActiveX DLL project from a Standard project provided it contains only Class modules by simply changing its type in the Project Properties dialog and then setting a few properties.

COM Terminology: Components, Libraries, and Objects

We are starting to bandy about a number of terms so its time to define what's what. Most everything in COM is some sort of an object. Because of this, it's appropriate to call a COM library an object and to consider each instance of a class an object. Although those might seem like very different things, recall the hierarchical nature of COM: the library is just a large object that contains other smaller objects. Then there is the term component; what does that mean? Essentially, the terms *COM component*, *COM library*, and *Object library* are synonyms intended to encompass a larger version of the term object. They all refer to the physical file, that is, the .EXE or .DLL file that can contain many classes of objects. Once an object is created as an .EXE or .DLL file, it is considered a COM or ActiveX component, which is just a large object. What about the term, ActiveX? *ActiveX* is the Microsoft brand name for all of the technologies that support COM on any level including Distributed COM (using COM over a network—see the "DCOM" section later in this chapter), Microsoft Transaction Server, COM+, and even ActiveX controls. In Microsoft literature the terms ActiveX and COM are frequently used interchangeably. However, industry-wide, most still call Microsoft's object technology, COM.

TO TRY THIS

Continuing with the same project used in our previous examples, follow these steps to convert the cTestClass class into an ActiveX component:

1. Make sure your project and all of its associated files for the Form and Class modules are saved into a location where you can easily locate them.

2. Remove the Form module from your project (ActiveX components cannot contain Form modules, only Class modules) by placing your cursor on it in the Project Explorer window and selecting **Remove** from the pop-up menu. Click **Yes** to "Save Changes?" when prompted (it will still ask this even if you have just saved it).

NOTE *Removing a form from a project does not delete it from your hard drive. It has been saved so it will still be there as an .frm file that can be imported into another project.*

3. Select the **Project ➤ Properties** menu item. The Project Properties dialog displays.

4. Make the following changes in the Project Properties dialog:

    • Change the Project Type to **ActiveX DLL**.

    • Change the Project Name to **cTestClassProj**. This will be the name of the Object library for this new component.

    • Change the Project Description to **Test Class Demo**. This will be the title of the component when you (eventually) select it from the Project References dialog from within another application.

    • Change the Startup object to **(None)**.

The Project Properties dialog should look like this:

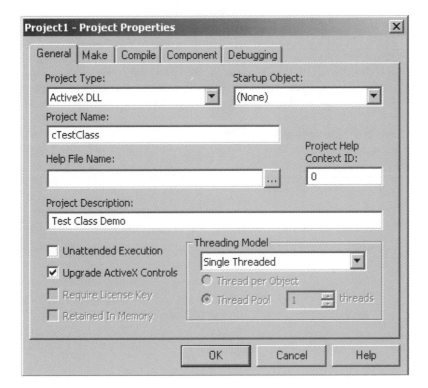

5. Click OK to close the Project Properties dialog.

NOTE *You will get a Message box indicating that the project Start mode has changed; this is simply informational, click* **OK** *to proceed.*

6. Now that this has been changed to an ActiveX DLL project, there is a new property added into the Properties window for the class: the Instancing property. Change the value of the **Instancing property** to **MultiUse**. This allows multiple instances of the class to be created once a reference to it has been set.

NOTE *The Instancing property actually has six possible values. Not all of them are available for every type of project. For example, only four are available for ActiveX DLL projects: Private, Public Not Creatable, MultiUse, and Global MultiUse. The Instancing property is very important to a class, as it specifies how the user of the class is allowed to use it. We have selected MultiUse because this value for the Instancing property will allow multiple applications to reference and use the class and will allow them to create multiple instances of this class as well. I highly recommend studying up on the Instancing property if you will be creating many ActiveX components of your own. For more information, see the "Instancing Property" section in Visual Basic Help.*

7. From the **File** menu, select the **Make** ProjectName.**DLL** menu item (the *ProjectName* will be whatever you saved it as earlier). You will be prompted to save the DLL. Save it into your own practice folder. Visual Basic compiles your module and notifies you if it finds any errors. If there are no errors, your DLL has been registered and recorded in the Windows Registry. (If there are errors, check your work against the Class-Demo.vbp file in the Chapter9\PracticeFiles folder.)

8. Save and close your project.

Once your ActiveX component has been successfully registered, you can find it in the Registry with an entry in the HKEY_CLASSES_ROOT hive (use the **RegEdit** from the **Start** ➤ **Run** menu item on the Windows Taskbar to open the Registry Editor). It will be registered under the project name cTestClassProj. To access your new DLL for use in a new project, you can create a new project and set a reference to the new component using the Project References dialog.

TO TRY THIS

NOTE *To accomplish this task, the previous "To Try This" examples must have been successfully completed.*

1. Create a new Visual Basic **Standard EXE** project.

2. Select the **Project ➤ References** menu item.

3. Check the checkbox next to the **Test Class Demo** item in the **Available References** list box. Click **OK** to close the Project References dialog. You can now explore this library using the Object Browser. The name of the library to select in the Object Browser is **cTestClassProj**.

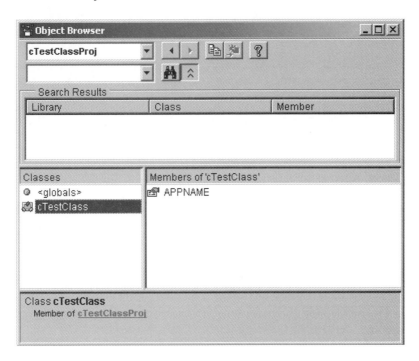

4. Now you can create an object of this class. Create a new button on the default form. Place the following code into the click-event of the button:

```
Private Sub Command1_Click()
    Dim myTestObj As cTestClass
    Set myTestObj = New cTestClass
    myTestObj.APPNAME = "My Appname"
    MsgBox "Hey it worked and here it is: " & myTestObj.APPNAME
End Sub
```

5. Run the program and click the button on the form. You should see the following Message box:

In the examples from this chapter so far, you have created a very simple and unsophisticated COM object. It's easy to make this object more useful by including more properties and methods for testing. In Exercise 9-1 you will create an ActiveX DLL (COM) component from a Standard project again, this time adding in a few useful methods and setting the stage to add many more of your own creation.

EXERCISE 9-1.

CREATING A TEST BED USING COM

In general, a tester is concerned with testing COM objects rather than creating them. However, as you go through the process of creating and using your own COM object, you gain valuable insight into how these objects actually work that can help you to develop effective test cases when testing other objects. It is also possible that you will occasionally find a need to create COM objects of your own that support the testing process. In previous chapters, you created and saved testing utilities into a Standard module. In Exercise 9-1, you will turn this Standard module into an ActiveX component and, in so doing, create a generic Test object for use on any testing project.

This exercise has four parts:

I.   Creating a New Class

II. Testing the New Class

III. Making an ActiveX (COM) DLL

IV. Using Your Test Utilities COM Object

Each part of this exercise builds on the previous part.

I. Creating a New Class

1. Create a new standard Visual Basic project.

2. Place your cursor in the Project window and right-click. Select **Add** ➤ **Class Module** from the pop-up menu.

3. Double-click on the **Class Module** template icon. Note that a new Class module icon now appears in your Project window. Also notice that a Code window for the new class opens.

4. In the Properties sheet for your new Class module, change the name of the Class module to **cLogUtilities**.

5. Right-click the Properties window again. This time, you will add an existing module into your project. Select **Add** ➤ **Module** and select the **Existing** tab.

6. Navigate to the Chapter9\Exercise9-1 folder. Double-click the file **LogUtil.bas** to import it into your project. You will now see the LogUtil Standard module file added into the Project window.

7. Review the code in the LogUtil Standard module. The LogUtil Standard module includes a full pathname to the file used for logging as referenced by a constant named LOGFILE. It also includes a reference to a constant called APPNAME in another module. When we convert this code to a class, we will change things so that these two constants become properties of the class. As properties, the application name and the log file name can then be changed as necessary by any project using the class. The subsequent steps will accomplish this.

8. Select and copy all the code in the **LogUtil.bas** Code window.

9. Switch to the cLogUtil Code window (you can do this by double-clicking the **cLogUtil** module in the Project Explorer window). Paste the code you copied from the LogUtil Code window into the cLogUtil Code window.

> **TIP** *To ensure you are in the right window, look at its caption. It will tell you which Code window you are working with.*

10. Select the **LogUtil** Standard module in the Code window. Right-click it and select **Remove** from the pop-up menu. If asked whether you want to save changes to it before removing, click **No**. You can now make changes manually to the class. However, we will let Visual Basic's Class Builder utility help us to do the conversion.

11. From the **Add-Ins** menu, select the **Add-Ins Manager**. The following dialog will appear:

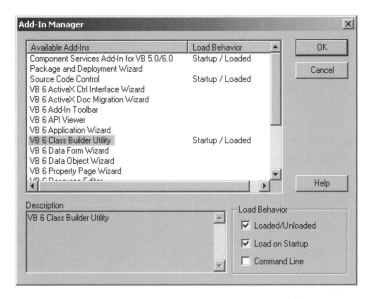

12. Select the **Class Builder Utility** and check the **Loaded/Unloaded** and **Load on Startup** checkboxes as shown. Click **OK** to close the dialog. Now the Class Builder utility will be added into the Add-Ins menu. You will use this utility to add two new properties to this class.

13. From the **Add-Ins** menu, select the **Class Builder Utility** menu item. (You may see a dialog warning you that the class was not initially created in the Class Builder utility; just click **OK** to bypass this warning. We can still add items such as properties to an existing class with this utility.) The Class Builder dialog is displayed.

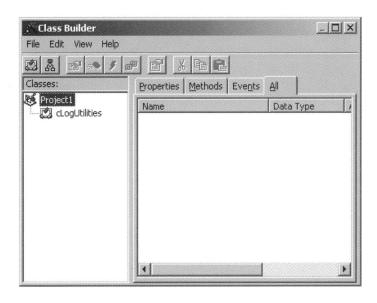

14. Select the **cLogUtil** class by clicking it. Click the **Methods** tab to display the routines listed in the Class module. In a Class module, the existing subroutines and functions are considered methods of the class.

15. Click the **Properties** tab. There are no Properties displayed. You will create two in the following steps.

16. Select the **File ➤ New ➤ Property** menu item. The Property Builder dialog displays:

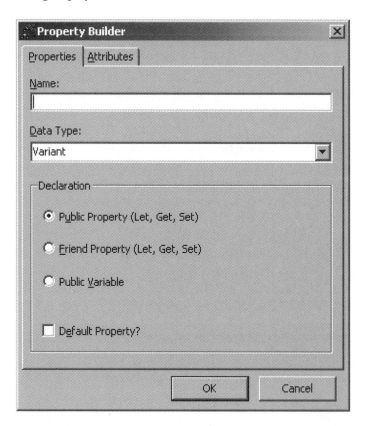

17. In the Property Builder dialog, type "**APPNAME**" in the Name text box. Select the String data type from the Data Type dropdown as shown. Leave the Declaration section with the **Public Property (Let, Get, Set)** option selected. The dialog should look like this:

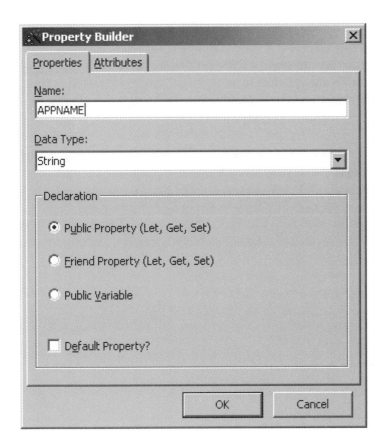

NOTE *Optionally, you can click on the **Attributes** tab of the Property Builder dialog and fill out a description of the property you are creating. Doing this will provide information that will be available to the user of the class in the Object Browser.*

18. Click **OK**. This will create a new property for the cLogUtilities class.

19. Repeat the steps 16 through 18 to create another new String property named **LOGFILE**.

20. Delete (or comment out) the original declaration of the Private Constant LOGFILE. You may also want to change the header comments to reflect the changes you have made.

21. Select **File ➤ Update Project** and then **File ➤ Exit** to close the Class Builder utility. (Click **Yes** if asked whether you want to update the project.)

The Class Builder utility has added new code to the cLogUtilities class Code window. Property Let and Property Get procedures have been added to the module for the two new properties. These properties can be modified to manage the values of the Private variables mvarAPPNAME and mvarLOGFILE. The code added for the two new properties is shown in Listing 9-2. As you can see, two new Private variables have been added along with their corresponding Property Let and Get procedures. This is similar to the code created previously in this chapter's "Creating Class Properties Using Property Let and Property Get" section. We could have written this code ourselves, but it is easier to let the Class Builder utility do it for us. This is especially useful when creating a significant number of properties.

Listing 9-2. Code added by the Class Builder utility when creating new properties.

```
Private mvarAPPNAME As String 'local copy
Private mvarLOGFILE As String 'local copy
Public Property Let LOGFILE(ByVal vData As String)
'used when assigning a value to the property, on the left side of an assignment.
'Syntax: X.LOGFILE = 5
    mvarLOGFILE = vData
End Property


Public Property Get LOGFILE() As String
'used when retrieving value of a property, on the right side of an assignment.
'Syntax: Debug.Print X.LOGFILE
    LOGFILE = mvarLOGFILE
End Property


Public Property Let APPNAME(ByVal vData As String)
'used when assigning a value to the property, on the left side of an assignment.
'Syntax: X.APPNAME = 5
    mvarAPPNAME = vData
End Property


Public Property Get APPNAME() As String
'used when retrieving value of a property, on the right side of an assignment.
'Syntax: Debug.Print X.APPNAME
    APPNAME = mvarAPPNAME
End Property
```

II. Testing the New Class

In this section, you will write code to access the APPNAME and LOGFILE properties and the LogToFile method just to verify that they are accessible and work properly.

1. Set a reference to the **Microsoft Scripting Runtime** library using the Project References dialog. (Select the **Project ➤ References** menu item.)

2. Switch to the form in the application. Create a button on the default form and place the following code in its click-event procedure:

```
Dim lg As cLogUtilities
Set lg = New cLogUtilities

lg.APPNAME = "Calc"
lg.LOGFILE = "c:\mylog.txt"

lg.LogToFile lg.Appname & ": This gets logged"
lg.ReadLog
```

This code creates an *instance*, in other words, a new object, of the cLogUtilities class. It then accesses two of the properties of the class and two of its methods. Now you can use the logging routines of this class when testing an application. You can also declare additional objects of the cLogUtilities class, allowing you to set different values for the log file and application name, if desired. There are even more advantages to using this class, as we will see once we convert it into a COM object.

3. Run the project and debug, as necessary. Save your work.

III. Making an ActiveX (COM) DLL

Converting your class into an ActiveX/COM DLL will allow you to link to this code dynamically as your test application runs. This saves compilation time and reduces the size of your executable. It also affords you the ability to easily set a reference to this code as you have done previously with the other COM objects, such as the Microsoft Scripting Run Time library and Microsoft Excel.

1. Right-click the default form in the Project Explorer window. Select **Save As** from the pop-up menu and save this form as **frmTest.frm**

> **NOTE** *You will use this form in a following section so remember where you have saved it!*

2. Remove the form from the project by right-clicking it in the Project Explorer window and selecting **Remove**.

3. Select the **Project** ➤ **Properties** menu item. The Project Properties dialog displays.

4. Make the following changes in the Project Properties dialog:

   • Change the Project Type to **ActiveX DLL**.

   • Change the Project Name to **cLogUtilitiesLib**.

   • Change the Project Description to **Test Utilities**.

   • Change the Startup object to **(None)**.

   The Project Properties window should look like the following graphic. Click **OK**.

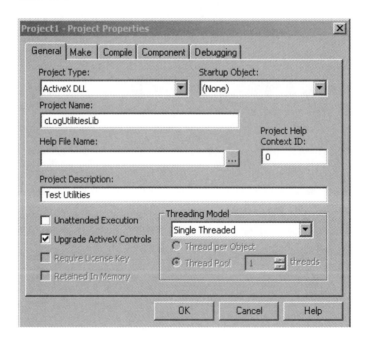

NOTE *You will get a Message box indicating that the project's Start mode has changed; this is just informational, click **OK** to proceed.*

5. Now that this has been changed to an ActiveX DLL project, there is a new property added into the Properties window for the class. Change the **Instancing** property to **MultiUse**. This allows multiple applications to access the component and multiple instances of the class to be created once a reference to it has been set.

6. From the **File** menu select the **Make cLogUtilitiesLib.DLL** menu item; the **Make Project** dialog displays. Save the DLL into your own folder (in general, DLLs are saved into the Windows System directory—you may save it there if desired).

7. Click **OK** to close the **Make Project** dialog. Visual Basic compiles your module and notifies you if it finds any errors. If there are no errors, your DLL has been registered and recorded in the Windows Registry. If there are errors, check your work against the answer in the Chapter9\Exercise9-1\Answer folder.

8. Close your cLogUtilitiesLib project. Save all items into your folder.

IV. Using Your Test Utilities COM Object

1. Start a new Visual Basic project. Delete the default form and add in the **frmTest.frm** form you saved and removed in Part Three of this exercise, "Making an ActiveX (COM) DLL," steps 1 and 2. (If you did not save it or can't find the form frmTest.frm, then keep the default form for this project, add a button, and type in the code from step 2, Part Two of this exercise, "Testing the New Class.")

2. From the **Project** menu, select the **Project References** menu item.

3. Set a reference to your new DLL by finding the **Test Utilities** checkbox and checking it as shown.

NOTE *The references dialog uses the Project Description you gave your DLL in its Project Properties dialog.*

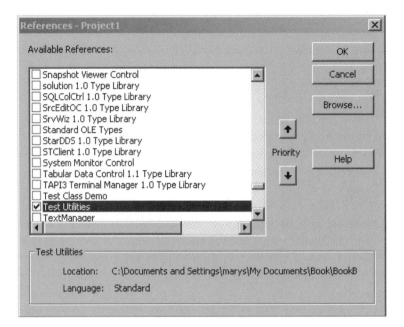

4. One last thing to do before running the new project: Open the **Project Properties** dialog and set the Startup form to **Form1**, then click **OK**. (When you deleted the default form, the project lost its Startup object. VB does not automatically use the form that you imported as the Startup object. You must manually set that in the Project Properties dialog.)

5. Run the project. Verify that the log file was created and properly written to.

6. Save your work. You can compare your work to the files contained in Chapter9\Exercise9-2\Answer folder.

NOTE *The answers file will also need to have the appropriate DLL project compiled and the references set in the Ex9_1.vbp project before it will run. Open the Ex9_1.vbp file in the Chapter9\Exercise9-1\Answer folder and read the comments for instructions on how to do this.*

Now you can add to your Test Utilities DLL as you develop additional routines for testing. To utilize your test routines, you just need to set a reference to this DLL. The Test Utilities DLL can be considered part of a basic testing *framework* for all of your future test projects. Framework is a term used in automated testing to refer to the code and utilities that surround and support the automated testing effort. These scripts and utilities are not tests themselves but provide the means to quickly and efficiently create and use test scripts. When you move to a new test project, you can use the framework you have created to streamline that new effort. (See the Chapter 5 section "Documenting your Tests.")

There is something more you can do in Visual Basic to speed up test development with your new Test Utilities DLL: create a template project that already has a reference set to your Test Utilities component. You do this by creating a project, setting the appropriate reference (you might even want to customize the initial form), then you simply save the form and project to the following folder: c:\Program Files\Microsoft Visual Studio\VB98\Template\Projects. When you then start Visual Basic, your project will show up with an icon in the New Project dialog! This makes it easy to start writing a new test project. I named my template project TestBed.

Testing COM Objects

Now that you know how to create and use a COM object, it's time to concentrate on how and why to test these objects. COM objects are, in general, a hidden part of a software application. If we were testing an application like Microsoft Excel, we could test its functionality manually or even programmatically by means of the user interface just as any user would. Why, then, would we choose to separately set a reference to and test Excel's Worksheet object? In other words, what is the benefit of separately testing individual objects within an application? While holistically testing an application is an important task, it also makes sense to test each unit as it is developed and modified throughout the lifetime of the application. It makes sense precisely because of the object-oriented nature of COM. In a COM-based application, a significant bug in a major object can cause problems that ripple throughout the entire system and can be difficult to isolate in a more holistic testing approach. Unit testing each major object for specific performance, functionality, and other key criteria can identify problems early before incorporating the new object into an otherwise well-functioning system.

Now let's get to the practical matters. If you are given the task of testing a COM object, where do you begin? The following steps summarize the overall process.

Basic Steps to Test COM Objects

1. Explore and study this Object library in the Visual Basic Object Browser and any available associated documentation, such as the software specification, the test plan, and any available Help files.

2. Create a new Visual Basic project and set up the initial framework by setting a reference to your own Test object. Locate and set a reference to the Object library you will be testing.

3. Develop and write the automated test scripts per the test plan and test cases to access the pertinent properties, methods, and events of the objects in the Object library.

Next, we'll take a look at an existing COM object, review a test case similar to one we might find within an actual test plan, and then review the solution and implementation of this test case in Visual Basic code. You will then implement the steps to test a COM object in the exercise for this section.

Case Study: Testing the Housing COM Object

Consider the simple Object library shown in Figure 9-4 that exposes a class used for a Housing application. This Housing application keeps track of various kinds of housing units, rental homes, apartments, condos, and calculates rental rates. The Housing object within this application, represents the individual rental unit and exports a few properties, such as rental rate and rental fee; and a method called ComputeFee for calculating rates; and a couple of events.

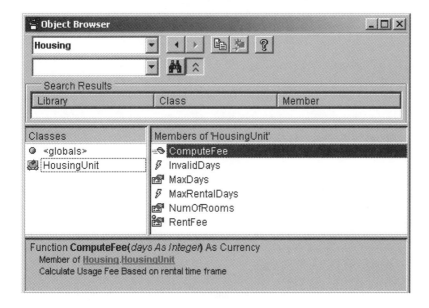

Figure 9-4. A simple, custom Object library.

Step 1: Review the Source Code and Object Library

Although you might not always be lucky enough to have access to the source code for an object you are going to test, it's helpful if you do. The source code for the Housing object is available in the Chapter 9 Practice Files for this book. It is also reprinted here in Listing 9-3.

Listing 9-3. The source code for the Housing COM Object case study.

```
Option Explicit
'*************************************************
'* Housing object
'* This is a demo COM object for testing purposes for
'* Chapter 9 VB for Testers.
'*************************************************
```

```
Public RentFee As Currency
'local variable(s) to hold property value(s)
Private mvarNumOfRooms As Integer 'local copy
'To fire this event, use RaiseEvent with the following syntax:
'RaiseEvent MaxRentalDays[(arg1, arg2, ... , argn)]
Public Event MaxRentalDays(strMessage As String)
Public Event InvalidDays(strMessage As String)
Private mvarMaxDays As Integer 'local copy
Public Property Let MaxDays(ByVal vData As Integer)
    mvarMaxDays = vData
End Property

Public Property Get MaxDays() As Integer
    MaxDays = mvarMaxDays
End Property

Public Property Let NumOfRooms(ByVal vData As Integer)
    mvarNumOfRooms = vData
End Property

Public Property Get NumOfRooms() As Integer
    NumOfRooms = mvarNumOfRooms
End Property

Function ComputeFee(days As Integer) As Currency
'calculates the rate for a given rental unit based on
'numbers of days * fee. The formula charges less per day for greater
'than 7 days. An event is raised if too many days are specified.
'An event is also raised if the object is given a negative # of days
'to rent
    If days > 7 Then
        If days > mvarMaxDays Then
            RaiseEvent MaxRentalDays("Max days were set to " & _
                    Str(mvarMaxDays) & " Defaulting to: " & Str(mvarMaxDays))
        End If
        days = mvarMaxDays
        ComputeFee = days * RentFee - (days * RentFee * 0.1)
    ElseIf days < 0 Then
        RaiseEvent InvalidDays("Days to rent cannot be negative")
    Else
        ComputeFee = days * RentFee
    End If
End Function
```

```
Private Sub Class_Initialize()
    mvarMaxDays = 30
End Sub
```

Notice that this code include properties using the Property Let and Get procedures you learned about in the preceding section. It also includes some events (see sidebar).

....

Adding Events to COM Objects

The code in the Housing object includes some events. Events can be added to a COM object with a declaration similar to one of those in the Housing object:

```
Public Event InvalidDays(strMessage As String)
```

This single line sets up the event-handling process between the object and the user of the object. When the object's user creates an instance of this object, he can specify that he wants this object *with events*. The object's events will then be exposed to the user and the programmer can write an event handler (or not) for the situation. The following line will create the object and allow access to all of its events:

```
Private WithEvents Cabin1 As HousingUnit
```

The keyword WithEvents is the operative one—without it, the events of the object will not be available.

The writer of the object determines when the event gets raised. When the writer wants to *raise* the event, he simply includes the following line somewhere in a method of the object:

```
RaiseEvent InvalidDays("Days to rent cannot be negative")
```

Raising the event means that when this line of code is executed at run time, Windows will immediately send a message to the user of the object indicating that this event has occurred. Then, if the user of the object has written an event handler for this event, that code will run next. Notice that this is exactly the same process that occurred when you wrote code for the event of a control in Visual Basic. When the event occurred, (such as the click-event of a button), if you wrote code for that event, your code ran when the button was clicked at run time. If you did not write any code for the button's click-event, nothing happened when the button was clicked. The following code is how the event handler might look for the InvalidDays event of the Housing object:

```
Private Sub Cabin1_InvalidDays(strMessage As String)
    MsgBox strMessage
    L.LogToFile "Invalid days error: " & strMessage
End Sub
```

What might constitute a relevant test for this object that could be performed by an automated test script? Well, one critical function of this object is to perform a calculation of a rental fee. The ComputeFee function performs this task. So, a possible set of tests might concern verifying the computation of this rental fee. The following test case is written in a format similar to what might be found in a test plan for this object.

TEST CASE ID:

HSG01 VERIFY COMPUTATION OF COMPUTERENTFEE METHOD

COMPONENT UNDER TEST: Housing Project. The Housing Project exposes a HousingUnit object containing properties, methods, and an event for managing a rental-housing unit.

METHOD UNDER TEST: ComputeFee*(days as integer) as Currency*. This method takes as an input the number of days to rent the unit. ComputeFee calculates the total fee required by the user to rent the unit. It returns a currency value.

DESCRIPTION: The purpose of this test is to verify the correctness of the ComputeFee method by processing values in the identified ranges and comparing the results to the results to those calculated in this test.

PROCEDURAL STEPS:

1. Create an instance of the housing unit:

   ```
   Dim Cabin1 As HousingUnit
   Set Cabin1 = New HousingUnit
   ```

2. Prompt tester for test values for the RentFee property of the HousingUnit object (later upgrade to read from file or database) and number of days to rent. RentalDays is an input to ComputeFee method.

PASS/FAIL CRITERIA: The correct computation is performed.

Test values for rental days should span the following ranges:

RENTALDAYS	EXPECTED CALCULATION BY COMPUTEFEE METHOD
< = 7	RentalDays * RentFee
> 7	RentalDays * RentFee * 10% discount

Step 2: Set up the Framework

In this step, you will set up your Visual Basic test script to reference your own Test object containing test utilities and set the appropriate reference to the COM library.

TO TRY THIS

Follow these steps to review the source code and examine the Object library for the Housing object.

1. In the Chapter9\Demos\Housing folder, double-click on the **HousingDLL.vbp** file. Review the code in this file. It creates several properties, methods, and events for a class, HousingUnit. *Do not make any changes!*

2. Select the **Project ➤ Housing Properties** menu item. The Project Properties dialog box appears. Note that the Project Name is Housing. Also note that the description for this object reads: Housing COM object Demo. Close the Project Properties dialog box by clicking **Cancel**.

3. Register this DLL by selecting the **File ➤ Make Housing.dll** menu item. The Make Project dialog box appears. Save this DLL into your Windows system directory.

4. Close the **HousingDLL.vbp** file by selecting **File ➤ Exit**, (you do not need to save).

5. Start a new Visual Basic **Standard EXE** project then select the **Project ➤ References** menu item. The Project References dialog displays.

7. Set a reference to the **Housing COM Object Demo** Object library by clicking the checkbox next to it. (Object libraries are listed in alphabetical order by their description so you might need to scroll down to find it.) Click **OK** to close the Project References dialog box.

8. Press **F2** to view the Object Browser. Select the **Housing** library. You will see the Housing Object library displayed similarly to Figure 9-4. Find and review the information on the **ComputeFee** method.

With the information found in the Object Browser, the source code, and the test case description, the next step is to create a test script to satisfy the test case.

Step 3: Implementing a Test Case for the Housing COM Object

Listing 9-4 shows one way to implement the test case described in this case study. Before this code will run, references must be set to the TestUtilities Object library and the Housing Object library.

Listing 9-4. The Visual Basic code to implement a test case for the Housing COM object.

```
'**************************************************************************
'*  Housing Unit Tests
'*  Test Case:  HSG01 Verify Value of ComputeRentFee Method
'*  Date:  12/1/2000
'*  Author: MRS
'*  Modification History:
'*  Date:           Automator:        Build#:        Remarks/Changes:
'*  3/1/2001        MRS               H2             Support new build
'*
'*  Inputs/Setup:   Set reference to Housing object
'*                  Set reference to TestUtilities object
'*  Outputs:  L.LOGFILE = "C:\houselog.txt"
'*  Component Under Test:  Housing Project.
'*     The Housing Project exposes a HousingUnit object containing
'*     properties, methods, and an event for managing a rental housing unit.
'*  Method Under Test:  ComputeFee(days as integer) as Currency.
'*    This method takes as an input the number of days to rent the unit.
'*    ComputeFee calculates the total fee required by the user for renting the unit.
'*    It returns a currency value.
```

```
'*  Description:  The purpose of this test is to verify the correctness of the
'*    ComputeFee method by processing values in the identified ranges and
'*    comparing the results to the results to those calculated in this test.
'*  Remarks:  See test case for Procedural Steps
'*********************************************************************
Option Explicit
Private WithEvents Cabin1 As HousingUnit
Private L As cLogUtilities


Private Sub Cabin1_InvalidDays(strMessage As String)
    MsgBox strMessage
    L.LogToFile "Invalid days error: " & strMessage
End Sub


Private Sub Cabin1_MaxRentalDays(strMessage As String)
    MsgBox strMessage
    L.LogToFile "Maximum rental days exceeded, object should set to default"
End Sub


Private Sub cmdTestBed_Click()
'Test case HSG01:  Verify value of ComputeRentFee method
    Dim curRentfee As Currency
    Dim curComputedFee As Currency
    Dim RentalDays As Integer
'set object
    Set Cabin1 = New HousingUnit
'prompt for test values
    curRentfee = Val(InputBox("Enter Rental Fee"))
    Cabin1.RentFee = curRentfee
    RentalDays = Val(InputBox("Enter # of Rental Days"))
'perform test
    StartLog
    L.LogToFile "Begin Tests HSG01"
    curComputedFee = Cabin1.ComputeFee(RentalDays)
    If RentalDays <= 7 And _
        (curComputedFee = RentalDays * curRentfee) Then
        L.LogToFile ("HSG01: Test passed; correct calculation")
    ElseIf RentalDays > 7 And (curComputedFee = _
            RentalDays * curRentfee - (RentalDays * curRentfee * 0.1)) Then
        L.LogToFile ("HSG01: Test passed; correct calculation")
    Else
        L.LogToFile ("HSG01: Test Failure incorrect calculation; " & _
                " Rental Days: " & RentalDays & " Rental Fee: " & curRentfee)
    End If
```

```
    L.LogToFile "End of Tests"
'end test; open the log file
    L.ReadLog
End Sub
Sub StartLog()
    Set L = New cLogUtilities
    L.APPNAME = "Housing Tests"
    L.LOGFILE = "C:\houselog.txt"
End Sub
```

In Listing 9-4, the calculations performed by the object to compute rental fees are verified by performing the same calculation in the automated test script and then comparing the results.

 TESTER'S TIP *Verifying the accuracy of certain important calculations done by an object can be one requirement for testing an object's performance. In fact, the script in Listing 9-4 is similar (although simplified) to an actual script used on a real test project. I feel compelled to note, however, that you must* not *try to replicate every function of the application in your test scripts because this effort can result in a duplication of the development effort and can be a significant time and resource waste. Only automate those functions that are deemed critical by the test planning team.*

Note that our own COM object, TestUtilities, created in this chapter accomplishes the work of logging. You can find the full project associated with this file in the Chapter9\PracticeFile\HousingDemo folder in the Practice Files.

TO TRY THIS

To view the test of the Housing COM object, you will first need to register it on your system. Then you can run the test application that will reference the object:

1. In the Chapter9\Demos\HousingEX folder, double-click on the **Rental.vbp** file. This file contains all the code from Listing 9-4. Review this code to see how it accesses the Housing object. Before this code will run, you will need to set some references.

2. Select the **Project ➤ References** menu item. Set a reference to the **Housing COM Object Demo** Object library by clicking the checkbox next to it. Object libraries are listed in alphabetical order by their description so you will need to scroll down to find it.

3. Select the **Test Utilities** Object library by clicking the checkbox next to it. Once the reference to *both* of these Object libraries has been set (as shown). Click **OK** to close the Project References dialog.

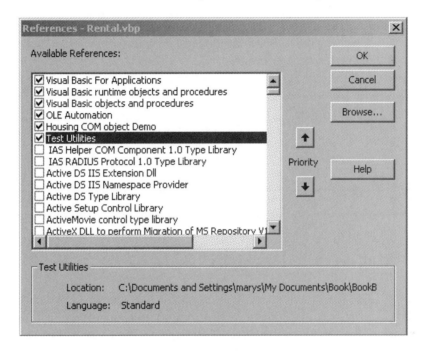

NOTE *If the Test Utilities Object library does not show up in the list, you will also need to register this item. To do so, open the* **Chapter9PracticeFile\Exercise9-1\Answer\cLogUtilitiesLib.vbp** *file by double-clicking it. Select the File ➤ Make cLogUtilitiesLib.dll; save the DLL into the Windows System directory and click OK.*

4. Now you should be able to run the tests by clicking **F5** to run the Rental.vbp project. Click the button on the default form as shown in the preceding graphic.

5. You will be prompted to enter a value for rental days and rental fees. Enter **75** for the Rental Fee into the Inputbox when prompted. You will then be prompted for rental days: enter **5**. The code then sends this information to the ComputeFee method of the Housing object and verifies its response. A notepad file displays with the test results.

6. Close notepad. Click the button on the test form again and enter different values. A test failure will be generated when the user (you) enters a negative value for rental days.

7. When you are finished entering test data, return to Design mode and review the code again.

NOTE *The code in the Rental.vbp file (Listing 9-4) is a simplified version of an actual test run. Rental2.vbp in the Chapter9\Demos folder contains a version that uses data input from a file instead of input manually as we have done here.*

Working with Collections

In the "COM Basics" section at the beginning of this chapter, I defined collections as a way to work with objects as a group. Many applications use collections in their object model. In fact, Visual Basic itself has many predefined collections that can be very useful to work with. For example, there is a collection that contains all of the installed printers, the Printers collection. There is also a Controls collection that contains the list of all controls on a form. In this section, we will explore how to access and test collections of objects.

The standard programming structure for holding lists of values has been the array (see "Creating Lists with Arrays" section in Chapter 6). Collections allow another more flexible way to group items together. The biggest difference between an array and a collection is that you do not have to redimension a collection in order to resize it. The collection automatically resizes itself when a member item is added or deleted. In an array, each element's index value remains the same but because of the dynamic sizing of a collection, when a member is deleted, the index is recalculated. Another big difference is that a collection does not have to be homogenous—each member of a collection can be of a completely different type, although, usually members of a collection are logically related.

Let's look at an example of a collection. Visual Basic's Controls collection can be very useful for returning and setting properties of controls collectively. The following code will loop through all the controls on the current form and print its Name property to the Immediate window.

```
Private Sub Form_Load()
    Dim MyCtrl As Control
    For Each MyCtrl In Controls
        Debug.Print MyCtrl.Name
    Next MyCtrl
End Sub
```

The declaration:

```
Dim MyCtrl As Control
```

...creates an object variable that can hold a reference to any control. For each pass through the For-Loop, the MyCtrl variable will be successively loaded with the next control until all the controls have been processed. We can use this object variable, MyCtrl, to access any property of the current control that can be read at run time. In this case, the Name property is read and printed to the Immediate window. We can use a similar method to access the properties of any collection. This can be useful to verify a specific number of items in a collection as well as specific property values.

TO TRY THIS

1. Create a new Visual Basic project. Add as many controls as you would like (at least three or four) to the default form.

2. Add the following code to the Form_Load event of the default form:

```
Private Sub Form_Load()
    Dim MyCtrl As Control
    For Each MyCtrl In Controls
        Debug.Print MyCtrl.Name
    Next MyCtrl
End Sub
```

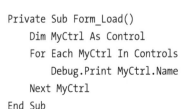

3. Run the project. Select the **View ➤ Immediate Window** menu item. Notice that the name of each control on the form has been printed into the Immediate window as shown here. You may have to scroll up in the Immediate window to see all of the names.

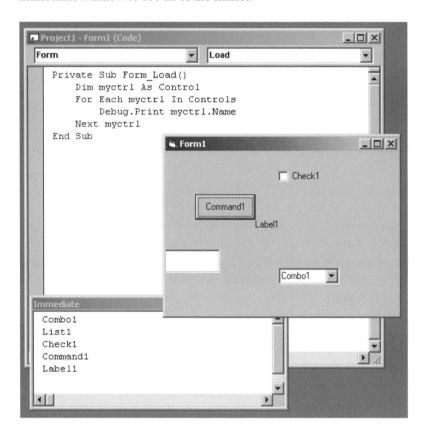

CASE STUDY:

THE INVOICES PROJECT—TESTING COLLECTIONS

Now we will consider an Object library that contains a collection. The InvoicesProject is an Object library used to manage a business's invoices. The invoices are grouped into sets by business. Each business groups together a logically related set of invoices and has a name for that group (for example, Invoiceset Entry), which is essentially just the name of the business.

The Object Browser shows three classes in the InvoicesProject library: cBusinesses, cInvoiceObject, and cInvoicesCollection (Figure 9-5).

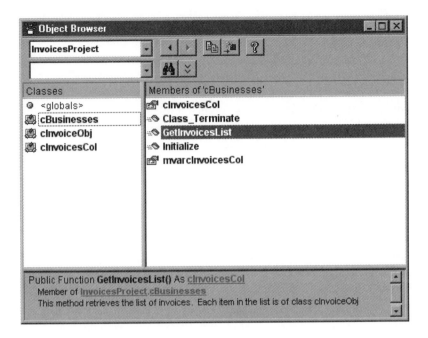

Figure 9-5. The Invoices project as viewed in the Object Browser.

Exploring the library yields the hierarchy displayed in Figure 9-6, which shows the same information we find in the Object Browser except that it is presented in a more graphical format.

Figure 9-6. The hierarchy for the Invoices project Object library as produced by the Class Builder utility.

It would be nice if the Object Browser would do this, but it doesn't. Figure 9-6 was produced using the Class Builder utility. In order to use the Class Builder to show a hierarchical representation of an Object library, you must have access to the source code for the library. While you may not be able to get access to the source code, sometimes the developers will have created an object hierarchy in documentation (such as the Help system or a design document) and that can also be helpful. If the developers have not provided one for you, it is usually well worth your time to create one for yourself once you have become familiar with the library.

The Invoices Project has a class called cBusinesses that can be considered the highest level of the Object library hierarchy. This is the overall object for managing invoices. Within the cBusinesses object, there are some important properties and methods to accomplish such management. CBusinesses also contains a collection of invoices called cInvoicesCol. Think of this collection as a group of many invoices. These invoices are each objects of a class called cInvoicesobj.

Let's presume that we have a test case, asking us to list and verify the items in the cInvoicesCol collection. What must we do to get to the list? Figure 9-5, displaying the Object Browser, shows a method called GetInvoicesList. The developer's description of the method reads: "This method retrieves the list of invoices. Each item in the list is of class cInvoiceObj." The Object Browser also gives us the syntax to access this method.

We must first create the necessary, higher-level object variables in order to get to objects lower in the hierarchy. Since the cInvoicesCol collection is contained within the cBusinesses object, we create the cBusinesses object first. The following code will create a new instance of the cBusinesses object. The colInvoices collection object is then created and set equal to the results of the GetInvoicesList method.

```
'Create and set the Businesses object
Dim oBusiness1 As cBusinesses
Set oBusiness1 = New cBusinesses

' Create the collection Object
Dim colInvoices As cInvoicesCol
' retrieve the Invoices collection
Set colInvoices = oBusiness1.GetInvoicesList
```

Notice that GetInvoicesList is a method of the highest-level object of the Object library hierarchy in the Invoices Project Object model. In the previous code, the object variable oBusiness1 holds the reference to this top-level object. The GetInvoicesList method returns a collection into the colInvoices object variable.

We have finally created and set the required variables in order to loop through the collection of invoices. The following code does just that and prints the name of the form by accessing its InvName property. Where did the InvName property come from? InvName is a property of the class cInvoiceObj. The collection we created is a collection of objects of this class so we can access the properties of an individual invoice using a cInvoiceObj object:

```
Dim MyInvoice as cInvoiceObj
For each MyInvoice in colInvoices
    Debug.print MyInvoice.InvName
Next MyInvoice
```

Does this code look familiar? Compare it to the code we used earlier when accessing Visual Basic's Controls collection—it is essentially the same! One of the nice things about working with collections and COM in general is that once you have learned how to access one collection, you can access others in a similar way no matter what application you are working with.

EXERCISE 9-2.

In Exercise 9-2, you will set a reference to an existing COM Object library, the Invoices Project. You will explore this library and using the test cases provided, write automated tests to exercise the properties and methods exposed by the objects.

This exercise has two parts:

I.   Creating a DLL

II. Testing the InvoicesProject Objects

I. Creating a DLL

1. In the Chapter9\Demos\InvoiceProjectDLL folder, open the InvoicesProject.vbp file. *You will not make changes to this project.*

2. Review the code in all of the Code modules in this project. (It is not a completely developed library; it contains just enough properties and methods for us to test.) Open the **Project ➤ Properties** menu item and note the Project Description.

   Write the Project Description here:

   _____

   Write the Project Name here:

   _____

   The Project Description is listed in the Project References dialog so you will need to know it when you want to set a reference to this Object library. The Project Name is the name of the library so you will need to know that when you want to view it in the Object Browser.

3. Click **Cancel** to exit the Project Properties dialog.

4.   In the Properties window, review the properties for each Class module, particularly the Instancing property. Look up Instancing in Help by placing your cursor on this property in the Properties window and pressing **F1**. Review the descriptions of the types of instancing available for a class.

5.   Select the **Add-Ins ➢ Class Builder Utility** menu item. Review the object model for the Invoices Project by clicking on each class in turn and looking at the properties and methods for each.

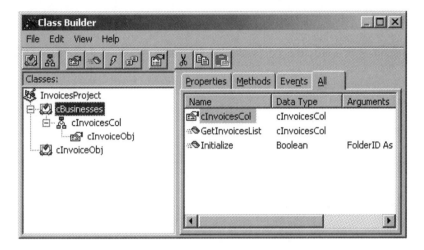

6.   Close the Class Builder dialog without making any changes.

7.   In order to register this DLL, you will compile it on your own computer. Compile the Invoices Project by selecting the **File ➢ Make InvoicesProject.DLL** menu item. The Make Project dialog displays.

8.   Click **OK** to compile and save the .DLL file. When it is finished compiling (this might take a minute or so), the DLL is now registered on your system. Close InvoicesProject.vbp.

II. Testing the InvoicesProject Objects

1.   Create a new Visual Basic Standard EXE project.

2.   Select the **Project ➢ References** menu item. In the Project References dialog, select your Test Utilities COM object from Exercise 9-1 so you can access your logging routines. Also find and select the Invoices Project Objects library. (Search for the description you wrote down in Part One,

step 2 of this exercise.) Make sure both items are checked and then click **OK** to close the Project References dialog.

3. Open the Object Browser and review the objects in the Test Utilities and Invoices Project libraries. (The Invoices Project will use the Project Name you wrote down in Part One, step 2 of this exercise.)

4. Study the following test case. Follow the procedural steps of the test case to *write the code to implement it in Visual Basic.*

TEST CASE ID:

INV1

COMPONENT UNDER TEST: Invoices Project.

The Invoices Project exposes sets of invoices by category.

METHOD: GetInvoicesList.

This method returns a collection of all available invoices.

PROCEDURAL STEPS:

- Create a new instance of the Invoices Manager object variable:

```
Dim oBusiness1 as cBusinesses
Set oBusiness1 = New cBusinesses
```

- Create an object variable of the form set collection class, cInvoicesCol:

```
Dim colInvoices as cInvoicesCol
```

- Set this object variable equal to the return value of the GetInvoicesList method.

```
Set colInvoices = oBusiness1.GetInvoicesList
```

- Write code to verify the number of expected invoices: **6**

TIP *Use the Count method of the colInvoices collection object: ColInvoices.Count.*

- Write code to print the InvName property of all existing invoices in the cInvoicesCol collection to the log file. (You do not need to write verification code for this):

    InvoiceEntry

    InvoiceSpecial

    InvoiceWeb

    InvoiceReport

    Unclaimed

    Root

- Use appropriate comments within your code to document your test script.

- Use appropriate error handling logic.

- Log all test results to a text file (using test utilities routines).

PASS/FAIL CRITERIA: The expected number of invoices should exist.

 TIP *Use the code examples in this chapter to help you write the code to implement the preceding test case. For more help, there are some projects accessing this same COM object in the Demos folder for Chapter 9 in the Practice Files.*

5. Open the log file you specified in your tests to determine whether or not the test passed and to ensure the list of invoices were printed correctly. Your results should look similar to the following:

```
InvoicesTests.txt - Notepad                                          _ □ ×
File  Edit  Format  Help
Starting Tests on  5/18/2001 4:18:29 PM
1 **Starting Tests:  Test Case INV1
2 Test Passed: Correct number of Expected Invoices in colInvoices collection
3 *** the following Invoices were found:
4 Unclaimed
5 Root
6 InvoiceEntry
7 InvoiceSpecial
8 InvoiceWeb
9 InvoiceReport
10 **Ending Test Case INV1 5/18/2001 4:18:30 PM
```

6. Compare your answer to the Ex9_2.vbp project in the Chapter9\Exercise9-2\Answer folder in the Practice Files

7. Name and save your files into your own folder.

Distributing COM Components

Now that you can create and use a component registered on a single computer, the next question is how to access that same object from another computer? Your first temptation might be to simply create the component on each individual computer by copying and compiling the code on each. That arrangement makes upgrading and management of these objects difficult and even chaotic, especially in large systems. A better solution is to have an object reside on a server with the ability to be accessed by multiple clients. There are several ways a developer can accomplish this. Microsoft provides DCOM, which is a set of program interfaces in which client components can request services from server components on a network. There are other ways to do this: for our Visual Basic components, we can also use MTS (Microsoft Transaction Server) or COM+.

The next section is an overview of COM and DCOM by guest author and Visual Basic expert, Walt Ritscher.

COM Components and DCOM

By Walt Ritscher

Reusing Code

Programmers are always looking for better methods to reuse code. The sub procedure and function are simple examples of reuse that are available in every major programming language. While reusable, sub and function procedures suffer from a very basic limitation: they must reside in the main application. If you wish to reuse a particular function—let's say the IsPrinterReady function—you need to copy the IsPrinterReady function to each project that needs it.

As a result, other schemes have evolved. One idea that gained popularity was storing reusable code in an external location and then linking to this external library. Class libraries and Include files are some examples of this approach. Using this tactic, developers could store their favorite utility code in one or more separate libraries, link their application to these external files, and then compile the combined results into a single executable. This single executable is often called a *monolithic application*. Since the libraries are reusable they can easily be linked and compiled into other applications.

There are still problems with this approach, however. One major problem of a monolithic application is the difficulty in modifying your application. Let's say that you want to make a couple of minor changes to one of your print routines. In the monolithic world, you need to open up the print library, change the code, test your changes, and save your work. Now comes the painful part—you must relink the files, recompile the entire application, and redistribute to your users. All this work for a couple of trivial changes.

Components

Components fulfill most of the wishes of software builders, at least as far as reusability is concerned. Components are binary, compiled libraries of code that can be easily replaced at any time. Imagine that instead of one large, solitary executable, you assemble your application out of many little code executables. This concept of constructing an application from separate executables is called *component architecture*. If you break your application up into these little pieces, you get some major benefits:

- **Building Blocks**: You can create little software blocks—I like to think of LEGOs—that you can assemble into finished products. Mix and match these existing blocks to create new products and tools.

- **Easy Replacement**: Suppose you need to change a component—perhaps to improve performance, fix bugs, or enhance features. Simply modify one of these mini-blocks, recompile, and plug the new version into the existing application. There is no need to recompile any of the other components in the application.

- **Rapid Application Development (RAD)**: Having a toolbox filled with well-crafted components allows for quick assembly of a new application. Buying parts from a reliable vendor is another strategy for RAD. If you don't have a component already built to handle a certain task, you probably can find a vendor who has one for sale. Usually, you can buy a tool cheaper than you can build it.

- **Run on Multiple Computers**: Since you have already split your application into numerous parts, it is much easier to deploy the pieces across multiple machines.

Component Implementations

When you consider that components offer so many advantages to developers, it should come as no surprise that they have taken a leading role in the modern development world. Many of the major players in the software development arena have embraced the ideas of components and created their own proprietary versions. Microsoft created the Component Object Model, better known as COM, as their way of distributing and using components. Sun countered with JavaBeans. Other companies have weighed in with their own versions but none have proven as popular as COM and JavaBeans. COM is currently the most widely-used component model available. According to the most recent Microsoft statistics, COM is available on over 150 million computers.

Microsoft offers several tools for building COM-based components. The two most widely used are Visual C++ and Visual Basic. Visual Basic specializes in easy-to-build, easy-to-compile versions of COM components. Most of the COM plumbing is hidden away and handled on your behalf. Visual C++'s strength is speed, performance, and greater control over the COM interfaces. Both tools have had a significant impact on modern application development.

DCOM

COM is a standard that allows software to communicate with other software. COM permits communication between any two COM components *as long as they are both on the same machine.* If you want to have your client component on your desktop computer and a library component running on a separate server, you need another standard. Several years after the debut of COM, Microsoft released a protocol that could handle this scenario. Microsoft provides Distributed COM (DCOM): a set of program interfaces in which client components can request services from server components on a network.

You should be aware that DCOM is not the only distributed component technology available. One competitor is EJB (Enterprise JavaBeans), developed by Sun Microsystems. Another is CORBA (Common Object Request Broker Architecture), which is sponsored by the OMG (Object Management Group). Each of these technologies permits the developer to distribute parts of the application to another machine. DCOM tends to be very Windows-centric; although, COM/DCOM can be installed on Mac and UNIX systems. EJB only works with Java components. CORBA has had little commercial success yet.

Location Transparency

One of the great concepts of COM is the idea of location transparency. When you use a component in your code, you don't need to do anything special or different based on where the component resides. For example, this next snippet of code uses an object located on your local computer:

```
Dim MyTest as cTest
Set MyTest = New cTest
```

The following code uses an object located on another machine on your network:

```
Dim MyTest as cTest2
Set MyTest = New cTest2
```

Notice that these two examples are syntactically identical. This is what is meant by *location transparency*. Obviously, the local computer is aware that these two classes are in different locations and is able to properly find the object template but you don't need to modify your coding syntax to compensate.

How Does DCOM Work?

One of the premier rules of Windows applications is that all software has to run in a Windows process (see the sidebar "What is a Process?" next). The components you write must follow this rule. There are really only two choices available to a component:

1. Create a new process for its own use, or

2. Find another process to serve as a host.

The first case, creating a separate process, requires us to build a COM EXE, also called an *out-of-process* component. The advantage of an out-of-process component is that because it is a separate process, it can be run stand-alone or it can be called from another application depending on how it's written. Microsoft Excel is an example of this. It can be run on its own or it can be called for use in another application (as you did in this chapter). The second case, employing a host process, requires a COM DLL otherwise known as an *in-process* component. An in-process component cannot be run stand-alone as an out-of-process component can. Its advantage is that it runs in the same process space as the application that uses it so the calls to it are faster. (An example of this is the Test DLL you created in Exercises 9-1 and 9-2. It cannot be run stand-alone.)

DCOM is supposed to allow us to create a client application on one computer and still deploy our COM component on a separate machine. As you can imagine, this is not a trivial undertaking. While most of the complex stuff is managed by DCOM, we still need to handle a few things before we can use the component. First, we need to decide whether to create our component as an in-process or out-of-process component. Second, we need to successfully deploy both parts of our application to their appropriate computers. Third, we need to notify the client machine that the component we desire is located elsewhere on the network.

What Is a Process?

Windows is a multitasking environment. Or, at least, it gives the appearance of running multiple applications at the same time. In reality, the OS doles out a few milliseconds of processing time to each application. When the OS determines that the time allocated has expired, it shuts down the application. Before loading another application, however, the OS stores the previous programs data in a safe place. Each application needs to be isolated from other applications so that its data can be safeguarded. The mechanism for this isolation is called a *process*. Another benefit from individual processes is that if (or some would say, when) a program crashes, it will not affect other running applications. Each Windows process gets its own 4 GB of virtual memory. Each process also manages its own files and threads.

DCOM Component as an EXE

The first step is to create an ActiveX EXE project and build your component. In order to get your component registered properly on the client machine, you need to add a .vbr file to the project. Prior to compiling the component, you select the **Component** tab on the Project References dialog (see Figure 9-7) and check the **Remote Server Files** checkbox. This will create the necessary .vbr file. The component EXE is then deployed to the server machine and registered. The client application is deployed and registered to the client machine. The last step involves notifying the client machine that the component is located on separate machine. On the client, you can use the CliReg32.exe application located in the Microsoft Visual Studio Common Tools folder to register the component. The Package and Deployment Wizard can also handle the redirection of the client registry so that it points to the server. Whichever method you choose, both use the .vbr file created by the Visual Basic compiler.

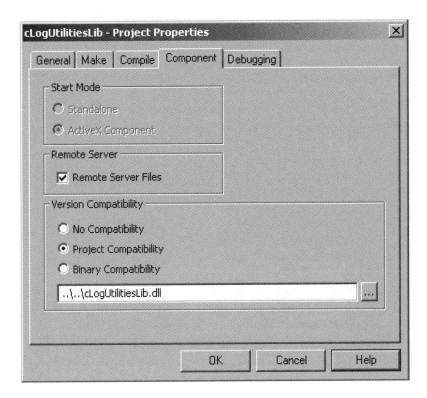

Figure 9-7. Check the Remote Server Files checkbox in the Project References dialog to create a .vbr file.

DCOM Component as a DLL

Building and compiling an ActiveX DLL project is the first step in creating an in-process DCOM component. It is not necessary for you to create a .vbr file as in-process DCOM components do not need one. Now that you have your ActiveX DLL, you need to deploy it to the server. Remember, however, that an in-process component needs a host/surrogate process in which to run. This is easy if the DLL is on the same box as the client code but can be a problem if the DLL is on a foreign machine. The DLL needs a host but where are we going to find one? Not to worry. Microsoft has created a surrogate application for you to use. If your server is running Windows NT 4, you can use Microsoft Transaction Server (MTS) as your surrogate. If you are running on Windows 2000, the surrogate is named COM+. COM+ is essentially a newer version of MTS. Setting up your component inside of MTS or COM+ is beyond the scope of this book. For further information, try these Microsoft Web sites:

```
http://msdn.microsoft.com/com
```

```
http://msdn.microsoft.com/library/psdk/cossdk/betaintr_6qan.htm
```

```
http://msdn.microsoft.com/library/psdk/mts20sp1/gettingstarted_1qjo.htm
```

As with the previous ActiveX EXE example, we deploy and register the client application to the client machine. We also need to add the component to the server and install it properly inside of MTS/COM+. The final step requires pointing the client machine to the server so that the client can find the component. MTS/COM+ can generate an executable file that manages this redirection. This is similar to the previous .vbr example except that MTS/COM+ creates the file instead of Visual Basic.

Summary

Let's recap what we've learned about COM and DCOM. COM is a Microsoft specification that describes and implements their component architecture. Via COM, we can split our application into many small executables and link these executables at run time. COM, like all component architectures, allows for easy replacement of components. Applications can be quickly assembled from sets of components.

DCOM is simply COM on a wire. All the benefits and features of COM are available with the added capability of distributing the components to clients and servers on your network.

TESTER'S CHECKLIST

- When testing a custom COM object, has Help been provided for the object's properties, methods, and events? If not, this can be written up as a bug or as a recommendation depending on test requirements.

- Look for objects that have not been properly released in source code. All object variables should be set equal to the keyword Nothing when they are no longer being used in the code. If you do not have access to source code and objects have not been released properly in the COM component, you may see "Out of Memory" or "File Locked" errors.

- Does the software under test use early or late-binding for object variables? In general, early binding is more efficient. (See the sidebar "Declaring Object Variables: Early versus Late Binding" earlier in this chapter.)

Chapter 9 Review

- Define Component Object Model.
  See page 293.

- What are the differences between a Class module, a Form module, and a Standard module?
  See the section "Creating a Class" on page 303. Also see Chapter 5.

- What is a collection? How is a collection similar to and different from an array?
  See page 338.

- What are the steps to test a COM object?
  See page 328.

- Define DCOM.
  See page 348.

CHAPTER 10

Testing the Web with Visual Basic

The Web is a big place. Testing the Web is a big topic. You can't and probably don't even want to test everything you need to test on a Web site using Visual Basic. That's because there are already many tools available, some of them free, for doing basic things such as checking that links work properly and for stress and load testing. The intent of this chapter is to show you some things you *can* use Visual Basic for in Web site testing. First, we will look at the three basic categories of Web pages and then we will examine some ways to test pages in those categories using Visual Basic. I will show you how to use the Internet Transfer control and the WebBrowser control to interrogate a Web site. I will also introduce you to VBScript so that you can use this subset of Visual Basic for testing as well. In the process, you will gain more understanding of the Web and acquire some Visual Basic code for accessing the Web.

 NOTE *I assume that you have a general knowledge of the Web and HTML. If not, there are many good references—see Appendix A: Resources and References for more information.*

Objectives

By the end of this chapter, you will be able to:

- View the raw data on a Web page using the Microsoft Internet Transfer control.

- Access and return pertinent information about a Web site using the WebBrowser control.

- Use Visual Basic code and the WebBrowser control to trap, save, and then send HTTP requests to a Web server.

- Understand the difference between a Get and Post HTTP request.

- State some of the differences and similarities between VBScript and Visual Basic.

- Name and locate multiple resources for Web testing.

- Use VBScript code to perform simple tasks.

Web Site Testing Basics

When testing a Web site, there are essentially three categories of pages to consider: static Web pages, Active Server Pages (ASP), and pages that include database access.

Static pages   These are sometimes called *brochureware* because they contain the same sort of information you might see on a company brochure. That is, they do not contain any data loaded from a database, just information typed directly into the Web page. There is little or no interaction between the user and the Web site other than very simple things such as links to other pages or the ability to e-mail the Webmaster.

ASP or CGI   ASP and CGI are two different ways a page can process information on the server side of the client-server relationship. Microsoft's Active Server Page (ASP) is a page in which an embedded script, usually VBScript or JavaScript, is executed on the server before the page is sent back to the client. With CGI, you can specify the name of a program to run on the server side in certain tags like the form tag. In this text, we will focus on ASP.

Database access   These are Web pages that access a database backend, usually on a separate server than the Web server. This category includes e-commerce Web sites that use databases to store their product information. However, they aren't limited to e-commerce sites since many kinds of Web sites can contain data from a database backend. This database access is usually performed through an ASP but I list it separately here since not every ASP performs database access.

A Web site can contain all three types of pages or be completely comprised of pages of just one type. Strategies for testing these categories of pages will differ so your first step is to determine what types of pages the Web site you will be testing includes.

Static Page Testing

Static pages are the easiest to test. Figure 10-1 shows a static page. Strategies for testing this page might include manually clicking on all links and images to verify that they jump to valid locations or writing code to do the same thing programmatically. You can also stress test the page using some of the available tools for stress testing. If there are any controls on the page that require input, like textboxes, you can use standard functionality testing to verify input.

Visual Basic can assist in Static page testing in several ways. For standard functionality testing, you can use the SendKeys function (see the "Simple GUI Testing Using SendKeys" section in Chapter 5) to send keystrokes to the page. If you need more advanced capability, you can use the SendMessage API (see Chapter 7). Testing the page in this way would be similar to what is done on a non-Web application (are there any of those these days?) so I will not cover it again here. Also, I mention these options only because I know of testers who have done some GUI and functionality testing of Web pages using SendKeys and SendMessage and have been satisfied with the results. However, their scripts were typically short and focused on a particular item that worked well for this type of test. For more typical projects (are there any of those either?), it is a lot of coding and a lot of time to test pages this way, especially given the number of tools available for testing Web pages (see the sidebar in this chapter, "Resources for Web Testing Tools"). In this section, we will explore the capabilities of the Microsoft Internet Transfer control for static page testing.

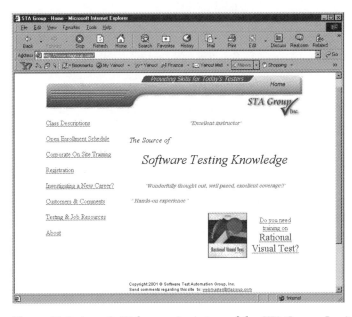

Figure 10-1. A static Web page (courtesy of the STA Group, Inc.).

Resources for Web Testing Tools

The World Wide Web consortium (W3C) is a resource primarily for Web developers (`http://www.W3C.org`). It's also a place that all testers should become familiar with since many, if not most, applications you test will have Web access. The mission of the W3C is to "lead the World Wide Web to its full potential by developing common protocols that promote its evolution and ensure its interoperability." The W3C Web site contains industry standards for Web page development, which can be useful in developing test cases for a Web site. Also of special interest to testers is the tools download area. This area includes many tools that are useful for Web site testing including tools for link checking, HTML validation, and tools to check a Web site for accessibility for users with special needs. The link to the tools page is `http://www.w3.org/WAI/ER/existingtools.html#Evaluation`.

Microsoft provides a free Web stress-testing tool called, appropriately, the Web Application Stress (WAS) tool. It can be downloaded from `http://homer.rte.microsoft.com`.

Of course, there are many commercially available tools for Web site testing as well. Becoming a member of the W3C will put you in touch with other Web testers and developers so you can compare notes on the best ones for your particular needs.

Using the Microsoft Internet Transfer Control

Microsoft's Internet Transfer control has the ability to connect to the Web using two of the most common protocols, FTP and HTTP. Perhaps the most common use of the Internet Transfer control is to be able to provide a browser to FTP sites. This can be handy for testers or anyone who needs to access FTP sites but it isn't a testing task per se. Some of the other uses of the Internet Transfer control are a bit more relevant for testing. For example, you can use the control to access a Web page and return raw data, such as the HTML used to render the page, or the directory of an FTP site. Retrieving the HTML code is useful to verify the accuracy of the page against its intended output. You could then parse this raw information to locate graphics references, links to other pages, or anything else relevant to your test cases.

The Internet Transfer control is not one of the standard controls in the toolbox, however, it does come with the Professional and Enterprise editions of Visual Basic so you can add it to the toolbox through the Components dialog.

TO TRY THIS

1. In a new Visual Basic project, select the **Project ➤ Components** menu item. The Project Components dialog displays. The Controls tab has the focus. This tab contains a list of the available components and sets of components that you can add to the Toolbox.

TIP *You can also open the Components dialog by right-clicking on the **Toolbox** window and then selecting **Components** from the pop-up menu.*

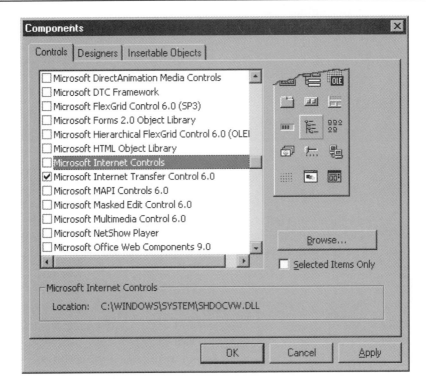

2. Check the box for the Microsoft Internet Transfer control. You will have to scroll down to see it because the controls are listed alphabetically. Click **OK** to close the Components dialog box. The new control is added to the Toolbox as shown.

TIP *When your cur∆sor is located inside the list of controls, you can press the letter "**m**" key (not case–sensitive) and it will immediately drop you down to the controls that start with the letter "m". Keep pressing "**m**" and it iterates through all of the controls starting with that letter. This saves you a lot of scrolling.*

3. Double-click on the **Internet Transfer control** in the Toolbox to add it to your form. This is a control that will be invisible on the form at run time so it really doesn't matter where on the form you place it. It simply adds the hooks to access the Internet. The default name for the new control is Inet1.

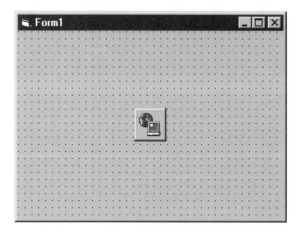

4. Run the program. You will not see anything on the form at run time. Close the program. Now that you are back in Design mode, you do see the control.

You can use the properties and methods of this control to do powerful work quite simply.

Returning Raw Data from a Web Page

Once the Internet Transfer control is on your form, you can use it to quickly attach to a Web page and return the HTML data behind it. The OpenURL method of the Internet Transfer control is a function can be used to access a Web page and return it's HTML code:

```
Text1.text = Inet1.OpenURL("www.yahoo.com")
```

> **NOTE** *If you retrieve text from a Web site using the OpenURL method into a textbox (as shown in the preceding line of code), be sure to change the MultiLine property of the textbox to True. Otherwise, the text will be retrieved as a single line no matter how you have sized the textbox and you will have to do a whole lot of scrolling to see the information!*

The full syntax of this command is:

InternetTransferControl.**OpenURL** URL [,datatype]

As you can see, the OpenURL method has two arguments. The first argument is required and is where you specify the URL (see the sidebar "URL [Uniform Resource Locator]" next) of a Web site, either an FTP or HTTP site, but you can also refer to a specific file on the site. The second argument is optional and is where you specify the kind of file you will retrieve. You can either return text, which is the default, or a byte array. To specify a byte array, provide the number 1 or the constant icByteArray. Byte arrays are useful for retrieving binary data like .exe and .zip files. We will look at both text and byte arrays in the examples in this section.

The following code will retrieve the directory of an FTP site into a Rich-TextBox control:

```
RichTextBox1.Text = Inet1.OpenURL("ftp://ftp.microsoft.com")
```

The URL of an FTP site is used so the directory is returned but if you give a specific file name, you can retrieve the text of just that file:

```
Text1.Text = Inet1. OpenURL("ftp://ftp.microsoft.com/disclaimer.txt")
```

What's really great about this control, among other things, is that it can not only access the Web with either of two different protocols, HTTP or FTP, but it will also automatically use the correct protocol. In the preceding line of code, the URL provided is to an FTP site, so the Internet Transfer control uses the FTP protocol automatically. If the provided URL is an HTTP site, then the HTTP protocol is used.

The OpenURL method is a function that will return either a text file or a byte array, which one is returned depends on the URL provided. If the URL provided to the OpenURL method is the directory of an FTP server or if the specified URL is a text file, the OpenURL will return text. If the specified URL is a binary file, then a byte array will be retrieved.

....

URL (Uniform Resource Locator)

The following is the definition of a URL from the Microsoft Visual Studio Help:

"Identifies the full path of a document, graphic, or other file on the Internet or on an intranet. A URL expresses the protocol (such as FTP or HTTP) to be accessed and the file's location. A URL may also specify an Internet e-mail address or a newsgroup."

Some examples of URLs are:

```
http://www.someones.homepage/default.html
ftp://ftp.server.somewhere/ftp.file
file://Server/Share/File.doc
```

....

The following shows the code to use the OpenURL method to download a binary file. Notice that the file that is accessed has a .zip extension. The code effectively retrieves the zip file from the FTP site to the local machine:

```
Dim b() As Byte          'a dynamic byte array
Dim strURL As String

    strURL = "ftp://ftp.microsoft.com/developr/drg/Win32/Autorun.zip"
    'Retrieve the file as a byte array.
    b() = Inet1.OpenURL(strURL, icByteArray)
    'the folllowing lines write the file to the local drive:
```

```
Open "C:\Temp\Autorun.zip" For Binary Access Write As #1
Put #1, , b()   'write the array to the file
Close #1
```

Listing 10-1 retrieves a URL specified by the user (it presumes the existence of a textbox called txtHTMLCode on the form that the user will fill with a valid URL). If the URL is valid, the OpenURL method will retrieve the HTML code for the Web page into a textbox.

Listing 10-1. Using the OpenURL method of the Internet Transfer control to retrieve the HTML code attached to a Web page.

```
Private Sub cmdGo_Click()
'this code presumes a form loaded with two text boxes named txtHTMLCode and txtURL
On Error GoTo errhand
    If txtURL.Text = "" Then
        MsgBox "You must enter a valid URL!"
    Else
        txtHTMLCode = Inet1.OpenURL(txtURL.Text)
    End If
Exit Sub
errhand:
    If Err.Number = -1610612736 Then
        MsgBox "You can't provide a file URL: " & Err.Description
    Else
        MsgBox " The following error occurred: " & Err.Number & " " & _
            Err.Description
    End If
End Sub
```

Where did Error −1610612736 come from? I found this error occurred whenever I typed a file URL. A file URL is an .htm file that resides on disk. So, I simply copied the error number and trapped for it. This is a common strategy for test scripting: you will find known errors as you write tests. You can then trap and log those errors as your tests run. (To keep it simple, this code does not do logging. Test results logging is covered in Chapters 5 and 9.)

TO TRY THIS

> **NOTE** *To run the examples in this chapter you will need to have an Internet connection and Internet Explorer 4 (or later). The examples in this text use Internet Explorer 5.*

1. Add a textbox control to a project that has an Internet Transfer control on the default form (see the previous "To Try This" in this chapter under "Using the Microsoft Internet Transfer Control").

2. In the Properties window, change the following properties of the textbox you just added:

   - Change the **Name** property of the textbox to **txtHTMLCode**.

   - Change the **MultiLine** property of the textbox control to **True**.

   - Change the **Scrollbars** property of the textbox to **Both.**

   - Change the **Height** property of the textbox so that it is at least **4000**.

   - Change the **Width** property so that it is at least **6000**.

3. Add a second textbox to the form. Place it just above the first textbox and size it so that it is just about as wide but do not change its height. Change the **Name** property of this second textbox to **txtURL**.

4. Add a Command button control to the form. Place it anywhere you like and size it any way you like. Add the code from Listing 10-1 to the **click-event** of this Command button.

5. Add the following code to the Form_Load-event:

   ```
   txtURL = "www.stagroup.com"
   txtHTMLCode = Inet1.OpenURL(txtURL.Text)
   ```

6. Run the program. The txtHTMLCode textbox will be loaded with the HTML text for the same Web site displayed in Figure 10-1. The following graphic displays output similar to what you will see:

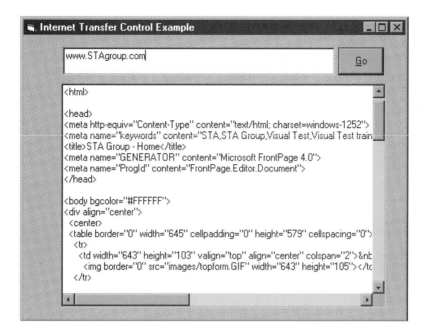

Now that you have the HTML code, you can write a routine using Visual Basic's string manipulation functions to parse this code and extract a list of links or images. Sample code for extracting items from the HTML source is included in the Chapter 10 Practice Files.

In the preceding examples, you saw that you could retrieve the HTML code from a Web page, the directory of an FTP site, and a binary file from an FTP site. In addition to what you have seen, the Internet Transfer control is a powerful tool that has many other valuable properties and methods. It can also trap server messages and perform other tasks on a Web site. The Help on the Internet Transfer control is very complete. Besides looking at the control description in Help, check out the section called "Using the Internet Transfer Control"—it contains a discussion with several examples of the uses of this control. For testing ASP, however, we will turn to the WebBrowser control. The WebBrowser control is also very powerful and has certain advantages over the Internet Transfer control when testing ASP, as we will see in the next section.

Testing ASP

ASP pages contain server-side processing. To test these pages, you could run all tests through the client, which does test the server-side processing somewhat. But to identify bugs that are solely on the server–side you should consider testing the server independently of the client. If you can trap the HTTP requests sent to the server, you can save them and then send them yourself through your own test utility, effectively bypassing the client. ASP pages communicate with the server by passing information through variables in HTTP requests.

Although several methods are available for sending data to an HTTP server, Get and Post are currently the most common. Get is a simpler method to use because in a Get request, the variable information, called the *QueryString*, is passed in the URL itself by appending the information onto the end of the URL. A "?" character separates the URL from the QueryString. For example, let's say there's a Web page with a textbox and a Submit button and the developer wants to send it to the server (Assume the information entered in the text box is "Mary Sweeney.") The Get request would look like the following:

```
GET
/SomeWebSite/SomeASPPage.asp?txtName=Mary+Sweeney&btnSubmit=Submit
HTTP/1.1 Accept: text/plain
```

In the request shown above, the QueryString is

```
txtName=Mary+Sweeney&btnSubmit=Submit
```

The Get request is easy for the developer to use and it is also easy to troubleshoot because the URL and all of the values that are passed show up in the address bar at the bottom of the browser. This also makes it an excellent technique for testers to use. (In HTML, the Get request is usually sent in the <Form> tag with a method = GET.) The only downside to the Get request is that it is cumbersome for passing a lot of information. The Post request is typically used instead to submit form data to an HTTP server when the data exceeds the maximum allowable transfer using the Get method. This maximum is approximately 2 KB. So, the Post request can send a lot more data but the price paid is a more complex request. The Post request includes the information associated with the request in the body of the request. It also includes a header. The Post request for the same information used in our Get example might look something like this:

```
POST /SomeWebSite/SomeASPPage.asp? HTTP/1.1 Accept: text/plain
...
Content-type: application/x-www-form-urlencoded
Content-length: 37
txtName=Mary+Sweeney&btnSubmit=Submit
```

The disadvantage to this method for testing is that the data, now called *form variables*, won't show up in the address bar of the browser. (This might be considered a plus for the Web page user since it might be less confusing.) It's not so bad, though, because the information is still available to us through the use of the Internet Transfer control and WebBrowser control, not to mention using the View ➤ Source menu item on the browser itself.

Although there are pros and cons to both kinds of HTTP requests, the reality for testing is that if you want to trap requests between the client and server, you need to allow for both since which to use is a Web developer's choice—you will definitely encounter them both. There are a number of ways to trap these values using Visual Basic. In the next section, we will see how to do so using the Web-Browser control.

Using the WebBrowser Control

In this section, you will learn how to use the WebBrowser control to access a Web site and return the messages being sent to and from the server. The WebBrowser control has a Browser window, which the Internet Transfer control does not. The WebBrowser control also supports sessions, which the Internet Transfer control does not. This makes the WebBrowser a likelier tool to use to create a testing utility. Like the Internet Transfer Control, the WebBrowser control is not in the standard set of tools so you will need to add it using the Project Components dialog.

NOTE *The WebBrowser control is a part of the Internet Explorer platform SDK. It actually installs along with Internet Explorer 4 and later versions. You will* not *find help available for the WebBrowser control in the Visual Basic documentation. If you installed the Internet Explorer platform SDK help, you will find it there. Otherwise, you can access Help on the WebBrowser control online at* `http://msdn.microsoft.com/workshop/browser/Webbrowser` `/reference/objects/Webbrowser.asp.`

TO TRY THIS

1. In a new Visual Basic project, select the **Project ➤ Components** menu item. The Project Components dialog displays. The Controls tab has the focus.

2. Check the **Microsoft Internet Controls** box and then click **OK** to close the Components dialog box. Adding this component to your Toolbox automatically creates a reference to an associated library, **shdocVWCtl** (great name, huh?). At this point, you may want to take a look at this library in the Object Browser.

> **NOTE** *Microsoft also recommends setting a reference to the Microsoft Internet Controls library through the* **Project ➤ References** *menu item. If you set the reference here as well, you will actually get two libraries. The other library is* **shdocVW**.

3. Double-click the **WebBrowser control** icon (in the shape of the world) in the Toolbox to add it to the default form.

4. Add the following to the **Form_Load** event:

```
WebBrowser1.Navigate2 "www.microsoft.com"
```

> **NOTE** *In place of* www.microsoft.com, *you can put your favorite Web site!*

5. Run the project. You will see the Web site displayed in your new custom browser. With one line of code, you created an instant browser. It's not very friendly at this point, but you can use the properties and methods of the WebBrowser control to create a custom interface for your Web browser.

6. Add a textbox control just above the WebBrowser control. Change its Name property to **txtURL**. Size it so that it is at least wide enough to contain a typical URL, for example:

```
"http://support.microsoft.com/support/kb/articles/Q167/6/58.ASP"
```

7. Add a Command button and change its Name property to **cmdGo**.
   Change its Caption property to **&Go**. Change its Default property to
   True. Your form should look similar to this:

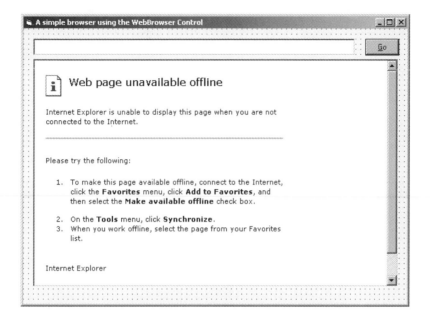

8. Add the following code to the click-event of the **cmdGo** Command
   button:

```
If txtURL.Text = "" Then
    MsgBox "You must provide a valid URL"
    Exit Sub
End If
WebBrowser1.Navigate2 txtURL.Text
```

9. Run your project. If you have an Internet connection, you can type a
   valid URL into the textbox and navigate to it by clicking the **Go** button.

Your new custom Web browser uses the Navigate2 method to access a Web
site. When the WebBrowser control performs the Navigate2 method successfully,
a BeforeNavigate2 event is generated. When this event triggers, some information available in the argument list of this event handler will be very useful for us.
Table 10-1 lists the arguments returned by the BeforeNavigate2 event (from the
MSDN Help).

Table 10-1. Arguments for the BeforeNavigate2 Event of the WebBrowser Control

ARGUMENT	DESCRIPTION
pDisp	An object that evaluates to the top level or frame of the WebBrowser object corresponding to the navigation.
URL	A string expression that evaluates to the URL to which the browser is navigating.
Flags	Reserved for future use.
TargetFrameName	A string expression that evaluates to the name of the frame in which the resource will be displayed or NULL if no named frame is targeted for the resource.
PostData	Data to send to the server if the HTTP POST transaction is being used.
Headers	A value that specifies the additional HTTP headers to send to the server (HTTP URLs only). The headers can specify things such as the action required of the server, the type of data being passed to the server, or a status code.
Cancel	A Boolean value that the container can set to TRUE to cancel the navigation operation or to FALSE to allow it to proceed.

The three arguments of special interest to us are the URL, PostData, and Headers arguments because these will allow us to trap the HTTP requests. For a Get request, all of the pertinent information will be returned in the URL argument. For Post requests, the critical information will be in the PostData and Headers arguments. Listing 10-2 shows the BeforeNavigate2 event of the Web-Browser. The relevant (for us) arguments, URL, PostData, and Headers, are automatically loaded with data when this event triggers.

Listing 10-2. Code in the BeforeNavigate2 event of the WebBrowser that will capture information from HTTP requests.

```
Private Sub WebBrowser1_BeforeNavigate2(ByVal pDisp As Object, URL As Variant, _
        Flags As Variant, TargetFrameName As Variant, PostData As Variant, _
        Headers As Variant, Cancel As Boolean)

        Dim lCount As Long
        Dim lLen As Long
        Dim strPostData As String

        lLen = LenB(PostData) ' Use LenB to get the byte count
        If lLen > 0 Then    ' If it's a post form, lLen will be > 0
            For lCount = 1 To lLen
            ' Use MidB to get 1 byte at a time:
```

```
            strPostData = strPostData & Chr(AscB(MidB(PostData, lCount, 1)))
         Next

      'now we can load text boxes on our form with the data returned from the server
         txtFormvariables.Text = strPostData
         txtHeaders.Text = Headers
      End If
      TxtURLReturned.Text = URL
End Sub
```

The values in the Headers and URL arguments can be directly loaded into textboxes on the form but the value in the PostData argument is a little more troublesome. It is must be converted from a binary format into a string. The information on how and why you must do this is available from the Microsoft Support Web site in an article called "HOWTO: Handle Data from a Post Form When Hosting WebBrowser Control." Basically, you have to do the conversion because this control was written for C++ programmers. Because of this, the PostData argument is in the form of a pointer to a binary array, a C++ structure (a SAFEARRAY for you C++-literate readers). The For-Next loop in Listing 10-2 converts the data to a string using the MidB, AscB, and Chr functions in succession. Don't worry about memorizing how to do this, you probably won't and why should you? You can just download the article from http://support.microsoft.com/support/kb/articles/Q256/1/95.asp.

Once you have the information from the URL, Headers, and PostData arguments, you can save this information either to a variable or to a file and formulate the request yourself in code later. You can change the values and create a variety of test cases. Catenating the correct values together is pretty straightforward except in the case of that troublesome Postdata argument. In this case, you will have to convert it back the other way, that is, from a string back into a binary format. It's a little easier going in this direction since the string can be converted to binary using the StrConv function, which is used to convert values from one data type to another. This can be done using an array of the data type Byte. The following code prepares a text value from a textbox into a Byte array using the StrConv function with the vbFromUnicode constant:

```
Dim abytPostData () as Byte
abytPostData = StrConv(txtFormVariables.Text, vbFromUnicode)
'if there are form variables, then this is a Post request
'so we must add a header
If txtFormVariables.Text <> "" Then
    TxtHeaders.Text= _
        "Content-type: application/x-www-form-urlencoded" & vbCrLf
End If
WebBrowser1.Navigate2 trim(txtURLReturned), 15, , abytPostData, txtHeaders
```

The necessity to create an array of the Byte data type and convert it using VB's StrConv function is outlined in another Microsoft Support article, "HOWTO: Use the PostData Parameter in WebBrowser Control" at

`http://support.microsoft.com/support/kb/articles/Q174/9/23.asp`.

In the preceding code, a header had to be added once it was determined that the request was a Post request. The header is always the same for a Post request so it is directly coded into script. The required header is:

`Content-Type: application/x-www-form-urlencoded`

As you can see from the previous example, the Navigate2 method has a few more arguments that allow you to specify the form variables and header associated with a Post request. If there is no such data, then Navigate2 presumes a Get request:

`WebBrowser1.Navigate2 trim(txtURLReturned), 15, , abytPostData, txtHeaders`

Table 10-2 lists all of the arguments for the Navigate2 method (from the MSDN Help).

Table 10-2. Arguments for the Navigate2 Method of the WebBrowser Control

ARGUMENT	DESCRIPTION		
URL	Required. A string expression that evaluates to the URL of the resource to display or the full path to the file location.		
Flags	Optional. A constant or value that specifies whether to add the resource to the history list, whether to read from or write to the cache, and whether to display the resource in a new window. It can be a combination of the following constants or values.		
	CONSTANT	**VALUE**	**MEANING**
	navOpenInNewWindow	1	Open the resource or file in a new window.
	navNoHistory	2	Do not add the resource or file to the history list. The new page replaces the current page in the list.
	navNoReadFromCache	4	Do not read from the disk cache for this navigation.
	navNoWriteToCache	8	Do not write the results of this navigation to the disk cache.
TargetFrameName	Optional. String expression that evaluates to the name of an HTML frame in the URL to display in the Browser window. The possible values for this parameter follow.		

(continued)

ARGUMENT	DESCRIPTION	
	VALUE	MEANING
	_blank	Load the link into a new unnamed window.
	_parent	Load the link into the immediate parent of the document the link is in.
	_self link	Load the link into the same window the was clicked in.
	_top	Load the link into the full body of the current window.
	<window_name>	A named HTML frame. If no frame or window exists that matches the specified target name, a new window is opened for the specified link.
PostData	Optional. Data to send to the server during the HTTP POST transaction. For example, the POST transaction is used to send data gathered by an HTML form to a program or script. If this parameter does not specify any post data, the Navigate2 method issues an HTTP GET transaction. This parameter is ignored if the URL is not an HTTP URL.	
Headers	Optional. A value that specifies additional HTTP headers to send to the server. These headers are added to the default Internet Explorer headers. The headers can specify things like the action required of the server, the type of data being passed to the server, or a status code. This parameter is ignored if the URL is not an HTTP URL.	

The second argument listed in Table 10-2, the Flags argument, is of particular interest to testers. We can set this value so that we do not impact the cache or the browser's history file.

ASP Resources

There are several articles on the Microsoft Support Web site that relate to what we are doing in this section. Here is a list of the ones we have mentioned so far, plus one more:

- "HOWTO: Automate Internet Explorer to POST Form Data,"
  http://support.microsoft.com/support/kb/articles/Q167/6/58.asp

- "HOWTO: Use the PostData Parameter in WebBrowser Control,"
  `http://support.microsoft.com/support/kb/articles/Q174/9/23.asp`

- "HOWTO: Handle Data from a Post Form When Hosting WebBrowser Control,"
  `http://support.microsoft.com/support/kb/articles/Q256/1/95.asp`

The tone of these articles expects the reader to have intermediate to advanced programming skills. Even if you don't, it's a good idea to be exposed to these topics. Hopefully, you have realized by now that the Microsoft Support articles and MSDN online are great resources and free, too.

ASP Today, at `http://www.asptoday.com`, is another first-rate resource for ASP developers and is helpful for testers as well since there is occasionally a testing-related article. One such article, "Automated Testing of ASP Pages using Visual Basic and the WebBrowser control," by Erik Slotboom, inspired this section. You must pay a fee to join this site to look at back articles but there are always a couple of free articles available on a daily basis.

The ASP Resource Index at `http://www.aspin.com` is a great place to start learning ASP and to find out just about anything. It is the place where the tutorial for the Get versus Post page is located (`http://www.asp101.com/samples/getpost.asp`). It is also the place where I have personally learned a great deal about ASP!

TO TRY THIS

1. Open the following file in the Practice Files:
   **Chapter10\Demos\WebBrowserDemo\
   WebBrowserDemo.vbp.** This project has a
   WebBrowser control added called WebBrowser1.
   Review this project and its code; it contains all of
   the code from this section. It also contains a textbox
   control, txtURL, for entering new URLs and a CommandButton control, cmdGO, that when clicked, executes a Navigate2 method to the value in the txtURL textbox. At the bottom of the form, there are three Label controls. These will display the full URL returned, the form variables, and the header. These last two are filled only when the request is a Post request. Finally, there is a Command button control called cmdSubmitRequest, which contains the code to resubmit the request using the values in the textboxes.

2. Run the project. The Form_Load event issues a
   Navigate2 method to a Web site containing an ASP tutorial at
   `http://www.asp101.com/samples/getpost.asp`. As long as you are here,
   read the page for a discussion of the differences between the Get and

Post HTTP requests. This site is a good one to use for checking the code in this simple utility. The page contains a button for submitting a Post request and another for submitting a Get request.

 NOTE *The ASP101 Web site at* `http://www.asp101.com` *is a great place to explore and learn more about ASP. If you are going to be testing a lot of ASP, you should definitely spend some time here.*

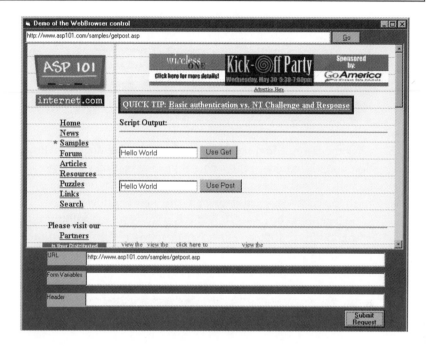

3. Inside the Browser window, change the text in the first textbox from "Hello World" to "**Hello Yourname.**" Click the **Use Get** button. Scroll down in the Browser window to read the output. Notice that the URL textbox on your form now contains text similar to the following:

   ```
   http://www.asp101.com/samples/getpost.asp?Text=Hello+YourName
   ```

   This is the URL and the Get HTTP request information trapped by the BeforeNavigate2 event.

4. Modify the text in the URL textbox, changing "YourName" to read "Elvis" so that it looks like the following:

   ```
   http://www.asp101.com/samples/getpost.asp?Text=Hello+Elvis
   ```

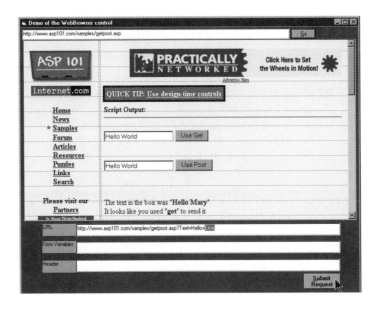

5. Click the **Submit Request** button. This will generate a new Browser window containing the same page, yet this navigation was generated by the code in the click event of the Submit Request button using the values from the textboxes. Scroll down in this new window to verify that it says: "The text in the box was '**Hello Elvis**'." You have just submitted a request with modified variable values. Now you can not only submit the same request but you can construct multiple tests modifying the input as required.

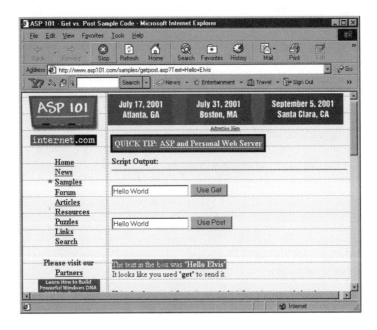

Close the additional Browser window. Try using the Post button as well. To really understand how this works, try steps 1 through 5 again using the Debugger (see "The Debugger" section in Chapter 4). Stepping through this line-by-line will help you see the process of trapping and submitting requests.

Listing 10-3 contains the full text of the Chapter10\Demos\WebBrowserDemo\WebBrowserDemo.vbp project.

Listing 10-3. The full code for the WebBrowserDemo project.

```
Option Explicit
'*******************************************************************
'* Chapter 10. WebBrowser Demo project. This code demonstrates the use
'* of the WebBrowser control for retrieving and sending Get and Post HTTP
'* requests.
'*******************************************************************
Private Sub Form_Load()
'this code amounts to having a "startup" Web site.
    WebBrowser1.Navigate2 "http://www.asp101.com/samples/getpost.asp"
    txtURL.Text = "http://www.asp101.com/samples/getpost.asp"
End Sub

Private Sub cmdGO_Click()
    If txtURL.Text = "" Then
        MsgBox "You must provide a valid URL"
        Exit Sub
    End If
    WebBrowser1.Navigate2 txtURL.Text
End Sub

Private Sub cmdSubmitRequest_Click()
    Dim iCount As Integer
    Dim abytPostData() As Byte
    abytPostData = StrConv(Trim(txtFormVariables.Text), vbFromUnicode)

    'if there are form variables, then this is a Post request
    'so we must add a header
    If txtFormVariables.Text <> "" Then
        txtHeaders.Text = _
            "Content-type: application/x-www-form-urlencoded" & vbCrLf
    End If
```

379

```
                  WebBrowser1.Navigate2 Trim(txtURLReturned), 15, , abytPostData, txtHeaders.Text
                  'the number 15 in the 2nd argument does the following:
                      'opens a new browser window
                      'specifies that this URL will NOT be written to the Browser History
                      'specifies that this navigation will not read from or write to the cache
         End Sub


         Private Sub WebBrowser1_BeforeNavigate2(ByVal pDisp As Object, URL As Variant, _
                  Flags As Variant, TargetFrameName As Variant, PostData As Variant, _
                  Headers As Variant, Cancel As Boolean)

                  Dim lCount As Long
                  Dim lLen As Long
                  Dim strPostData As String

                  lLen = LenB(PostData) ' Use LenB to get the byte count

                  If lLen > 0 Then      ' If it's a post form, lLen will be > 0
                      For lCount = 1 To lLen
                      ' Use MidB to get 1 byte at a time:
                          strPostData = strPostData & Chr(AscB(MidB(PostData, lCount, 1)))
                      Next

                  'now we can load text boxes on our form with the data returned from the server
                      txtFormVariables.Text = strPostData
                      txtHeaders.Text = Headers
                  End If
                  txtURLReturned.Text = URL
         End Sub
```

Detecting Errors

Now you know how to trap and send an HTTP request. For a proper test case, you will also need to determine if the request produced any errors. The demonstration created in the last example allows for only a visual check on your part. It would be preferable to automate the check for errors. If a page generates an error, the server will issue an Internal Server error in the response header. Unfortunately, the WebBrowser control is not able to access the server responses. Another strategy to determine errors would be to interrogate the inner text of the returned Web page. If the returned page is in error, it will usually contain the word "error," literally, in its HTML text or its title. This isn't optimal since it isn't exact but it provides a way to do a first pass for errors. The HTML text can be parsed to search for any text that will represent an error.

The DownLoadComplete event of the WebBrowser executes after the page is downloaded, just as it name implies. The following code accesses the Document object of the WebBrowser control to retrieve the title of the downloaded page and its inner HTML text. Then, Visual Basic's InStr function is used to determine if the word "error" appears anywhere in the returned code:

```
Private Sub WebBrowser1_DownloadComplete()
    Dim lError As Long
    Dim lErrorTitle As Long

    lError = InStr(LCase(WebBrowser1.Document.documentelement.innerhtml), "error")
    lErrorTitle = InStr(LCase(lblTitle.Caption), "error")
    If lError > 0 Then
        lblResult.Caption = "Fail: 'Error' in HTML"
    ElseIf lErrorTitle > 0 Then
        lblResult.Caption = "Fail: 'Error' in Title"
    Else
        lblResult.Caption = "Pass: No Errors detected in HTML"
    End If
    lblTitle.Caption = WebBrowser1.Document.Title
End Sub
```

We can turn the WebBrowserDemo project into a testing utility by adding a few more bells and whistles to it. For example, it would be advantageous to browse the Web site you want to test, trapping and logging all of the HTTP requests into a file. Then, you could submit those requests yourself from script, testing various combinations of variables and types of requests. It would also be nice to make the interface more user-friendly and more like a standard browser. For example, you might like to have a menu that allows you to browse and find an .asp or .html file to test. In order to add this kind of capability, you will need to use a few more controls than we have covered so far. In the next section, I will show you how to add a menu and a common dialog control; these controls can be useful on any project.

Adding a Menu to Your Project

In this book, I have deliberately not introduced a great many different controls. That's because the intent of this book is to concentrate more on getting information quickly and simply and less on providing a fancy user interface for your projects (unlike developers who *must* do that). As the chapters have progressed, though, the projects are getting more complex and the addition of certain controls can make the user interface for your own Visual Basic projects more friendly, making life easier for *you!* One of the more common controls to add is a menu because it is such a standard item that we all expect one to exist. Visual Basic 6 has a simple Menu Editor that makes it easy and fast to add a basic menu.

TO TRY THIS

1. Within the **Chapter10\Demos\WebBrowserDemo\ WebBrowserDemo.vbp** project, make sure you are in Design mode and the Form Designer window is showing. (If not, the Menu Editor will be disabled.) Select the **Tools ➤ Menu Editor** menu item. You can also get to the Menu Editor by pressing **Ctrl-e** or clicking the **Menu Editor** icon in the Standard toolbar. The Menu Editor dialog displays.

> **NOTE** *You may want to save the form and project with a different name before going further.*

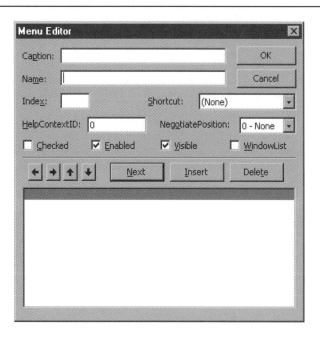

2. Type **&File** into the Caption textbox and **mnuFile** into the Name textbox. Notice that the window at the bottom of the dialog now contains the text "&File". This window will contain a hierarchy of the menu structure you will create.

3. Place your cursor in the window at the bottom of the dialog just below the "&File" line and **click**. It may look like the values you typed into the textboxes in the last step have disappeared. They are still there—to get them back, click on the **&File** line again. When you click below the &File line, you are opening up a new spot to place a menu item. So, now you can type in Name and Caption properties for the next menu item.

4. Type **&Browse** into the Caption textbox and **mnuFileBrowse** into the Name textbox. Your menu should look something like this:

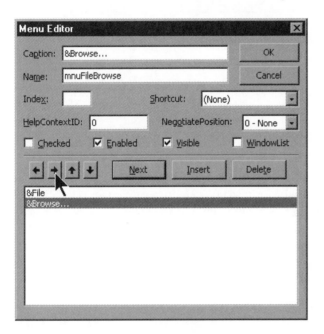

5. You have two menu items but the Browse menu item should be a subitem to the File menu item. To make this a submenu item, indent it by clicking the **right-arrow** button on the dialog. (In the preceding graphic, the cursor is pointing to the right-arrow button on the dialog.) If you click this button while a menu item is highlighted in the large window on the dialog, it will indent it and make it a submenu item to the one above it.

6. Repeat steps 4 and 5 but this time create a menu item with the following values for the Caption and Name properties: Caption: **E&xit**; Name: **mnuFileExit.** Make sure to indent the item so that it is a submenu item to the File menu. Your menu should look like this:

7. Click **OK** to close the Menu Editor. Even in Design mode, your menu is displayed on the form so you can drop it down and click the items. When you do this in Design mode, the form's Code window will open with your cursor in the click-event for the menu item you selected. Click on the **File ➤ Exit** menu item you just created on the *frmWeb-BrowserDemo* form. The mnuFileExit_Click event is displayed in the form's Code window as shown.

```
WebBrowserDemo - frmWebBrowserDemo (Code)                     _ □ ×
mnuFileExit                          ▼   Click                        ▼

    Private Sub mnuFileExit_Click()

    End Sub


    Private Sub WebBrowser1_BeforeNavigate2(ByVal pDisp As Object, URL
            Flags As Variant, TargetFrameName As Variant, PostData
            Headers As Variant, Cancel As Boolean)

        Dim lCount As Long
        Dim lLen As Long
        Dim strPostData As String

        lLen = LenB(PostData)  ' Use LenB to get the byte count

        If lLen > 0 Then      ' If it's a post form, lLen will be >
            For lCount = 1 To lLen
                ' Use MidB to get 1 byte at a time:
```

8. Type the following code into the mnuFileExit_Click-event:

```
Unload Me               'unloads the form from main memory
```

Run the program. Click on the **File ➤ Exit** menu item of the WebBrowser Demo. Now that you are in Run mode, the code executes and the form is closed.

In the next section, you will add the code for the File ➤ Browse menu item as well, but first, you will need to know a little about common dialogs.

The Menu Editor has more capabilities—for example, you can add Access keys (the ability to access a menu item with a control sequence such as Ctrl-Alt-K—sometimes called shortcut keys). For more information about the Menu Editor's capabilities, see the Visual Basic Help system, particularly the topics, "Menu Basics" and "Creating Menus with the Menu Editor." You should try to make your interface conform to basic Windows standards for menus. This will make it consistent and intuitive for your users. See the MSDN Web site (msdn.microsoft.com) for more information on standards for Windows applications.

NOTE *There will* not *be a Menu Editor in Visual Basic's next version, VB.Net, in which menu handling is done via a Menu control. See Chapter 11 for more information.*

Using the Common Dialog Control in Your Project

In the last section, we created a menu with a Browse menu item but did not write any code for it. You might want to add the capability to browse for a file of type .htm, .html, or .asp so you can view the page in your utility. You could create your own form for browsing and open it using the *formname*.Show method, as learned in Chapter 5. There is an easier way that you'll see next.

The dialog box for opening a file is a very standard one, just run any Microsoft accessory, like the Notepad accessory, and click on the **File ➤ Open** menu to see an example. When the Open dialog displays, it's a familiar sight, there is a List box with a list of files and an Open button. In fact, opening virtually any Windows application yields a File menu with an Open subitem. The dialog looks virtually the same in every application. This is good because it provides the user with a common way to accomplish a task across multiple applications. In fact, the Open dialog is such a standard dialog, like the Print and Save dialogs, that Microsoft provides a control that allows access to these prewritten, common dialogs. The control that provides this access is aptly named the Common Dialog control. You can add this control to your Visual Basic form and use its properties and methods to add the functionality of common dialogs to your application. You could actually add these dialogs via calls to the Microsoft Windows Commdlg DLL, which is part of the Microsoft Windows API (see Chapter 7 for information on how to access the Windows API libraries). Using the Common Dialog control greatly simplifies the coding involved, so it's better to use it.

There are six dialogs you can get to with the Common Dialog control; each is accessed via a method of this control. Table 10-3 shows the six common dialogs available.

Table 10-3. Dialogs That Can Be Accessed Using Methods of the Common Dialog Control

DIALOG DISPLAYED	METHOD
Open	ShowOpen
Save As	ShowSave
Color	ShowColor
Font	ShowFont
Print	ShowPrinter
Help	ShowHelp

TO TRY THIS

1. In Design mode, **right-click** on the Toolbox. Select the **Components** menu item from the pop-up menu. This is the same Components dialog you have heretofore accessed with the **Project ➢ Components** menu item.

2. In the Components dialog, check the box to select the **Microsoft Common Dialog** control and then click **OK** to close the Components dialog. The icon of the Common dialog control appears in the Toolbox window.

3. **Double-click** on the new icon in your Toolbox as shown. A Common Dialog control is added to your form. This is a control that will never be visible to the user of the program. It is there solely to add hooks into the Microsoft Windows Dynamic Link Library, Commdlg.DLL.

NOTE *Because this control is not visible to the user at run time, it doesn't matter where on the form you place it, even on top of another control.*

4. Examine the properties of this new control using the Properties window. Notice that the name of the control is CommonDialog1. You can change this to a shorter value if desired, just don't forget what you've called it. All of the code in this text will use the default name CommonDialog1. There are some other properties that we will change soon but in general, it's a better idea to change property values in code rather than using the Properties window. Doing it in code is self-documenting—it is easier to tell which properties have been modified and which have not.

5. **Double-click** on the Common Dialog control on your form: the Code window opens but your cursor is not placed in an event for the Common Dialog. Surprise! There aren't any events for this control. You will add code to access it from one of the event handlers for the menu items you created in the last section, "Adding a Menu to Your Project." Use the Object dropdown in the Code window to find the **mnuFileBrowse** object. Since the only event for menu items is the click-event, your cursor is placed in the middle of the mnuFileBrowse_Click event handler:

```
Private Sub mnuFileBrowse_Click()
|
End Sub
```

6. Add the following code to the mnuFileBrowse_Click event:

```
CommonDialog1.ShowOpen
```

7. Run the project and click on the **File ➤ Browse** menu item. The Open dialog displays. (Depending on which version of Windows you are running, the dialog may look slightly different.) This looks familiar but there are some things missing.

8. Navigate to a file of your choice, any file, and click it. Its name shows up in the Filename textbox on the dialog. Now click the **Open** button. What happens? The dialog closes but the file doesn't open. That's because you have only added a line of code to open the dialog but you haven't yet told it what to do with the file! There are other things missing as well— for example, there isn't a filter for the dialog where you can specify the kinds of files you want to see. You will also probably want to specify a starting directory so that this dialog starts in the same directory each time.

9. Return to the Code window of the form and modify the click-event of the mnuFileBrowse menu item so that it looks like the following:

```
Private Sub mnuFileBrowse_Click()
    CommonDialog1.DialogTitle = "My Custom Dialog"
    CommonDialog1.Filter = "*.asp;*.htm;*.html|*.asp;*.htm;*.html|All Files (*.*)|*.*"
    CommonDialog1.InitDir = App.Path
    CommonDialog1.ShowOpen
    txtURL.Text = CommonDialog1.FileName
End Sub
```

The lines you added just above the ShowOpen method add a custom title, specify two filters for the dialog, and set the initial directory of the dialog to the path of the application. (App.path is the directory where the application is located.) The line after the ShowOpen method is executed only after the user clicks the Open button on the dialog; it assigns the file the user selected to the txtURL textbox on the form. This line is ignored if the user clicks Cancel.

10. Run the program again and try using the Open dialog to navigate to a file with an .asp or an .html extension.

You can use the same Common Dialog control to access any of the six available common dialogs listed in Table 10-3 simply by setting and using its properties and methods. To learn more about how to use this control see "Using the Common Dialog Control" in the Visual Basic Help system.

An ASP Testing Utility

The WebBrowserDemo has become a little more user-friendly with the addition of a menu and an Open dialog. This demo has been useful to learn how to use the WebBrowser control but it can't be considered much of a test tool unless it can store HTTP requests it retrieves in a file (rather than just to a form) and allows you to send them when needed. This would incorporate data-driven test techniques into the utility (see the sidebar, "Data-Driven Testing," next). In Chapter 5, you learned how to use the Microsoft Scripting Library to add code to log test results to a file and to read those results back again when needed. You can use this same knowledge to add file-handling capability to the demo project and create a simple test tool. To add this capability, you will first need to set the reference to the Microsoft Scripting Library using the Project References dialog. You can then add a button to the form to add the information returned from an HTTP request.

Listing 10-4 displays code to update the General Declarations section of the form with the proper File System Objects and to update the Form_Load event to initialize these objects. The code for a new button, cmdAddtoTC (add to test case), is shown.

Listing 10-4. Code to add file access to the WebBrowserDemo.

```
'The next 2 lines are added to the General Declaration section of the form

Private fs As FileSystemObject
Private tsTestCase As TextStream

Private Sub Form_Load()
    'set up objects for creating a list of HTTP requests:
    Set fs = CreateObject("Scripting.FileSystemObject")    'set up to log to URL's list
```

```
    Set tsTestCase = fs.CreateTextFile(App.Path & "\ASPTestURLs.txt")
    tsTestCase.Close
    Set tsTestCase = Nothing

    WebBrowser1.Navigate2 "http://www.asp101.com/samples/getpost.asp"
    txtURL = "http://www.asp101.com/samples/getpost.asp"
End Sub

Private Sub cmdAddtoTC_Click()    'new button adds code to write request to a file
    Set tsTestCase = fs.OpenTextFile(App.Path & "\ASPTestURLs.txt", ForAppending)
    tsTestCase.WriteLine txtURLReturned.Text & "," & txtFormVariables.Text
    tsTestCase.Close
    MsgBox "URL Added to Request List"
End Sub
```

Data-Driven Testing

Data-driven testing, as defined by Mark Fewster and Dorothy Graham in their very practical and informative book, *Software Test Automation,* "stores test inputs in a separate data file rather than in the script itself." This allows the tester to use the same test script multiple times with different data rather than create a single test for each atomic piece or set of data. The demonstration utility used in this book creates such a file of HTTP requests and allows the tester to submit them at will. This is one form of data-driven testing. Data-driven testing is often associated with load and stress testing since large amounts of data input can be loaded from a file quickly and applied against an application but it not necessarily limited to that. The file-handling techniques discussed in Chapter 5 and used in this chapter as well as those discussed in Appendix C can be used to implement data-driven testing. Accessing a database with data inputs can also be a part of data-driven testing. Database access techniques are discussed in Chapter 8. For more information on data-driven testing techniques as well as other test automation techniques, I recommend the Fewster and Graham text. It has some helpful examples and is a good adjunct to this book, which teaches you the skills needed to create the algorithms in theirs.

The next step is to add code to read the file. To do this, a button is added to read from the file once each time it is clicked. Listing 10-5 displays the code for a new button called cmdTest that reads the file of stored requests created by the code in Listing 10-4.

Listing 10-5. Code for reading stored HTTP requests.

```
Private Sub cmdTest_Click()
'**************************
'* This code reads from the app.path & "\ASPTestURLs.txt" test file to
'* execute the HTTP requests stored there.
'**************************
    Dim strInputURL As String
    Dim strURL As String
    Dim strFormVariables As String
    Dim abytPostData() As Byte
    Dim strHeader As String

    If bTestStarted = False Then
        bTestStarted = True
        Set tsTestCase = fs.OpenTextFile(App.Path & "\ASPTestURLs.txt", ForReading)
        cmdTest.Caption = "Tests &Started; Click again for next request "
    End If


    If Not tsTestCase.AtEndOfStream Then
        strInputURL = tsTestCase.ReadLine

        strURL = Left(strInputURL, InStr(strInputURL, ",") - 1)
        strFormVariables = Mid(strInputURL, InStr(strInputURL, ",") + 1)
        ' the form variables must be converted from Unicode into the required format
        abytPostData = StrConv(strFormVariables, vbFromUnicode)

        'if there are form variables, then this is a
        'Post request so we must add a header
        If Len(strFormVariables) > 0 Then
            strHeader = "Content-type: application/x-www-form-urlencoded" & vbCrLf
        Else
            strHeader = ""
        End If
        Debug.Print "strURL: '" & strURL & "' strHeader: '" & strHeader & "'"
        WebBrowser1.Navigate2 strURL, 14, , abytPostData, strHeader
    Else
        MsgBox "End of file reached; click again to start over", _
                                   vbInformation, "ASP Test"
        tsTestCase.Close
        Set tsTestCase = Nothing
        bTestStarted = False
        cmdTest.Caption = "&Start URL Request Submission"
    End If
End Sub
```

The updated code for this new utility is in the Practice Files in the project Chapter10\ Demos\ASPTesting\ASPTesting.vbp. It has much of the same code for accessing a Web site and retrieving HTTP requests as the WebBrowserDemo project but it is has some additions to make it more functional. It has added file access for storing and retrieving the HTTP requests instead of simply retrieving the requests to the form. It contains all the menu items added in this section plus a couple more. It has code to retrieve the HTML for the Web page. Additional user-friendly features have been added, such as a Stop button to end a navigation that takes too long.

TO TRY THIS

Rather than change the WebBrowser demo, in these steps, you will run a finished version complete with all the code added for enhancements. You will then take this new utility through a test of some ASP sites.

1. Open the file
    Chapter10\ Demos\ASPTesting\ASPTesting.vbp. Review the code in this project.

2. Run the project. The Testing ASP Utility dialog displays with the ASP101 Web site loaded in the WebBrowser control window. Click the **Use Get** button on the Web page. The functionality has been changed so that the Web page is not generated in a new window but is loaded back into the WebBrowser control itself. This might not seem as fun but it simplifies the execution of multiple tests. Take note of the values loaded into the textboxes.

3. Click the **Add Information to Request List** button on the Testing ASP Utility window. A Message box displays indicating the request has been added to your test file. Click **OK** to dismiss the Message box.

4. Click the **View Request List** button to see the way the Get request was added into your test file. The Notepad accessory displays with the Get request showing. Notice the name and location of the test file. You can change that here by clicking **File ➤ Save As** on the Notepad menu—however, the utility will not be able to use it once it is renamed. One feature that could be added to this utility would be to allow the user to select the name and file location for this test file. Another menu item and the Common Dialog control would take care of that. **Close** the Notepad window.

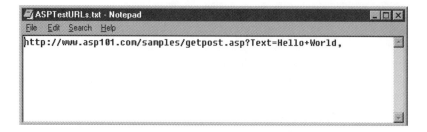

5. On the Web page, click the **Use Post** button, and then click the **Add Information to Request List** button again. The Post request has also been added to the test file.

6. Now navigate to the AOL Web site by typing "**www.aol.com**" into the first textbox on the Testing ASP utility and click **Go**. The AOL Members Sign In Web page appears.

7. On the **AOL Members Sign In** page, type the following invalid user name into the **ScreenName** textbox: "**InvalidUser**". Now click the **Go** button on the AOL Members Sign In page (*not* on the test utility!). Since you have entered an invalid logon, you have received an error page from the server. In the Test Result label at the bottom of the form, you will see that the utility has correctly trapped this error.

8. Click the **Add Information to Request List** button once more. If you like, click the **View Request List** button to see the differences in the way the three requests were logged into the file. The code logged Get requests by placing a comma after the URL and then nothing after it (a "?" character is separates the URL from the QueryString in the Get request when it comes back from the server). The Post requests were logged by placing a comma between the URL and the form variable values. Close the Notepad. You have added three HTTP requests to the test file. It's now time to start the test!

```
ASPTestURLs.txt - Notepad                              _ □ ×
File  Edit  Search  Help
http://www.asp101.com/samples/getpost.asp?Text=Hello+World,
http://www.asp101.com/samples/getpost.asp,Text=Hello+World
http://my.screenname.aol.com/_cqr/login/login.psp?error=6000&siteId=aolcomprod&screenname
=invalidname&siteState=,
```

9. Click the **Clear** button on the form. This does not clear the WebBrowser but simply clears all of the textboxes and labels on the form just to make sure we start clean.

10. Click the **Start URL Request Submission** button. You will see the first request submitted and the new results returned to the fields on the form. Click this button twice more, as it repeats the steps you took but submits the requests behind the scenes, using the test file. Note the values each time you click.

11. Click the **Start URL Request Submission** a fourth time and you will receive a Message box indicating that the test file is completed. Click **OK** to dismiss this Message box.

This utility has become more useful but is still mostly for demonstration purposes. It could use some additional features such as the ability to prompt for test file location and name. It could also use some Back and Forward buttons like a standard browser would have. For simplicity, I also left out logging test results to a separate file. Test results logging is covered in detail in Chapter 5 and then again in Chapter 9 when we created a Test object with logging utilities. Error handling should also be added (see Chapter 6). With this code and the information learned in previous chapters, you should be able to create a very functional utility. Further modifications are left to the reader!

Considerations for Databases

The strategies for testing databases connected to Web sites are similar to those for any data-based application. As long as you have programmatic access to the backend database and it is ODBC-compliant, you can use Visual Basic to attach to the database to test it. When the database is attached to a Web page, your Visual Basic test scripts may include accessing both the Web page (as we have done in this chapter) and the database with a separate connection to perform data verification testing and application functionality with respect to the data. This can be considered a part of end-to-end testing, which is the concept of testing data as it travels from the front-end application through any and all middleware components to the database back-end and returns again. Visual Basic scripts, using much of the syntax from previous chapters of this book, can be used to return information at each step since Visual Basic code can be used in all of the phases the data travels (see Figure 10-2).

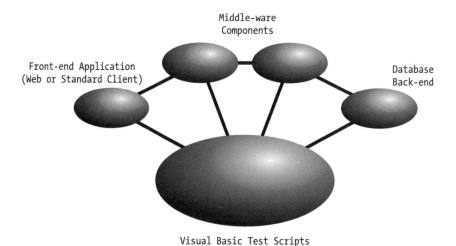

Figure 10-2. Visual Basic test scripts can be used during multiple phases of end-to-end data testing.

One company I worked with tested the interoperability of a COM component with the database back-end. Visual Basic scripts were used to perform both tasks since there were no commercial tools available able to provide the necessary functionality. The COM components were tested by setting a reference to their code libraries similar to the way we accessed COM components in Chapter 9. The same scripts also used ADO code to access the back end, similar to the scripts used in Chapter 8. The application had multiple ways to access the application including a Web-client front end. Although a commercial tool was used largely for the front-end testing, a few Visual Basic scripts were used to simulate HTTP requests as well. This demonstrated for us the full flexibility and capability of Visual Basic as a tool for test script development.

Additional Resources for Web Testing

We have looked at some ways to test the three basic types of Web pages. There are some other things you may need to do when testing a Web application. For example, determining when a Web site is available and when it is down is of key interest to Web site owners and users. A number of Visual Basic scripts for testing Web site availability and other metrics have been developed by Web site developers and testers alike. Rather than having to create them yourself, you can download and adapt many existing scripts from several locations. The best I have found for testing relevancy so far is Randy Birch's VBNet at `http://www.mvps.org/vbnet/` because it has a many scripts that are useful for testing purposes. Figure 10-3 shows just some of the articles available on Randy's VBNet Web site.

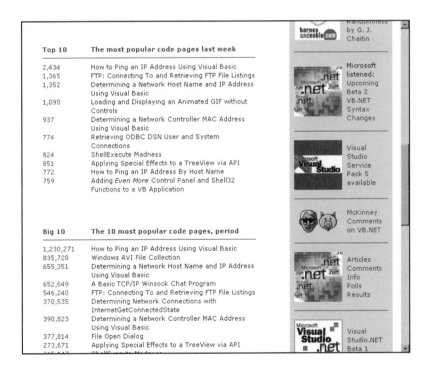

Figure 10-3. Some of the articles available on Randy Birch's VBNet Web site.

One of the most popular and useful pages available on the VBNet Web site is "How to Ping an IP Address Using Visual Basic." This article shows you how to verify that a host computer can connect to the TCP/IP network. It's also useful for isolating network and incompatibility problems. This article and the others available on the VBNet Web site are for intermediate to advanced programmers. Many of the articles are useful for Web testing applications but others deal with networking and other thorny issues. It's a great resource for tricky problems but not for the faint-hearted or lightweight programmer.

To help out the entry-level Visual Basic programmer, there are a number of great Web sites—Carl and Gary's Visual Basic Home page at http://www.cgvb.com/, for one—but not many have any additional relevancy for testing. There is only one (that I am aware of) written by an experienced tester and that is Jason Herres' Visual Monkey Web site. In fact, Jason has set up a special directory for readers of this book at http://www.visualmonkey.com/vb4testers/. At this location, he will also post items of interest to the test automator (that's you). Jason has written an excellent front end to the VBNet article on pinging an IP address called VBPing (see Figure 10-3), which is available on the Visual Monkey Web site. Figure 10-4 displays the initial form for the VBPing project.

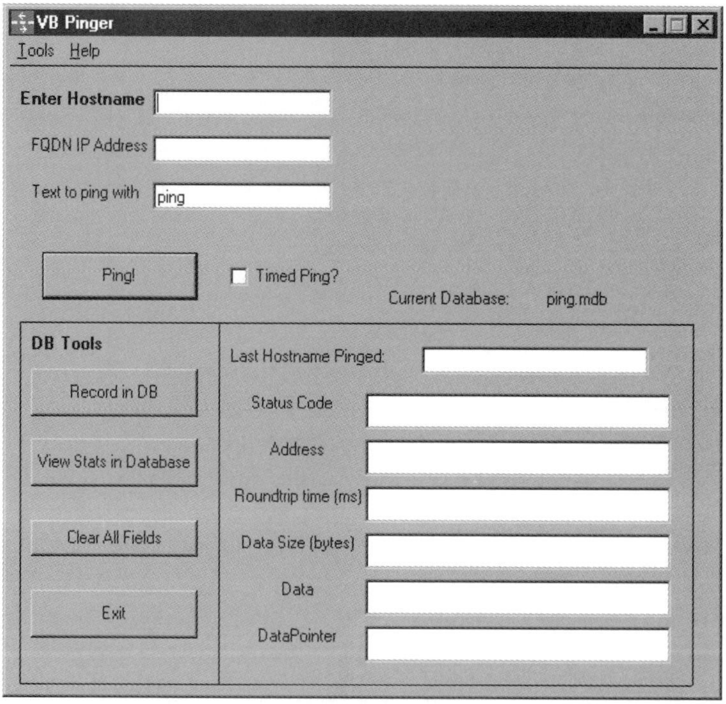

Figure 10-4. The VBPing project is available at http://www.visualmonkey.com.

Introduction to VBScript

Microsoft Visual Basic Scripting edition, otherwise known as VBScript, is a widely available lightweight subset of Visual Basic. Its advantage for testing is its availability and the fact that because it is very lightweight, it does not take much memory to run.

 TESTER'S TIP *One concern of automated testing always is to attempt to reduce your "footprint," that is, to minimize your impact on the platform you test. If you run a very large and cumbersome test script, it can take up enough memory to impact the application you are testing, perhaps making it behave differently. This is a good reason for using VBScript where possible, especially in situations where the impact of low-memory conditions on an application is being tested.*

I am covering VBScript in this chapter because VBScript is used as a scripting language within HTML. Consequently, knowing VBScript can help you to read and interpret the code behind Web pages that use it, which is always an advantage for Web testers. However, VBScript's use is not limited to working with Web pages. You can type VBScript code into the Notepad and execute it to retrieve a list of files. You can also create objects to connect to a database.

Because VBScript is a small language, it's fairly easy to learn and if you know Visual Basic, you pretty much already know VBScript. Your main stumbling block will be trying statements in VBScript that work in Visual Basic but are not supported in VBScript. On the other hand, most coding in VBScript will port over to Visual Basic quite nicely so you should be able to use some scripts in both, if desired. Perhaps the biggest downside to using VBScript is also its upside: it is small and therefore not nearly as powerful as its bigger cousin, Visual Basic. Also, you do not have the help in writing the code that the Visual Basic IDE gives you, such as automatic syntax checking and the automatic quick-info that fills drop-down lists of available properties and methods while you type code. There are many good books available on VBScript (see Appendix A: Resources and References) so here, I will present only a brief introduction to VBScript so you can start to use it.

VBScript Essentials

First, there is only one kind of variable in VBScript: a variant. A variant can store any kind of data. Visual Basic's rich set of data types allow you to avoid mixing kinds of data that can lead to confusion and errors. Since VBScript doesn't have this, you will have to be much more careful with your use of variables. You can create a variable with the Dim, Private, and Public statements but you just leave off the data type. It's still a good idea to name them appropriately for the kind of data they will contain. For example:

```
Dim strName
Dim iCount
Dim bFlag
```

Just to show you how easy this is, let's start with a very simple script.

TO TRY THIS

1. Open the Notepad accessory and type the following code into it:

```
Dim iInput

iInput = _
Inputbox("Hello there, please enter your favorite number")
msgbox "Here is your favorite number back again: " & iInput
```

> **NOTE** *By now you are used to having Visual Basic's IDE change the case of your code as you type but you should be aware that case-sensitivity is not an issue for Visual Basic or VBScript. You do not need to worry about case as you type.*

2. Save your Notepad file to the desktop with a .vbs extension by clicking **File ➤ Save As** and typing the following as the filename: **"myfirstvbscript.vbs"**

>
> **WARNING** *You* must *type the quotation marks! Otherwise, the Notepad accessory will attach a .txt extension to the end of your file and it will be called myfirstvbscript.vbs.txt.*

3. Close the Notepad accessory. **Double-click** the icon on the desktop for your new .vbs file. It should execute and display an Inputbox.

 NOTE *If the Inputbox does not appear, you may have to set the file association for VBS. You can do this by opening Windows Explorer and selecting* **Tools** ➣ **Folder Options** *(or* **View** ➣ **Folder Options** *for Windows 95/98 systems). Select the* **File Types** *tab. Navigate to the .vbs extension and change its "Opens With" property to* **c:\winnt\system32\wscript.exe "%1" %*** *for WinNT and Win2K systems or* **c:\windows\system32\wscript.exe "%1" %*** *for Windows 95/98.*

So, now you just need to know what statements and syntax are available in VBScript. Tables 10-4 contain a list of all VBScript statements. Compared to Visual Basic, there aren't many but there are enough to write a pretty sophisticated script. Most of these should be familiar to you from previous chapters. This isn't the whole language there are still plenty of functions and methods available too, though again, not as many as full Visual Basic, of course.

Table 10-4. VBScript Statements (from MSDN Help)

STATEMENT	DESCRIPTION
Call	Invokes a subroutine.
Const	Declares a constant value.
Dim	Declares variables.
Do/Loop	Executes a loop until or while a condition is True.
Erase	Reinitializes the contents of a fixed-size array and frees all of the memory allocated to a variable-sized array.
For/Next	Executes a loop while iterating a variable.
For Each/Next	Executes a loop while iterating through a collection of objects.
Function/End Function	Declares a routine that will return a value.
If/Then/Else/End If	Conditionally executes one set of statements or another.
On Error Resume Next	Takes the specified action if an error condition arises.
Option Explicit	Requires that all variables must be declared before their use.
Private	Declares private variables.
Public	Declares public variables.
Randomize	Initializes the random-number generator.

(continued)

STATEMENT	DESCRIPTION
ReDim	Changes the size of an array.
Select Case/End Select	Chooses a single condition from a list of possible conditions.
Set	Assigns a reference to an object or creates a new object.
Sub	Declares a subroutine.
While/Wend	Executes a loop while a condition is True.

Notice that you can still do good modular programming because you can create subroutines and functions as well as provide error handling. This is not all of the language, you also have functions and methods available but, again, it is not the full complement. For example, none of the financial functions are available.

At first, another disadvantage of VBScript may seem to be the lack of Help since it does not have its own IDE. However, if you installed the Enterprise edition of Visual Basic and have the Visual Studio Help, then you have an excellent amount of Help installed, including a tutorial. If you don't have this, you can still get Help online from the Microsoft Developer's Network at http://msdn.microsoft.com/scripting/vbscript. It includes the same tutorial, the full language reference, and a number of examples as well.

Accessing Objects with VBScript

One of the most powerful things you can do with VBScript is access a COM object. You can use the CreateObject function to return a reference to an available library. The following code connects to the Excel Application object to open a spreadsheet:

```
on error resume next
Dim strInput
Dim oApp
Dim oWorkBook
StrInput = InputBox("Input the name of a spread sheet you would like to open")
Set oApp = GetObject(, "Excel.Application") 'look for a running copy of Excel
If Err.Number <> 0 Then 'If Excel is not running then
    Set oApp = CreateObject("Excel.Application") 'run it
End If
Err.Clear   ' Clear Err object in case error occurred.
Set oWorkBook = oApp.Workbooks.Open(strInput)
oApp.visible = true
MsgBox "Opened Excel successfully!"
```

This is virtually the same code from an example in Chapter 9. This code is available in the file Chapter10\Demos\VbscriptDemos\excel.vbs. If you have Excel installed, just double-click it to run it. You can open the file from within the Notepad accessory to view its contents.

In the preceding example, the Err object was used. In-line error handling as done with the `On Error Resume Next` statement is the only kind of error handling available in VBScript. So you will not be able to use an error-handler and the other Resume statements that you learned about in Chapter 6. In addition to the Err object, you have a few others available; Table 10-5 contains a list of all of the intrinsic objects in VBScript.

Table 10-5. VBScript Objects

OBJECT	DESCRIPTION
Class Object	Provides access to the events of a created class.
Dictionary Object	Object that stores the data key and item pairs.
Err Object	Contains information about run-time errors.
FileSystemObject Object	Provides access to a computer's file system.
Match Object	Provides access to the read-only properties of a regular expression match.
Matches Collection	Collection of regular expression Match objects.
RegExp Object	Provides simple, regular expression support.

Notice that our old friend the File System Object is available. That means we can do file access in VBScript.

TO TRY THIS

1. Open the Notepad accessory and type the following code into it:

```
Dim fs    'file system object
Dim ts    'text stream
Set fs = CreateObject("Scripting.FileSystemObject")
Set ts = fs.CreateTextFile("c:\testfile.txt", True)
ts.WriteLine("Test Passed!! ")
ts.Close

set ts = Nothing
set fs = Nothing
msgbox " To see your work check the file in c:\testfile.txt "
```

2. Save your Notepad file to the desktop with a .vbs extension by clicking **File ➤ Save As** and typing the following as the filename: **"fso.vbs"** (including the quotes!).

3. Close the Notepad. **Double-click** the icon on the desktop for your new .vbs file. Open the Notepad again. Navigate to and open the file **c:\testfile.txt** to verify that your VBScript file worked.

With these examples, you should feel more confident that you already know a lot about VBScript. It's nice to know you have such a flexible and easy tool at your disposal. Most books and examples concentrate on VBScript for use within a Web page but, as you can see, it is much more versatile than that.

TESTER'S CHECKLIST

There are so many things to check for on a Web site—and so many of them subject to the *type* of Web site—that it would be futile to attempt to list them all here. Additionally, not all of these items can be readily done with Visual Basic. A good place to start is the World Wide Web Consortium (`http://www.w3.org/`), which lists standards for Web sites. A good reference for further information on Web site testing is *Testing Applications on the Web* by Hung Nguyen.

Chapter 10 Review

- What are the three categories of Web page?
  See page 397.

- Name a few ways that Visual Basic can be used in Web site testing.
  See pages 359–380 and 391–395.

- Can Visual Basic be used to support all types of Web site testing? Why or why not?
  No, there are many good tools for testing Web sites that may be superior or take less time than test scripts written in Visual Basic. Research is required to find the best uses.

- Name two Visual Basic controls that can be useful in Web site testing.
  The WebBrowser control and the Internet Transfer control.

- Name some resources for further information on testing the Web.
  See page 358.

CHAPTER 11

VB.NET:
Brave New World

You just finished learning all about Visual Basic 6 and now here's a chapter on the next version already. Hold on because VB.NET is much more than just a new version—it's a whole new game altogether. Let's deal with the question on everyone's mind: why a new Visual Basic—what's wrong with Visual Basic 6? Sure, we can all think of improvements to VB6 and the Visual Basic community has never been shy about suggestions for the next release. But VB.NET? There are those who claim that VB.NET is not VB at all but a whole *new* language that is, well, VB-like. I have to confess that I am a member of that group. That's because Microsoft really didn't take Visual Basic 6 as a base and modify it—it's entirely new. Oh, yes, many of the same capabilities are there and it looks somewhat familiar but the underlying run time has changed. VB.NET is as close to Visual Basic 6 as the new VW Beetle is to the classic Beetle. They look a bit alike but we can all tell the difference right away.

So, again, why a new Visual Basic? Well, in spite of what we in the VB community may think, we are not the whole world. Microsoft has for years been supporting vastly different kinds of programmers with fundamentally different products. This has had its benefits. Visual Basic, up to this point, has been the most successful programming language ever, drawing into the programming world quasi-technical types, like us testers for example, who would never have ventured so far if we hadn't been lured by the sexy simplicity and elegance of Visual Basic. The C++ developers have been able to do what they do best: get down pedal-to-the-metal writing the code that makes the Windows world go-round. Perhaps this has caused a kind of corporate schizophrenia that they wanted to remedy but they really do want to provide the fabulous parts of each product to the whole programming community. And trying to upgrade Visual Basic to include more complex features created workarounds that were getting increasingly rickety. To keep growing Visual Basic for an era where the Web is becoming the delivery platform of choice, Microsoft had to make a big change at some point. That time is now.

What are those fabulous new things we get with VB.NET? With each release of Visual Basic, users have demanded more object-oriented capability. Visual Basic will be a fully object-oriented language with the release of .NET, or at least as much so as one can be to date. We get some confusing parts of Visual Basic fixed, too. For example, having to understand why we had to use Let and Set for object variables was a pain (Chapter 9)—Let and Set are eliminated in VB.NET. Web development is vastly improved, which is something the Visual Basic community has been wanting for years. And we will get the all-important inter-operability with other Windows languages since all .NET languages are the same at the core. In particular, VB.NET code will run as fast as C++ or C# code on the .NET platform: VB is no longer a second-class citizen. So, we're getting what we asked for. Conversely, C++ language developers will gain the ease of RAD (Rapid Application Development) using the best elements of Visual Basic's great IDE that we have enjoyed. ASP developers gain huge new features and performance with ASP.NET. And .NET adds much greater capacity for Intranet and Internet applications. Combining these features into a common development environ-ment on top of a common language core—called the Common Language Runtime (CLR)—is risky and courageous. Will it pay off? I think it will. But it will be a long time before Visual Basic 6 is gone. So, for those of us in the testing com-munity, don't throw out your VB test scripts just yet. Even though Visual Basic is scheduled to be released this year, we've got awhile. A transition this big will take a long time.

Now, for some of the changes: The VB.NET IDE will look familiar with similar windows so it should only take a little stumbling before you can drag and drop a button on the form. There are some new windows. (You'll see more on all of this later in this chapter.) As far as languages changes, readers of this book will find that since much of what we covered was general programming, we won't have to change much. There are some exceptions to that, which you will find mostly annoying but not terribly problematic; here's a sampling:

- There's no `Debug.Print`; it is now `Debug.Writeline` and it goes to the new Output window and not the Immediate window. The Immediate window is still there but is used to enter and check values. You also can't use it to evaluate expressions except when the program is in Break mode (as was the case with early versions of VB).

- The default data type is Object, not Variant:

```
Dim myvar as Variant    'old
Dim myvar as Object     'new
```

- There are no fixed-length strings in the first implementation of VB.NET, they will be implemented in a later version. You can still do fixed-length strings as a workaround using a compatibility class that Microsoft has added. So, the old way of declaring fixed-length strings:

```
Dim MyStr As String * 10
```

will now be:

```
Dim MyStr As New VB6.FixedLengthString(10)
```

- The Integer data type is changing from 16 bit to 32 bit and the Long data type will change from 32 bit to 64 bit. There is a new integer data type called Short, which is 16 bit. This means that wherever you would have declared:

```
Dim x As Integer
Dim y As Long
```

you should now declare:

```
Dim x As Short
Dim y As Integer
```

- Declaration of a UDT (Chapter 7) has been changed. The UDT was a confusing name, anyway, and it's been eliminated. User-defined types are now called Structures. Instead of declaring a UDT like this:

```
Type MyType
    MyInt As Integer
End Type
```

you will declare your Structure like this:

```
Structure MyType
    Dim MyInt As Short    ''notice the use of the Dim statement here!
End Structure
```

NOTE *I am working with a beta version so there may be changes to the items I mention here prior to release. Although there is no official schedule for release of VS.NET, expectations are that it will be available by December 2001.*

Again, this is just a sampling and probably doesn't seem too bad. Nonetheless, there are definitely some more significant changes. The following are the top changes that I believe will most greatly and immediately affect those of us using Visual Basic to write automated test scripts:

- Less work with the Windows API DLLs (Chapter 10). Much of what we will want to know about the operating system is available in the CLR. This will make life easier for us, I believe, in the long run.

- New error handling (Chapter 6). Your `On Error Goto` statements will still work but there is a different and better way of doing error handling that will be more efficient in the long run called *structured exception handling*. It uses a Try-Catch-Finally syntax. It's going to provide us with a common way to catch all run time errors. Demonstrating it here wouldn't be possible without an entire chapter but there are already some good introductory articles available. Try an excellent article, "Error Handling the VB.NET Way: Living with Exceptions" (at `http://www.pinnaclepublishing.com/vb`), by Gary Cornell and Jonathan Morrison from their forthcoming book with Apress (`http://www.apress.com`).

- The language gains full object orientation, including inheritance. (Although this may not affect our own test scripts, it will affect the Visual Basic programs we test so we will have to be more fully informed on these topics.)

- There is now automatic garbage collection of objects. (The downside of this is that the programmer has to cleanup certain objects so we will have to watch for that in applications we test.)

There will indeed be other major changes that will affect us, including Web access and COM development but their impact for testing will remain to be seen. With so many changes, what will be adopted and adapted by developers? The answer will also be the answer to what will affect we testers the most.

The rest of this chapter will cover VB.NET in greater detail. It is actually two chapters adapted from a new book by Gary Cornell and Jonathan Morrison, *Programming VB.NET: A Guide for Experienced Programmers* (forthcoming from Apress in 2001). Gary Cornell is the cofounder of Apress and a winner of the Visual Basic Programmer's Journal Award for his book, *Visual Basic from the Ground Up*. He's a well-known and respected expert in all things Visual Basic. His coauthor, Jonathan Morrison, has written a book on *C++ for VB Programmers* (Apress, 2000) and currently works for Microsoft's Solution Integration Engineering team. Gary and Jonathan have graciously allowed me to take advantage of their extensive research on VB.NET by giving me permission to publish these two chapters, which discuss the new features of VB.NET and demonstrate the new IDE.

Introduction
to VB.NET

by Gary Cornell and Jonathan Morrison

This is Chapter 1 of Programming VB.NET: A Guide for Experienced Programmers *by Gary Cornell and Jonathan Morrison (forthcoming from Apress, 2001).* **From this point on, all references to other chapters and appendices are to those from the Cornell and Morrison book and** **not** *to chapters and appendices within* **Visual Basic for Testers.**

We hope this book will be profitably read by experienced programmers of all languages, but this introduction is primarily aimed at Visual Basic programmers. Other programmers can jump to the section entitled "The VB.NET IDE: Visual Studio.NET" later in this chapter to begin delving into an incredibly rich integrated development environment (IDE) backed by the first, modern, fully object-oriented language in the BASIC[1] family. Programmers accustomed to Visual Basic for Windows may need some convincing. Hence, this chapter.

Visual Basic Then and Now

Visual Basic for Windows is a little over ten years old. It debuted on March 20, 1991. There is no question that Visual Basic caused a stir. Our favorite quotes came from Steve Gibson, who wrote in *InfoWorld* that Visual Basic was a "stunning new miracle" and will "dramatically change the way people feel about and use Microsoft Windows." Charles Petzold, author of one of the standard books on Windows programming in C, was quoted in the *New York Times*: "For those of us who make our living explaining the complexities of Windows programming to programmers, Visual Basic poses a real threat to our livelihood." Petzold's comments are ironic, considering the millions of VB books sold since that fateful day in 1991. But another quote made at Visual Basic's debut by Stewart Alsop is more telling: Alsop described Visual Basic as "the perfect programming environment for the 1990s."

---

1. Read BASIC as meaning "very readable-with no ugly braces…"

But we don't live in the 1990s anymore, so it should come as no surprise that Visual Basic.NET is as different from Visual Basic for Windows as Visual Basic for Windows version 1 was from its predecessor, QuickBasic. While we certainly feel there's a lot of knowledge you can carry over from your Visual Basic for Windows programming experience, there are as many changes in programming for the .NET *platform*[2] using Visual Basic.NET (or VB.NET for short) as there were in moving from QuickBasic for DOS to VB1 for Windows.

The Versions of Visual Basic

The first two versions of Visual Basic For Windows were quite good for building prototypes and demo apps—but not much else. Both versions were relatively easy languages to learn with relatively small feature sets. When VB3 was released, the first reaction of many people was, "Oh great, they've messed up VB!" Well, with the benefit of hindsight, the database features added to VB3 were necessary for it to grow beyond the toy stage into a serious tool. With VB4 came a limited ability to do object-oriented programming that was further enhanced with versions 5 and 6. But the structure was getting pretty rickety and the designers of VB saw that, if they were going to have a VB-ish tool for their new .NET platform, more changes were needed.

We feel that the hardest part of dealing with the various changes in VB over the years is not so much that the IDE changed a little or a lot, or that there were a few new keywords to learn. The pain was in having to change the way that you thought about your VB programs. In particular, to take full advantage of VB5 and VB6, you had to begin to move from an *object-based* language to an *object-oriented* one.

Many VB programmers who grew up with the product had never programmed with objects before. When classes were introduced in VB, probably 80 percent or more of VB programmers had no idea what a class really was—never mind why they would ever want to use one. But once you learned how to use

---

2. Microsoft takes the word platform seriously. It's the Windows platform remember.

them, you could do neat things like banish the evil Select Case statement from maintenance hell. That is, object-oriented principles let you banish code that worked more or less like this:

```
Select Case KindOfEmployee
Case Secretary
    Raise Salary 5%
Case Manager
  RaiseSalary (10%)
Case Programmer
    Raise Salary(15%)
Case Architect
    RaiseSalary(20%)
'etc
End Select
```

which was a pain to maintain, because whenever you added a new type of employee you had to change all the corresponding Select Case statements.

Starting with VB5, you simply use the magic of classes and collections and write code like this:

```
For Each Employee in Employees
    Employee.RaiseSalary
Next
```

secure in the knowledge that the compiler would look inside your classes to find the right RaiseSalary method.

Classes let you create VB apps in a much more efficient and maintainable manner. We can't imagine writing a serious VB app without them.

The .NET Mentality Shift

What does all of this have to do with .NET? Quite a lot. You see, .NET is going to change the way you design your applications as much as the introduction of classes to VB changed how you built your VB for Windows applications. And just as we VB programmers suffered through the change between the classless to class-enabled incarnations of VB, so will we feel some pain in the transition to .NET![3]

---

3. There's a conversion tool supplied with VB.NET, but we guarantee it won't ease the pain much. Any serious program won't convert well—you're better off redoing them from scratch.

With that in mind, let's look at some of the things to watch out for—or, more important, that you can take advantage of—when switching from VB6 to VB.NET.

The Common Language Runtime

Visual Basic has always used a runtime, so it may seem strange to say that the biggest changes to VB that comes with .NET is the change to a Common Language Runtime (CLR) shared by *all* NET languages. The reason is that, while on the surface the CLR is a runtime library just like the C Runtime library or the VB Runtime library, it is so much larger and has so much more functionality as to make it seem like you are writing to a whole new operating system API.[4]

For example, think about what it means to have all languages that are .NET-compliant use the *same* CLR: there is no need for a language-specific runtime to be present. What's more, that code that is common-runtime-compliant code can be written in *any* language and still be used equally well by *all* .NET languages.[5] Your VB code can be used by C# programmers and vice versa with no extra work *and will run as fast as the code written in C++ or C#*. (See the chapter *InterOp, Native Calls, and Deployment*[6] for more on this.)

Next, there is a common file format for .NET executable code, called *Microsoft Intermediate Language* (MSIL or just IL). IL is a semi-compiled language that gets compiled into native code (not interpreted) by the .NET runtime at execution time. So .NET languages combine the best features of interpreted languages with the best features of compiled languages.

Completely Object Oriented

The object-oriented features in VB5 and VB6 were (to be polite) "somewhat limited." The key issues were that these versions of VB couldn't initialize the data inside a class automatically when creating an instance of a class. This led to classes being created in an indeterminate (in other words, buggy) state. To resolve this, VB.NET adds an important feature called *parameterized constructors* (see the *Objects and Classes* chapter).

---

4. Dan Appleman, the wizard of the VB API, intends to write a book called something like *The VB.NET Programmers Guide to Avoiding the Windows API*. The .NET framework is so full-featured that you almost never need the API.

5. Thus, the main difference between .NET and Java is that with .NET, you can use any language, as long as you write it for the CLR; with Java, you can write for any platform (theoretically at least—in practice there are some problems) as long as you write in Java. We think .NET will be successful precisely because it leverages existing language skills.

6. Note from Mary Sweeney: Remember, throughout the rest of this chapter, all references to *other* chapters and appendices are to those from the Cornell and Morrison book and *not* to chapters and appendices within *Visual Basic for Testers*.

The next problem was the lack of true *inheritance*. We'll cover inheritance in the chapter, *Inheritance and Interfaces*, but you should know that this is not the be-all end-all of object-oriented programming, as some people would have you believe.

Automatic Garbage Collection: Fewer Memory Leaks

Visual Basic always had a problem with memory leaks from what are called *circular references*. The *garbage collection* feature built into the CLR eliminates this problem. Of course, this extra power comes at a cost, and the *Objects and Classes* chapter will explain what the benefits and downside of automatic garbage collection are. (It will also explain what a circular reference is, if you don't already know about them.)

Structured Exception Handling

All versions of Visual Basic use a form of error handling that dates back to the first Basic written almost forty years ago. To be charitable, it had problems. To be uncharitable, it was simply stupid to use On Error GoTo with all the spaghetti code problems that ensued in a modern programming language. Visual Basic adds *structured exception handling* (see the chapter entitled *Exceptions*), the most modern and most powerful version of handling errors.

True Multithreading

Multithreaded programs seem to do two things at once. E-mail programs that let you read old e-mail while downloading new e-mail are good examples. Users expect them, but earlier versions of VB couldn't really deliver them. In the *InterOp, Native Calls, and Deployment* chapter, we introduce the pleasures and pitfalls of this incredibly powerful feature of VB.NET.

Why You Will Need to Learn a Whole Lot of New Concepts to Use VB.NET

You may be tempted to think that you can use the conversion tool and a little bit of fiddling to move your VB programs to VB.NET. Don't go down this path. To really take advantage of VB.NET, you need to understand object-oriented principles *and* how the .NET frameworks works. Note that we don't mean you have to memorize the twenty-five thousand or so methods that are in the .NET framework. But, in order to read the documentation or to take advantage of the

IntelliSense feature of the IDE, you really do need to understand how the framework "ticks." To use the various Windows and Web Forms designers in the IDE, you *really* have to understand these issues.

The best ways to help you see this is to remind you of the code you got when you added an active button to a form in earlier versions of VB. All you needed to do (and all you saw as a result) was a simple print statement inside a Button1_Click event procedure.

Fair warning: if you add a button to a form in VB.NET, you'll get a *lot more* code generated by the VB.NET IDE. One of the main purposes of this book is to show you why all this extra code is worth understanding—and of course, how to understand it as easily as you can the simple Button1_Click of yore.

Here is the code for simply adding a button to a form:

```
Public Class Form1
    Inherits System.Windows.Forms.Form

#Region " Windows Form Designer generated code "

   Public Sub New()
       MyBase.New()

       'This call is required by the Windows Form Designer.
      InitializeComponent()

       'Add any initialization after the InitializeComponent() call
   End Sub

   'Form overrides dispose to clean up the component list.
   Public Overrides Sub Dispose()
       MyBase.Dispose()
       If Not (components Is Nothing) Then
           components.Dispose()
       End If
   End Sub
 Private WithEvents button1 As System.Windows.Forms.Button

   'Required by the Windows Form Designer
   Private components As System.ComponentModel.Container

   'NOTE: The following procedure is required by the Windows Form Designer
   'It can be modified using the Windows Form Designer.
   'Do not modify it using the code editor.
   Private Sub <System.Diagnostics.DebuggerStepThrough()>
InitializeComponent()
```

```
Me.button1 = New System.Windows.Forms.Button()
Me.button1.Location = New System.Drawing.Point(112, 224)
Me.button1.TabIndex = 0
Me.button1.Text = "button1"
Me.AutoScaleBaseSize = New System.Drawing.Size(6, 16)
Me.ClientSize = New System.Drawing.Size(292, 268)
Me.Controls.AddRange(New System.Windows.Forms.Control() {Me.button1})
Me.Text = "Form1"

    End Sub
```

And here is the equivalent of the simple Click event procedure:

```
Private Sub button1_Click(ByVal sender As System.Object, _
                    ByVal e As System.EventArgs) Handles button1.Click

End Sub
```

and there is actually a little more code needed:

```
#End Region

    End Class
```

Should You Use C# and Not Bother with VB.NET?[7]

There is certainly something to be said for switching to C#.[8] Most of the .NET framework is written in it, so one can argue that C# *is* the .NET language. Although C# is a wee bit more powerful than VB.NET, 99 percent of programmers will never use those extra features.

But for those who have never programmed in a C-style language, C# will look strange and be much harder to learn than VB.NET. Besides, there are some definite plusses to VB.NET over C#. Here's our top five countdown:

5. **A compatibility layer** that gives you the old VB/VB Script Functions such as Mid, Sin(x) instead of Math.Sin(x), or FormatNumber instead of the more cryptic functions in the .NET frameworks.

---

7. Dan Appleman has an e-book that goes into this question at some length (available at http://www.desaware.com). Still, if you are browsing this chapter in a bookstore trying to decide, we hope the following are sufficient reasons for choosing VB.NET.

8. We are writing a book tentatively entitled *C# for the Experienced (VB) Programmer* for those who want to do this, but VB remains *our* first love, which is why we wrote this book first.

4. **Readability**. VB.NET uses human-readable words for everything. For example, C# uses a ":", and VB.NET uses "inherits" or "implements." C# uses words like abstract, sealed, and virtual, while VB.NET uses MustInherit, NotInheritable, Overridable, Overrides, Shadows. Which are clearer to you—even without knowing what the terms mean?

3. You still have **background compilation** of your code. This means you get immediate feedback from the compiler. (This is much better than simply parsing your code, as is done in C#.)

2. VB.NET is **case insensitive and has a smart editor** that changes the case to reflect your declarations. C#, like all languages in the C family, is case sensitive, which, for those inexperienced with case-sensitive languages, is guaranteed to drive you nuts.

And the #1 reason in our opinion is:

1. It still looks pretty much like Visual Basic 6, the most popular programming language in the world!

The VB.NET IDE: Visual Studio.NET

by Gary Cornell and Jonathan Morrison

This is Chapter 2 of Programming VB.NET: A Guide for Experienced Programmers.

If you are accustomed to using an earlier version of VB, then the .NET IDE (integrated development environment)—Visual Studio.NET—will look somewhat familiar. The concept of a rapid application development (RAD) tool with controls that you drag onto forms is certainly still there, and F5 will run your program. But much has changed, mostly for the better. For example, the horrid Menu Editor that has essentially been unchanged since VB1 has been replaced by an in-place menu editing system (see the *Windows Forms and Web Forms* chapter) that is a dream to use.

VB.NET is capable of building many other kinds of applications than just GUI-intensive ones. For example, you can build Web-based applications, server-side applications, and even Console-based (in what looks like an old-fashioned DOS window) applications. Moreover, there's finally a unified development environment for all of the "Visual" languages from Microsoft. The days when there were different IDEs for VC++, VJ++, Visual Interdev, Visual Basic, and DevStudio are gone. (Actually, Visual Interdev is now subsumed into VS.NET.) Another nice feature of the new IDE is the new macro and enhanced customization possible through an enhanced extensibility model. VS.NET can be a set up to look much like the IDE from VB6, or any of the other IDEs if you like those better.

Finally, keep in mind the purpose of this chapter is to give you an overview of the IDE, not to bore you to death with details. The best way to get comfortable with the IDE is to use it, working with the on-line help as needed. We suggest skimming this chapter and returning to it for reference as needed. Also, note that the parts of the IDE that are connected with specific programming elements such as GUI design are covered in greater depth in later chapters.

 NOTE *If you have never used Visual Basic before, you may need to read this chapter more closely.*

Getting Started

Users of earlier versions of VB (like us for example) will probably want the IDE to resemble and work like the traditional VB6 IDE as much as possible. This is done by selecting "Visual Basic Developer" from the Profile drop-down list on the "My Profile" link on the "VS Home Page," as shown in Figure 11-1. Notice that you can also customize the keyboard and the window layout for the IDE, and that you can save these in different profiles.

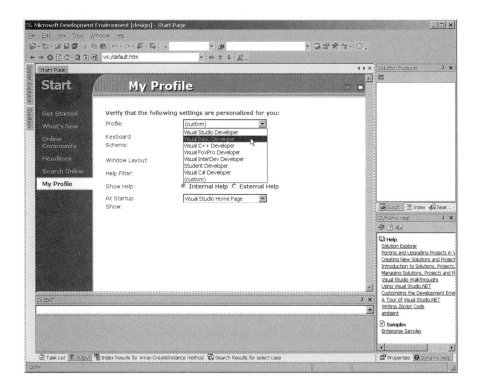

Figure 11-1. Visual Studio "Home Page."

In VB.NET, every project is part of what Microsoft calls a *solution*. You can't do anything in the VB.NET IDE without your code being part of a specific "solution." Think of a solution as the container that holds all information about a given set of projects and its associated files that will eventually be compiled into the program. A solution can contain multiple projects; various miscellaneous files such as images; *metadata* (data that describes data); and just about anything else you can think of. Although cumbersome at first, and in all honesty, always cumbersome for small projects, once you get used to solutions, enterprise development will be much easier. They do this by allowing you to dictate what should go along with the files you deploy in order to solve a specific problem.

Creating a New Solution

The first step in creating a new solution is to select File ➤ New. At this point you have two choices: you can create a New Project or a Blank Solution. Note that even when you choose "New Project," you get a solution. The difference is that the VS.NET IDE builds a bunch of bookkeeping files and adds them to the solution container if you choose a specific type of project. (What kind of files you get depends on what kind of project you choose.)

Most of the time you'll choose New Project. When you do so, you will see a dialog box like the one shown in Figure 11-2, which shows the many different kinds of projects VB.NET can build. (As we write this, there are *ten* types.) These project templates work in much the same way as templates did in VB6. For example, they often contain skeleton code but always contain bookkeeping information.

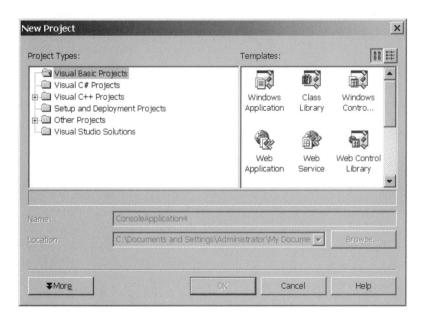

Figure 11-2. New Project dialog box.

To focus on the new features of the VB.NET language, we will discuss building Console Applications in the first part of this book. These are text-based applications that write and read to what is for all practical purposes a DOS window (they read from standard in and write to standard out). You don't see the template for a Console Application listed in Figure 11-2, but you can scroll down with the arrow keys in this dialog box until you do. Notice that when you choose Console Application (or any item but the last one, which is called "New Project in Existing Solution") from the dialog box shown in Figure 11-2, you are not asked if you want to create a solution. This is because when you create a new project outside of an existing solution, the IDE creates the basic structure of the solution for you. (Most .NET programmers put each solution in a separate directory whose name matches the name of the solution, and this is the default behavior for solutions created in the IDE.)

We named this sample solution `vb_ide_01`, but any legal file name is acceptable. So, if you prefer spaces or capital letters in your solution names, that's fine. Of course, like everything in the Windows file system, case is ignored (but retained for readability). The IDE then automatically creates a subdirectory for the solution using the name of the solution in the home directory you specify. In this case, our choices lend to a directory named something like: `C:\vb net book\Chapter 2\vb_ide_01`. At this point, your IDE should look very similar to Figure 11-3.

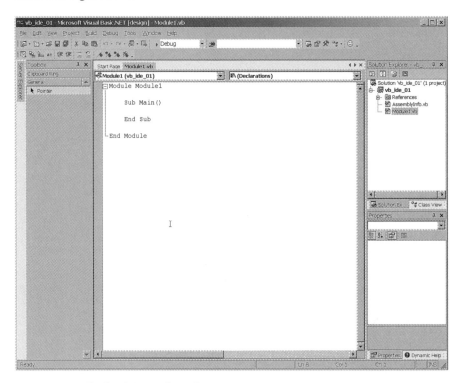

Figure 11-3. The basic Visual Studio IDE.

TIP *Remember that the IDE has context sensitive help. For example, Figure 11-4 shows you roughly what you'll see if you hit F1 when the focus is in the Solution Explorer. There's also a "Dynamic Help" (use Ctrl+F1) feature that automatically monitors what you are doing and attempts to place likely help topics into focus. Figure 11-5 shows the list of dynamic help topics you see when you are starting to work with a project. The downside to dynamic help is that it is CPU intensive. Once you get comfortable with the IDE, you might want to turn it off to improve performance.*

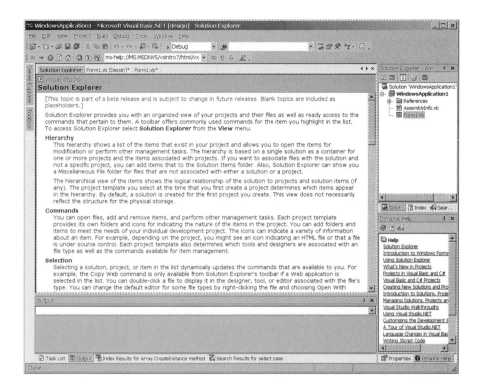

Figure 11-4. Context-sensitive help at work.

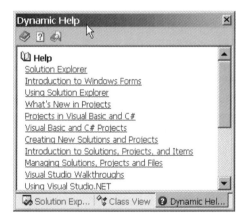

Figure 11-5. Dynamic Help at work.

The View menu on the main menu bar is always available to bring a specific window of the IDE into view (and into focus). Note that all windows on the IDE can be dragged around and actually "free float." Interestingly enough, these are not MDI child windows—you can move any window in the IDE outside the main window.

Another cool feature is that, if you choose to dock a window and it completely overlaps an existing window, you are not as lost as you sometimes were in VB6. The reason is that you automatically see the hidden windows as tabs. As an example, notice where the cursor is pointing in Figure 11-6. To reveal one of the hidden windows, simply click and drag on the tab for that window. To recombine windows—for example, to preserve real estate—simply drag one on top of the other. The use of tabs in this way is a welcome change to the VB6 IDE, where over-zealous docking occasionally caused the IDE to become practically unusable, forcing you to tweak the registry in order to get things back to normal. Also note the use of tabs in the main window to allow you a quick way to access the IDE Start page.

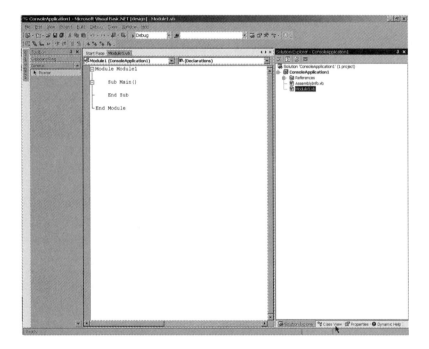

Figure 11-6. Docked windows with tabs.

A Tour of the Main Windows in the IDE

We cover the basic windows in this section and address specialized windows such as the ones for debugging later in this chapter or in subsequent chapters. Before we go any further, however, we want to remind you that in the VS.NET IDE, as with most modern Windows applications, you get context menus by right-clicking. We strongly suggest that you do a little clicking to become comfortable with each context menu. For example, here is the context menu available in the editor:

As you can see, it has a mixture of editing tools and debugging tools available.

Next, the various icons on the menu bars have tool tips.[9] A few of the icons have little arrows on them indicating they actually serve as mini-menus. For example, the second menu bar icon (Add New Item), has a list of the items you can add to a solution, as you can see here:

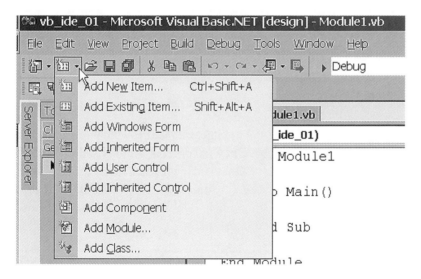

---

9. It has struck us from time to time that the need for tool tips shows that GUIs have their limitations. We wonder if the next trend in UI design will be to have these things called *words* on buttons dispensing with the icons completely?

TIP *If you are accustomed to earlier versions of VB, note the incredibly useful Comment Block and Uncomment Block tools are again available in the Text Editor toolbar. Now, however, these default to being available in the standard toolbars that show up in the IDE as opposed to being on the Edit toolbar.*

Finally, the Toolbox is used mostly for GUI applications, but it also holds the new *Clipboard Ring* that we describe in the next section. You can also store code fragments directly on the toolbox. We cover these features, too, in the next section.

The Editor

The code editor has all the features you might expect in a program editor, such as cut, paste, search, and replace.[10] You access these features via the usual Windows shortcuts (Ctrl+X for cut, Ctrl+V for paste, and so on). If you like icons, you have them as well, on the context menu inside the code window or the Edit menu. Check out this menu for the keyboard shortcuts or look at the Help topic on *editing, shortcut keys* for a full list). The shortcut Ctrl+I activates an incremental search facility, for example.

NOTE *Certain options, such as "Option Explicit," are now the defaults and do* not *show up in your code window as they did in VB6. (Although we still have a habit of putting them in to make sure!) See the* Language Issues *chapter for more on these options.*

You also have the amazingly useful IntelliSense feature, which tells you what methods are available for a given Object or what parameters are needed for a function, as you can see in Figure 11-7. You usually see IntelliSense at work when you hit the "**.**" that is ubiquitous in accessing functionality in Visual Basic. If you need to get directly to IntelliSense, simply right-click immediately after a period and choose "List Member" from the context menu.

---

10. You can even automatically add line numbers by working with the dialog box you get by choosing Tools ➤ Option ➤ Text Editor.

```
Module Module1

    Sub Main()
        System.Console.|
    End Sub

End Module
```

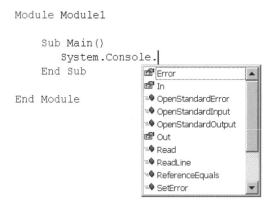

Figure 11-7. IntelliSense at work.

You usually get the global features of the editor by working with the Tools ➤ Options dialog box and choosing the Text Editor option, as shown in Figure 11-8. Notice this options dialog box is quite a bit different then its counterpart in earlier versions of VB6 and we suggest exploring it carefully. To actually set things like tab stops, click on the Text Editor option shown in Figure 11-8. Once you do that, you can either set them on a language-by-language basis or solely for VB. You can also change how the indentation of the previous line effects the next line from None, to Block (where the cursor aligns the next line with the previous line), to a "Smart" setting. In the Smart setting, the body of a loop is automatically indented, as good programming style would indicate. (You can select tabs and apply smart formatting after the fact using Ctrl+K, Ctrl+F or via the Edit ➤ Advanced ➤ Format Selection option.)

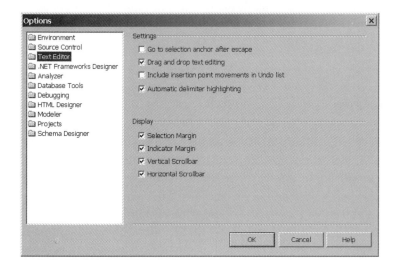

Figure 11-8. The Options dialog box.

One neat new feature in the Editor is the ability to "collapse" regions of code so that all you see is the header. Notice the lines of code in Figure 11-9 with the + signs next to them. Clicking on one of these would expand the *region,* as it is called in VS.NET. Hovering the mouse over the ellipses (the three dots) would show the collapsed code. The Edit ≻ Outlining submenu controls this feature.

```
Public Class Form1
    Inherits System.Windows.Forms.Form

#Region " Windows Form Designer generated code "                    I

    Public Sub New()...

    'Form overrides dispose to clean up the component list.
    Public Overrides Sub Dispose()...

    'Required by the Windows Form Designer
    Private components As System.ComponentModel.Container

    'NOTE: The following procedure is required by the Windows Form Designer
    'It can be modified using the Windows Form Designer.
    'Do not modify it using the code editor.
    Private Sub <System.Diagnostics.DebuggerStepThrough()> InitializeComponent()...

Private Sub Form1_Load(ByVal sender As System.Object, ByVal e As System.EventArgs) Handles MyBase.Loa

#End Region

End Class
```

Figure 11-9. Collapsed regions in the Editor.

There are a few other nifty features of the VS Editor that will be new to experienced VB programmers, and we take them up next.

 TIP *The on-line help topic called "Editing Code and Text" and its various links is particularly useful. There are quite a few nifty navigation features available to you, for example.*

The Clipboard Ring

You now have (much like in Word 2000) the ability to collect multiple items in a *Clipboard Ring.* Whenever you cut or copy text, it goes into the Clipboard Ring that is available on the Toolbox. You can see what's in the Clipboard Ring by clicking the Clipboard Ring tab on the Toolbox. The ring holds the last fifteen pieces of text that you cut or copied. To use the Clipboard Ring:

- Use Ctrl+Shift+V to paste the current item into the current document.

Repeatedly pressing Ctrl+Shift+V lets you cycle through the Clipboard Ring. Each time you press Ctrl+Shift+V, the previous entry you pasted from the Clipboard Ring is replaced by the current item.

Code Fragments

You can store any piece of code for instant reuse in the Toolbox. (Most people use the General tab for this, but you can easily create your own tab by right-clicking and choosing Add Tab from the context menu.). This is incredibly useful with code that you repeatedly use, such as Dim i As Integer. You get code fragments here by highlighting them and dragging them to the toolbox (see Figure 11-10). The fragments remain in the Toolbox until you delete them through the context menu. To reuse text simply drag the text back to the correct insertion point in the Code Window.

Figure 11-10. Text stored in the Toolbox.

Task List and TODO, HACK, and UNDONE Comments

Visual Studio now comes with a Task List feature that it inherits from Visual InterDev and Visual J++. The idea is that you can use comments and special keywords embedded at the beginning of the comment, including TODO, HACK, and UNDONE. The IDE keeps track of these comments in the Task List window, which you get by choosing View ➤ Other Windows ➤ Task List (or Ctrl+Alt+K). An example is shown in Figure 11-11.

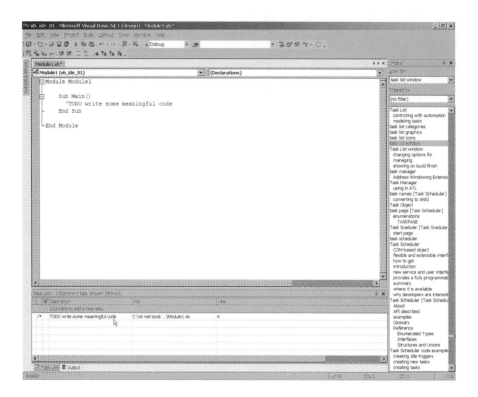

Figure 11-11. Task List at work.

Here's how to set up a custom keyword for use in the Task List:

1. Select Tools ➤ Options ➤ Environment ➤ Task List.

2. Enter a Name for your custom token (this enables the Add button).

3. Select the priority level.

4. Click Add and then OK.

The Solution Explorer

The Solution Explorer window, shown in Figure 11-12, allows you to browse the files that make up your solutions. The default name of the solution is the same as the first project created in it. As you can see in the Solution Explorer window, we also have a project named vb_ide_01, which contains a file named Module1.vb.

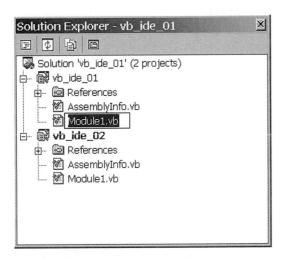

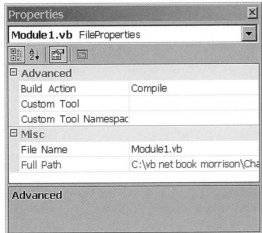

Figure 11-12. Solution Explorer and Properties Windows for file properties.

Note that in VB.NET, the .vb file extension is what is used for *all* VB.NET files, regardless of their type: no more .frm, .bas, or .cls files. One important feature is unchanged, however: .vb files are still text files, just as in VB6. (And, in fact, the free .NET SDK comes with a stand-alone VB compiler that can easily compile programs written with a text editor.)

NOTE *Later in the book you'll see how the IDE deals with designing forms and how it knows which parts of a file are visual and which parts are not. For now, you need only know that all VB.NET files end in .vb.*

TIP *You can create an empty solution without first creating a project by choosing the Visual Studio Solutions* ➤ *Blank Solution option from the New Project dialog box. Using this option is the easiest way to create a solution when you don't want the solution to have the same name as one of the projects.*

Properties Window

The Properties Window in VS.NET (also shown in Figure 11-12) is now more than the place where you go set properties of controls. The item you select determines what the Properties Window shows. The text box at the top of the Properties Window describes the item you are working with. To edit a property, click in the cell to its right and start typing. The usual Windows editing shortcuts work within the Properties Window.

As you can see in Figure 11-12, the Properties Window now lets you set the properties of the Module1.vb file. You can also use it to set the properties of designers such as the ones you use for building Web applications or server-side solutions.

ICON	DESCRIPTION
	Gives an alphabetized list of all properties and property values arranged by category. Categories can be collapsed or expanded at will. Moves the focus to the Properties Window. The context menu for this item allows you to quickly clear a property value.
	Gives a categorized list of all properties and property values arranged by category. Categories can be collapsed or expanded at will.
	Moves the focus to the property currently selected..
	Displays a Property Page for the property if one is supplied. (As in VB6, Property Pages are an aid to setting more complicated properties.)

References and the Reference Window

If you look at the list of files in the Solution Explorer, you can see that there is a branch of the Solution Explorer tree named *References*. (Think of the references in a VB.NET solution as being analogous to the COM libraries that you may have imported into your VB6 project through the References dialog box.) This is a list of all of the external files that we are currently using in our solution. With the trivial application we have just built, all these libraries are basic .NET framework libraries that are automatically made part of any VB.NET applications.

If you expand the tree by clicking on the + icon, you should see something similar to Figure 11-13. Notice that almost all of the files that we are *importing* are named System <Something>. (Importing a library makes the code in that library available for your solution.)

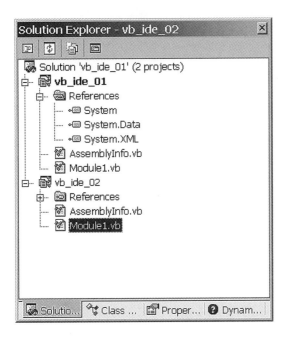

Figure 11-13. Drilling down in the Solution Explorer.

Now right-click on the "References" branch of the "Solution Explorer" tree and choose "Add Reference." (You can also choose Project ➤ Add Reference.) You will see a dialog box like the one pictured in Figure 11-14. Notice that there are three available types of references that we can add: ".NET," "COM," and "Projects."

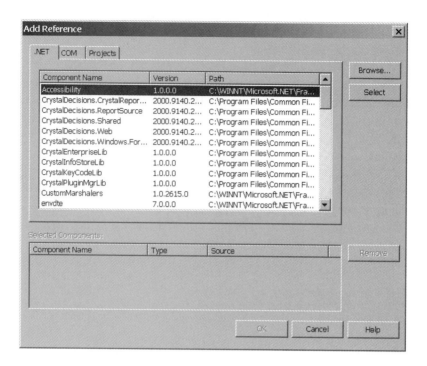

Figure 11-14. The References tabbed dialog box.

NOTE *Yes, you can use traditional COM components in your .NET apps and thus use ActiveX controls, including ones you may have built yourself. This is done through the magic of "interop" (see the* Threading *chapter). Now, as with most things, just because you can do something does not necessarily mean that you should do it. Using COM components in .NET applications adds significant overhead.*

Output Window and Command Window

The Output Window (choose View ➤ Other Windows or Ctrl+Alt+O) is where you see status messages. When you (try to) build a solution (see the section on this later in this chapter), this is where you see the results of the compilation process, both good and bad.

The Command Window (choose View ➤ Other Windows or Ctrl+Alt+A) is analogous to VB6's Immediate Window and remains incredibly useful when debugging (more on this next). However, it *has* lost the ability to evaluate simple expressions in design mode—so nothing like ? 2+2 is allowed. On the other hand, it has gained the ability to interact with the environment. You can actually issue commands like this:

```
File.AddNewProject
```

which brings up the New Project dialog box. By the way, IntelliSense works when you use the Command Window.

The Command Window has two modes: Command and Immediate. You switch back and forth between them by typing either `immed` into the window without the greater than sign or typing a greater than sign followed by `cmd` into the window. You can navigate through the command window using the following keystrokes.

Move through the list of previously entered commands: Up or Down Arrow
Scroll up the window: Ctrl+Up Arrow
Scroll down the window: Ctrl+Down Arrow

TIP *You can copy part or all of a previously issued command to the current action line by scrolling to it, highlighting it, and then pressing ENTER.*

Working with a Solution

At this point, the folder containing the vb_ide_01 solution (which you can view via Windows Explorer) has quite a few files and folders that were created automatically. Here's a list of everything in our folder:

```
            943 AssemblyInfo.vb
<DIR>           bin
             79 Module1.vb
<DIR>           obj
          1,354 vb_ide_01.sln
          7,168 vb_ide_01.suo
          3,008 vb_ide_01.vbproj
          1,643 vb_ide_01.vbproj.user
          6 File(s)        14,195 bytes
```

As you can see, there are two subdirectories named `bin` and `obj` that are used for compiled code, plus the four files that make up the solution. The `obj` directory contains a subdirectory for debugging code. The `Module1.vb` file contains the source code. In this case, all you would see if you looked at it in a text editor is the following (we'll explain how to put meaningful code into the file in the chapter, *Language Issues*):

```
Module Module1
    Sub Main()
    End Sub
End Module
```

The `vb_ide_01.sln` file is the equivalent of the .vbp project file from VB6. It contains all the bookkeeping information needed to compile your solution. For example, this file contains information about all of the projects and files in the solution. It will look something like this when viewed in a text editor:

```
Microsoft Visual Studio Solution File, Format Version 7.00
Project("{F184B08F-C81C-45F6-A57F-5ABD9991F28F}") = "vb_ide_01",
"vb_ide_01.vbproj", "{F40E94D3-09CA-4E17-9DEA-7A514E991F93}"
EndProject
Project("{F184B08F-C81C-45F6-A57F-5ABD9991F28F}") = "vb_ide_02",
"..\vb_ide_02\vb_ide_02.vbproj", "{926DC073-167F-49D0-8A30-AF27E27BA2B4}"
EndProject
Global
GlobalSection(SolutionConfiguration) = preSolution
        ConfigName.0 = Debug
        ConfigName.1 = Release
    EndGlobalSection
    GlobalSection(ProjectDependencies) = postSolution
    EndGlobalSection
    GlobalSection(ProjectConfiguration) = postSolution
        {F40E94D3-09CA-4E17-9DEA-7A514E991F93}.Debug.ActiveCfg = Debug|.NET
        {F40E94D3-09CA-4E17-9DEA-7A514E991F93}.Debug.Build.0 = Debug|.NET
        {F40E94D3-09CA-4E17-9DEA-7A514E991F93}.Release.ActiveCfg = Release|.NET
        {F40E94D3-09CA-4E17-9DEA-7A514E991F93}.Release.Build.0 = Release|.NET
        {926DC073-167F-49D0-8A30-AF27E27BA2B4}.Debug.ActiveCfg = Debug|.NET
        {926DC073-167F-49D0-8A30-AF27E27BA2B4}.Debug.Build.0 = Debug|.NET
        {926DC073-167F-49D0-8A30-AF27E27BA2B4}.Release.ActiveCfg = Release|.NET
        {926DC073-167F-49D0-8A30-AF27E27BA2B4}.Release.Build.0 = Release|.NET
    EndGlobalSection
    GlobalSection(ExtensibilityGlobals) = postSolution
    EndGlobalSection
    GlobalSection(ExtensibilityAddIns) = postSolution
    EndGlobalSection
EndGlobal
```

The file named `vb_ide_01.vbproj`, which is actually written in XML,[11] contains information about the project, including descriptions of properties. These can usually be changed by choosing Project ≻ Properties or by right-clicking on the project name in the Solution Explorer.

> **NOTE** *XML is actually omnipresent used throughout .NET. Wherever possible, items built with .NET are described (and even transported over the Web) via XML.*

Here's what a project file looks like in text form. Notice the constant repetition of the keyword "Assembly." Assemblies are connected with how .NET projects are deployed—we cover them in a subsequent chapter. We explain the other important keywords used here, `Imports` and `Namespaces`, in the *Objects and Classes* chapter:

```
<VisualStudioProject>
    <VisualBasic
        ProjectType = "Local"
        ProductVersion = "7.0.9148"
        SchemaVersion = "1.0"

    >

        <Build>
            <Settings
                ApplicationIcon = ""
                AssemblyKeyContainerName = ""
                AssemblyName = "vb_ide_01"
                AssemblyOriginatorKeyFile = ""
                AssemblyOriginatorKeyMode = "None"
                DefaultClientScript = "JScript"
                DefaultHTMLPageLayout = "Grid"
                DefaultTargetSchema = "IE50"
                DefaultServerScript = "VBScript"
```

---

11. XML stands for *extensible markup language*. Think of it as an extension of HTML that can describe both data and program functionality. A good source of basic information about XML is http://msdn.microsoft.com/xml/general/intro.asp; Apress will be publishing a complete treatment of XML in .NET in the fall of 2001. Still, we can't resist pointing out that in a way, all XML is a vast generalization of the e-mail convention that lets you better convey emotions. For example, you might surround text with <grin> </grin> where you wanted to know the person you were grinning about it!

```
                DefaultSessionState = "True"
                DelaySign = "false"
                OutputType = "Exev"
                OptionCompare = "Binary"
                OptionExplicit = "On"
                OptionStrict = "On"
                RootNamespace = "vb_ide_01"
                StartupObject = "vb_ide_01.Module1"
            >

            <Config
                Name = "Debug"
                BaseAddress = "0"
                DefineConstants = ""
                DefineDebug = "true"
                DefineTrace = "true"
                DebugSymbols = "true"
                Optimize = "false"
                OutputPath = "bin\"
                RemoveIntegerChecks = "false"
                TreatWarningsAsErrors = "false"
                WarningLevel = "1"
            />
            <Config
                Name = "Release"
                BaseAddress = "0"
                DefineConstants = ""
                DefineDebug = "false"
                DefineTrace = "true"
                DebugSymbols = "false"
                Optimize = "false"
                OutputPath = "bin\"
                RemoveIntegerChecks = "false"
                TreatWarningsAsErrors = "false"
                WarningLevel = "1"
            />
        </Settings>
        <References>
            <Reference Name = "System" />
            <Reference Name = "System.Data" />
            <Reference Name = "System.XML" />
        </References>
        <Imports>
            <Import Namespace = "Microsoft.VisualBasic" />
            <Import Namespace = "System" />
```

```
            <Import Namespace = "System.Collections" />
            <Import Namespace = "System.Data" />
            <Import Namespace = "System.Diagnostics" />
        </Imports>
    </Build>
    <Files>
        <Include>
            <File
                RelPath = "AssemblyInfo.vb"
                BuildAction = "Compile"
            />
            <File
                RelPath = "Module1.vb"
                SubType = "Code"
                BuildAction = "Compile"
            />
        </Include>
    </Files>
    </VisualBasic>
</VisualStudioProject>
```

The file named vb_ide_01.suo is a binary file that contains user settings for the solution, such as current breakpoints and open documents. If you delete the SUO file, you'll lose these cached settings, but it won't break the solution. The analogous VBPROJ.USER file is for user settings at the project-level, such as how and where to start it and in which debug mode to run it. Notice how it, too, is written in XML:

```
<VisualStudioProject>
    <VisualBasic>
        <Build>
            <Settings
                OfflineURL = "/vb_ide_01_Offline"
                ReferencePath = ""
            >
                <Config
                    Name = "Debug"
                    EnableASPDebugging = "false"
                    EnableASPXDebugging = "false"
                    EnableUnmanagedDebugging = "false"
                    EnableSQLServerDebugging = "false"
                    StartAction = "Project"
                    StartArguments = ""
                    StartPage = ""
                    StartProgram = ""
```

```
                    StartURL = ""
                    StartWorkingDirectory = ""
                    StartWithIE = "false"
                />
                <Config
                    Name = "Release"
                    EnableASPDebugging = "false"
                    EnableASPXDebugging = "false"
                    EnableUnmanagedDebugging = "false"
                    EnableSQLServerDebugging = "false"
                    StartAction = "Project"
                    StartArguments = ""
                    StartPage = ""
                    StartProgram = ""
                    StartURL = ""
                    StartWorkingDirectory = ""
                    StartWithIE = "false"
                />
            </Settings>
        </Build>
        <OtherProjectSettings
            CopyProjectDestinationFolder = ""
            CopyProjectUncPath = ""
            CopyProjectOption = "0"
            ProjectView = "ProjectFiles"
        />
    </VisualBasic>
</VisualStudioProject>
```

Adding Projects to a Solution

Adding an existing project to a solution is easy. With the previous solution still open, simply select File ➤ New ➤ Project. You should see the now-familiar New Project dialog box, but if you look closely at Figure 11-15, you'll see that two radio buttons have been added that let you choose whether to Close Solution or Add to Solution. If you choose "Close Solution," you get a new project within a new solution as before. But if you choose "Add to Solution," the IDE adds the new project to the already open solution.

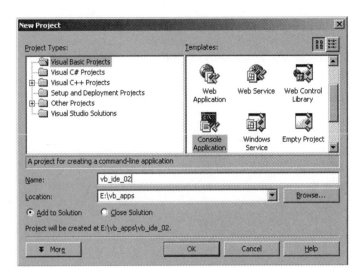

Figure 11-15. Adding to an existing solution.

Suppose you choose Add to Solution and then select Console Application as before. At this point, as you can see in Figure 11-16, a new project named vb_ide_02 has been added to our vb_ide_01 solution. So, we have a solution named vb_ide_01, which contains two projects named vb_ide_01 and vb_ide_02, respectively. This is similar to a Project Group in VB6. These multiple projects can interact with each other and you could use them for testing components, for example, in the IDE.

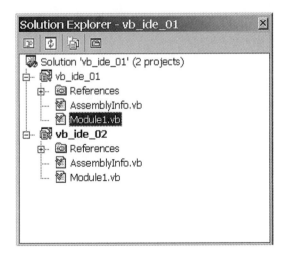

Figure 11-16. Multiple projects, single solution.

Compiling

As we mentioned earlier, when you compile .NET code, you first get to an intermediate language called MSIL, which is then compiled into native code. Suppose we wanted to create an executable from our solution. In this case, we have two *compilation* units—our two projects. We can create an executable from either project; each project is capable of being independently compiled. The easiest way to do this is to right-click on one of the projects in the Solution Explorer window and select "Build" or "Rebuild" from the menu. Choosing Build tells the compiler to compile only those parts of the project that have changed since the last build, while Rebuild recompiles all parts of the project. Using Build is often better, because it is faster than Rebuild. (If you choose F5 to run the project, the project gets "Built" not "Rebuilt.")

Once the project is compiled, you can see how things went during the build process by looking at the Output window. When we compiled the vb_ide_01 project, we got the output shown in Figure 11-17.

Figure 11-17. Output of a successful build.

As Figure 11-17 shows, our project compiled successfully. What happens if things don't go so well? Figure 11-18 shows a build after a bogus function call.

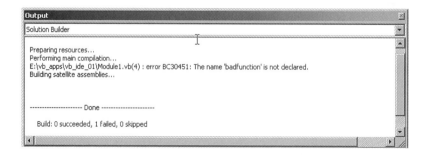

Figure 11-18. Output of an unsuccessful build.

Next, you can get detailed information in the Output window as well as a task-oriented view of the build errors in the Task List window, as shown in Figure 11-19. This is much more detailed than the output from the VB6 compiler.

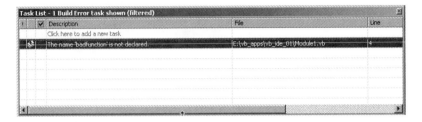

Figure 11-19. Details of a unsucessful build in the Task List window.

 TIP *If you double click on any item in the Task List build errors list, you'll be taken to the code that caused the error.*

Multiple Compilations

You will occasionally want to build all or some of the projects in a given solution without having to do individual builds of each part. This is where the Build Solution and Batch Build features of VB.NET come into play. When you select Build ➤ Build Solution, *all* projects in the solution will be compiled. We do this when we are close to the end of the development process and getting ready to build all of the projects in our solution for deployment (see the *Threading* chapter for more on deployment).

The Batch Build option lets you select which projects in the solution you want to build. This cool feature is especially useful when you are working on one or two projects and you don't want to have to wait for a Build Solution compilation but also don't want to have to build each project by hand. When we used Build Solution on the vb_ide_01 solution, the Output window looked like Figure 11-20.

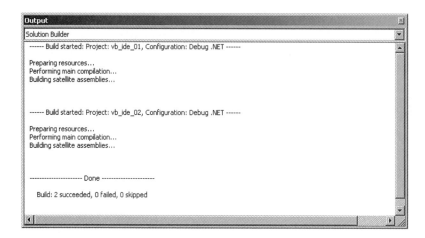

Figure 11-20. Details of a multiple build.

In this case, you can see that both of the projects in our solution have been built successfully. Had there been errors in either of the projects in the solution, they would have been tagged in the Output window.

If you choose Select Build ➤ Batch Build, then you see the dialog box shown in Figure 11-21. If you ever have a solution with several projects and have problems with one or two of the projects, you will really grow to love the Batch Build option.

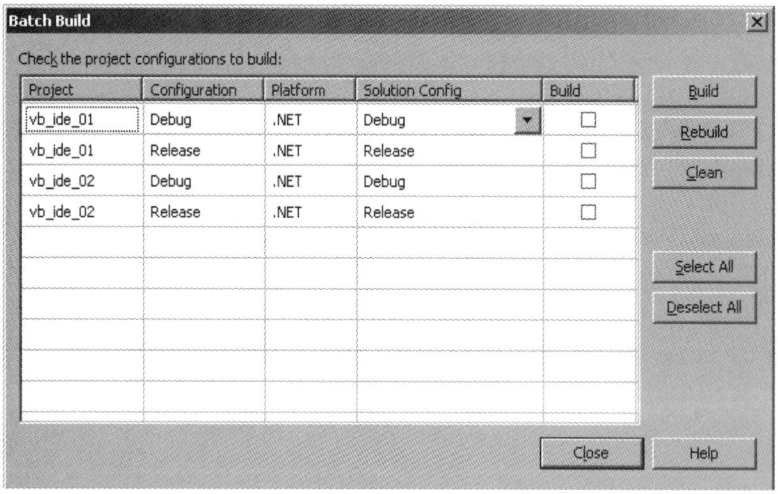

Project	Configuration	Platform	Solution Config	Build	
vb_ide_01	Debug	.NET	Debug	☐	**Build**
vb_ide_01	Release	.NET	Release	☐	**Rebuild**
vb_ide_02	Debug	.NET	Debug	☐	**Clean**
vb_ide_02	Release	.NET	Release	☐	

Figure 11-21. Selecting what to build.

Most of the general options for compiling a project are available by right-clicking the name of the project in the Solution Explorer and choosing Properties (or Project ➤ Properties). This opens up the Property Pages screen shown in Figure 11-22. We cover the most important ones pertaining to building projects here, but we encourage you to explore all the possibilities available in the Common Properties and Configuration Properties items. For example, you can:

- Set the Application Icon (Common Properties ➤ Build).

- See the libraries that are automatically imported (or change them) (Common Properties ➤ Imports).

- Control various features of the "Assembly" and "Namespace" that your project will become part of (Common Properties ➤ General, see the chapter on *Objects and Classes* for more on these important topics).

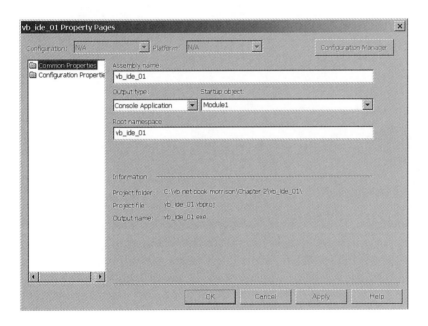

Figure 11-22. Project properties.

NOTE *The default names used for the Assembly Name and Root Namespace are derived automatically from the name of your solution. These can't have spaces in them so VB.NET automatically inserts underscores if needed in place of spaces.*

Build Options

Now that you have seen the different ways to compile projects and solutions, we want to show you the options for compiling an individual project. If you right-click on a project in the Solution Explorer window and choose Properties ➤ Configuration Properties ➤ Build, you will see the options that are available to you when you compile. For example, the Debugging option lets you set command line arguments.

Figure 11-23 shows the available build options for our project.

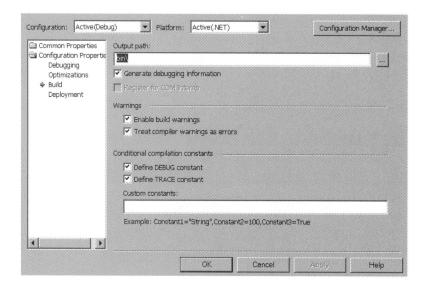

Figure 11-23. Build options.

Note how few options there are compared to VB6. This is because of the CLR and is *not* necessarily a bad thing, since the CLR handles a lot of stuff that you had to worry about in VB6. The main options are that you can choose whether or not to create debug info (which we cover next), define the DEBUG and TRACE constants and whether or not you want to see warnings.[12] The point of

---

12. We can't imagine a situation where you would disable this option and we'll offer a free glow-in-the-dark Apress T-shirt for the first rational answer.

defining the DEBUG and TRACE constants is similar to why you would have done so in VB6: they let you write conditionally compiled code like this:

```
#If DEBUG Then
        Console.WriteLine("Debug")
#End If

#If TRACE Then
        Trace("Debug")
#End If
```

By clicking on the Optimizations item in the Configuration Properties list box, you can turn off integer overflow checks—again, not a real good idea. Hopefully, Microsoft will add more optimizations before the final version of VB.NET is released or provide them in service packs.[13]

Debug versus Release Versions

At the top of the Project Properties ➤ Configuration Properties ➤ Build dialog box is a drop-down list box called Configuration, with three options: Release, Debug, and All Configurations. Having these settings available is simply a matter of convenience. They let you set different options for different kinds of builds. For example, when you get ready to ship, you may want to change some of the options you previously set for a Debug build. In this case, you choose Release build and reconfigure the options. Clicking the Configuration Manger button lets you set the Build options for multiple projects at once.

 TIP *Generally, the difference between these two builds will be the inclusion of debugging info or the turning on or off of optimizations. We suggest you do all development under the debug configuration and then build your shipping product under a release build configuration. For example, in a debug configuration, you may want to turn on the "Treat warnings as errors" feature. You may want to turn it off in your release configuration.*

---

13. <advertisement>Remember to register for free electronic updates to this book at
http://www.apress.com</advertisement>

Output Files

What do you get when you finally compile a project? Figure 11-24 shows the directory structure generated by the IDE for our vb_ide_01 solution. As we mentioned previously, the source files are kept in the root of the vb_ide_01 folder. The bin folder gets the binary output files after compilation—in this case, we get an .exe file and a .pdb file. The .pdb file is the debug info file that gets created whenever you choose to create debugging info via the project build options dialog box.

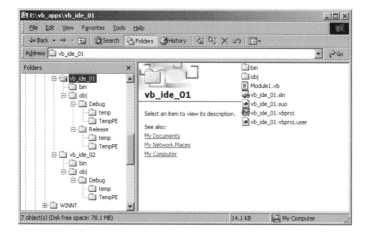

Figure 11-24. Directory structure after a build.

Debugging in VB.NET

We will cover this important topic in more depth in later chapters when we have some meaningful code to debug! Still, we want to give you a quick overview of the changes and features of VB.NET debugging. Of course, some things haven't changed: you still have the cool *Edit and Continue* feature that lets you make changes while a program is stopped in Break Mode and then continue running the program with those changes having gone into effect. And the various forms of stepping through or breaking your program are still available, such as procedure stepping or conditional breakpoints.

Yet without a doubt, the existence of a common debugger for all of VS.NET, whose power is at the level of the VC++ editor, is one of the greatest improvements that was made in VB.NET over previous versions of VB. You now have much tighter control over all elements of your applications while you are debugging them. You can drill down to the loaded module and thread level. You can also debug multiple processes at the same time in the same debugger session!

NOTE *To take advantage of the power of the debugger, you need to make sure the .pdb file is created with Debug Symbols. You do this by making sure "Generate symbolic debug information" on the build options dialog box is checked. The .pdb file contains the information necessary for the debugger to know what line you are on in the source code, and what the values of your variables are. Without symbolic debug information, you are usually forced to resort to looking at assembly listings to figure out what the heck has gone wrong in your application.*

New Debugger Features

The VB.NET debugger has several cool features that were not available in VB6. Here's an overview.

Memory Window

After waiting ten years, we finally have a memory window in VB. A memory window lets you look at a memory address or a variable so that you can see what is actually there, byte by byte. This is amazingly helpful in some situations, such as when you have to go through the assembly and try to figure out what is going on. You access the memory window by selecting Debug ➤ Windows ➤ Memory ➤ Memory1 (or 2 through 4). When you do this, you see a window similar to Figure 11-25. When you right-click on the memory window, you get lots of choices about how you want the memory displayed, such as 1–64 byte display, No data display, and Unicode display.

```
Memory 2                                                              ×
Address 0x030d1674                          ▾ (↩)  Cols Auto ▾         ▾
0x030D1674  5e 5f 8b e5 5d c3 00 00 1c 45 5e 03 00 00 00   ^_..]....E^....    ▲
0x030D1683  00 80 30 ae 02 55 8b ec 50 89 4d fc ff 15 3c   ..0..U..P.M...<
0x030D1692  31 ae 02 8b e5 5d c3 00 00 00 00 00 00 00 00   1....]..........
0x030D16A1  00 00 00 24 45 5e 03 00 00 00 00 e8 30 ae 02   ...$E^......0..
0x030D16B0  55 8b ec 83 ec 08 57 56 33 f6 33 ff 90 be e8   U.....WV3.3....
0x030D16BF  03 00 00 33 ff ff 15 40 31 ae 02 90 5e 5f 8b   ...3...@1...^_.
0x030D16CE  e5 5d c3 00 00 00 00 00 00 00 00 00 00 00 00   .]............
0x030D16DD  00 00 00 00 00 00 00 00 00 00 00 00 00 00 00   ..............
0x030D16EC  00 00 00 00 00 00 00 00 00 00 00 00 00 00 00   ..............    ▓
0x030D16FB  00 00 00 00 00 00 00 00 00 00 00 00 00 00 00   ..............
0x030D170A  00 00 00 00 00 00 00 00 00 00 00 00 00 00 00   ..............
0x030D1719  00 00 00 00 00 00 00 00 00 00 00 00 00 00 00   ..............
0x030D1728  00 00 00 00 00 00 00 00 00 00 00 00 00 00 00   ..............
0x030D1737  00 00 00 00 00 00 00 00 00 00 00 00 00 00 00   ..............
0x030D1746  00 00 00 00 00 00 00 00 00 00 00 00 00 00 00   ..............
0x030D1755  00 00 00 00 00 00 00 00 00 00 00 00 00 00 00   ..............    ▼
```

Figure 11-25. The memory window.

Process Debugging

Technically, every time you debug, you are debugging a process. Prior to VB.NET, however, only C++ programmers could drill into a running process and start debugging it. Selecting Debug ➤ Processes gives you the dialog shown in Figure 11-26.

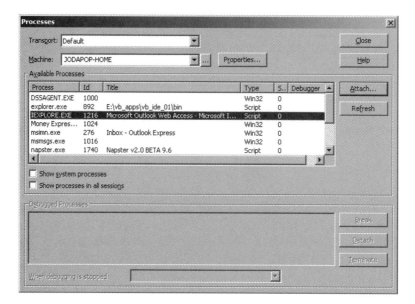

Figure 11-26. Process debugging.

To start debugging, select a process from the list and click Attach. Once attached, you select Break to see the current state of the application. If you haven't generated debug symbols, you will be looking at a disassembly listing of the code. Also, after you click Attach, you will get a dialog that asks what you want to debug (for instance, Native code, CLR code, script, etc.). In most cases, you will want to debug either native code or CLR code. As an example, we started an instance of Notepad.exe and attached to it from the VB.NET debugger so we could "debug" it. Figure 11-27 is was what we saw.

It's pretty ugly, because we don't have debug symbols for Notepad.exe. If we did have them, we would have seen the source line and function names of the functions that were in call when we stopped the application to look at it in the debugger.

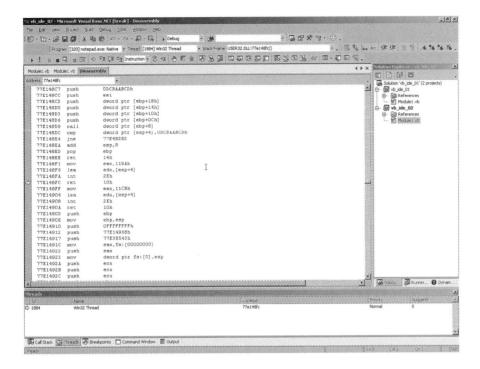

Figure 11-27. Process debugging of Notepad.

Threads

Another cool feature of the VB.NET debugger is the ability to view all running threads for an application. When you are trying to debug multithreaded applications, the ability to switch threads in the debugger is invaluable. We will look a bit more at this feature in the *InterOp, Native Calls, and Deployment* chapter, which deals with multithreaded programming.

Exception Flow Management

This seems like an esoteric feature until you are stuck in a situation where you have numerous exceptions (see the *Exceptions* chapter) occurring during testing and want to fine-tune what happens. You manage exception flow by selecting Debug ➤ Windows ➤ Exceptions—see Figure 11-28. From this dialog box you can control what the debugger does when specific exceptions occurred. For instance, say you're trying to track down an access violation in your application. You would select the Win32 Exceptions ➤ 0xc0000005 exception and then select the "Break into the debugger" radio button under the "When the exception is thrown" frame. This would cause the debugger to activate every time an 0xc0000005 access violation occurred. You would then know exactly what line of code caused the access violation to occur.

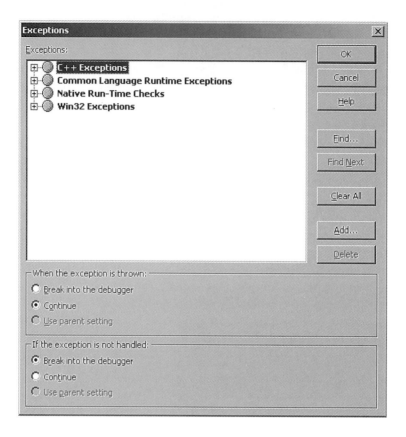

Figure 11-28. Exception management.

Debugging Managed versus Unmanaged Code

Managed code is what .NET calls code that is run through the CLR and is "safe." There's no use of pointers and you let the CLR manage memory. Unmanaged code (which C# and C++ can build but VB.NET cannot create) is code that breaks out of the boundary of the CLR.

When you are working with totally managed code, some debugging options may be difficult to use. The reason is that the CLR runtime environment optimizes a lot of the code that it runs. This can make it hard for the debugger to build good stack frames (the addresses of all of the functions currently in call). Also, depending on what you are doing, your code may be so optimized that you will only have the assembly to look at for debugging purposes. At any rate, these few problems are negligible compared with the benefits of the new debugging environment in VB.NET.

From Tester to Tester: Advice to the Visual Basic Automator

You have made it through eleven chapters on Visual Basic and testing. If you started at Chapter 1, you have covered the basics of how to write a Visual Basic program all the way to using it for testing COM objects, databases, and even a bit of the Web. Along the way, you also learned a little about what it is like to be a software developer because you encountered the same sort of problems they do—running into frustrating bugs and encountering all kinds of new technology that you need to get familiar with *fast*. In many ways, both programming and testing continually run into that age-old problem, what comes first, the chicken or the egg? In our case, it's which technologies do we learn first, COM, ODBC, or the new DotNet? It seems that we need to know about all of them to fully comprehend the systems we test. You should have enough to get you started, though, and plenty of references to continue your learning. So, now you are ready to face the world of automated testing. Or are you? If you have not read through Appendix D, please take the time to do so. There are many pitfalls and problems you may encounter unless you take the time to learn from the experts. I have some recommendations and lessons of my own that I would like to offer as you start your own adventures in automated testing but first I will allow some of the testers who have contributed code, advice, and reviewing for this book to speak their minds. I asked them what they would say to the test engineer, test lead, or test manager who had just learned how to use Visual Basic and wants to apply that knowledge in an automated software test project. Here's the advice they have for you.

From Jason Herres

I would say some of the major concerns are:

Knowledge: Know the limitations of Visual Basic's automation capabilities.

It's a great tool and it supports a lot of automation—but it is not SilkPerformer, it is not designed to be responsible for unit testing an entire ERP implementation. It is a tool to be used by testers to move them toward more efficient testing.

Know the testability of your product.

Visual Basic can only automate as much as an application will let it. If your APIs are closed and poorly documented, then VB may not help with unit testing. But, given a very testable product, which exposes its controls and APIs, VB becomes a very useful tool to know.

Take advantage of Visual Basic's strengths.

Microsoft has built a lot of functions into VB that are not always taken advantage of. For example, to convert a WMF into a BMP is an arduous process—until you discover that only one picture box and two lines of code will make the conversion for you. The more you know about those types of tricks, the more VB can help you.

Clearly define expectations.

Make sure the automators and the managers on your team have agreed on the expectations from automation before the project has begun. If the automators think they are responsible for automating the install testing—and management thinks they are automating the installation process for the entire lab, eliminating downtime—the automators are doomed to fail before they start. Clear, written specifications of the goals of the automation should be done before one line is written.

From Lee Wallen

Depending on project length, one good thing to avoid is trying to make something too generic. Projects come and go and there will always be another project where you can extend how generic your code is. It is easy to miss deadlines because you've spent most of your time trying to develop something that can handle everything when your code will never have to handle *everything*.

NOTE FROM MARY SWEENEY *Lee makes a great point also made by Bret Pettichord in his article, "Seven Steps to Successful Test Automation"—see Appendix A. The point is that you can overdo the idea of planning for code reuse and spend way too much time trying to make code generic. Common sense should prevail.*

From Harvin Queen (Technical Reviewer for *Visual Basic for Testers*)

I can speak from experience from several "nightmare" projects on this one:

1. Prioritize up front what product functionality is necessary and which is "nice to have." When time crunches occur (and they will) and decisions must be made on what needs to be finished and what is for the next version, then knowing your priorities up front will help the project stay on course.

2. The "basic rules of code development" should also include *standardization*. This book talks about naming conventions and uses them in its examples—I reiterate that testers should be:

   - Commenting their code—this is *very* important.

   - Using the same naming conventions for their variables.

   - Declaring their variables in the *same* places in the same way so that code can easily be moved around if necessary. I can tell you stories of late nights spent trying to relearn my own code because I didn't comment it well or of code that worked well separately but was fatally broken when integrated together because the styles of the code were very different.

3. CODE REVIEWS. And let me say it again...*code reviews*. Make certain that automators take time to look over each other's code before it is officially "checked in." Without doing this, having several automators on a project will lead to problems—Eventually, someone will write code that fundamentally doesn't work with someone else's program and by the time it's noticed, it will be too late and time is lost. If the dev's (test automators) coordinate their efforts from the beginning as well as make certain that code is efficient (this promotes standardization, too), then less time is lost.

4. If the automation tool is something that is a *deliverable* (meaning, it is to be delivered to the customer), make certain that a functional spec is written *before* you begin writing code. If the developer and the client have not formally agreed and don't have a clear-cut understanding of what the tool will do (and *not* do), then expectations can cause the code to be written . . . and rewritten . . . and rewritten again—and that is just a waste of time. Do not write code without knowing exactly what you are trying to write. Know exactly what your tool *must* be able to do. Know exactly what your tool *cannot* do. Without this, you have no way of gauging your progress or knowing that you are done.

NOTE FROM MARY SWEENEY *Harvin has written a significant test tool in C++ that was sold to a customer. His experience on that project is reflected in the point he makes here.*

5. Finally, the GUI. The Interface. The most important piece to any program is the interface and automation is no exception. If the program is Windows-based, make certain that the automated test tool you write follows Windows conventions:

- Hierarchical menu choices.

- An easy way to terminate the program.

- Easily accessible Help files.

- Self-explanatory names for buttons, menu items, etc.

I am living proof and the leader of the parade that the items I have listed are vitally important to the success of any project where code is written for the purpose of either being a deliverable or meant for internal reuse. I have made the mistakes, drawn the roadmap, led the tour, bought the T-shirt, have the scars, and am hoping to help others avoid a similar fate.

From Dan Hodge

Over the last few years, I've had the opportunity to teach Visual Test on site at many companies. Often enough, these companies have very small, say, three to five people that make up their testing department. Starting out, I always ask them why they're getting into automation and what their goals are. More often than not I hear, "We don't have enough people to accomplish the amount of testing we need so we hope to automate at least part of it." This idea sounds reasonable until you start figuring in real-life dynamics. If the testers feel that they don't have enough time to fully test the product by hand, how are they going to find enough time to write automated tests and still get the product out on schedule? When testers engage in automated testing, much of their time is spent really playing the role of a programmer. Sure, they may get a small percentage of the testing accomplished by the mere fact that creating a test program requires looking at the product. But this is a very small percentage compared to what they would accomplish if they were testing manually full time. The problem is that management is not usually willing to push back the release date of a product to make enough time for the testers to develop automated tests *and* test the product by hand. While management might like the idea of automated tests and saving time, when it comes down to it, what they really want is the bottom line— to see a cash flow. This means get the product tested as quickly as possible and out the door. I've never seen a company where automated testing took precedence over manual testing. For those just getting into automation, it needs to be understood that testers can't test and develop automated tests at the same time. Because of this, many advocate ensuring that enough time is placed in the schedule to do both. I agree but, again, management wants to see the product out as quickly as possible. Automation, while planned for in the schedule, is usually placed on the back burner in an effort to get the product out quicker. In almost all situations that I've seen, companies that are successful at automation invest in additional people to write the automated tests so that they still have a full complement of manual testers. Once the automated tests are in place, perhaps then the amount of people needed to automate can be scaled back. People are expensive, which makes automation expensive. Being successful at automation means being willing to invest up front to receive the pay off later.

From Kevin Ingalls

My input is that it is more important to know what not to automate than what to automate. The problem with automation testing is not in its application but in its misapplication. Draw clear boundaries between what will be tested manually and what will be attempted with automation. This list will change as the project goes along. Make it visible to those affected and update it as necessary.

Code comments are bad but module comments are good. Unless you are doing something unexpected or tricky ("tricky" should be avoided, if possible, of course), the code should not be commented but the module should be. This is standard Black Box, loosely-coupled, highly-cohesive stuff. That way, I can make mods to the code (but not the intent of the module) without having the comments go stale. As we know, stale comments are worse than no comments, as they mislead.

The key thing for programmers/developers/automation testers to remember is that they should be sure to get on projects that are well managed. Good trick, I know. I'm suggesting that they be rewarded for doing things the "right" way rather than simply for pounding out code as quickly as possible. Developers and automators will still be asked to write code at three in the morning with the assurance that it will never be used again, knowing full well that they will be maintaining it until they leave the company. Sadly, I think the failure of Ada to catch on is partly attributable to this mentality.

 NOTE FROM MARY SWEENEY *Kevin and I taught Ada, an embedded-systems programming language, for many years for Boeing.*

From Marshall Peabody

I hope your book has something in it about starting small. If you try to jump in and automate *everything*, there's the risk that you'll never get anything accomplished! Your automation tool might just be relegated to shelfware. Start small, automate the easy stuff first, and then spend your time on the more complicated items. If you start off with the hard stuff, there's the risk that you'll spend all your time and budget without accomplishing even minimum payback.

From Alan Corwin

My favorite bit of advice is to make sure that you design your tests when you design your software. And further, to build your tests at the same time you build your software. Otherwise, it doesn't get done.

From Elisabeth Hendrickson

NOTE FROM MARY SWEENEY *Elisabeth Hendrickson is a well-known author, lecturer, and expert in software testing. Her advice for Visual Basic automators is also in Appendix D. I think it appropriate to print it here, as well.*

Most of my advice about learning Visual Basic is rather generic, I'm afraid. If you can use it, you're welcome to it:

- Consider taking a class if you learn well in a classroom setting.

- Find someone with whom you get along well that has done a fair bit of VB programming and is willing to help you.

- Try changing sample programs as a way to learn the language rather than trying to write code from scratch.

- Start simple—it's okay if your first from-scratch program doesn't do anything more useful than displaying some text in a dialog box.

- Make a habit of testing out key bits of your programs in isolation. I often create dumb little test programs just to see how the language really works or how my implementation will work in practice.

- MsgBox is your friend. When still working the kinks out of a program, I often use MsgBox to display values. I find that easier than stepping through programs with a debugger.

I have three reasons why every tester should have at least basic Visual Basic skills:

- If you plan to use Visual Test or Rational Robot, you'll end up having to learn VB anyway, so you might as well learn it early.

- If your product has an API that can be accessed through VB, it's a great way to drive your product for a variety of types of tests (including hammer tests).

- If you use MS Office products for tracking test results and bugs, you can use your VB knowledge to automate the gathering and sending of test results and bug stats.

General Recommendations and Lessons Learned

When I wrote the original paper on the topic, "Automated Testing Using Visual Basic" (`http://www.data-dimensions.com/Testers'Network.htm`), I included a list of recommendations that some of our clients and staff involved in automated test projects using Visual Basic told me they wished they had to make the project go easier. I reprint that list here:

- **Acquire appropriately experienced personnel.**
  A three to five day Visual Basic course will not automatically turn a tester into a Visual Basic professional. Hire knowledgeable automation testers with Visual Basic experience if possible. And if you plan an aggressive Visual Basic automation project, make sure your staff is fully trained in advanced topics like COM and API calls.

- **Implement effective source code control.**
  Keeping track of the test code, versioning it, and knowing what is current can be an enormous administrative task that will sink an automation project quickly if not done well. Plan for and enforce effective source code control.

- **Allocate sufficient time.**
  Allocate sufficient time to bring Visual Basic automation code into accord with your current test processes. Development of Visual Basic test scripts should follow the basic rules of software development since that's exactly what it is. This means allowing sufficient time for requirements analysis, design, code, testing, and maintenance of your test scripts.

- **Plan for reuse.**
  Building your Visual Basic code with a plan for reuse means creating standard and class modules with generic, reusable code. Without this, the team ends up writing the same things repeatedly. This implies the use of effective project management and source control.

 NOTE *Use common sense, of course—see Lee Wallen's advice. The operative words here are "effective project management."*

I have a few other points I would like to add to this list gleaned from more recent experiences:

- **Don't hold on for a hero.**
  In his paper, "Enough About Process, What We Need Are Heroes" (http://www.satisfice.com), James Bach advocates that heroes step forward to produce quality software. His point is that the right people can make any project and process work. My caveat to this is: just make sure you don't start *expecting* the hero. On a recent project I was involved in, a couple of consultants were asked to be available to the team but it was then made it clear that the use of these consultants was expensive so the directive was to limit their use to "as necessary." In order to make budget and not appear unqualified, the team rarely called on the two experts— until the end of the project when everything was behind. Of course, then the two consultants (okay, I was one) had to come in blind without much time to understand the intricacies of the effort. This was frustrating for everyone. In a post mortem, the manager agreed that he should have made clear that the consultants should have been kept up-to-date all along and used regularly. There can't be any heroes in this kind of a situation.

- **Don't over-estimate your heroes.**
  Joe Tester performed brilliantly on one contract receiving many kudos from the customer. So, Joe Tester was placed on another very critical project. Flush from his success, Joe exuded the confidence that he could handle the lead position. But Joe didn't use his staff much and didn't ask for help; he had never been a lead before. Joe's manager was confident in Joe's capabilities. Too confident. Everyone, including Joe, expected another miracle. As the project got further and further behind, others were brought in but the project had to be scaled back significantly. The moral of this story? Keep tabs on your heroes, too. It's rare for lightning to strike twice so make sure that they actually have the skill set to handle the next project. And just like any other profession, being a great technician doesn't necessarily make you a great leader.

- **Don't let "just in time" training become "no time for training."**
  On another project, most of the team needed extensive training with a particular tool in order to accomplish the test effort. A basic training class of two days was provided but it was clear that the team needed more extensive training. The question was, when to do it? The project kept getting delayed so management delayed the training. Once the project actually started, of course, it had a short deadline due to the previous delays. Now there was "no time for training." The end result was that the one person who knew the tool spent all her time writing templates and

debugging scripts for the others. This project eventually completed but ended up being saved only by the "hero model" (see the previous bullet): a truly heroic effort by two of the team members. Not surprisingly, shortly after the project completed, one of the heroes left for another job. The other members of the team were no wiser than when they started and were left feeling frustrated and unqualified and no better prepared for the next project with the same tool.

Conclusions

I know that most advice we get seems to always be on the negative side: "stay away from this," "don't do that." That's because the good things are usually easy to see, such as increased productivity and enhanced capability. In fact, it's just too easy to get starry-eyed about the use of technology. I hope the preceding advice didn't scare you too much. You just need to be aware of some of the problems you might encounter. Now that you are, keep on investigating and learning. I will close with the following paragraph also from my original paper. It reflects where I see Visual Basic fitting into Software Test.

I once worked with a company that had a very expensive test tool in-house; still, they were creating large Visual Basic programs to test their application. When I asked them why, the response was, "We couldn't get the tool to test the COM objects. It does a lot of things but it won't do that." So, they were writing the code themselves. The expensive test tool was being put to good use to test the things it was designed to test but Visual Basic was being used to fill in the gaps. That is where Visual Basic belongs in the testing arena: filling in the gaps to provide a broader, more thorough test effort.

Appendixes

APPENDIX A
Resources and References

This appendix contains both a bibliography of references that I have used in the writing of this book (References) and also a list of resources for you to get more information on the myriad topics we have touched upon in this text—things like ASP, SQL, and so on. My hope is that you can use this book *and* this list as a springboard to further your career as an automated software tester.

References

These are sources that I have used in the writing of this book. All of them do double-duty as valuable resources.

Testing Books

- Dustin, Elfriede, Jeremy Rashka, and John Paul. *Automated Software Testing: Introduction, Management and Performance.* Addison-Wesley Publishing Company, 1999.

  Elfriede wrote a foreword for Visual Basic for Testers (see front pages). She is an established expert in the field of automated software testing and this book is an excellent resource. She also has a new book: *Quality Web Systems: Performance, Security, and Usability.* Addison-Wesley Publishing Company (available in August, 2001).

- Fewster, Mark and Dorothy Graham. *Software Test Automation: Effective Use of Test Execution Tools.* Addison-Wesley Publishing Company, 1999.

- Kaner, Cem, Jack Falk, and Hung Nguyen. *Testing Computer Software.* Van Nostrand Reinhold, 1993.

- Kit, Edward. *Software Testing in the Real Word: Improving the Process.* Addison-Wesley Publishing Company, 1995.

- Marick, Brian. *Craft of Software Testing: Subsystems Testing Including Object-Based and Object-Oriented Testing.* Prentice Hall PTR/Sun Microsystems Press. 1997.

- Nguyen, Hung. *Testing Applications on the Web: Test Planning for Internet-Based Systems.* Van Nostrand Reinhold, 1993. John Wiley & Sons, 2000

Visual Basic Books

- Appleman, Dan. *Developing COM/ActiveX Components.* Sams, 1999.

- Appleman, Dan. *Visual Basic 5.0 Programmer's Guide to the WIN32 API.* Ziff-Davis Press/Macmillan Computer Publishing USA, 1997.

  I refer to this book many times, especially in Chapter 7, as a required reference for testers. You will frequently use API calls when using Visual Basic 6 and this is the best reference around for that purpose. Dan just explains things very well.

- Cornell, Gary. *Visual Basic 6 from the Ground Up.* Osborne/McGraw-Hill, 1998.

  There are a lot of good Visual Basic books but Gary's book is the best one to learn Visual Basic 6 on your own. It's the perfect adjunct to this book.

- Cornell, Gary. *Learn Microsoft Visual Basic Scripting Edition Now.* Microsoft Press, 1998.

- Microsoft Corporation. *Mastering Microsoft Visual Basic 6.0 Development.* Microsoft Press, 1999.

General Software Design and Development

- Beck, Kent and Martin Fowler. *Planning Extreme Programming.* Addison-Wesley Publishing Company, 2000.

  I considered recommending old standards like Yourdon and Constantine, but I read this book and got a lot out of it. I think you will too. Keep in mind that it doesn't say much of anything about testing but does give a great perspective on software development and plenty of great advice on planning, developing, and implementing an effective software system. It's short and well worth the read.

Articles/Journals/Periodicals

- Dustin, Elfriede. "Lessons in Test Automation." *STQE* Vol 1. Issue 5 (October, 1999)

- Hendrickson, Elisabeth. "Build It or Buy It?" *STQE* Vol 2. Issue 3 (May, 2000)

Web Articles Referenced

- *ASP101*: "Get vs. Post." http://www.asp101.com/samples/getpost.asp

- *ASP Today*: "Automated Testing of Web Pages Using Visual Basic and the WebBrowser Control." Erik Slotboom. http://www.asptoday.com/content/articles/20001107.asp

- *The Common Controls Replacement Project*: Timers Downloads link. http://www.mvps.org/ccrp/

- *The Development Exchange*: "Run with Scissors.NET?" James E. Fawcette. http://www.devx.com/free/hotlinks/2001/ednote011001.asp

- *StickyMinds.com*: "Bang for the Buck Test Automation." Elisabeth Hendrickson. http://www.StickyMinds.com

- *VBNet Visual Basic Developer's Resource Center*: "How to Ping an IP Address Using Visual Basic." Randy Birch. http://www.mvps.org/vbnet/

Microsoft Product Support Services: Multiple Articles

- "HOWTO: Automate Internet Explorer to Post Form Data." http://support.microsoft.com/support/kb/articles/Q167/6/58.asp

- "HOWTO: Use the PostData Parameter in WebBrowser Control." http://support.microsoft.com/support/kb/articles/Q174/9/23.asp

- "HOWTO: Handle Data from a Post Form *when* Hosting WebBrowser *control*." http://support.microsoft.com/support/kb/articles/Q256/1/95.asp

Resources

These are my recommendations for places to learn more about the topics in this text, *in addition* to those already listed in References (since those are great too). This is not just a list of books and Web sites that I got from someone else. These resources are ones that are tried and true by me, personally, and my colleagues and students. I believe they will give you the most information, clearly and effectively.

Recommended Testing Web Sites

- *Quality Tree Software, Inc.*: Elisabeth Hendricksen.
  http://www.qualitytree.com/

  Excellent articles on automated testing. Check out Elisabeth's Articles and Automation Advice links. I especially like "Build It vs. Buy It" and "Bang for the Buck Test Automation."

- *Satisfice, Inc.*: James Bach. http://www.satisfice.com/

  James also wrote a foreword for *Visual Basic for Testers*. He is a noted expert in the field of software testing. His paper, "Test Automation Snake Oil," is in Appendix D of this book because it's a classic and a must-read for all testers. Check out his other articles on his Web site. He also offers training and consulting.

- *STA Group, Inc.*: Dan Hodge. http://www.stagroup.com/

  Dan's company has been a premiere training organization for Rational Visual Test and basic testing topics for years. His company provides consultation and training. This is also a good Web site for testing resources and white papers.

- *StickyMinds.com*: http://www.StickyMinds.com

  Don't let the odd name fool you. This is quickly becoming the premiere Web site for software testing resources and information.

- *Software Testing Hot List*: Editor: Bret Pettichord.
  http://www.io.com/~wazmo/qa/#test_automation

  Bret's article "Seven Steps to Test Automation Success" is in Appendix D of *Visual Basic for Testers*. It's a thorough and informative article that anyone doing automated software testing should read.

- *Software Testing Resources on the Web*:
  http://www.aptest.com/resources.html

- *Visual Monkey*: Jason Herres. http://www.visualmonkey.com/vb4testers/

  Special location for readers of this book. Front-end for VBPing is there.
  See Chapter 10 in this book for a description of the VBPing project.

- *World Wide Web Consortium*: http://www.w3.org/

  If you do any Web testing or Web development, you need to be here on a
  regular basis. This site contains the standards for all things Web-related,
  including HTML and XML. There are tools for testing Web sites, many
  free.

- *Quality Assurance Forums*. www.QAForums.com

  QA forums is a great place to communicate with other testers.
  It includes a segment just for automated testing.

Recommended Visual Basic Web Sites

- *Carl and Gary's Visual Basic Home Page*: http://www.cgvb.com/

- *Whatis.com*: http://www.whatis.com

  This is not specifically a VB Web site, but you can get a lot of essential
  programming terminology definitions here. This site will not only help
  you get definitions of basic computer terms but it also contains links to
  the appropriate Web sites for these terms.

- *Microsoft Developer's Network*: http://msdn.microsoft.com and the library
  at http://msdn.microsoft.com/library/

  The Developer's Network and its associated library is one of the first
  places to go for information on any Microsoft product. The library has
  essentially all of the Help files you will need regardless of what you have
  installed.

Recommended Database Design and SQL Resources

- Hernandez, Michael J. *Database Design for Mere Mortals*. Addison-
  Wesley Publishing Company, 1997.

  The "Mere Mortals" books by Hernandez are highly recommended by
  my students at Bellevue Community College. They far surpass other
  books on these topics for clarity.

- Hernandez, Michael J. *SQL Queries for Mere Mortals*. Addison-Wesley Publishing Company, 2000.

Recommended Web and ASP Resources

- *ASP 101*: http://www.asp101.com/

  If you want to know about ASP, you can learn it here. I used one of the samples in Chapter 10 of *Visual Basic for Testers* but his site has all kinds of code from easy to hard with good explanations.

- *World Wide Web Consortium*: http://www.w3.org/

  If you do any Web testing or Web development, you need to be here on a regular basis. This site contains the standards for all things Web-related, including HTML and XML. There are tools for testing Web sites, many free.

Recommended Testing Publications

Both of the following publications continually publish articles by leaders in the Software Test and Quality Assurance industries. If you prefer reading from paper rather than from a Web page, these are excellent resources:

- *The Journal of Software Testing Professionals*. International Institute for Software Testing. Published Quarterly. Inver Grove Heights, MN.

- *Software Testing and Quality Engineering Magazine*. Software Quality Engineering. Published bimonthly. Orange Park, FL.

Recommended Visual Basic Publications

- *Visual Basic Programmer's Journal*. Fawcette Technical Publications. Published monthly. Palo Alto, CA.

  I usually learn enough in just one edition to pay for the entire year's subscription.

More Controls

In the introduction and Chapter 1, I explained that this book is different than other Visual Basic books because our goal is not to design a fancy interface but to learn how to get information quickly. Consequently, we have not covered many controls. Table B-1 lists the controls we have covered and their corresponding chapters.

Table B-1. Controls Covered in Chapters 1 through 10

CONTROL	CHAPTER COVERED
Command button	Multiple chapters
Textbox	Multiple chapters
Label control	Multiple chapters
Timer control	Chapter 5
List box	Chapter 6
Menu control	Chapter 10
Common dialog	Chapter 10

It's very likely that you will need and want to use more than just this limited set. In this appendix, I will present a few more essential controls:

- Option button

- Checkbox

- Frame control

- Combo box

Figure B-1 displays the location of these controls in the Toolbox.

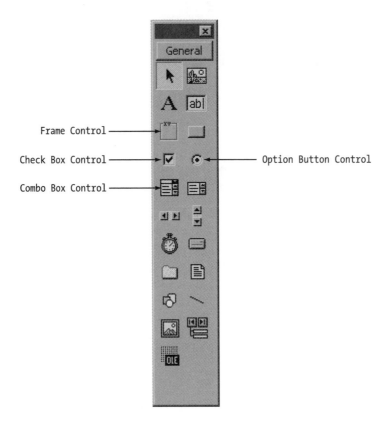

Frame Control

Check Box Control

Combo Box Control

Option Button Control

Figure B-1. The Option button, Checkbox, Combo box, and Frame control locations in the Toolbox window.

There are many more that I could cover but once you are familiar with the essentials, it is fairly straightforward to pick up the rest. At the end of this appendix, I will show you how to find even more controls.

All but one of these controls, the Frame control, are used to give the user a choice. While it is possible to let users continue to enter values into Input boxes and textboxes to make choices, providing these controls will allow you to manage the values available to the user. For example, if users are allowed to enter a choice into a Textbox control, they have the latitude to make many spelling mistakes—and you will have to write a lot of code to make sure the data is what you need. With a Combo Box control, you can give the user a predefined and limited set of choices. It can make your program much more robust (error free) and easier to maintain and use.

Option Buttons and Checkboxes

Figure B-2 displays the Find dialog of Internet Explorer 5. You can get to this dialog from the **Edit** ➤ **Find (on this page)** menu item within IE 5.

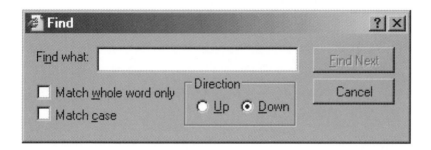

Figure B-2. A dialog from Internet Explorer 5 containing Frame, Option button, and Checkbox controls.

Option buttons and checkboxes are both used for making choices, as you can see. The standard difference between them is that Option buttons (sometimes referred to as Radio buttons) are used for mutually exclusive choices, for example, in the Find dialog you can search either Up or Down but not both. Checkboxes are used for nonmutually exclusive choice. For example, in the dialog, it would make sense to check "Match Whole Word Only" and "Match Case." It would also be possible to select either or both of those choices. Although both specify search criteria, they are completely independent of each other. This is the way you should use these kinds of controls in your applications—otherwise, it will confuse the user.

You can place Option Button and Checkbox controls by double-clicking their icons in the Toolbox. (They are easy to find in the Toolbox since their icons show exactly how they display.) The important property of the Option Button and Checkbox controls is their Value property. For Option buttons, the Value property will be either True or False. If the user has selected the Option button, it's Value property evaluates to True. By default it's False. To create a default option, you can set the Value property of one of the Option buttons to True prior to loading the form. You can do this either by selecting the Value property for the Option button in the Property window or by executing the following line of code in the Form_Load event:

```
Option1.Value = True
```

While the Option Button control has only two possible states: it's either selected (True) or it's not (False), the Checkbox control actually has three possible states. Checkbox controls can be checked, not checked, or grayed. The third state, grayed, is for times when a choice is only partially True. Because of these three states, the Checkbox control's Value property is not True or False but is either 1, 2, or 3 instead. Table B-2 shows the three possible states for a Checkbox control along with some Visual Basic intrinsic constants you can choose to set the Value property

Table B-2. The Three Possible States for the Checkbox Control

VALUE	DESCRIPTION	CONSTANT
0	Unchecked	vbUnchecked
1	Checked	vbChecked
2	Grayed	vbGrayed

Using the constants makes your code more clear. The following two lines of code are equivalent for setting the initial value of a Checkbox control so that it displays as checked:

```
Check1.Value = 1
Check1.Value = vbChecked
```

There are a lot of properties, methods, and events available for both the Option Button and Checkbox controls but to make a simple choice, just check for the Value property. In the Practice Files, there is a folder associated with this appendix (Appendix B), which contains a project called OptChkDemo.vbp. This contains a form with checkboxes and Option buttons. It's an example of how you might use these controls on a form to determine the logging options you may want to provide for your tests. Figure B-3 displays the window of the OptChkDemo.vbp project.

I am not going to claim that this is the best way to set logging options. Mostly, I just want demonstrate how to use them. In this project, the user is given a selection of "levels" of logging. You may want to choose levels associated with the severity of a bug. These levels are mutually exclusive so the Option Button control is used for them. The user is also given a choice of logging test results to a file or to the Immediate window. By using checkboxes for these choices, the user is allowed to do both. The project uses the code in Listing B-1 to evaluate the Value property of these controls and then take action accordingly.

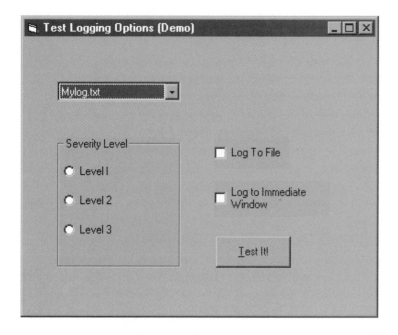

Figure B-3. The OptChkDemo.vbp project demonstrates the use of Option Button, Checkbox, Combo Box, and Frame controls.

Listing B-1. Code to manipulate Option buttons and Checkbox controls of the OptChkDemo.vbp program.

```
Dim strlevel As String
If optLevel1.Value = True Then
    strlevel = "REALLY bad bug"
ElseIf optLevel2 = True Then
    strlevel = "Bad bug"
Else
    strlevel = "Not so bad bug"
End If

If chktoImmediate = vbChecked Then
    LogIt "Test data; Level: " & strlevel
End If
If chktoFile = vbChecked Then
    LogToFile "Test data; Level :" & strlevel
    ReadLog
End If
```

The Frame Control

Notice in Figure B-3 that the Option buttons appear within a square box. This is actually a Frame control. Visually, the Frame control makes it easy to set the Option buttons apart and allows you to name the set. This is user-friendly. There is an additional value in using the Frame control with Option buttons, though. The Frame control allows you to place multiple sets of Option buttons, different from each other, onto the form. Without the Frame control, all Option buttons on a form would be mutually exclusive of each other. If you want multiple sets of Option buttons, you can place each set inside of a Frame control. (*Any* control can go inside of a Frame control to set it apart, by the way.) To take advantage of the Frame control's ability to set apart Options, however, you must make sure that the Options buttons are completely contained by the Frame. This means that you must initially draw the controls that you want directly inside of the frame. You can't do that by creating a control and simply dragging it into the Frame control. You must draw the control within the Frame completely when you create it. Another, easier way is to create the control as usual—by double-clicking its icon in the Toolbar—then cut it, select the Frame control, and paste so that it appears in the Frame. Moving the Frame control in Design mode will move any controls inside of it as well.

The Combo Box Control

The Combo Box control is similar in use to the List Box control used in Chapter 6. It allows you to provide the user with a set of predefined choices. The List Box control can take up a lot of room on a form. The Combo Box control can take up just as much space as a textbox, but still provide the flexibility of multiple choices because the choice list drops down only when the user selects it. The OptChkDemo.vbp program uses one to allow the user a limited selection of file names. Of course, this probably isn't the best way to choose file names in your own projects; the Common Dialog control is better for that (see Chapter 10). The Combo box is used here for demonstration purposes—you will find many uses for it.

The Combo Box control is so named because it's really a combination of the Textbox control and the List Box control. Like the Textbox control, you can enter values; and like the List Box control, you can also select from a list of possible values. So, the Combo Box control has all of the properties of the Textbox control plus those of the List Box control. Now, having said this, I am really talking about just one style of the Combo box, the default style, which is the dropdown Combo box. There are actually three possible styles of Combo box: the default style, a simple combo, and a read-only style. You determine which style you want by setting the Style property in the Properties window at design time. Table B-3 lists the available styles of the Combo box.

Table B-3. Combo Box Styles

STYLE	DESCRIPTION
0	Dropdown combo—The default. Allows you to type your own value as well as select from the list.
1	Simple combo—Like the Dropdown combo but not used as much. Looks like the selection in Font dialogs.
2	Dropdown list—Essentially, a read-only Combo box. Users can't enter a value, they must select from the list.

To load the Combo box with values, use its AddItem method:

```
Combo1.AddItem "Test1"
```

One of the key properties of the Combo box is the Text property. You can use this property to specify the default value of the Combo box. For example, in the following code, assume there is a Combo box with the name cmbLogFileChoice. The code loads the Combo box with three file names: Mylog.txt, Logfile.txt, and Anotherchoice.txt. The last line sets the Text property of the Combo box to "Mylog.txt." That will make MyLog.txt the default value of the Combo box. That means it will show up in the Combo box first but the user can change it easily by selecting another value from the Combo box's dropdown list:

```
Private Sub Form_Load()

    cmbLogFileChoice.AddItem "Mylog.txt"  'first Item In the combo box
    cmbLogFileChoice.AddItem "Logfile.txt" 'second Item
    cmbLogFileChoice.AddItem "Anotherchoice.txt" 'third Item

    cmbLogFileChoice.Text = "Mylog.txt"  'specifies the default value

End Sub
```

You can use the Text property to retrieve the value also. The following code places the selected file into a string variable:

```
    LogUtil.LOGFILE = App.Path & "\" & cmbLogFileChoice.Text
```

The OptChkDemo.vbp demonstration project also contains a Combo box and contains the preceding code.

Even More Controls

The Visual Basic Help system contains a lot of information on controls so I recommend taking a look at the *Programmer's Guide* within the Help system, particularly the subsection "Forms, Controls and Menus" for more information. Although Help is where I recommend starting, most other VB books go into great detail on the rich set of controls you can use in Visual Basic. My personal favorite is Gary Cornell's *Visual Basic 6 from the Ground Up*. He has a chapter called "Finishing the Interface," which pretty much says it all.

Additionally, there are many third-party controls available from other vendors. Don't worry, if you have a license to own Visual Basic, you will be hearing from them! The downside to third-party controls, though, is that you may find yourself stuck if there are problems. For the most part, Microsoft will not support a third-party control with technical support—you will have to rely on the third-party vendor. I use third-party controls with caution. You can find out from Visual Basic User's groups which ones to try. My recommendation for additional controls is the Common Controls Replacement Project (CCRP). See their Web site at http://www.mvps.org/ccrp/.

File Access and Management

I did not want to divert from the topics in the chapters to discuss file access and management in depth but it is an important topic for testing. You will frequently find yourself working with files. Visual Basic has many ways to manage files and we introduced the preferred way, the File System Object (FSO), in Chapter 5. In this appendix, I will go into the traditional methods of file access. First, I will show you some essential commands for file management.

File Management in Visual Basic

Visual Basic's developers knew you would be working with files enough to warrant placing file management commands directly into the language rather than making you work with the Windows API libraries to perform file management tasks. The following Visual Basic commands mirror some DOS commands for creating, deleting, and copying files:

MkDir	Creates a new directory.
RmDir	Removes a directory or folder.
ChDir	Changes the current directory or folder.
Kill	Deletes a file.
Name	Renames a file or folder. You can rename into a new location by changing the path along with its name.
FileCopy	Copies a file.
CurDir	Returns the current directory.

The following code uses many of these to demonstrate file management:

```
Option Explicit
' to get the most out of this demo
' you should step through it using the debugger

Private Sub cmdTest_Click()
    Debug.Print "current directory is: " & CurDir
    Debug.Print "app path is: " & App.Path

    MkDir "MyTestDir"

    Open CurDir & "\MyTestDir\MyTestFile.txt" For Output As 1
    Print #1, "my stuff; you should delete this file. It's in c:\mytestfile.txt"
    Close #1

    FileCopy CurDir & "\MyTestDir\MyTestFile.txt", "c:\mytestfile.txt"

    Kill CurDir & "\MyTestDir\MyTestFile.txt"   'cleaning up
    RmDir "MyTestDir"
    MsgBox "Done"
    Shell "notepad " & "c:\mytestfile.txt", vbNormalFocus
End Sub
```

Standard File Access

Chapter 5 introduced the File System Object from the Microsoft Scripting Runtime library as a way to access a file. Eventually, Microsoft plans to phase out the traditional forms of file access I'll be showing you here in favor of the FSO. The FSO works well and is very powerful but is still not flexible enough to handle all file types, such as binary files. So, the following methods are still necessary in some situations. There are three types of file access in Visual Basic: sequential, random, and binary.

To open one of the three standard files, use the Open statement. For example, the following line opens a sequential file for writing:

```
Open "c:\testresults.txt" for output as 1
```

And this statement opens a random file:

```
Open "TESTFILE" For Random As #1 Len = Len(Test)
```

The general form of the command is:

Open *filename* For *FileMode* as *FileNum* [Len =*length of record*]

The parts of the Open statement are:

- **Open** The keyword used to signify that a file is to be opened. The Open statement is used for opening any of the three file access methods.

- **Filename** The full pathname to the file. If you open the file for writing, or if the file does not exist, it is created.

- **FileMode** Output and Append are the two modes used for writing to sequential files. The difference between them is that Output mode deletes any existing information in the file, Append places the cursor at the end of the existing data and writing begins there. Random specifies that the file is open for Random access for both reading and/or writing and the Binary mode specifies that the file is open for binary access for both reading and/or writing.

The file modes for the three file access methods are displayed in Table C-1.

Table C-1. File Modes for the Three Standard File Access Methods

FILE ACCESS METHOD	FILE MODES FOR READING	FILE MODES FOR WRITING
Binary	Binary	Binary
Random	Random	Random
Sequential	Input	Output/Append

- **FileNum** The system will refer to the file as a number after opening it. You are allowed to specify what this number will be: it must be an integer between 1 and 511.

- **Len=*Length of record*** This clause is for random access files only and specifies the size of each record.

The Sequential File

Sequential files are stored just as it sounds, sequentially. Each record in the file can be of any length. The sequential file is the method originally developed for use with magnetic tape. The file is written directly onto the tape in sequence. Think of it as similar to recording onto a cassette tape. Once the artist has recorded songs onto the tape, you must rewind or fast-forward the tape to get to a particular selection again. Because each song is stored sequentially, the length of each song does not matter. It's the same with the sequential files you create: the length of each record can be as long or short as you want. The start and end of each record is marked by the system.

All text files are sequential files, these files can have almost any extension but familiar extensions are .txt, .dat and .log. It's the fastest mode of access when you want to quickly store a lot of data and read the entire file later. Thus, it is good for test results logging.

Writing to a Sequential File

To write to a sequential file, first you open it and then you can print to that file using either the Print or Write statements. When the file is opened, you must assign a file number to it. This number must be an integer between 1 and 511. Use file numbers in the range of 1 through 255, inclusive, for files private to your own application—that is, inaccessible to other applications. Use file numbers in the range of 256 through 511 for files that you want to be accessible from other applications. You can open many files at the same time. To avoid using a number that may already be used by another open file, the function Freefile can be used to return the next available file handle. (So, if the number 1 is already in use, Freefile returns the number 2)

The following code opens a file for writing using the *Append File* mode. If the file already exists, the Append File mode opens the file, preserving the existing data. Your statements will write to the end of the file. (The Output File mode would erase existing data. Both file modes will create the file if it does not already exist.)

```
Dim fHand as Integer
fHand = Freefile
Open "c:\testresults.txt" for append as fHand
```

The following is an alternate logging subroutine for the Logging Utilities module, LogUtil, used in Chapter 5:

```
Public LOGFILE = "c:\testlog.txt"
Sub LogtoFile(strLogText As String)
'Logging to a sequential file
  Static lLogNum As Long
  Dim fHand As Long
  fHand = FreeFile
  lLogNum = lLogNum + 1

  Open LOGFILE For Append As fHand
  'write a header record:
  If lLogNum = 1 Then
    Print #fHand, "Starting Tests ", Now
  End If
  Print #fHand, lLogNum, strLogText, Now
  Close fHand
End Sub
```

Reading a Sequential File

Reading a sequential file can be even more important to a tester than writing to one. Many applications write information to text files, for example, application log files. In testing, we may need to verify the information written to these files.

The following code reads the information from the log file that we created for our preceding test results:

```
Sub ReadLog()
'The following routine writes to the immediate 'window and also opens notepad to
display the 'output
  Dim fHand As Long
  Dim strHold$
  fHand = FreeFile
  Debug.Print "Output from File: "
  Open LOGFILE For Input As fHand
  Do While Not EOF(fHand)
    Line Input #fHand, strHold
    Debug.Print strHold
  Loop
  Close fHand
  'open notepad and display the current output
  Shell "notepad.exe " & LOGFILE, vbNormalFocus
End Sub
```

The previous example shows writing to a sequential file using Print # and reading from it using Line Input#. This is standard Basic programming. Visual Basic also has another combination of statements that allows you to create a more complex record. If you write to a file using the Write# statement, you can print each record with a comma-delimited list of variables. To read from this kind of sequential file back into a variables list, use the Input# statement. Listing C-1 shows writing to and reading from a sequential file using the Write# and Input# statements.

Listing C-1. Writing to and reading from a sequential file with Write# and Input#.

```
Option Explicit

Private Sub CmdTest_Click()
    Open App.Path & "\TESTFILE2.txt" For Output As #1    ' Open file for output.
    Dim Testnum As Integer
    Dim TestPassed As Boolean
    Dim TestDate As Date
    Dim TimeElapsed As Double

    Testnum = 1
    TestPassed = False
    TestDate = Now
    TimeElapsed = 1.55555

    ' Assign Boolean, Date, Null, and Error values.
    ' Boolean data is written as #TRUE# or #FALSE#. Date literals are
    ' written in universal date format, for example, #1994-07-13#
    'represents July 13, 1994. Null data is written as #NULL#.
    ' Error data is written as #ERROR errorcode#.
    Write #1, Testnum, TestPassed, TestDate, TimeElapsed  'write using variables
    Write #1, 2, True, Now, 1.333              'write using literals

    Close #1   ' Close file.

    Shell "notepad " & App.Path & "\TESTFILE2.txt", vbNormalFocus
    'now reopen the file for reading
    Open App.Path & "\TESTFILE2.txt" For Input As #1   ' Open file for input.
    Do While Not EOF(1)   ' Loop until end of file.
        Input #1, Testnum, TestPassed, TestDate, TimeElapsed
        Debug.Print Testnum, TestPassed, TestDate, TimeElapsed   ' Print
    Loop
    Close #1   ' Close file.
End Sub
```

Sequential file access is quick—unless you want to search for just a single record. Just like a cassette tape, you must read the file until you find the desired record. Because of this, sequential files are mostly used for quickly writing and reading data when you need to read and write the entire file. A good example might be to write test results out to a sequential file and then read the file to print it out in a report-like format. If you want to frequently read a specific record, this isn't the best file access method to use because you have to read through all preceding items before you get to the one you want. If you have a data file in which you frequently need to read a specific record, in order to work with this file, choose either the random access file method or use COM (Chapter 9) to write to a spreadsheet or ADO to store the information in a database (Chapter 8).

The Random Access File

The random storage method allows you to store fixed-size records that contain fields of various data types. A UDT type is used to define the fields in the record (UDTs were introduced in Chapter 7). The following UDT is one we might consider using to specify the information stored for test logging:

```
Type TestDataType    ' Define user-defined type.
   TestNum As Integer
   TestName As String * 20
   TestResult as String * 6
   TestTimeElapsed as Double
End Type
```

The length of a record of this data type can be calculated because the size for each of the data types is known. The Integer data type stores values in 2 bytes and the Double data type stores values in 8 bytes. The two strings are declared as fixed length so they are 20 and 6 bytes long, respectively. That makes the total length of this record:

2 + 20 + 6 + 8 = 36 bytes

You will see the importance of this in the next section.

Writing to and Reading from a Random Access File

When you open a random file, it is opened for both reading and writing at the same time because when you open the file, you must specify the length of the record you are storing. Since the length of the record is known, the system can calculate the exact location of each record easily. So, unlike sequential files, you can go directly to a specific record number in the file. When you write or read from that record, it does not affect any other records, as it would in sequential file where the length of each record is unknown (so writing a new value could potentially overwrite the next record—this is why you must open a sequential file for either reading *or* writing). If you can think of a sequential file as a cassette tape, think of the random access file as more like a CD. You can go directly to a particular selection, like the fifth song on a CD, without having to read through the others before it.

Listing C-2 shows code to open a random access file, write three records into it, and then, without closing the file, read the third record.

Listing C-2. Writing to and reading from a random access file.

```
Option Explicit
'UDT definitions go in the General declarations section of a module
Private Type TestDataType    ' Define user-defined type.
    TestNum As Integer
    TestName As String * 20
    TestResult As String * 6
End Type


Private Sub cmdTest_Click()
    Dim Test As TestDataType
  ' Open file for random access.
    Open "TESTFILE" For Random As #1 Len = 36  'length of the record
  ' or you could use the len function to retrieve the length:  len = len(test)
    Test.TestNum = 1              ' Define Test Number.
    Test.TestName = "ABCTest1"
    Test.TestResult = "Passed"
    Put #1, 1, Test                     ' Write first record to file.
    Test.TestNum = 2              ' Define Test Number.
    Test.TestName = "ABCTest2"
    Test.TestResult = "Failed"
    Put #1, 2, Test                    ' Write second record to file.
    Test.TestNum = 3              ' Define Test Number.
    Test.TestName = "ABCTest1"
    Test.TestResult = "Passed"
    Put #1, 3, Test                     ' Write third record to file.
```

```
'You can read from the file without closing it
Dim HoldRecord As TestDataType
Get #1, 3, HoldRecord    ' Read third record.

Debug.Print HoldRecord.TestName, HoldRecord.TestNum, HoldRecord.TestResult
MsgBox "View Immediate window to see result of the read"
Close #1    ' Close file.

End Sub
```

You might wonder why you should go to all of this trouble when you could just store the information in a database (Chapter 8) or spreadsheet (Chapter 9). In those file storage systems, you can get a lot more power for manipulating and reporting on the data. You are correct to wonder and, in many cases (especially for large amounts of data), you will likely want to choose those storage methods. The advantage to the random access file is that it takes up less overhead for both memory and storage. For small files, it is still a viable option.

The Binary Access File

Binary access is the only method that will allow you to read a file byte-by-byte. You may have occasion to read a file this way when you are comparing files or looking for file anomalies. A binary file, like a random file, can be open for reading and writing but you don't need to provide a file length. In fact if you do, it is ignored:

```
Option Explicit
Private Sub cmdBinary_Click()
    Dim strVarstring As String
    Open App.Path & "\binarydemo" For Binary As 1  'open for writing

    strVarstring = "Mary Sweeney"
    Put #1, , strVarstring$

'variables used for reading the file
    Dim b As Byte
    Dim iCount As Integer
    Dim lFileLen As Long

    lFileLen = Len(App.Path & "binarydemo")
```

```
For iCount = 1 To lFileLen 'read file a byte at a time
        Get #1, iCount, b
        Debug.Print Chr(b);
    Next iCount
    Debug.Print
    Close #1

End Sub
```

For more information on file access in Visual Basic other than the FSO, see the Visual Basic Help system topic, "Processing Files with Older File I/O Statements and Functions."

Required Reading: Automated Testing Essays

To automate software testing effectively, it isn't enough to know how to write code to extract information—you need an effective strategy. There are just too many possible problems that can make your efforts a waste of time, money, and energy. I know, I have run into many of them myself. Fortunately, there are a number of experts around who are willing to help the rest of us by thoughtfully sharing strategies and techniques for avoiding problems and setting up successful projects.

There are numerous essays I recommend that you read by authors that include Elfriede Dustin, Elisabeth Hendrickson, Brian Marick, Boris Beizer, and Linda Hayes. These people can help you avoid the common problems and pitfalls associated with automating software testing. Appendix A: Resources and References lists what I consider to be some of the best articles I've read so far. It was difficult to choose which to reprint here. I had to decide which articles are the best to get you started as an effective software test automator.

I chose the first article, "Seven Steps to Test Automation Success," by Bret Pettichord because it compiles the information from many excellent sources into one logical, thoughtful, and practical essay. The second article, "Test Automation Snake Oil" by James Bach, is a classic that debunks the myths surrounding automated software testing and sets realistic expectations. Thirdly, I asked Elisabeth Hendrickson for her recommendations for software test automators using Visual Basic. Her advice is reprinted here.

About the Authors

My sincere thanks goes out to all three authors for giving me their permission to reprint their articles.

Bret Pettichord is a consultant specializing in software testing, test automation, and testability. Familiar with many test tools, he helps teams to develop test automation strategies and architectures. He has helped develop automated tests for such companies as Texas Instruments, Rational, Netpliance, Whisper-wire, Managemark, Tivoli, Unison, BMC, Segue, and Interleaf. He also provides training in automated testing architectures and design.

Bret is the editor of the Software Testing Hotlist (http://www.io.com/~wazmo/qa/) and is a frequent speaker. He is the founder of the Austin Workshop on Test Automation and a founding participant in the Los Altos Workshop for Software Testing. He sits on the advisory board of Stickyminds.com and is certified in Software Quality engineering by the American Society of Quality. He is also a member of the IEEE Computer Society. Bret has a bachelor's degree in Philosophy and Mathematics from New College in Sarasota, Florida.

James Bach is founder and principal consultant of Satisfice, Inc. (http://www.satisfice.com) James cut his teeth as a programmer, tester, and SQA manager in Silicon Valley and the world of market-driven software development. He has worked at Apple, Borland, a couple of start-ups, and some consulting companies, including a stint as chief scientist at ST Labs, an independent software-testing laboratory. He was part of the team that defined the body of knowledge covered by the Certified Software Quality Engineer program for the American Society for Quality. He has also served on curriculum advisory boards for the Rochester Institute of Technology and the International Technological University.

Elisabeth Hendrickson is my favorite author because her articles are full of common sense and insight. Elisabeth has over twelve years experience as a practitioner and manager in software development, with an emphasis on quality assurance and testing. She is the founder of Quality Tree Software, Inc. and creator of the Quality Tree Web site (http://www.qualitytree.com), a resource for software professionals interested in automated testing and quality. Elisabeth is a published author and frequent conference speaker.

Seven Steps to Test Automation Success

By Bret Pettichord

bret@pettichord.com
http://www.pettichord.com
Revised version of a paper originally presented at STAR West conference, San Jose, California. November 1999.
Version of 11 June 2001.

Abstract

Test automation raises our hopes yet often frustrates and disappoints us. Although automation promises to deliver us from a tough situation, implementing automated tests can create as many problems as it solves. The key is to follow the rules of software development when automating testing. This paper presents seven key steps: improve the testing process, define requirements, prove the concept, champion product testability, design for sustainability, plan for deployment, and face the challenges of success. Follow these steps as you staff, tool, or schedule your test automation project, and you will be well on your way to success.

A Fable

I've seen lots of different problems beset test automation efforts. I've worked at many software companies, big and small. And I've talked to people from many other companies. This paper will present ways to avoid these problems. But first we need to understand them. Let me illustrate with a fable.

Once upon a time, we have a software project that needs test automation. Everyone on the team agrees that this is the thing to do. The manager of this project is Anita Delegate. She reviews the different test tools available, selects one and purchases several copies. She assigns one of her staff, Jerry Overworked, the job of automating the tests. Jerry has many other responsibilities, but between these, he tries out the new tool. He has trouble getting it to work with their product. The tool is complicated and hard to configure. He has to make several calls to the customer support line. He eventually realizes that they need an expert to set it up right and figure out what the problem is. After more phone calls, they finally send an expert. He arrives, figures out the problem and gets things working. Excellent. But many months have passed, and they still have no automation. Jerry refuses to work on the project any further, fearing that it will never be anything but a time sink.

Anita reassigns the project to Kevin Shorttimer, who has recently been hired to test the software. Kevin has a recent degree in computer science and is hoping to use this job as a step up to something more challenging and rewarding. Anita sends him to tool training so that he won't give up in frustration the way Jerry did. Kevin is very excited. The testing is repetitive and boring so he is glad to be automating instead. After a major release ships, he is allowed to work full time on test automation. He is eager for a chance to prove that he can write sophisticated code. He builds a testing library and designs some clever techniques that will support lots of tests. It takes longer than planned, but he gets it working. He uses the test suite on new builds and is actually able to find bugs with it. Then Kevin gets an opportunity for a development position and moves on, leaving his automation behind.

Ahmed Hardluck gets the job of running Kevin's test suite. The sparse documentation he finds doesn't help much. It takes a while for Ahmed to figure out how to run the tests. He gets a lot of failures and isn't sure if he ran it right or not. The error messages aren't very helpful. He digs deeper. Some of the tests look like they were never finished. Others have special setup requirements. He updates the setup documentation. He plugs away with it. He finds that a couple failures are actually due to regression bugs. Everyone is happy that the test suite caught these. He identifies things in the test suites that he'd like to change to make it more reliable but there never seems to be the time. The next release of the product has some major changes planned. Ahmed soon realizes that the product changes break the automation. Most of the tests fail. Ahmed works on this for a while and then gets some help from others. They realize that it's going to take some major work to get the tests to run with the new product interface. But eventually they do it. The tests pass, and they ship the product. And the customers start calling right away. The software doesn't work. They come to realize that they reworked some tests so that error messages were being ignored. These tests actually failed, but a programming error had dismissed these errors. The product is a failure.

That's my fable. Perhaps parts of the story sound familiar to you. But I hope you haven't seen a similar ending. This paper will suggest some ways to avoid the same fate. (James Bach has recounted similar stories of test automation projects [Bach 1996].)

The Problems

This fable illustrates several problems that plague test automation projects:

> **Spare time test automation**. People are allowed to work on test automation on their own time or as a back burner project when the test schedule allows. This keeps it from getting the time and focus it needs.

> **Lack of clear goals**. There are many good reasons for doing test automation. It can save time, make testing easier and improving the testing coverage. It can also help keep testers motivated. But it's not likely to do all these things at the same time. Different parties typically have different hopes. These need to be stated, or else disappointment is likely.

> **Lack of experience**. Junior programmers trying to test their limits often tackle test automation projects. The results are often difficult to maintain.

> **High turnover**. Test automation can take awhile to learn. But when the turnover is high, you lose this experience.

> **Reaction to desperation**. Problems are usually lurking in the software long before testing begins. But testing brings them to light. Testing is difficult enough in itself. When testing is followed by testing and retesting of the repaired software, people can get worn down. Will the testing ever end? This desperation can become particularly acute when the schedule has dictated that the software should be ready now. If only

it weren't for all the testing! In this environment, test automation may be a ready answer, but it may not be the best. It can be more of a wish than a realistic proposal.

Reluctance to think about testing. Many find automating a product more interesting than testing it. Some automation projects provide convenient cover stories for why their contributors aren't more involved in the testing. Rarely does the outcome contribute much to the test effort.

Technology focus. How the software can be automated is a technologically interesting problem. But this can lose sight of whether the result meets the testing need.

Follow the Rules of Software Development

You may be familiar with the five-step maturity models that can be used to classify software development organizations. The Capabilities Maturity Model from the Software Engineering Institute is a well-known example. Jerry Weinberg has his own organizational model, in which he adds an additional level, which he calls Pattern Zero. A Pattern Zero organization is *oblivious* to the fact that it is actually developing software; there is no distinction between the users and the developers [Weinberg 1992]. This is the place that test automation often finds itself. Thus, dedicating resources to test automation and treating it like a development activity elevates it to the first level. This is the core of the solution to the problems of test automation. We need to run test automation projects just as we do our other software development projects. Like other software development projects, we will need to have developers dedicated to developing our test automation. Like other software development projects, test automation automates a task in which the programmer is probably not an expert. Therefore, expert testers should be consulted and should provide the requirements. Like other software development projects, test automation benefits if we design our approach before we start coding. Like other software development projects, test automation code needs to be tracked and safeguarded. Therefore, we need to use source code management. Like other software development projects, test automation will have bugs. Therefore, we need to plan to track them and test for them. Like other software development projects, users will need to know how to use it. Therefore, we need user documentation.

It's not my place to tell you how to develop software. I assume that you are part of a software organization that already has some idea as to what reasonable and effective methods should be used for developing software. I am simply urging you to abide by whatever rules are established for software development in your own test automation. This paper will be organized by the normal steps that we all use for our software development projects, making special notes of the considerations and challenges that are particular to test automation.

1. Improve the Testing Process

2. Define Requirements

3. Prove the Concept

4. Champion Product Testability

5. Design for Sustainability

6. Plan for Deployment

7. Face the Challenges of Success

Step 1. Improve the Testing Process

If you are responsible for improving the efficiency of a business task, you first want to make sure that the process is well defined. You also want to see if there are simple and cheap ways to make things go easier before you invest the time and money in automating the system using computers. The same, of course, holds for test automation. Indeed, I like to think that the term "test automation" refers to anything that streamlines the testing process, allowing things to move along more quickly and with less delay. Automated test scripts running on a machine are just one alternative.

For example, many teams start by automating their regression tests. These are the tests that are frequently run and rerun, checking to make sure that things that used to work aren't broken by new changes. They are run often and are tedious. How well are your regression tests documented? It is common to use lists of features that are to be checked. This is a great start. A reminder of what you need to test suits someone who knows the product and understands the test approaches that need to be used.

But before you start to automate, you'll need to improve this documentation. Make your test approach explicit. Specify what names and data should be used for the tests or provide guidelines for making them up. It is probably safe to assume that the tester has basic product knowledge. This is surely documented elsewhere. But you need to be specific about the details of the test design. You also need to state the expected results. This is often unstated, suggesting that the tester should know. Too many testers don't realize what they are missing or are too embarrassed to ask. This kind of detailed documentation is going to be an immediate benefit to your team because now anyone who has a basic understanding of the product can execute the tests. It is also going to need to be done before you do a more thorough automation of the tests. Your test design is going to be the primary requirements statement for your automation, so it's important that it be explicit. It's possible to go overboard here and spell out every step that needs to be taken to execute the test. It is safe to presume that someone who understands how to operate the software will execute the tests. But don't assume that they understand your ideas on how it should be tested. Spell these out.

I once had the job of automating tests for a software module. This module had some features that made it hard to automate. When I realized that I wasn't going to be finished in a short amount of time, I decided I needed a detailed regression test design. I went through the closed defects for the module and for each one I wrote a description of a test that would have been able to find the defect. My plan was that this would provide me with a detailed list of automation requirements that would help me decide what parts of the module most needed automation support. Well, I never got a chance to write the automation. But when we needed to run a full regression on the module, we were able to give the test specifications to a couple people who knew the product but had no experience testing it. Using the detailed test descriptions, they were able to go off and test independently. They found bugs. This required almost no supervision. In a way, it was great automation. Indeed, on this project we had better luck handing off these documented test cases, than we did the automated test scripts we had for other product modules. We learned that the automated scripts required too much training for others to just pick them up and run them. If the automated tests were better designed, this wouldn't have been a problem, but we found that it was much easier to create well-designed test *documentation* than it was to create well designed test *automation*.

Another easy way to improve the efficiency of the testing is to get more computers. Many testers can easily keep a couple of machines busy. This is an obvious point, but I make it because I've seen some misguided automation attempts that resulted from trying too hard to maximize the testing done on a single machine. Test automation can be an expensive and risky way of dealing with an equipment shortage. Better, would be to focus on making a case for the equipment you need.

My final suggestion for improving the testing process is to improve the product to make it easier to test. There are many improvements that will help both the users and the testers. Later, I'll discuss testability needs for automation. Here, I want to suggest identifying product improvements that will help manual testing.

Some products are hard to install, and testers find themselves spending lots of time installing and reinstalling. Rather than automating the install process, maybe it would be better to improve the install program. That way, the customer gets the benefit, too. Another way of putting this is to consider developing your automation in a form that can be delivered with the product. Indeed, there are many commercial tools available that are specifically designed to create install programs.

Another product improvement can be to utilize tools for scanning install or execution logs for errors. Visually scanning through pages and pages of logs looking for error messages gets tedious very quickly. So, let's automate it, right? Writing a scanning tool is easy if you know exactly what form the error messages will take. But if you aren't sure, you are setting yourself up for disaster. Remember the fable about the test suite that missed the failures? Customers don't want to scan through logs looking for errors either. Adding an error scanner to the product will likely result in a more reliable scanner, possibly requiring modifications to the error logging system itself to ensure all errors are caught. This is a tool your testing can depend on.

Performance is another area where product improvement can help the testing. Surely this is obvious. If product sluggishness is delaying your testing, identify the slow functionality, measure it, and report it as a defect that's blocking testing.

These are some of the things you can do to improve test efficiency without having to build a test automation system. Improving the test process may buy you some time for test automation and will certainly make your automation project go more smoothly.

Step 2. Define Requirements

In our fable, we saw that automators can have different goals than the sponsors. To avoid this situation, we'll need to make sure we have agreement on the requirements for test automation. We'll have test requirements, which will describe what needs to be tested. These will be detailed in our test designs. And we will have automation requirements, which will describe the goals for automation. Too many people think test automation is obviously the right thing and don't bother to state what they hope to get. There are several reasons why people choose to automate tests:

- Speed up testing to accelerate releases.

- Allow testing to happen more frequently.

- Reduce costs of testing by reducing manual labor.

- Improve test coverage.

- Ensure consistency.

- Improve the reliability of testing.

- Allow testing to be done by staff with less skill.

- Define the testing process and reduce dependence on the few who know it.

- Make testing more interesting.

- Develop programming skills.

Goals will often differ between development management, test management, the testers themselves and whoever is automating the tests. Clearly, success will be elusive unless they all come to some agreement.

Of course, some of these automation goals will be easier to meet than others. Test automation often actually increases the required skill level for testers, as they must be able to understand the automated tests sufficiently that they can reproduce the defects found. And automation can be a frustrating means of extracting test knowledge from your staff. Regardless, be clear in advance on what people will count as success.

Manual testers do a lot of things that can go unnoticed when they run tests. They plan and obtain required resources. They setup and execute tests. They notice if anything unusual happens. They compare test results. They log results and reset the system to get ready for the next test. They analyze failures and investigate curious behavior. They look for patterns of failure and devise and execute additional tests to help locate defects. And then they log defect reports in order to get fixed and summary reports so that others can know what's been covered.

Don't feel compelled to automate every part of the tests. Look for where you are going to get the biggest payback. Partial automation is okay. You may find it's best to automate the execution and leave the verification to be done manually. Or you may choose to automate the verification and leave the execution to be done manually. I've heard some people say that it's not real automation unless it does everything. That's hogwash. If you are simply looking for challenge, then you can try to do it all. But if you are looking for success, focus on where you can quickly get automation that you can use again and again.

Defining requirements for your test automation project will force these various tradeoffs to be made explicit. It will also help set different parties' expectations reasonably. By defining your goals, you have taken another step towards test automation success.

Step 3. Prove the Concept

In our fable, we saw that the automators dived into the automation project without knowing for sure where they were headed. But they also got mixed support for their project.

You may not realize it, but you have to prove the feasibility of your test automation project. It always takes longer than people would like. To get the commitment it needs, you'll need the support of various people in your organization.

Many years ago, I worked on a test automation project where we had all kinds of great ideas. We designed a complex testing system and worked hard on many of its components. We periodically gave presentations describing our ideas and the progress we were making. We even demonstrated the pieces we had working. But what we didn't do was demonstrate actual tests. Eventually, the project was canceled. It's a mistake I haven't repeated since.

You'll need to validate your tools and approach as soon as possible. Is it even possible to automate tests for your product? It's often difficult. You need to find the answer to this question as soon as possible. You need to find out whether your tools and approach will work for your product and staff. What you need is a proof of concept – a quick, meaningful test suite that demonstrates that you are on the right track. Your proof-of-concept test suite will also be an excellent way to evaluate a test tool.

For many people, test automation means GUI test automation. That's not my meaning. I've done both GUI and non-GUI automation and I've been surprised to learn that most of the planning concerns are shared by both. But GUI test tools are much more expensive and finicky. It is hard to predict what difficulties they will encounter. Consequently, choosing the right GUI test tool is an important decision. Elisabeth Hendrickson has provided excellent guidelines for selecting one [Hendrickson 1999]. I can suggest that your proof-of-concept will be an important part of your evaluation. This will require at least a one-month trial license for the tool. You may even want to purchase one copy now and wait to buy additional copies until after the evaluation. You want to find the tool problems before you've shelled out the big bucks. You'll get better help from the vendor and you won't feel trapped if you find you have to switch to a different tool.

Here are some candidates for your proof of concept:

Regression testing. Do you have tests you run on every build? These kinds of tests are excellent candidates for automation.

Configuration tests. How many different platforms does your software support? And are you expected to test them all? Some automation may help.

Test-bed setup. The same setup procedures may be used for lots of different tests. Before automating the tests, automate the setup.

Non-GUI testing. It's almost always easier to automate command line and API tests than it is to automate GUIs.

Whatever your approach, define a demonstrable goal and then focus on it. Proving your test automation concept will move you one step further on the road to success.

Step 4. Champion Product Testability

Three different interfaces a product might have are command-line interfaces (CLIs), application-programming interfaces (APIs), and graphical user interfaces (GUIs). Some may have all three, but many will have only one or two. These are the interfaces that are available to you for your testing. By their nature, APIs and command-line interfaces are easier to automate than GUIs. Find out if your product has either one; sometimes these are hidden or meant for internal use only. If not, championing product testability may require you to encourage your developers to include a CLI or API in your product.

But first, let me talk a little more about GUI test automation. There are several reasons why GUI test automation is more difficult than people often realize. The first reason is that GUI test automation requires some manual script writing. Most GUI automation tools have a feature called 'record and playback,' or 'capture replay.' The idea is great. You execute the test manually while the test tool sits in the background and remembers what you do. It then generates a script that you can run to re-execute the test. It's a great idea that rarely works. Many authors have concluded that although usable for learning and generating small bits of code, various problems prevent recorders from being effectively used for complete test generation [Bach 1996, Pettichord 1996, Kaner 1997, Linz 1998, Hendrickson 1999, Kit 1999, Thomson 1999, and Groder 1999]. As a result, you will need to create your GUI tests primarily by hand.

A second reason for the difficulty of GUI test automation regards the technical challenge of getting the tool to work with your product. It often takes considerable expertise to get GUI test tools to work with the latest user interface technologies. This difficulty is also one of the main reasons why GUI test tools are so expensive. They have a hard job. Nonstandard or custom controls can present added difficulties. Solutions can usually be found, but often require modifications to the product source code or updates from the tool vendor. Bugs in the test tool may require analysis and patches or workarounds. The test tool may also require considerable customization to make it work effectively with customized elements of your product interface. The difficulty of this work often comes as a surprise. You may also find yourself redesigning your tests to avoid difficult controls.

A third complication for GUI test automation involves keeping up with design changes made to a GUI. GUIs are notorious for being modified and redesigned throughout the development process. This is often a very good idea as the first version of the GUI can be awful. But keeping the automation running while the GUI keeps changing can feel like running in place. You can spend a lot of time revising your tests to match the changing interface. Yet, you don't want to be in the position of arguing against helpful improvements. I've been in this situation and it is mighty uncomfortable to be suggesting that improvements be withheld from the product just so that the tests can keep running. Programmable interfaces tend to exhibit less volatility after the original design has been worked through.

These are reasons not to depend on GUI test automation as the basis for testing your product functionality. The GUI still needs to be tested, of course, and you may choose to automate these tests. But you should have additional tests you can depend on to test core product functionality that will not break when the GUI is redesigned. These tests will need to work through a different interface: a command line or API. I've seen people choose GUI test automation because they didn't want to have to modify the product. But they eventually learned that product modification was necessary to get the GUI test automation to work. Automation is likely to require product modification whichever way you go. So, demand a programmable interface that will be dependable.

To make it easier to test an API, you may want to bind it to an interpreter, such as TCL or Perl or even Python. This enables interactive testing and should also speed up the development cycle for your automated tests. Working with APIs may also allow you to automate unit tests for individual product components.

An example of a possibly hidden programmable interface regards Install-Shield, a popular tool for developing install programs. InstallShield has command line options that enable what's called a silent install. This allows install options to be read from a response file you've created in advance. Using this is likely to be easier and more dependable than automating the InstallShield GUI itself.

Another example of how you could avoid GUI automation relates to Web-based software. GUI tools are available to manipulate Web interfaces through a browser. But it can be easier to directly test the HTTP protocol that Web browsers use to communicate to Web servers. Perl is but one language tool that can directly connect to a TCP/IP port, enabling this kind of automation. Applications using advanced interface technology, such as client-side Java or ActiveX won't be able to take advantage of this kind of approach. But when this approach is suitable, you may find that your automation is cheaper and easier than working through a GUI.

I was once hired to write automated tests for a product GUI. The product also had a command-line interface for which they already had automated tests. After some investigation, I learned that it wasn't hard to find GUI bugs, but that the customers didn't care much as they were happy using the CLI. I also learned that we had no automation for the latest features (which could be accessed from either the GUI or the CLI). I decided to put off the GUI test automation and extended the CLI test suite to cover the latest features. Looking back, I sometimes think of this GUI test automation project I chose not to do was one of my bigger successes, because of all the time and effort that could have been wasted on it. They were all ready for the GUI automation; they had bought a tool and everything. But I know it would have faced various difficult obstacles, while providing extremely limited value.

Whether you need support for GUI, CLI, or API automation, you are going to be much more successful in getting your testability features designed right into the product if you ask early, while the product is still being designed. Enlightened developers will realize that testability is a product requirement. Getting an early start on your test automation project puts you on the road to success.

Step 5. Design for Sustainability

We saw in our fable that test automation efforts are prone to being dropped. This happens when automators focus on just getting the automation to work. Success requires a more long-term focus. It needs to be maintained and expanded so that it remains functional and relevant as new releases of your product are developed. Concern for the future is an important part of design. The integrity of the tests is also paramount. People must trust that when the automation reports a test as passed, it actually did. I have seen far too many cases where parts of tests were silently skipped over or where errors failed to be logged. This is the worst kind of automation failure. It's the kind of failure that can lead to disaster for the whole project. Yet, it can happen when people build test automation that is poorly designed or carelessly modified. This can often happen as a result of a misguided focus on performance or ease of analysis.

> **Performance.** Improving code performance often increases its complexity, thus threatening its reliability. This is a particular concern with test automation because rarely is much attention placed on testing the automation itself. My analysis of test suite performance has also shown that many test suites spend most of their time waiting for the product. This places a limit on how much the test execution can be sped up without improving the performance of the product. I suspect that the concern I've seen amongst test automators with performance stems from overemphasis of this characteristic in computer science curriculums. If test suite performance is a genuine concern, get more hardware or reduce the number of tests in your test suite. They often contain a fair amount of redundancy.

Ease of Analysis. A common bugbear is what to do when automated tests fail. Failure analysis is often difficult. Was this a false alarm or not? Did the test fail because of a flaw in the test suite, a mistake in setting up for the tests, or an actual defect in the product? I see several ways to aid failure analysis, one of which can lead to problems. You could improve the reliability of the test suite by having it explicitly check for common setup mistakes before running tests. You could improve the serviceability of the test suite by improving its error reporting. You could repair known problems in your test harness. You could train people on how to analyze failures. You might even be able to find unreliable tests that can be safely removed because they are redundant or test obsolete functionality. These are all positive ways of reducing false alarms or improving test analysis. A mistaken approach would be to build a results post-processor that conducted its own analysis and filtered the information. Although this approach can be made to work, it complicates the test automation system. Moreover, bugs in the post-processing could seriously impair the integrity of the tests. What happens if it dismisses or mischaracterizes bona fide failures? I've seen this approach taken a couple times by groups wary of modifying the test suites and reluctant to conduct training. This misguided tactic can be very appealing to managers looking for testing that occurs at the push of a button. Resist suggestions to hide the complexity of your tests.

That said, let's focus on what it takes to make a sustainable test suite. It takes reviewability, maintainability, integrity, independence and repeatability.

Reviewability. A common situation is to have an old test suite that's been around for years. It was built before the current staff was on the project. We could call this a "wise oak tree" [Bach 1996]. People depend on it, but don't quite know what it does. Indeed, it invariably turns out that the test suite is rather modest in its accomplishments, but has attained oracular status with time. These wise oak test suites suffer from poor reviewability. It is hard to determine what they actually test, and people tend to overestimate their abilities. It's critical that people be able to review a test suite and understand what is being tested. Good documentation is one way to achieve this. Code coverage analysis is another. I used a variation of this on one project. I instrumented the test suite to log all product commands. We then analyzed the logs to determine which commands were being exercised and with what options. It provided a nice summary of what was and wasn't being covered by the tests. Without reviewability, it's easy to become overly dependent on a test suite you don't really understand. You can easily start thinking that it is doing more than it really is. Being able to review your test suite also facilitates peer review.

Maintainability. I once worked with a test suite that stored all the program output to files. These output files would then be compared to previously generated output files, termed "gold files." The idea was that this would be a good way to detect any regression bugs. But this approach was so sensitive that it generated many false alarms. The problem was that with time, the developers intentionally made small changes to many of the output messages. A test failure would result whenever one of these changed messages appeared in the test output. Clearly, the gold files needed to be updated, but this required lots of analysis. A more maintainable approach would only select specific product outputs to be checked. Rather than comparing all the output, the tests could just compare the output relating to the specific features being tested. Product interfaces can also change and prevent old tests from running. I mentioned that this is a particular challenge for GUI automation. Building an abstraction barrier to minimize the changes to your tests due to product interface changes is a common approach for addressing this problem. This can take the form of a library used by all the tests. Product changes will then only require that this library be updated to make the tests current.

Integrity. When your automation reports that a test passed, did it really? This is what I call test suite integrity. In our fable, we saw a dramatic example of what could happen when due attention isn't given to the integrity of the tests. How well can you depend on its results? False alarms can be a big part of this problem. People hate it when test suites fail and it just turns out to be just a problem with the tests or the setup. It's hard to do much about false alarms. You want your tests to be sensitive and report a failure if things don't look right. Some test harnesses help by supporting a special test result for when the test isn't setup right to run. They have PASS, FAIL, and a third result called something like NOTRUN or UNRESOLVED. Whatever you call it, it's handy to be able to easily sort the tests that were blocked from the tests that ran but failed. Getting the correct result is part of integrity. The other part is making sure that the right test was run. I once found a bug in a test dispatcher that caused it to skip parts of some tests. No errors were generated. I stumbled across this bug while reviewing the code. Had I not noticed this, I imagine that we could have been running partial tests for a long time before we realized something was wrong with the automation.

Independence. Automation cannot truly replicate manual tests. A written manual test procedure assumes you have an intelligent, thinking, observant human being running the tests. With automation, a dumb computer will be running the tests instead. You have to tell it what a failure looks like. And you have to tell it how to recover so that it can keep running the test suite. Automated tests need to be able to be run as part of a suite or individually. The only way to reliably implement this is to make tests independent. Each test needs to setup its test environment. Manual regression tests are usually documented so that each test picks up after the preceding test, taking advantage of any objects or records that may already have been created. Manual testers can usually figure out what is going on. A common mistake is to use the same approach with automated tests. This results in a "domino" test suite. A failure in one test will topple successive tests. Moreover, these tests also cannot be run individually. This makes it difficult to use the automated test to help analyze legitimate failures. When this happens, people will start questioning the value of automated tests in the first place. Independence requires adding repetition and redundancy to the tests. Independent tests will be convenient for developers to use when diagnosing reported defects. It may seem inefficient to structure tests this way, but the important thing is to maintain independence without sacrificing reliability. If the tests can be run unattended, efficiency becomes less of a concern.

Repeatability. There's not much that can be done with a failure report that only hits an error intermittently. So, you need to make sure that your tests work the same way every time they are run. This principle indicts careless use of random data. Random numbers built into common language libraries often hide the initialization process. Using this can make your tests run differently each time. This can frustrate failure analysis. There are two ways of using random number generators to avoid this. One would be to use a constant value to initialize the random number generator. If you wanted to generate a variety of tests, you could set this up to vary in a predictable and controlled way. The other technique would be to generate your random test data ahead of time in a file or database. This is then fed to your test procedure. This may seem obvious enough, but I've seen too many violations of this principle. Let me explain what I've seen. When you execute tests manually, you often make up names for files and records on the fly. What do you do when you automate this test? One approach would be to define a fixed name for the records in the test. If they are going to persist after the test completes, you'll need to use a naming convention to ensure that different tests don't collide. This is usually the wise thing to do. However, I've seen several cases where the tests randomly generated the names for the records. Unfortunately, this turned out to be an unreliable way of avoiding name collisions that also impaired the repeatability of the tests. The automators had apparently underestimated the likelihood of a name collision. In two cases, four-digit numbers were used as random elements of record names. Some basic probability calculations show that it only takes 46 of such records to generate a 10% chance of a name collision. With 118 records, the odds go up to 50%. I suspect that these tests used random names in a lazy attempt to avoid having to write code to clean out old test records before rerunning the tests. But this only introduced problems that damaged the reliability and integrity of the tests.

Placing a priority on these design concerns will help ensure that your automated test suite will continue to be usable for the life of the product it tests.

Let me now turn to discussing a few test automation architectures that have been used to support these design goals:

Libraries. A common strategy is to develop libraries of testing functions that can be used in lots of different tests. I've reviewed a lot of these libraries and have written my own. These can be particularly helpful when they allow tests to be insulated from product-interface design changes. But my general observation is that these tend to be overdeveloped. The libraries are overly ambitious in what they cover and are under-designed. They are often poorly documented and tests that use them can be hard to follow. When problems are later found, it is hard to tell whether the error lies in the function or its usage. Because of their complexity, maintainers can be reluctant to modify them even when they look broken. The obvious conclusion is to make sure your libraries are not poorly designed. But the practical conclusion is to realize that test automation often doesn't get the luxury of having well-designed libraries. I often find that open coding is a better option than using under-designed libraries. I've also seen too many libraries that included functions that were unused or only used once. This squares with the Extreme Programming principle, "You're not going to need it." [Jeffries 1997] This may result in some duplication of code between test cases, but I've found that small variations may still exist that are difficult to handle elegantly with library functions. You want to have some variety amongst your test cases and open coding makes this easier to do. If I have several tests that do some of the same things, I use cut and paste to duplicate my code. Some people think that this practice is heresy. Oh well. It allows me to modify the common code as needed, and I don't have to try and guess how I'm likely to reuse code ahead of time. I think my tests are easier to read, because the reader doesn't have to know the semantics of some library. Another advantage of this approach is that it is easier for others to understand and extend the test suite. Rather than writing from scratch, most programmers find code that does something similar to what they want to do and then modify it. This is an excellent approach for writing test suites that open coding actually encourages. I do like to write small libraries of functions I'll be using again and again. These need to be conceptually well defined and well documented, especially with regard to start and end states. And I test them thoroughly before I use them in my tests. This is, of course, all a matter of balance. But don't plan a large testing library with the hope that hordes of test automators will come someday to write lots of tests. They aren't coming.

Data-Driven Tests. A technique that is becoming widely discussed allows tests to be written in a simplified table format. This is know variously as table-driven, data-driven or even "third generation" automation. It requires that a parser be written to interpret and execute test statements. One of the primary benefits of this architecture is that it allows tests to be specified in a format that is easy to write and review. It's well suited for test teams with domain experts who may not be strong programmers. However, a data-driven test parser is basically a test library with a small language on top. Thus, the comments I made about test libraries apply here as well. There is also the difficulty of designing, developing, and testing a small language for the tests. Invariably, these languages grow. A tester decides that they want to use the output from the first part of a test as input to a second part. Thus, variables are added. Then someone decides that they want to repeat something a hundred times. So loops are added to the language. You can end up with yet another language. If it looks like you are headed down this route, it's probably better to hook in a publicly available language like Perl, Python or TCL than to try and design your own.

Heuristic Verification. I've seen some test automation with no real results verification. This resulted from the difficulty of doing complete verification and the fact that the test design specifications failed to indicate expected results. Clearly, this is unfortunate. It's okay to depend on manual log verification, but this needs to be advertised. When I write tests that depend on external verification, I place a note to this effect in the execution logs. Gold files are another approach for results verification. The program output is captured, reviewed manually, and then archived as "gold." Later, results are then compared against it. The problem with this is that many of the differences will be due to changes in time, configuration, or product messages that are not indicative of problems. It leads to many false alarms. The best approach for verification is to look at specified portions of the output or results and then to make reasonable comparisons. Sometimes it is hard to know in advance what a correct result looks like, but you know what a wrong one looks like. Developing useful heuristics can be very helpful. I suspect that some people are reluctant to develop anything short of comprehensive results verification because of a fear that tests will be faulted if they let anything slip by. But, of course, we always make tradeoffs when we test, and we always need to face the risk we may have missed something. Automation doesn't change this. Automators who aren't used to making these kinds of tradeoffs need to have someone available to consult with on verification strategies. Creativity is often required as well. Many techniques are available that can find defects without raising false alarms.

By focusing on design goals of long-term sustainability and choosing an appropriate architecture, you will be moving along on the road to success.

Step 6. Plan for Deployment

In our fable, we saw some of the problems that can occur when automators defer packaging test suites for others to use. It doesn't happen, and then the next person needing to run the tests has to reverse engineer them to figure out how they should work.

As the automator, you know how to run the tests and analyze the failures. But to really get the payoff from test automation, the tests need to be packaged so that other people can use them. This will mean documenting the setup and maybe even making the test suite easier to install and run. Make sure you give helpful error messages in situations where the resources necessary for testing are unavailable.

Think of your test suite as a product. You'll have to test it, and make sure it doesn't depend on any special libraries or services you have installed on your machine.

Get someone else to use your test suite as soon as it's ready. Make sure that it does the testing in a way they think is appropriate. And make sure they understand the test results and can analyze failures. Some training and documentation may be in order.

As a manager, you want a chance to identify and remedy any major issues with the test suite before the automator moves on. Sooner or later they will, and then you won't have time to address this issue. If you don't address it, you risk owning another abandoned test suite.

A good test suite has many uses. Clearly, it can be used to test new versions of the product. It can also be handy to assist with certifying your product on new platforms. Having a test suite that is easy to run can support a nightly build process or even one whereby developers are expected to run standard tests on their code before they check it in.

It can be hard to foresee which people might want to use your test suite. So, make it widely available to the entire product team. Making it downloadable from an internal Web site is often ideal. People shouldn't have to talk to several people just to find out how to obtain a copy of the test suite. And too many test suites are kept secret because their owner doesn't think they are "ready." Finish the test suite and move on. It doesn't have to be perfect.

Planning for deployment and making your tests widely available sets you on the path to successful test automation that will be used again and again.

Step 7. Face the Challenges of Success

You're done. Your test suite is documented and delivered. People understand the tests and how to run them. The tests are used regularly as your product is developed and maintained. Your success now brings additional challenges. Although you have certainly made some things easier, automation invariably complicates the testing process. Staff will need to learn how to diagnose failures found by the automated tests. If this doesn't happen, the people running the tests are apt to presume that failures are automation problems and the automators will be called in to help diagnose every run. Developers are also prone to suspecting automation code they are unfamiliar with. So, testers will need to learn how to reproduce failures either manually or with minimal test scripts.

The work with the test suites is not over. Tests will need to be added to improve the coverage or to test new features. Old tests will need to be repaired if broken or removed if redundant. Tests themselves may need to be ported to newly supported platforms. Ensuring that the test suites improve over time can be difficult. One idea is to plan a formal review of the test suites after each major release. If you already conduct a post-mortem as part of your process, make sure you include time to identify weaknesses of the test suite and then carry out the required improvements. Don't let the "old oak syndrome" set in. Just because a test suite has been around for a while doesn't mean it doesn't have blind spots.

With time, your tests are likely to stop finding problems. Developers will learn the tests and discover how to pass the tests the first time through. This phenomenon is known as the pesticide paradox. Your developers have improved their design and practices to the point where they are no longer making the kinds of errors that your tests are designed to detect. Some people may doubt whether your tests are still working correctly. You may need to assess whether it is time to raise the bar.

Previously, I mentioned the fantasy in which all the testing is done at the push of a button. I don't think that can ever really happen. There will always be a role for manual testing. For one, it is the only real way to sanity-test your automation itself.

The other reason for manual tests is that there will always be tests that are justified by the specific circumstances motivating the tests. This testing is often best done in an exploratory manner. And it's hard to say in advance that tests are worth repeating. There is always a cost involved. Don't fall into the classic error of trying to automate everything. [Marick 1997]

I've been urging you to maintain your investment in test automation. But a particular challenge lies in the timing for when test automation should be done. Test automation must be released to the testing staff in time for it to be useful. It's nice to release some automation early, but there comes a point where no new automation can be used, except for requested fixes. When the test effort is in full swing, testers can't afford to spend any time learning new tools or diagnosing tool errors. Identify this date in the project plan and let everyone know that you plan to meet this milestone. But after this date has been met, what should automators do? The focus on delivering the current release of the product may pull the automators into helping the test effort and executing tests. But once the testers know how to use the automation, it's a good time for automators to get a jump on the next release and improve the test tools and libraries. This is often the time when some developers start designing features for the next product release. The test automation is well served if the design work for new automation features also begins now. The idea is to keep the automators synchronized with the development cycle, rather than the testing cycle. Not doing this will result in fewer opportunities for improvement to the test automation. Explain the benefits of this schedule to the testers so they don't resent the fact that the automators aren't focusing on the release that is approaching its ship date.

Continuing to invest in automation will help you face the challenges of success and ensure that the road remains clear for continuing success as test automation becomes a dependable basis for your testing process.

Acknowledgments

Earlier versions of this paper were presented at the STAR West conference in San Jose, California, November 1999; Lucent Technologies' Automated Software Testing conference in Naperville, Illinois, November 1999; the Practical Software Quality Techniques conference in Austin, Texas, March 2000; and the Rational User's Conference in Philadelphia, Pennsylvania, August 2000.

Carol Schiraldi, Noel Nyman, Brian Marick, and James Bach provided helpful comments on early drafts.

References

Bach, James. 1996. "Test Automation Snake Oil."
Windows Technical Journal, (October): 40-44.
http://www.satisfice.com/articles/test_automation_snake_oil.pdf

Dustin, Elfriede. 1999. "Lessons in Test Automation."
Software Testing and Quality Engineering (September): 16-22.

Fewster, Mark and Dorothy Graham. 1999. *Software Test Automation*. Addison-Wesley.

Groder, Chip. "Building Maintainable GUI Tests" in [Fewster 1999].

Kit, Edward. 1999. "Integrated, Effective Test Design and Automation." *Software Development* (February).
http://www.sdmagazine.com/articles/1999/9902/9902b/9902b.htm

Hancock, Jim. 1997. "When to Automate Testing." *Testers Network* (June).
http://www.data-dimensions.com/Testers'Network/jimauto1.htm

Hendrickson, Elisabeth. 1999. "Making the Right Choice: The Features You Need in a GUI Test Automation Tool." *Software Testing and Quality Engineering Magazine* (May): 21-25.

Hoffman, Douglas. 1999. "Heuristic Test Oracles: The Balance Between Exhaustive Comparison and No Comparison at All." *Software Testing and Quality Engineering Magazine* (March): 29-32.

Kaner, Cem. 1997. "Improving the Maintainability of Automated Test Suites." Presented at Quality Week.
http://www.kaner.com/lawst1.htm

Linz, Tilo and Matthias Daigl. 1998. "How to Automate Testing of Graphical User Interfaces." European Systems and Software Initiative Project No. 24306 (June).
http://www.imbus.de/html/GUI/AQUIS-full_paper-1.3.html

Jeffries, Ronald E. 2001. "XPractices"
http://www.XProgramming.com/Practices/xpractices.htm

Marick, Brian. 1998. "When Should a Test Be Automated?" Presented at Quality Week.
http://www.testing.com/writings/automate.pdf

Marick, Brian. 1997. "Classic Testing Mistakes." STAR West conference.
http://www.testing.com/writings/classic/mistakes.html

Pettichord, Bret. 1996. "Success with Test Automation." Presented at Quality Week (May).
http://www.io.com/~wazmo/succpap.htm

Thomson, Jim. "A Test Automation Journey" in [Fewster 1999].

Weinberg, Gerald M. 1992. *Quality Software Management: Systems Thinking*. Vol. 1. Dorset House.

Test Automation Snake Oil

By James Bach

Item #1: A product is passed from one maintenance developer to the next. Each new developer discovers that the product's design documentation is out of date and that the build process is broken. After a month of analysis, each pronounces it to be poorly engineered and insists on rewriting large portions of the code. After several more months, each quits or is reassigned and the cycle repeats.

Item #2: A product is rushed through development without sufficient understanding of the problems that it's supposed to solve. Many months after it is delivered, a review discovers that it costs more to operate and maintain the system than it would have cost to perform the process by hand.

Item #3: $100,000 is spent on a set of modern, integrated development tools. It is soon determined that the tools are not powerful, portable, or reliable enough to serve a large scale development effort. After nearly two years of effort to make them work, they are abandoned.

Item #4: Software is written to automate a set of business tasks. But the tasks change so much that the project gets far behind schedule and the output of the system is unreliable. Periodically, the development staff is pulled off the project in order to help perform the tasks by hand, which makes them fall even further behind on the software.

Item #5: A program consisting of many hundreds of nearly independent functions is put into service with only rudimentary testing. Just prior to delivery, a large proportion of the functions are deactivated as part of debugging. Almost a year passes before anyone notices that those functions are missing.

These are vignettes from my own experience, but I bet they sound familiar. It's a truism that most software projects fail and for good reason—from the outside, software seems so simple. But, the devil is in the details, isn't it? And seasoned software engineers approach each new project with a wary eye and skeptical mind.

Test automation is hard, too. Look again at the five previous examples. They aren't from product development projects. Rather, each of them was an effort to automate testing. In the eight years I spent managing test teams and working with test automation (at some of the hippest and richest companies in the software business, mind you), the most important insight I gained was that test software projects are as susceptible to failure as any other software project. In fact, in my experience, they actually fail much more often, mainly because most organizations don't apply the same care and professionalism to their testware as they do to their shipping products.

Strange, then, that almost all testing pundits, practicing testers, test managers, and of course, companies that sell test tools *unreservedly recommend* test automation. Well, perhaps "strange" is not the right word. After all, CASE tools were a big fad for a while, and test tools are just another species of CASE. From object-orientation to "programmerless" programming, starry-eyed advocacy is nothing new to our industry. So maybe the poor quality of public information and analysis about test automation is less strange than it is simply a sign of the immaturity of the field. As a community, perhaps we're still in the phase of admiring the cool idea of test automation, and not yet to the point of recognizing its pitfalls and gotchas.

Having said that, let me hasten to agree that test automation is a very cool idea. Most full-time testers and probably all developers dream of pressing a big green button and letting a lab full of loyal robots do the hard work of testing, freeing themselves for more enlightened pursuits, such as playing head-to-head Doom. However, if we are to achieve this Shangri-la, we must proceed with caution. This article is a critical analysis of the "script and playback" style of automation for system-level regression testing of GUI applications.

Debunking the Classic Argument for Automation

"Automated tests execute a sequence of actions without human intervention. This approach helps eliminate human error and provides faster results. Since most products require tests to be run many times, automated testing generally leads to significant labor cost savings over time. Typically a company will pass the break-even point for labor costs after just two or three runs of an automated test."

This quote is from a white paper on test automation published by a leading vendor of test tools. Similar statements can be found in advertisements and documentation for most commercial regression test tools. Sometimes they are accompanied by impressive graphs, too. Notice how the same argument could be applied to the idea of using software to automate any repetitive human activity. The idea boils down to just this: computers are faster, cheaper, and more reliable than humans. Therefore, automate.

At least with regard to system testing of Windows applications, this line of reasoning rests on many questionable assumptions:

1. **Everything important that people do when manually testing can be mapped to a definable "sequence of actions."**

   Most skilled hand testing is not preplanned in detail, but is rather a guided exploration and reasoning process. This process is therefore not a sequence of actions, but rather a heuristic search. Sure, this process can be projected into a sequence of very specific test cases with very specific pass/fail criteria, but the resulting hundreds or thousands of test cases would be, at best, an adjunct to skilled hand testing, not a replacement.

2. **That sequence of actions is useful to repeat many times.**

   Once a specific test case is executed a single time, and no bug is found, there's only a remote chance that same test, executed again, will find a bug, unless a new bug is introduced into the system. If there is variation in the test cases, though, as there usually is when tests are executed by hand, there is a greater likelihood of revealing problems both new and old. Variability is one of the great advantages of hand testing over script and playback testing. When I was at Borland, the spreadsheet group used to track whether bugs were found through automation or manual testing—consistently, over 80% of bugs were found manually, despite several years of investment in automation. Their theory was that hand tests were more variable and more directed at new features and specific areas of change where bugs were more likely to be found.

3. **That sequence can be automated.**

   Some tasks that are easy for people are hard for computers. Probably the hardest part of automation is interpreting test results. For GUI software, it is very hard to automate that process so as to automatically notice all categories of significant problems while ignoring the insignificant problems.

   The problem of automatability is compounded by the high degree of uncertainty and change in a typical innovative software project. In market-driven software projects, it's common to use an incremental development approach, which pretty much guarantees that the product will change, in fundamental ways, until quite late in the project. This fact, coupled with the typical absence of complete and accurate product specifications, make automation development something like driving through a trackless forest in the family sedan: you can do it, but you'll have to go slow, do a lot of backtracking, and you might get stuck.

Even if we have a particular sequence of operations that can in principle be automated, we can only do so if we have an appropriate tool for the job. Information about tools is hard to come by, though, and the most critical aspects of a regression test tool are impossible to evaluate unless we create or review an industrial-size test suite using the tool. Here are some of the factors to consider when selecting a test tool. Notice how many of them could never be evaluated just by perusing the user's manual or watching a trade show demo:

- *Capability*: does the tool have all the critical features we need, especially in the area of test result validation and test suite management?

- *Reliability*: does the tool work for long periods without failure, or is it full of bugs? Many test tools are developed by small companies that do a poor job of testing them.

- *Capacity*: beyond the toy examples and demos, does the tool work without failure in an industrial environment? Can it handle large-scale test suites that run for hours or days and involve thousands of scripts?

- *Learnability*: can the tool be mastered in a short time? Are there training classes or books available to aid that process?

- *Operability*: are the features of the tool cumbersome to use, or prone to user error?

- *Performance*: is the tool quick enough to allow a substantial savings in test development and execution time versus hand testing?

- *Compatibility*: does the tool work with the particular technology that we need to test?

- *Non-Intrusiveness*: how well does the tool simulate an actual user? Is the behavior of the software under test the same with automation as without?

4. **Once automated, the process will go faster, because it does not require human intervention.**

   All automated test suites require human intervention, if only to diagnose the results and fix broken tests. It can also be surprisingly hard to make a complex test suite run without a hitch. Common culprits are changes to the software being tested, memory problems, file system problems, network glitches, and bugs in the test tool itself.

5. **Once automated, human error is eliminated.**

   Yes, some errors are eliminated. Namely, the ones that humans make when they are asked carry out a long list of mundane mental and tactile activities. But other errors are amplified. Any bug that goes unnoticed when the master compare files are generated will go systematically unnoticed every time the suite is executed. Or an oversight during debugging could accidentally deactivate hundreds of tests. The dBase team at Borland once discovered that three thousand tests in their suite were hard-coded to report success no matter what problems were actually in the product. To mitigate these problems, the automation should be tested or reviewed on a regular basis. Corresponding lapses in a hand testing strategy, on the other hand, are much easier to spot using basic test management documents, reports, and practices.

6. **It is possible to measure the relative costs and benefits of manual testing versus automated testing.**

   The truth is, hand testing and automated testing are really two different processes, rather than two different ways to execute the same process. Their dynamics are different, and the bugs they tend to reveal are different. Therefore, direct comparison of them in terms of dollar cost or number of bugs found is meaningless. Besides, there are so many particulars and hidden factors involved in a genuine comparison that the best way to evaluate the issue is in the context of a series of real software projects. That's why I recommend treating test automation as one part of a multifaceted pursuit of an excellent test strategy, rather than an activity that dominates the process, or stands on it own.

7. **The value of automated testing will duplicate or surpass that of manual testing.**

   This is true only if all of the previous assumptions are true, and if there is also no value in having testers spend time actually using the product.

8. **The cost to automate the testing will be less than three times the cost of a single, manual pass through the same process.**

   This loosey-goosey estimate may have come from field data or from the fertile mind of a marketing wonk. In any case, the cost to automate is contingent on many factors, including the technology being tested, the test tools used, the skill of the test developers, and the quality of the test suite. Writing a single test script is not necessarily a lot of effort, but constructing a suitable test harness can take weeks or months. As can the process of deciding which tool to buy, which tests to automate, how to trace the automation to the rest of the test process, and, of course, learning how to use the tool and then actually writing the test programs. A careful approach to this process (i.e., one that results in a useful product, rather than gobbledygook) usually takes months of full-time effort, and longer if the automation developer is inexperienced with either the problem of test automation or the particulars of the tools and technology.

9. **For an individual test cycle, the cost of operating the automated tests, plus the cost of maintaining the automation, plus the cost of any other new tasks necessitated by the automation, plus the cost of any remaining manual testing will be significantly less than the cost of a comparable, purely manual test pass.**

   This is yet another reckless assumption. Most analyses of the cost of test automation completely ignore the special new tasks that must be done just because of the automation:

   - Test cases must be documented carefully.

   - The automation itself must be tested and documented.

   - Each time the suite is executed, someone must carefully pore over the results to tell the false negatives from real bugs.

   - Radical changes in the product to be tested must be reviewed to evaluate their impact on the test suite, and new test code may have to be written to cope with them.

   - If the test suite is shared, meetings must be held to coordinate the development, maintenance, and operation of the suite.

   - The headache of porting the tests must be endured if the product being tested is subsequently ported to a new platform, or even to a new version of the same platform. I know of many test suites that were blown away by hurricane Win95.

These new tasks make a significant dent in a tester's day. Every group I ever worked in that tested GUI software tried at one point or another to make all testers do part-time automation, and every group eventually abandoned that idea in favor of a dedicated automation engineer or team. Writing test code and performing interactive hand testing are such different activities that a person assigned to both duties will tend to focus on one to the exclusion of the other. Also, since automation development is software development, it requires a certain amount of development talent. Some testers aren't up to it. One way or another, companies with a serious attitude about automation usually end up with full-time staff to do it, and that must be figured in to the cost of the overall strategy.

I've left for last the most thorny of all the problems that we face in pursuing an automation strategy: it's always dangerous to automate something that we don't understand. It's vital to get the test strategy clearly outlined and documented, not to mention the specification of the product to be tested, before introducing automation. Otherwise, the result will be a large mass of test code that no one fully understands. As the original developers of the suite drift away to other assignments, and others take over maintenance, the suite gains a kind of citizenship in the test team. The maintainers are afraid to throw any old tests out, even if they look trivial, because they might actually be important. It continues to accrete new tests, becoming an increasingly mysterious oracle, like some old Himalayan guru or talking oak tree. No one knows what the suite actually tests, and the bigger it gets, the less likely anyone will go to the trouble to find out.

This situation has happened to me personally (more than once before I learned my lesson), and I have seen and heard of it happening to many other test managers. Most don't even realize that it's a problem, until one day a development manager asks what the test suite covers and what it doesn't, and no one is able to give an answer. Or, one day when it's needed most, the whole test system breaks down and there's no manual process to back it up. The irony of the situation is that an honest attempt to do testing more professionally can end up assuring that it's done blindly and ignorantly.

A manual testing strategy can suffer from confusion too, but when tests are created dynamically from a relatively small set of principles or documents, it's much easier to review and adjust the strategy. It's a slower testing method, yes, but it's much more visible, reviewable, flexible, and it can cope with the chaos of incomplete and changing products and specs.

A Sensible Approach to Automation

Despite the concerns raised in this article, I do believe in test automation. Just as there can be quality software, there can be quality test automation. To create good test automation, though, we have to be careful. The path is strewn with pitfalls. Here are some key principles to keep in mind:

- Maintain a careful distinction between the automation and the process that it automates. The test process should be in a form that is convenient to review and that maps to the automation.

- Think of your automation as a baseline test suite to be used in conjunction with hand testing, rather than as a replacement.

- Carefully select your test tools. Gather experiences from other testers and organizations (Usenet or CompuServe can be good for this). Try evaluation versions of candidate tools before you buy.

- Put careful thought into buying or building a test management harness. A good test management system can really help make the suite more reviewable and maintainable.

- Assure that each execution of the test suite results in a status report that includes what tests passed and failed versus the actual bugs found. The report should also detail any work done to maintain or enhance the suite. I've found these reports to be indispensable source material for analyzing just how cost effective the automation is.

- Assure that the product is mature enough so that maintenance costs from constantly changing tests don't overwhelm any benefits provided.

Conclusion

One day, a few years ago, there was a blackout during a fierce evening storm, right in the middle of the unattended execution of our wonderful test suite. When my team arrived at work the next morning, we found that our suite had automatically rebooted itself, reset the network, picked up where it left off, and finished the testing. It took a lot of work to make our suite that bulletproof, and we were delighted. The thing is, we later found, during a review of test scripts in the suite, that out of about 450 tests, only about 18 of them were truly useful. It's a long story how that came to pass—basically, the wise oak tree scenario—but the upshot of it was that we had a test suite that could, with high reliability, discover nothing important about the software we were testing. I've told this story to other test managers who shrug it off. They don't think this could happen to them. Well, it can happen if the machinery of testing distracts you from the craft of testing.

Make no mistake. Automation is a great idea. To make it a good investment as well, the secret is to think about testing first and automation second. If testing is a means to the end of understanding the quality of the software, automation is just a means to a means. You wouldn't know it from the advertisements, but it's only one of many strategies that support effective software testing.

Advice for Automated Testers Learning Visual Basic

By Elisabeth Hendrickson

 NOTE FROM MARY SWEENEY *Elisabeth graciously provided me with this list via e-mail. See Elisabeth's Web site at* http://www.qualitytree.com *for her articles on building versus buying automated testing tools and other ruminations on test topics.*

About learning Visual Basic, most of my advice is rather generic, I'm afraid. If you can use it, you're welcome to it:

- Consider taking a class if you learn well in a classroom setting.

- Find someone with whom you get along well that has done a fair bit of VB programming and is willing to help you.

- Try changing sample programs as a way to learn the language rather than trying to write code from scratch.

- Start simple—it's okay if your first from-scratch program doesn't do anything more useful than displaying some text in a dialog box.

- Make a habit of testing out key bits of your programs in isolation. I often create dumb little test programs just to see how the language really works or how my implementation will work in practice.

- MsgBox is your friend. When still working the kinks out of a program, I often use MsgBox to display values. I personally find that easier than stepping through programs with a debugger.

I have three reasons why every tester should have at least basic VB skills:

- If you plan to use Visual Test or Rational Robot, you'll end up having to learn it anyway, so you might as well learn it early.

- If your product has an API that can be accessed through VB, it's a great way to drive your product for a variety of types of tests (including hammer tests).

- If you use MS Office products for tracking test results and bugs, you can use your VB knowledge to automate the gathering and sending of test results and bug stats.

Index

Symbols

! (exclamation point) shortcut, 107
" " (quotation marks), using with
    VBScript, 400
(pound sign) shortcut, 107
$ (dollar sign) shortcut, 107
& (ampersand), 42, 107
% (percent) shortcut, 107
, (comma), using between arguments,
    144
() (parentheses)
    in arrays, 192, 196
    using with function calls, 149
. (dot) before extensions, 88
[] (square brackets) in command
    syntax, 64–65
| (pipe) in command syntax, 65

A

Access Keys
    assigning and displaying, 50–51
    combining with label controls and
      tab order, 53–54
accessibility testing, 52
ActiveX components
    converting classes to, 310–311
    converting cTestClass to, 311–314
ActiveX DLL projects, creating,
    310–311, 323–325, 354
activities
    adding control, 73
    creating simple program, 70–71
    saving files, 74
    using Message box, 71–72
Add Module dialog box, 151–154
AddItem method, using with list boxes,
    198
ADO (ActiveX Data Objects)
    architecture basics, 266–267
    testing, 264–265

ADO library, accessing, 266–267, 272
ADVAPI32.DLL, 215, 222
Alias keyword, 234
Allen, Paul, 40
ampersand (&), 52, 107
ANSI versus Unicode, 235
Any keyword, 234
AOL Web site, using with ASP testing
    utility, 394
API (application programming
    interface)
    calling routines in, 216–222
    libraries, 214–215
    location of files for, 214
    return values, 235–237
API Text Viewer tool, locating, 217–218
API wrappers, writing, 237–239
Append File mode, 482
Application-level variables, 108–111
application settings, creating and
    retrieving, 187
applications, testing for user-
    friendliness, 51
appname argument for SaveSetting
    Registry statement, 188
Appname global module-level
    constant, adding to Calculator
    accessory, 179
APPNAME variable, changing to
    Private scope from Public
    scope, 306–307
Apress Web Site, 70
ApTest Web site, finding GUI testing
    tools on, 169
arguments, 88
    for OpenURL method, 363
    for SaveSetting Registry statement,
      188
    using, 143–147
    for Windows API, 231–233
arrays
    creating lists with, 192–193
    displaying return values of,
      197–198

B

C

D

G

H

I

Q

R

T

W

X

Z